Struts:
The Complete Reference

About the Author

James Holmes is a leading Struts authority. He is a committer on the Struts project and creator of the most popular Struts development tool, Struts Console. Additionally, *Oracle Magazine* named him "2002 Java Developer of the Year" for his work with the Struts framework and JDeveloper.

James is an independent consultant who develops server-side applications for complex transactional environments, including ADP, Bank of America, IBM, and UPS. For information on retaining James for Struts and Java development projects, contact him via e-mail at james@jamesholmes.com. You can also visit his Web site at http://www.JamesHolmes.com/.

About the Contributor

Bill Siggelkow is a systems development and design consultant who specializes in enterprise-caliber Java-based applications. Bill is an active member of the Atlanta Struts User Group and frequently serves as a presenter for the group. With nearly 20 years of development experience, he has designed and developed systems for the manufacturing, energy marketing, e-commerce, and financial service industries. Bill enjoys training and mentoring developers in the art of programming.

About the Technical Editor

James Mitchell is a self-described "Open Source Evangelist" and can be found roaming the halls of the Apache and Sourceforge mailing lists. He is one of a handful of committers on the Struts project at Apache. James is currently working as an independent consultant in the Atlanta, GA, area specializing in Struts-based J2EE application development and is available on a contract basis. James has built Struts-based enterprise applications in B2B, banking, industrial, and telecommunications industries.

For more information or to contact James Mitchell, send your inquiries to jmitchell@apache.org. You can also reach him at 678/910-8017.

About the Editor

Herbert Schildt is a leading authority on the C, C++, Java, and C# languages, and is a master Windows programmer. His programming books have sold more than 3 million copies worldwide and have been translated into all major foreign languages. He is the author of numerous bestsellers, including *Java 2: The Complete Reference, The Art of Java, Java 2: A Beginner's Guide, Java 2 Programmer's Reference, C++: The Complete Reference, C: The Complete Reference,* and *C#: The Complete Reference.* Schildt holds a master's degree in computer science from the University of Illinois. He can be reached at his consulting office at 217/586-4683.

Struts:
The Complete Reference

James Holmes

Edited by
Herbert Schildt

McGraw-Hill/Osborne

New York   Chicago   San Francisco
Lisbon   London   Madrid   Mexico City
Milan   New Delhi   San Juan
Seoul   Singapore   Sydney   Toronto

The McGraw·Hill Companies

McGraw-Hill/Osborne
2100 Powell Street, 10th Floor
Emeryville, California 94608
U.S.A.

To arrange bulk purchase discounts for sales promotions, premiums, or fund-raisers, please contact **McGraw-Hill**/Osborne at the above address. For information on translations or book distributors outside the U.S.A., please see the International Contact Information page immediately following the index of this book.

Struts: The Complete Reference

234567890 DOC DOC 0198765

ISBN 0-07-223131-9

Publisher Brandon A. Nordin	**Contributing Editor** Bill Siggelkow
Vice President & Associate Publisher Scott Rogers	**Copy Editor** William McManus
Editorial Director Wendy Rinaldi	**Proofreader** Marian Selig
Project Editor Janet Walden	**Indexer** Valerie Robbins
Acquisitions Coordinator Athena Honore	**Compsition** Lucie Ericksen, Tara A. Davis
Editor Herbert Schildt	**Illustrators** Kathleen Edwards, Melinda Lytle
Technical Editor James Mitchell	**Series Design** Peter F. Hancik, Lyssa Wald

This book was composed with Corel VENTURA™ Publisher.

To my mother, who once chided me
for spending so much time behind the computer,
but who has stood behind me steadfast
and given me the platform
from which to flourish.

Contents at a Glance

Contents

Part IV Applying Struts

Acknowledgments

Writing this book has been one of the most challenging endeavors I've taken on and it would not have been possible without the help and support from several people. I'd like to thank everyone at McGraw-Hill/Osborne for being so kind and supportive. In particular, I want to thank Wendy Rinaldi for giving me the opportunity to write this book and for introducing me to and giving me the opportunity to work with Herb Schildt, whom I'd also like to thank. Not only has Herb been the editor on this book, providing me with endless insight and wisdom, he has become a great friend and a mentor. Thank you all!

Special thanks also to Bill Siggelkow for providing the initial drafts for Chapters 19 and 20. His efforts are sincerely appreciated.

PART I

The Struts Framework

## CHAPTER 1

An Introduction to Struts

Struts is the premier framework for building Java-based Web applications. Using the Model-View-Controller (MVC) design pattern, Struts solves many of the problems associated with developing high-performance, business-oriented Web applications that use Java servlets and JavaServer Pages. At the outset, it is important to understand that Struts is more than just a programming convenience. Struts has fundamentally reshaped the way that Web programmers think about and structure a Web application. It is a technology that no Web programmer can afford to ignore.

This chapter presents an overview of Struts, including the historical forces that drove its creation, the problems that it solves, and the importance of the Model-View-Controller architecture. Many of the topics introduced here are examined in detail by subsequent chapters.

A Brief History of Web Application Development

In order to fully understand and appreciate the need for and value of Struts, it's necessary to shed some light on how Web application development has evolved over the past several years. Initially the Internet was used primarily by the academic and military communities for sharing research information, most of which was in the form of static documents. Thus, originally, the Internet was mostly a mechanism for sharing files.

In 1995 the commercialization of the Internet began and there was an explosion of content made available on the Web. Similar to the research content that was being shared on the Web, the early commercial content was principally comprised of text mixed with simple graphics. Hyperlinks were used to connect the content together. Although hyperlinks enabled the user to move from page to page, the contents of each page was still a static document that did not support other forms of user interaction. It wasn't long, though, before businesses wanted to be able to offer dynamic content that offered the user a richer, more interactive experience.

Before continuing, it will be helpful to explain precisely what is meant by *dynamic content*. In short, dynamic content is data that is specifically targeted for a particular user. For example, a user may want to check the price and availability of some item in an online store. The user enters the item name and the server supplies the response. The response is generated on-the-fly based on the request, and is thus dynamic content.

To fill the dynamic-content void, Web server software began to support the use of CGI scripts for creating applications that could run on a Web server and generate dynamic content back to a browser. CGI, or *Common Gateway Interface,* allowed Web servers to accept a request and execute a server-side program that would perform some action and then generate output on standard out. Web server software would then read that output and send it back to the requesting browser. Initially, many of these CGI scripts were written in Perl or other Unix-based scripting languages. Over time, though, as the applications being built to run as CGI scripts grew in complexity, more application-oriented languages like C and C++ were being used to create larger, more robust applications. With the advent of HTML forms, CGI scripts also were able to receive data from the browser and process it. As most readers know, HTML forms allow data entry on a Web page. That data could be sent to a CGI script on the server and then manipulated, stored, or otherwise processed.

Around the same time that CGI-based application development was becoming popular on the server side, the Java programming language was introduced, with an initial focus on applets. Applets gave the Web developer the ability to add rich, dynamic functionality to Web pages. Because Java offered the promise of "write once and run anywhere" programs, any browser that supported Java could run the applets. For the first time, developers could easily include dynamic content on a Web page.

For the same reasons that Java began to blossom on the client side with applets, Java also began to make inroads on the server side with the advent of servlet technology in 1997. Servlets solved many of the shortcomings of CGI, such as portability and efficiency, and offered a Java-based solution for the Web application paradigm. Servlets are portable across operating systems and can run on any server that has a Java Virtual Machine (JVM). Thus, they also benefit from Java's "write once, run anywhere" philosophy. Servlets have a more efficient execution model than CGIs because they are multithreaded instead of requiring a new process for each request. Servlets also have access to Java's vast libraries, including the JDBC APIs.

After servlets were introduced, Sun released the *JavaServer Pages (JSP)* technology as an extension to the servlet technology. JSPs take the reverse approach from servlets to building Web applications by having Java code intermingled in an HTML-based page. When a request is made to the server for a JSP, the Java server container checks if the JSP has already been compiled into a servlet. If it has, it proceeds to execute the servlet. If the JSP has not yet been compiled into a servlet, the server container converts the JSP code into a Java source file and then compiles that source so that subsequent requests to the JSP will find the servlet already compiled and ready to execute.

The nice thing about this approach is that changes to the JSP HTML can be made without having to manually recompile the code. The server container manages the compilation and will recognize that the HTML in the JSP has changed and recompile the JSP into a servlet for you. JSPs solve the problem of presentation code (HTML) being embedded in servlets, which made development cumbersome because HTML authors had to wade through Java code to edit HTML (not a good separation of responsibilities). In contrast, HTML developers can work on JSPs directly without interfering with Java code.

As the preceding discussion shows, many of the changes in Web-based development that have occurred over the past few years have been driven by the desire to efficiently include dynamic content in a Web page. Streamlining the use of dynamic content has been, and remains, one of the more important issues associated with the Internet and the applications that use it. As you will see, Struts is part of the solution to the dynamic-content problem.

Two Development Models

When Sun introduced JSP technology, it provided a development road map for working with it and defined two models for building JSP-based Web applications. The two models are known as *Model 1* and *Model 2* and they prescribe different approaches to designing JSP-based Web applications. Model 1, the simpler of the two, was the primary solution implemented when JSPs were first introduced. However, over time, Model 2 has been accepted as the best way for building JSP-based Web applications and, as you'll see, is the inspiration for MVC-based Web frameworks like Struts. Following is an overview of both architectures.

Model 1 Architecture Overview

The Model 1 architecture is very simple, as you can see in Figure 1-1. A request is made to a JSP or servlet and then that JSP or servlet handles all responsibilities for the request, including processing the request, validating data, handling the business logic, and generating a response. Although conceptually simple, this architecture is not conducive to large-scale application development because, inevitably, a great deal of functionality is duplicated in each JSP. Also, the Model 1 architecture unnecessarily ties together the business logic and presentation logic of the application. Combining business logic with presentation logic makes it hard to introduce a new "view" or access point in an application. For example, in addition to an HTML interface, you might want to include a Wireless Markup Language (WML) interface for wireless access. In this case, using Model 1 will unnecessarily require the duplication of the business logic with each instance of the presentation code.

FIGURE 1-1   Model 1 architecture

Model 2 Architecture Overview

Model 2, or as it is most commonly referred to today, *Model-View-Controller (MVC)*, solves many of the inherent problems with the original Model 1 design by providing a clear separation of application responsibilities (see Figure 1-2). In the MVC architecture, a central servlet, known as the *Controller*, receives all requests for the application. The Controller then processes the request and works with the *Model* to prepare any data needed by the *View* (which is usually a JSP) and forwards the data to a JSP. The JSP then uses the data prepared by the Controller to generate a response to the browser. In this architecture, the business and presentation logic are separated from each other. Having the separation of business and presentation code accommodates multiple interfaces to the application, be they Web, wireless, or GUI (Swing). Additionally, this separation provides excellent reuse of code.

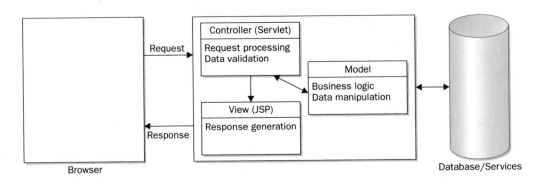

FIGURE 1-2   Model 2 architecture

A Closer Look at the Model-View-Controller Architecture

Because an understanding of the Model-View-Controller architecture is crucial to understanding Struts, this section takes a closer look at each of its parts. As a point of interest, MVC is based on an older graphical user interface (GUI) design pattern that has been around for some time, with its origins in the Smalltalk world. Many of the same forces behind MVC for GUI development apply nicely to Web development.

Model Components

In the MVC architecture, model components provide an interface to the data and/or services used by an application. This way, controller components don't unnecessarily embed code for manipulating an application's data. Instead, they communicate with the model components that perform the data access and manipulation. Thus, the model component provides the business logic. Model components come in many different forms and can be as simple as a basic Java bean or as intricate as Enterprise JavaBeans (EJBs) or Web services.

View Components

View components are used in the MVC architecture to generate the response to the browser. Thus, a view component provides what the user sees. Often times the view components are simple JSPs or HTML pages. However, you can just as easily use WML or another view technology for this part of the architecture. This is one of the main design advantages of MVC. You can use any view technology that you'd like without impacting the Model (or business) layer of your application.

Controller Components

At the core of the MVC architecture are the controller components. The Controller is typically a servlet that receives requests for the application and manages the flow of data between the Model layer and the View layer. Thus, it controls the way that the Model and View layers interact. The Controller often uses helper classes for delegating control over specific requests or processes.

Enter Struts

Although the Model-View-Controller architecture is a powerful means of organizing code, developing such code can be a painstaking process. This is where Struts comes in. Struts is a Web application framework that streamlines the building of Web applications based on the MVC design principles. But what does that mean? Is Struts an MVC Web application that you just add on to or extend? Is Struts just some libraries? Actually, Struts is a little bit of both. Struts provides the foundation, or *framework,* for building an MVC-oriented application along with libraries and utilities for making MVC development faster and easier.

You could create a new Controller servlet every time you wanted to use the MVC design pattern in your Web application. Additionally, you'd need to create the management/flow logic for getting data to and from the Model and then routing requests to the View. You'd also need to define interfaces for interacting with your Model objects and all the utility code that goes along with using the MVC design pattern. However, instead of going through this process each time you create a new application, you can use Struts. Struts provides the basic structure and outline for building that application, freeing you to concentrate on building the business logic in the application and not the "plumbing."

To better understand the benefits of Struts, consider the following analogy. If you were to create a GUI application in Java, you wouldn't write a textfield widget and a dropdown widget yourself. You would use Java's Swing API that already has standardized, fully functional code that provides these controls. Not only are the Swing controls ready-to-use, but they are also understood by all Java programmers. Struts provides the same type of advantages: Struts supplies a standard way of implementing an MVC application, the Struts code is tried and true, and the techniques required to use Struts are well known and documented.

In addition to providing the foundation for MVC applications, Struts provides rich extension points so that your application can be customized as you see fit. This extensibility has led to several third-party add-ons being made available for Struts, such as libraries for handling application workflow, libraries for working with view technologies other than JSP, and so on.

Struts Is Open Source

Struts was originally created by Craig R. McClanahan and then donated to the Jakarta project of the Apache Software Foundation (ASF) in 2000. In June of 2001, Struts 1.0 was released. Since then, many people have contributed both source code and documentation to the project and Struts has flourished. Today, Struts has become the de facto standard for building Web applications in Java and has been embraced throughout the Java community. As of the writing of this book, the current version of Struts is 1.2, and Struts is continuing to evolve.

When Craig McClanahan donated Struts to the Apache Jakarta project, it became *open source software.* This means that anyone can download the source for Struts and modify that code as he or she sees fit. Of course, such changes affect only that developer. The standard code provided by ASF remains unaltered.

Slowly, additional developers were added to the Struts project and were authorized to make changes to the code. These people are known as *committers,* since they have commit access to the source control repository for Struts. Only ten or so people have this access, and each picks an area of interest and works on that part of the code that he or she is interested in.

One of the advantages of open source software is that bugs can be fixed in a timely fashion. For ASF projects, bugs are handled by the committers, but anyone can fix a bug and provide a patch that the committers will then evaluate and "commit" if they deem it appropriate. Thus, open source enables rapid development and maintenance cycles. Being open source, Struts is completely free of charge and allows you to make changes to it without any consequence so long as you abide by and preserve the ASF license.

Support for Struts comes in three forms. First is the API documentation that comes with Struts. Second, Struts has a very active mailing list where you can get support for virtually any question. Third, several third-party consulting companies specialize in Struts support and development.

Basic Components of Struts

The Struts framework is a rich collection of Java libraries and can be broken down into the following major pieces:

- Base framework
- JSP tag libraries
- Tiles plugin
- Validator plugin

A brief description of each follows.

Base Framework

The base framework provides the core MVC functionality and is comprised of the building blocks for your application. At the foundation of the base framework is the Controller servlet: **ActionServlet**. The rest of the base framework is comprised of base classes that your application will extend and several utility classes. Most prominent among the base classes are the **Action** and **ActionForm** classes. These two classes are used extensively in all Struts applications. **Action** classes are used by **ActionServlet** to process specific requests. **ActionForm** classes are used to capture data from HTML forms and to be a conduit of data back to the View layer for page generation.

JSP Tag Libraries

Struts comes packaged with several JSP tag libraries for assisting with programming the View logic in JSPs. JSP tag libraries enable JSP authors to use HTML-like tags to represent functionality that is defined by a Java class.

Following is a listing of the libraries and their purpose:

- **HTML**   Used to generate HTML forms that interact with the Struts APIs.
- **Bean**   Used to work with Java bean objects in JSPs, such as accessing bean values.
- **Logic**   Used to cleanly implement simple conditional logic in JSPs.
- **Nested**   Used to allow arbitrary levels of nesting of the HTML, Bean, and Logic tags that otherwise do not work.

Tiles Plugin

Struts comes packaged with the Tiles subframework. Tiles is a rich JSP templating framework that facilitates the reuse of presentation (HTML) code. With Tiles, JSP pages can be broken up into individual "tiles" or pieces and then glued together to create one cohesive page. Similar to the design principles that the core Struts framework is built on, Tiles provides excellent reuse of View code. As of Struts 1.1, Tiles is part of and packaged with the core Struts download. Prior to Struts 1.1, Tiles was a third-party add-on, but has since been contributed to the project and is now more tightly integrated.

Validator Plugin

Struts comes packaged, as of version 1.1, with the Validator subframework for performing data validation. Validator provides a rich framework for performing data validation on both the server side and client side (browser). Each validation is configured in an outside XML file so that validations can easily be added to and removed from an application declaratively versus being hard-coded into the application. Similar to Tiles, prior to Struts 1.1, Validator was a third-party add-on, but has since been included in the project and is more tightly integrated.

Acquiring Struts

Struts is available free of charge and can be downloaded from the Apache Jakarta site at:

http://jakarta.apache.org/struts/

Because Struts is open source, you have a couple of options when downloading the Struts framework software. You can download the software in binary, precompiled form or you can download the source code for compiling on your own. For most cases, the binary distribution will suffice; however, if you want to make changes to the Struts source code, the source distribution is available.

If you choose to download a binary distribution of Struts, you have a couple of options. You can download a released version of the code, which has been rigorously tested and certified as being of good quality, or you can download a nightly build of the code, which is less stable and not intended for production use. Opting to use a nightly build allows you to get access to the latest enhancements and bug fixes that have been made to the Struts framework ahead of an official release. However, it's important to point out again that nightly builds have no guarantee on quality because adding a new feature to Struts could potentially break another feature that has been stable for some time.

Similar to downloading a binary distribution of Struts, if you choose to download a source distribution, you have a couple of options. You can download the source for an officially released version of Struts or you can choose to get the "latest and greatest" version of the Struts source code directly from the Struts CVS source control repository. Just as with the binary distribution, choosing to download the latest Struts source code can get you the newest enhancements and bug fixes to the software, but it may also be laden with new bugs.

What You Get (Binary)

Since Struts is a Web application framework and not a stand-alone application, Struts distributions are principally comprised of the Struts API libraries and their associated files, such as Document Type Definitions (DTDs) for XML configuration files and JSP Tag Library Descriptor (TLD) files. Additionally, Struts comes with several sample Web applications that illustrate how to use the Struts framework. One of the sample Web applications, **struts-blank.war**, is typically used for new Struts applications because it provides a basic template for a Struts application, including all the necessary **.jar** files, and so on. Struts distributions also come with a sample Web application, **struts-example.war**, that illustrates the basic structure of a Struts application.

What You Get (Source)

Similar to the binary distribution, the source distribution is comprised of the Struts API libraries and sample Web applications. The major difference, however, is that all of the code for the libraries and sample applications is in source form. This is particularly useful for projects where the source code may need to be changed or where you may want access to the source code for debugging an application and so on.

Getting Started with Struts

Now that the theoretical foundation for Struts has been covered, it is time to move on to actually writing Struts code. The next chapter walks through an example Struts application. Before then, you will need to choose one of the two Struts distribution options just discussed and download it.

Building a Simple Struts Application

Now that you've reviewed the history of Web application development and the fundamentals of the Struts framework, it's time to move beyond theory and into practice. As you will see, a Struts application is a composite of several interrelated parts. The goal of this chapter is to give you a general understanding of these parts and show how they work together to form a complete program. To accomplish that goal, this chapter develops a simple application that highlights each Struts component. In the process, several key elements of Struts are introduced. Once you understand how this simple Struts application works, you will be able to easily understand other Struts programs because all share a common architecture. Subsequent chapters discuss in detail the many concepts introduced here.

This chapter also describes the steps necessary to compile, package, and run the application. You will use the same general procedure with the other examples in this book.

Application Overview

The sample application in this chapter deviates from the stereotypical "Hello World" program found in most programming books. Instead, a bit more sophisticated example is needed to illustrate the components of Struts and the process required to build a Struts-based application. The example that we will use is a simple human resources (HR) application. Creating a full-blown HR application is a large undertaking that requires several pieces of functionality, from employee management to benefits management, so the sample application in this chapter will support only one common subset of functionality: Employee Search.

The sample application is called *Mini HR* and it will have a basic opening page that links to an Employee Search page. From the Employee Search page, users can search for employees by name or social security number. After executing the search, the Search page will be redisplayed with a list of employees that match the search criteria. Although quite simple, and limited in scope, this example illustrates the key features common to any Struts-based Web application.

The Mini HR Application Files

All Struts applications are comprised of several files, which contain the various parts of a Struts program. Some are Java source files, but others contain JSP and XML. A properties file is also required. Because of the relatively large number of files required by a Struts application, we will begin by examining the files required by Mini HR. The same general types of files will be needed by just about any Struts application.

The following table lists each file required by Mini HR and its purpose.

File	Description
index.jsp	Contains the JSP that is used as a gateway page for the Mini HR application and provides a link to the Employee Search page.
search.jsp	Contains the JSP that is used for performing employee searches and displaying the search results.
SearchForm.java	Contains the class that captures and transfers data to and from the Search page. This is a View class.
SearchAction.java	Contains the class code that processes requests from the Search page. This is a Controller class.
EmployeeSearchService.java	Contains the class that encapsulates the business logic and data access involved in searching for employees. This is a Model class.
Employee.java	Contains the class that represents an employee and encapsulates all of an employee's data. This is a Model class.
web.xml	Contains the XML that is used to configure the Java Web application properties for the Mini HR application.
struts-config.xml	Contains the XML that is used to configure the Struts framework for this application.
ApplicationResources.properties	Contains properties that are used to externalize application strings, labels, and messages so that they can be changed without having to recompile the application. This file is also used for internationalizing the application.

The following sections examine each of the Mini HR application files in detail, and in many cases line by line. First, though, it's necessary to explain where each file should be placed in a directory hierarchy. Because this application (and all other Struts applications) will be deployed to a J2EE servlet container, the application files have to be arranged in the standard J2EE Web Archive (.war) format, which is simply a Java Archive (.jar) file with a different extension (.war). The Web Archive format also specifies a few key requirements for the .jar file:

- There must be a directory at the root level of the archive named **WEB-INF**. At run time this is a protected directory and thus any files beneath it will be inaccessible to browsers.

- There must be a Web application deployment descriptor file named **web.xml** beneath the **WEB-INF** directory. This file will be explained later in this chapter in the "web.xml" section.

- Any libraries needed by the application should be under a directory called **lib** located beneath the **WEB-INF** directory.

- Any class files needed by the application, which are not already packaged in a .jar file, should be under a directory called **classes** located beneath the **WEB-INF** directory.

For the Mini HR application, you will create a directory called **MiniHR**. In principle, you can place this directory anywhere, but to follow along with this example, put it at **c:\java**. You'll use the **c:\java\MiniHR** directory as the root of your Web application so that you can easily create a Web Archive file later. Following is the layout of the **c:\java\MiniHR** directory, shown in Figure 2-1, and the location of each file examined in this section. You will need to place the files in this exact structure.

FIGURE 2-1   The c:\java\MiniHR directory layout

```
c:\java\MiniHR\index.jsp
c:\java\MiniHR\search.jsp
c:\java\MiniHR\WEB-INF\web.xml
c:\java\MiniHR\WEB-INF\struts-config.xml
c:\java\MiniHR\WEB-INF\classes\com\jamesholmes\minihr\ApplicationResources.properties
c:\java\MiniHR\WEB-INF\lib
c:\java\MiniHR\WEB-INF\src\com\jamesholmes\minihr\Employee.java
c:\java\MiniHR\WEB-INF\src\com\jamesholmes\minihr\EmployeeSearchService.java
c:\java\MiniHR\WEB-INF\src\com\jamesholmes\minihr\SearchAction.java
c:\java\MiniHR\WEB-INF\src\com\jamesholmes\minihr\SearchForm.java
c:\java\MiniHR\WEB-INF\tlds
```

index.jsp

The **index.jsp** file, shown here, is a very simple JSP that is used to render Mini HR's opening screen:

```
<%@ taglib uri="/WEB-INF/tlds/struts-html.tld" prefix="html" %>

<html>
<head>
<title>ABC, Inc. Human Resources Portal</title>
</head>
<body>

<font size="+1">ABC, Inc. Human Resources Portal</font><br>
<hr width="100%" noshade="true">

&#149; Add an Employee<br>
&#149; <html:link forward="search">Search for Employees</html:link><br>

</body>
</html>
```

You'll notice that **index.jsp** is comprised mostly of standard HTML, with the exception of the JSP tag library definition at the top of the file and the "Search for Employees" link. The **index.jsp** file uses Struts' HTML Tag Library to render the Search link. Before you can use the HTML Tag Library, you have to "import" it into the JSP with the following line at the top of the JSP:

```
<%@ taglib uri="/WEB-INF/tlds/struts-html.tld" prefix="html" %>
```

This line associates the tag library located at **/WEB-INF/tlds/struts-html.tld** with a prefix, or "handle," of html. That way, any time a tag from the Struts HTML Tag

Library is used, it will be prefixed with html. In **index.jsp**'s case, the **link** tag is used with the following line:

```
<html:link forward="search">Search for Employees</html:link>
```

Of course, if you wanted to use another prefix for the tag library, you could do so by updating the **prefix** attribute of the tag library import on the first line of the file.

The HTML Tag Library's **link** tag is used for rendering an HTML link, such as http://www.jamesholmes.com/. The **link** tag goes beyond basic HTML, though, by allowing you to access link, or *forward* definitions, from the Struts configuration file, **struts-config.xml**, which is covered later in this chapter in the "struts-config.xml" section. In this case, the tag looks for a forward definition named "search" defined in the **struts-config.xml** file to use for the link being generated. If you skip ahead to the "struts-config.xml" section of this chapter, you'll see that the forward definition is as follows:

```
<!-- Global Forwards Configuration -->
<global-forwards>
  <forward name="search" path="/search.jsp"/>
</global-forwards>
```

Forward definitions allow you to declaratively configure the location to which a link points instead of hard-coding that information into your JSP or application. As you'll see in Chapter 5, forward definitions are used throughout Struts to direct the flow of an application from the Struts configuration file.

The following is the source code generated after **index.jsp** has been requested in the browser. Notice that the Search page link has been converted into a standard HTML link.

```
<html>
<head>
<title>ABC, Inc. Human Resources Portal</title>
</head>
<body>

<font size="+1">ABC, Inc. Human Resources Portal</font><br>

<hr width="100%" noshade="true">

&#149; Add an Employee<br>
&#149; <a href="/MiniHR/search.jsp">Search for Employees</a><br>

</body>
</html>
```

Here is how **index.jsp** looks in the browser.

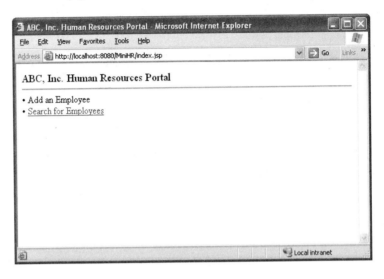

search.jsp

The **search.jsp** file is responsible for the bulk of the Employee Search functionality in the Mini HR application. When the Employee Search link is selected from the **index.jsp** page, **search.jsp** is executed. This initial request for **search.jsp** renders the basic Employee Search screen shown here:

Each time a search is performed, Struts' Controller servlet is executed and eventually **search.jsp** is executed to handle the rendering of the Employee Search screen, with the search results, as shown here:

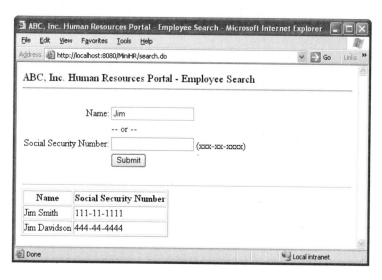

Similarly, if there are any errors with the search criteria when the search is submitted, **search.jsp** is executed to report the errors, as shown here:

The contents of **search.jsp** are

```
<%@ taglib uri="/WEB-INF/tlds/struts-bean.tld" prefix="bean" %>
<%@ taglib uri="/WEB-INF/tlds/struts-html.tld" prefix="html" %>
<%@ taglib uri="/WEB-INF/tlds/struts-logic.tld" prefix="logic" %>

<html>
<head>
<title>ABC, Inc. Human Resources Portal - Employee Search</title>
</head>
<body>

<font size="+1">
ABC, Inc. Human Resources Portal - Employee Search
</font><br>
<hr width="100%" noshade="true">

<html:errors/>

<html:form action="/search">

<table>
<tr>
<td align="right"><bean:message key="label.search.name"/>:</td>
<td><html:text property="name"/></td>
</tr>
<tr>
<td></td>
<td>-- or --</td>
</tr>
<tr>
<td align="right"><bean:message key="label.search.ssNum"/>:</td>
<td><html:text property="ssNum"/> (xxx-xx-xxxx)</td>
</tr>
<tr>
<td></td>
<td><html:submit/></td>
</tr>
</table>

</html:form>

<logic:present name="searchForm" property="results">

<hr width="100%" size="1" noshade="true">

<bean:size id="size" name="searchForm" property="results"/>
<logic:equal name="size" value="0">
```

```
<center><font color="red"><b>No Employees Found</b></font></center>
</logic:equal>

<logic:greaterThan name="size" value="0">
<table border="1">
<tr>
<th>Name</th>
<th>Social Security Number</th>
</tr>
<logic:iterate id="result" name="searchForm" property="results">
<tr>
<td><bean:write name="result" property="name"/></td>
<td><bean:write name="result" property="ssNum"/></td>
</tr>
</logic:iterate>
</table>
</logic:greaterThan>

</logic:present>

</body>
</html>
```

Because of its size and importance, we will examine it closely, line by line.

Similar to **index.jsp**, **search.jsp** begins by declaring the JSP tag libraries that will be used by the JSP:

```
<%@ taglib uri="/WEB-INF/tlds/struts-bean.tld" prefix="bean" %>
<%@ taglib uri="/WEB-INF/tlds/struts-html.tld" prefix="html" %>
<%@ taglib uri="/WEB-INF/tlds/struts-logic.tld" prefix="logic" %>
```

In addition to the HTML Tag Library used by **index.jsp**, **search.jsp** uses Struts' Bean and Logic libraries. These additional tag libraries contain utility tags for working with Java beans and using conditional logic in a page, respectively.

The next several lines are comprised of basic HTML tags:

```
<html>
<head>
<title>ABC, Inc. Human Resources Portal - Employee Search</title>
</head>
<body>

<font size="+1">
ABC, Inc. Human Resources Portal - Employee Search
</font><br>
<hr width="100%" noshade="true">
```

Immediately following this basic HTML is this **errors** tag definition:

```
<html:errors/>
```

Recall that **search.jsp** is used to render any errors that occur while validating that the search criteria are sound. The HTML Tag Library's **errors** tag will emit any errors that are passed to the JSP from the **SearchForm** object. This is covered in more detail in the "SearchForm.java" section in this chapter.

The next several lines of **search.jsp** are responsible for rendering the HTML for the search form:

```
<html:form action="/search">

<table>
<tr>
<td align="right"><bean:message key="label.search.name"/>:</td>
<td><html:text property="name"/></td>
</tr>
<tr>
<td></td>
<td>-- or --</td>
</tr>
<tr>
<td align="right"><bean:message key="label.search.ssNum"/>:</td>
<td><html:text property="ssNum"/> (xxx-xx-xxxx)</td>
</tr>
<tr>
<td></td>
<td><html:submit/></td>
</tr>
</table>

</html:form>
```

Before discussing the specifics of the search form, let's review the use of the Bean Tag Library in this snippet. This snippet uses the library's **message** tag, as shown here:

```
<td align="right"><bean:message key="label.search.name"/>:</td>
```

The **message** tag allows externalized messages from the **ApplicationResources .properties** file to be inserted into the JSP at run time. The **message** tag simply looks up the key passed to it in **ApplicationResources.properties** and returns the corresponding message from the file. This feature is especially useful to internationalize a page and to allow easy updating of messages outside the JSP. *Internationalization* is the process of providing content specific to a language, locale, or region. For instance, internationalization would be to create both English and Spanish versions of the same JSP.

NOTE *The acronym I18N is sometimes used in place of the word* internationalization, *because it is such a long word to type. I18N represents the first letter i, followed by 18 characters, and then the final letter n. The I18N acronym is used occasionally in this book.*

Now, it's time to examine the form. Struts' HTML Tag Library has a tag for each of the standard HTML form tags, such as

    <form>

    <input type="">

and so on. Instead of using the standard HTML tags, you'll use the HTML Tag Library's equivalent tag, which ties the form to Struts. For example, the **text** tag (**<html:text>**) renders an **<input type="text" ...>** tag. The **text** tag goes one step further, though, by allowing a property to be associated with the tag, as shown here:

```
<td><html:text property="name"/></td>
```

The property "name" here corresponds to the field named **name** in the **SearchForm** object. That way, when the tag is executed, it places the value of the **name** field in the HTML at run time. Thus, if the **name** field had a value of "James Holmes" at run time, the output from the tag would look like this:

```
<td><input type="text" name="name" value="James Holmes"></td>
```

At the beginning of this next snippet, the HTML Tag Library's **form** tag is used to render a standard HTML **<form>** tag. Notice, however, that it specifies an **action** parameter of "/search" as shown here:

```
<html:form action="/search">
```

The **action** parameter associates an **Action** object mapping from the **struts-config.xml** file with the form. That way, when the form is submitted, the processing will be handled by the specified **Action** object.

The final section of the **search.jsp** file contains the logic and tags for rendering search results:

```
<logic:present name="searchForm" property="results">

<hr width="100%" size="1" noshade="true">
```

PART I

```
<bean:size id="size" name="searchForm" property="results"/>
<logic:equal name="size" value="0">
<center><font color="red"><b>No Employees Found</b></font></center>
</logic:equal>

<logic:greaterThan name="size" value="0">
<table border="1">
<tr>
<th>Name</th>
<th>Social Security Number</th>
</tr>
<logic:iterate id="result" name="searchForm" property="results">
<tr>
<td><bean:write name="result" property="name"/></td>
<td><bean:write name="result" property="ssNum"/></td>
</tr>
</logic:iterate>
</table>
</logic:greaterThan>

</logic:present>
```

The beginning of this snippet uses Struts' Logic Tag Library for using conditional logic in a JSP. The Logic Library's **present** tag checks an object to see if a particular property is present. In this case, the **logic** tag checks to see if the **results** field of the **SearchForm** has been set. If so, then all of the HTML and JSP tags inside the **<logic:present ...>** tag will be executed. Otherwise, they will be ignored.

The rest of the tags in this snippet are responsible for rendering the search results. First, the Bean Library's **size** tag gets the size of the **results ArrayList** from the **SearchForm** object. Next, the size is checked to see if it is 0 using the Logic Library's **equal** tag. If the size is in fact 0, then a "No Employees Found" message will be rendered. Otherwise, each of the employees returned from the search will be displayed. The Logic Library's **iterate** tag is used to iterate over each of the search results. Each search result is assigned to a variable named **result** by the **iterate** tag. Inside the **iterate** tag the Bean Library's **write** tag is used to access the **result** variable's **name** and **ssNum** fields.

SearchForm.java

The **SearchForm** class, shown next, is a View class that is used to capture and transfer data to and from the Employee Search page. When the HTML form on the Search page is submitted, Struts' **ActionServlet** will populate this class with the data from the form. Notice that there will be a one-to-one mapping between fields on the page and fields in the class with getter and setter methods. Struts uses encapsulation and Java's reflection mechanism to call the method corresponding to each field from a page. Additionally, when **SearchAction** (the Controller class for the Search page) executes, it will populate this object with the search results so that they can be transferred back to the Search page.

```java
package com.jamesholmes.struts;

import java.util.List;

import javax.servlet.http.HttpServletRequest;

import org.apache.struts.action.ActionError;
import org.apache.struts.action.ActionErrors;
import org.apache.struts.action.ActionForm;
import org.apache.struts.action.ActionMapping;

public class SearchForm extends ActionForm
{
  private String name = null;
  private String ssNum = null;
  private List results = null;

  public void setName(String name) {
    this.name = name;
  }

  public String getName() {
    return name;
  }

  public void setSsNum(String ssNum) {
    this.ssNum = ssNum;
  }

  public String getSsNum() {
    return ssNum;
  }

  public void setResults(List results) {
    this.results = results;
  }

  public List getResults() {
    return results;
  }

  // Reset form fields.
  public void reset(ActionMapping mapping, HttpServletRequest request)
  {
    name = null;
```

```
    ssNum = null;
    results = null;
  }

  // Validate form data.
  public ActionErrors validate(ActionMapping mapping,
    HttpServletRequest request)
  {
    ActionErrors errors = new ActionErrors();

    boolean nameEntered = false;
    boolean ssNumEntered = false;

    // Determine if name has been entered.
    if (name != null && name.length() > 0) {
      nameEntered = true;
    }

    // Determine if social security number has been entered.
    if (ssNum != null && ssNum.length() > 0) {
      ssNumEntered = true;
    }

    /* Validate that either name or social security number
       has been entered. */
    if (!nameEntered && !ssNumEntered) {
      errors.add(null,
        new ActionError("error.search.criteria.missing"));
    }

    /* Validate format of social security number if
       it has been entered. */
    if (ssNumEntered && !isValidSsNum(ssNum.trim())) {
      errors.add("ssNum",
        new ActionError("error.search.ssNum.invalid"));
    }

    return errors;
  }

  // Validate format of social security number.
  private static boolean isValidSsNum(String ssNum) {
    if (ssNum.length() < 11) {
      return false;
    }

    for (int i = 0; i < 11; i++) {
      if (i == 3 || i == 6) {
```

```
      if (ssNum.charAt(i) != '-') {
        return false;
      }
    } else if ("0123456789".indexOf(ssNum.charAt(i)) == -1) {
      return false;
    }
  }

  return true;
  }
}
```

ActionForm subclasses, including **SearchForm**, are basic Java beans with a couple of extra Struts-specific methods: **reset( )** and **validate( )**. The **reset( )** method is used to clear out, or "reset," an **ActionForm**'s data after it has been used for a request. Because Struts reuses **ActionForm**s instead of creating new ones for each request, this method is necessary to ensure that data from different requests is not mixed. Typically, this method is used to just set class fields back to their initial states, as is the case with **SearchForm**. However, as you'll see in Chapter 4, this method can be used to perform other necessary logic for resetting an **ActionForm** object.

The **validate( )** method of **ActionForm** is called to perform basic validations on the data being transferred from an HTML form. In **SearchForm**'s case, the **validate( )** method first confirms that a name and social security number have been entered. If a social security number has been entered, **SearchForm** goes one step further and validates the format of the social security number with the **isValidSsNum( )** method. The **isValidSsNum( )** method simply ensures that an 11-character string was entered and that it conforms to the following format: three digits, hyphen, two digits, hyphen, four digits (e.g., 111-22-3333). Note that business-level validations, such as looking up a social security number in a database to make sure it is valid, are considered business logic and should be in a Model layer class. The validations in an **ActionForm** are meant to be very basic, such as just confirming that data was entered, and should not be used for performing any real business logic.

You'll notice that the **validate( )** method returns an **ActionErrors** object and the validations inside the method populate an **ActionErrors** object if any validations fail. The **ActionErrors** object is used to transfer validation error messages to the screen. Remember from the discussion of **search.jsp** that the HTML Tag Library's **errors** tag will emit any errors in a JSP if they are present. Following is the snippet from **search.jsp**:

```
<html:errors/>
```

Here in the **ActionForm** class, you simply place the keys for messages into the **ActionErrors** object, such as "error.search.criteria.missing". The **errors** tag will use these keys to load the appropriate messages from the **ApplicationResources.properties** file, discussed in the section of the same name later in this chapter.

Note that the **validate( )** method will be invoked only if the **validate** parameter of the **<action>** tag is set to "true" in the **struts-config.xml** file.

SearchAction.java

The **SearchAction** class, shown next, is a Controller class that processes requests from the Search page:

```java
package com.jamesholmes.struts;

import java.util.ArrayList;

import javax.servlet.http.HttpServletRequest;
import javax.servlet.http.HttpServletResponse;

import org.apache.struts.action.Action;
import org.apache.struts.action.ActionForm;
import org.apache.struts.action.ActionForward;
import org.apache.struts.action.ActionMapping;

public final class SearchAction extends Action
{
  public ActionForward execute(ActionMapping mapping,
    ActionForm form,
    HttpServletRequest request,
    HttpServletResponse response)
    throws Exception
  {
    EmployeeSearchService service = new EmployeeSearchService();
    ArrayList results;

    SearchForm searchForm = (SearchForm) form;

    // Perform employee search based on what criteria was entered.
    String name = searchForm.getName();
    if (name != null && name.trim().length() > 0) {
      results = service.searchByName(name);
    } else {
      results = service.searchBySsNum(searchForm.getSsNum().trim());
    }

    // Place search results in SearchForm for access by JSP.
    searchForm.setResults(results);

    // Forward control to this Action's input page.
    return mapping.getInputForward();
  }
}
```

Remember from the discussion of **search.jsp** that the HTML form on the page is set to post its data to the "/search" action. The **strut-config.xml** file maps the search action to this class so that when **ActionServlet** (Controller) receives a post from the Search page, it delegates processing for the post to this **Action** subclass. This mapping is shown here:

```
<!-- Action Mappings Configuration -->
<action-mappings>
  <action path="/search"
          type="com.jamesholmes.struts.SearchAction"
          name="searchForm"
          scope="request"
          validate="true"
          input="/search.jsp">
    <forward name="results" path="/results.jsp"/>
  </action>
</action-mappings>
```

Struts' **Action** subclasses manage the processing of specific requests. You can think of them as mini servlets assigned to manage discreet Controller tasks. For instance, in the preceding example, **SearchAction** is responsible for processing employee search requests and acts as a liaison between the Model (**EmployeeSearchService**) and the View (**search.jsp**).

SearchAction begins by overriding Struts' **Action** class **execute( )** method. The **execute( )** method is the single point of entry for an **Action** class by Struts' **ActionServlet**. You'll notice that this method takes an **HttpServletRequest** object and an **HttpServletResponse** object as parameters, similar to a servlet's **service( )**, **doGet( )**, and **doPost( )** methods. Additionally, **execute( )** takes a reference to the **ActionForm** associated with this **Action** and an **ActionMapping** object reference. The **ActionForm** reference passed to this **Action** will be an instance of **SearchForm**, as discussed in the previous section, "SearchForm.java." The **ActionMapping** reference passed to this **Action** will contain all of the configuration settings from the **struts-config.xml** file for this **Action**.

The **execute( )** method begins by instantiating a few objects, and then the real work gets underway with a check to see what search criteria was entered by the user. Notice that the **ActionForm** object passed in is cast to its native type: **SearchForm**. Casting the object allows you to access **SearchForm**'s methods for retrieving the search criteria. Based on the criteria entered, one of **EmployeeSearchService**'s methods will be invoked to perform the employee search. If an employee name was entered, the **searchByName( )** method will be invoked. Otherwise, the **searchBySsNum( )** method will be invoked. Both search methods return an **ArrayList** containing the search results. This **results ArrayList** is then added to the **SearchForm** instance so that **search.jsp** (View) can access the data.

The **execute( )** method concludes by forwarding control to **SearchAction**'s input page: **search.jsp**. The input page for an action is declared in the **struts-config.xml** file, as shown here for **SearchAction**, and is used to allow an action to determine from which page it was called:

```
<action path="/search"
        type="com.jamesholmes.struts.SearchAction"
        name="searchForm"
        scope="request"
        validate="true"
        input="/search.jsp">
```

EmployeeSearchService.java

EmployeeSearchService is a Model class that encapsulates the business logic and data access routines involved in searching for employees. The **SearchAction** Controller class uses this class to perform an employee search and then shuttles the resulting data to the View layer of the Mini HR application. **EmployeeSearchService** is shown here:

```
package com.jamesholmes.struts;

import java.util.ArrayList;

public class EmployeeSearchService
{
  /* Hard-coded sample data. Normally this would come from a real data
     source such as a database. */
  private static Employee[] employees =
  {
    new Employee("Bob Davidson", "123-45-6789"),
    new Employee("Mary Williams", "987-65-4321"),
    new Employee("Jim Smith", "111-11-1111"),
    new Employee("Beverly Harris", "222-22-2222"),
    new Employee("Thomas Frank", "333-33-3333"),
    new Employee("Jim Davidson", "444-44-4444")
  };

  // Search for employees by name.
  public ArrayList searchByName(String name) {
    ArrayList resultList = new ArrayList();

    for (int i = 0; i < employees.length; i++) {
      if(employees[i].getName().toUpperCase().indexOf(name.toUpperCase())
          != -1)
      {
        resultList.add(employees[i]);
      }
    }
```

```
      return resultList;
   }


   // Search for employee by social security number.
   public ArrayList searchBySsNum(String ssNum) {
     ArrayList resultList = new ArrayList();

     for (int i = 0; i < employees.length; i++) {
       if (employees[i].getSsNum().equals(ssNum)) {
         resultList.add(employees[i]);
       }
     }

     return resultList;
   }
}
```

In order to simplify Mini HR, the **EmployeeSearchService** class will not actually communicate with a real data source, such as a database, to query employee data. Instead, **EmployeeSearchService** has some sample **Employee** data hard-coded at the top of the class, as shown here:

```
/* Hard-coded sample data. Normally this would come from a real data
   source such as a database. */
private static Employee[] employees =
{
  new Employee("Bob Davidson", "123-45-6789"),
  new Employee("Mary Williams", "987-65-4321"),
  new Employee("Jim Smith", "111-11-1111"),
  new Employee("Beverly Harris", "222-22-2222"),
  new Employee("Thomas Frank", "333-33-3333"),
  new Employee("Jim Davidson", "444-44-4444")
};
```

The sample data is comprised of a few **Employee** objects. As you'll see in the next section, the **Employee** class is a simple class for encapsulating employee data.

The **searchByName( )** and **searchBySsNum( )** methods use the hard-coded data when performing a search. The **searchByName( )** method loops through each of the **Employee** objects in the **employees** array looking for any employees that match the name specified. If a match is found, it is added to the return **ArrayList** that will eventually be used by **search.jsp** to display the results. Note that the name search is case insensitive by virtue of uppercasing the **String**s before comparison. You should also note that the use of **String**'s **indexOf( )** method allows for partial matches instead of only exact matches.

Similar to the **searchByName( )** method, **searchBySsNum( )** loops through the hard-coded employee list looking for any employees that match the specified social security number. Note that **searchBySsNum( )** will capture only exact matches. Because social security numbers are unique to an individual, only one match should ever be returned for a social security number–based search.

Employee.java

The **Employee** class, shown next, is a simple bean for encapsulating the data for an employee. The class is straightforward, comprised simply of setters and getters for the **Employee** class data.

```
package com.jamesholmes.struts;

public class Employee
{
  private String name;
  private String ssNum;

  public Employee(String name, String ssNum) {
    this.name = name;
    this.ssNum = ssNum;
  }

  public void setName(String name) {
    this.name = name;
  }

  public String getName() {
    return name;
  }

  public void setSsNum(String ssNum) {
    this.ssNum = ssNum;
  }

  public String getSsNum() {
    return ssNum;
  }
}
```

This class is used by **EmployeeSearchService** for transferring employee search results data from the Model (**EmployeeSearchService**) to the View (**search.jsp**). Oftentimes, this "transfer" object is referred to as a Data Transfer Object (DTO) or Value Object (VO) and has the simple responsibility of being a data container and abstracting the Model from the View.

web.xml

The **web.xml** file, shown next, is a standard Web Archive deployment descriptor used to configure the Mini HR application. Because the file contains several configuration details, it will be reviewed section by section.

```xml
<?xml version="1.0"?>

<!DOCTYPE web-app PUBLIC
  "-//Sun Microsystems, Inc.//DTD Web Application 2.3//EN"
  "http://java.sun.com/dtd/web-app_2_3.dtd">

<web-app>

  <!-- Action Servlet Configuration -->
  <servlet>
    <servlet-name>action</servlet-name>
    <servlet-class>org.apache.struts.action.ActionServlet</servlet-class>
    <init-param>
      <param-name>config</param-name>
      <param-value>/WEB-INF/struts-config.xml</param-value>
    </init-param>
    <load-on-startup>1</load-on-startup>
  </servlet>

  <!-- Action Servlet Mapping -->
  <servlet-mapping>
    <servlet-name>action</servlet-name>
    <url-pattern>*.do</url-pattern>
  </servlet-mapping>

  <!-- The Welcome File List -->
  <welcome-file-list>
    <welcome-file>/index.jsp</welcome-file>
  </welcome-file-list>

  <!-- Struts Tag Library Descriptors -->
  <taglib>
    <taglib-uri>/WEB-INF/tlds/struts-bean.tld</taglib-uri>
    <taglib-location>/WEB-INF/tlds/struts-bean.tld</taglib-location>
  </taglib>
  <taglib>
    <taglib-uri>/WEB-INF/tlds/struts-html.tld</taglib-uri>
    <taglib-location>/WEB-INF/tlds/struts-html.tld</taglib-location>
  </taglib>
  <taglib>
    <taglib-uri>/WEB-INF/tlds/struts-logic.tld</taglib-uri>
```

```
    <taglib-location>/WEB-INF/tlds/struts-logic.tld</taglib-location>
  </taglib>

</web-app>
```

The following is the first section of the **web.xml** file. It declares the Struts Controller servlet, **ActionServlet**, and configures it.

```
<!-- Action Servlet Configuration -->
<servlet>
  <servlet-name>action</servlet-name>
  <servlet-class>org.apache.struts.action.ActionServlet</servlet-class>
  <init-param>
    <param-name>config</param-name>
    <param-value>/WEB-INF/struts-config.xml</param-value>
  </init-param>
  <load-on-startup>1</load-on-startup>
</servlet>
```

This declaration starts by assigning a name to the servlet that will be used in the next section for mapping the servlet to specific application requests. After defining the servlet's name and class, the **config** initialization parameter is defined. This parameter tells Strut's **ActionServlet** where to find its central configuration file: **struts-config.xml**. Finally, the **<load-on-startup>** tag is used to instruct the servlet engine how many instances of the servlet should be instantiated when the server starts.

The second section of the **web.xml** file causes **ActionServlet** to respond to certain URLs:

```
<!-- Action Servlet Mapping -->
<servlet-mapping>
  <servlet-name>action</servlet-name>
  <url-pattern>*.do</url-pattern>
</servlet-mapping>
```

Notice that the **<servlet-name>** tag references the same name declared in the previous section. This associates the previous servlet declaration with this mapping. Next, the **<url-pattern>** tag is used to declare the URLs that **ActionServlet** will respond to. In this case, it is saying that **ActionServlet** should process any requests for pages that end in **.do**. So, for example, a request to

http://localhost:8080/MiniHR/page.do

or a request to

http://localhost:8080/MiniHR/dir1/dir2/page2.do

will be routed to Struts' **ActionServlet** for processing.

The next section of the **web.xml** file declares the Welcome File list that the Mini HR application will use:

```
<!-- The Welcome File List -->
<welcome-file-list>
  <welcome-file>/index.jsp</welcome-file>
</welcome-file-list>
```

The Welcome File list is a list of files that the Web server will attempt to respond with when a given request to the Web application goes unfulfilled. For example, in Mini HR's case, you can enter a URL of **http://localhost:8080/MiniHR/** and **index.jsp** will be executed, because no page has been specified in the URL. The servlet engine detects this and references the Welcome File list for pages that should be tried to respond to the request. In this case, the servlet engine will try to respond with a page at **/index.jsp**. If that page is unavailable, an error will be returned. Note that the Welcome File list can span several pages. In that case, the servlet engine will iterate through the list until a file is found that can be served for the request.

The final section of the **web.xml** file declares the JSP tag libraries that should be available to JSPs in the Mini HR application:

```
<!-- Struts Tag Library Descriptors -->
<taglib>
  <taglib-uri>/WEB-INF/tlds/struts-bean.tld</taglib-uri>
  <taglib-location>/WEB-INF/tlds/struts-bean.tld</taglib-location>
</taglib>
<taglib>
  <taglib-uri>/WEB-INF/tlds/struts-html.tld</taglib-uri>
  <taglib-location>/WEB-INF/tlds/struts-html.tld</taglib-location>
</taglib>
<taglib>
  <taglib-uri>/WEB-INF/tlds/struts-logic.tld</taglib-uri>
  <taglib-location>/WEB-INF/tlds/struts-logic.tld</taglib-location>
</taglib>
```

A tag library definition associates a URI (or simple identifier) with the actual location of a ***.tld** file beneath a Web application, so essentially they are aliases. Using these aliases allows JSPs to reference an alias for a Tag Library Descriptor instead of the actual descriptor location. That way, the actual location of the tag library definitions can change without each JSP having to be changed as long as the aliases stay consistent.

Notice in the **web.xml** file that the URI (alias) and the actual location of the TLD files are the same. This is done for simplicity's sake and is a common practice. Note, despite the fact that the URL and location are the same, the definitions in **web.xml** are necessary for JSPs to access the tag libraries.

struts-config.xml

The **struts-config.xml** file, shown next, is the central location for all of a Struts application's configuration settings. Remember from the previous description of the **web.xml** file that the **struts-config.xml** file is used by **ActionServlet** to configure the application. The basic configuration information is covered here, but a complete description will have to wait until you know more about Struts. (A complete discussion of configuration is found in Chapter 16.)

```xml
<?xml version="1.0"?>

<!DOCTYPE struts-config PUBLIC
    "-//Apache Software Foundation//DTD Struts Configuration 1.1//EN"
    "http://jakarta.apache.org/struts/dtds/struts-config_1_1.dtd">

<struts-config>

  <!-- Form Beans Configuration -->
  <form-beans>
    <form-bean name="searchForm"
               type="com.jamesholmes.minihr.SearchForm"/>
  </form-beans>

  <!-- Global Forwards Configuration -->
  <global-forwards>
    <forward name="search" path="/search.jsp"/>
  </global-forwards>

  <!-- Action Mappings Configuration -->
  <action-mappings>
    <action path="/search"
            type="com.jamesholmes.minihr.SearchAction"
            name="searchForm"
            scope="request"
            validate="true"
            input="/search.jsp">
    </action>
  </action-mappings>

  <!-- Message Resources Configuration -->
  <message-resources
    parameter="com.jamesholmes.minihr.ApplicationResources"/>

</struts-config>
```

Struts configuration files are XML-based and should conform to the Struts Configuration Document Type Definition (DTD). The **struts-config.xml** file just shown begins by declaring its use of the Struts Configuration DTD:

```
<!DOCTYPE struts-config PUBLIC
   "-//Apache Software Foundation//DTD Struts Configuration 1.1//EN"
   "http://jakarta.apache.org/struts/dtds/struts-config_1_1.dtd">
```

Next, is the Form Beans Configuration section, which is used to specify all of the **ActionForm** objects used in your Struts application. In this case, you're only using one Form Bean: **SearchForm**. The definition of the Form Bean, shown here, allows you to associate a name or alias of "searchForm" with the **SearchForm** object:

```
<form-bean name="searchForm"
           type="com.jamesholmes.minihr.SearchForm"/>
```

That way, the application code (i.e., JSPs, **Action** objects, and so on) will reference "searchForm" and not "com.jamesholmes.minihr.SearchForm". This allows the class definition to change without causing the code that uses the definition to change.

The next section of the file, Global Forwards Configuration, lists the forward definitions that your application will have. Forward definitions are a mechanism for assigning a name to the location of a page. For example, for the Mini HR application, you assign the name "search" to the "search.jsp" page:

```
<forward name="search" path="/search.jsp"/>
```

Similar to Form Beans, the use of forward definitions allows application code to reference an alias and not the location of pages. Note that this section of the file is dedicated to "Global" forwards, which are made available to the entire Struts application. You can also specify action-specific forwards that are nested in an **<action>** tag in the config file:

```
<action ...>
  <forward .../>
</action>
```

The issue of action-specific forward definitions is examined later in this book.

After the Global Forwards Configuration section comes the Action Mappings Configuration section of the file. This section is used to define the **Action** classes used in your Struts application. Remember from the previous section on **SearchAction.java** that **Action** objects are used to handle discreet Controller tasks. Because the **SearchAction** mapping, shown here, has many settings, each is examined in detail.

```
<action path="/search"
        type="com.jamesholmes.minihr.SearchAction"
        name="searchForm"
        scope="request"
        validate="true"
        input="/search.jsp">
</action>
```

The first part of the Action Mappings Configuration section defines the path associated with this action. This path corresponds to the URL used to access your Struts application. Remember from the "web.xml" section that your application is configured to have any URLs ending in **.do** be handled by **ActionServlet**. Setting the path to "/search" for this action essentially says that a request to "/search.do" should be handled by **SearchAction**. Struts removes the **.do** from the URL (resulting in "/search") and then looks in the **struts-config.xml** settings for an Action Mapping that corresponds to the URL.

The next **<action>** attribute, **type**, specifies the **Action** class that should be executed when the **path** is requested. The **name** attribute corresponds to the name of a Form Bean defined in the **struts-config.xml** file. In this case, "searchForm" corresponds to the Form Bean you set up earlier. Using the **name** attribute tells Struts to populate the specified Form Bean with data from the incoming request. The **Action** object will then have access to the Form Bean to access the request data.

The next two attributes, **scope** and **validate**, are related to the Form Bean defined with the **name** attribute. The **scope** attribute sets the scope for the Form Bean associated with this action. For example, use "request" for request scope or "session" for session scope. The **validate** attribute is used to specify whether or not the Form Bean defined with the **name** attribute should have its **validate( )** method called after it has been populated with request data.

The final **<action>** attribute, **input**, is used to inform the **Action** object what page is being used to "input" data to (or execute) the action; in this case, it is "search.jsp".

The last section of the file, Message Resources Configuration, is used to define the location of the **ApplicationResources.properties** file. Notice that the file is specified using Java's package mechanism: package.package.class (i.e., "com.jamesholmes.minihr .ApplicationResources"). This allows **ActionServlet** to load the properties file from the same place that classes are loaded.

ApplicationResources.properties

The **ApplicationResources.properties** file, shown next, is based on Java's Resource Bundle functionality for externalizing and internationalizing application strings, messages, and labels.

```
# Label Resources
label.search.name=Name
label.search.ssNum=Social Security Number
```

```
# Error Resources
error.search.criteria.missing=<li>Search Criteria Missing</li>
error.search.ssNum.invalid=<li>Invalid Social Security Number</li>
errors.header=<font color="red"><b>Validation Error(s)</b></font><ul>
errors.footer=</ul><hr width="100%" size="1" noshade="true">
```

You'll notice that this file is simply comprised of name-value pairs, where the name is a key and the value is a message corresponding to the key. Each of the name-value pairs is then used by your Struts application whenever a string, message, or label needs to be displayed. Externalizing these strings in a separate file instead of embedding them in your application allows the strings to be changed without having to recompile the application (separation of concerns). Externalizing the strings also allows your application to support internationalization so that it can be tailored to different locales. As you'll see in Chapter 10, I18N with Struts is straightforward and easy with the use of properties files for strings, messages, and labels.

Compiling, Packaging, and Running the Application

Now that you have examined the sample application in detail, it's time to compile, package, and run the application. First, though, download and install the Struts and Tomcat software if you have not already done so. Tomcat is a free servlet engine available for download from the Internet and will be used in the examples in this book for running Struts applications. Tomcat is also the reference implementation for the JSP and servlet specifications from Sun. Of course, you don't have to use Tomcat to run the examples, but it is the only method described by this book. So, to follow along, it is strongly suggested that you use Tomcat.

Each of the following sections is dedicated to a step of the process. First, you will set up the Struts and Tomcat software. Next, you'll compile the application. Then, you'll package the application in a standard Web Archive file. Finally, you'll see how to deploy and run the application with Tomcat.

Downloading and Installing Struts and Tomcat

As mentioned, both Struts and Tomcat are freely available for download from the Internet. Following are the Web sites for each:

- **Struts**   http://jakarta.apache.org/struts/
- **Tomcat**   http://jakarta.apache.org/tomcat/

After you have downloaded the Struts and Tomcat software distributions, you will need to choose a directory to install them to. After selecting a directory, extract the files of each distribution to that directory. For example, if you choose to install the distributions in a directory called **c:\java**, then the Struts files would be located at **c:\java\jakarta-struts-1.1** and Tomcat would be installed at **c:\java\jakarta-tomcat-4.1.27**.

Compiling the Application

The Mini HR application is comprised of several files; however, only the Java source
code files need to be compiled before you package and run the application. Because the
Java source code files use the servlet and Struts APIs, you need to add these libraries
to your Java classpath. You could do this by updating your CLASSPATH environment
variable. Alternatively, you can just specify the classpath when you compile the Mini
HR application.

In addition to the files that you created and reviewed earlier in this chapter, you
also need to copy the following files to the **c:\java\MiniHR\WEB-INF\lib** directory.
These **.jar** files contain the Struts and associated library class files that are necessary
for the Mini HR application to run once it is packaged as a **.war** file.

```
c:\java\jakarta-struts-1.1\lib\commons-beanutils.jar
c:\java\jakarta-struts-1.1\lib\commons-collections.jar
c:\java\jakarta-struts-1.1\lib\commons-lang.jar
c:\java\jakarta-struts-1.1\lib\commons-logging.jar
c:\java\jakarta-struts-1.1\lib\commons-validator.jar
c:\java\jakarta-struts-1-1\lib\digester.jar
c:\java\jakarta-struts-1.1\lib\fileupload.jar
c:\java\jakarta-struts-1.1\lib\jakarta-oro.jar
c:\java\jakarta-struts-1.1\lib\struts.jar
```

Add the following files to the **c:\java\MiniHR\WEB-INF\tlds** directory:

```
c:\java\jakarta-struts-1.1\lib\struts-bean.tld
c:\java\jakarta-struts-1.1\lib\struts-html.tld
c:\java\jakarta-struts-1.1\lib\struts-logic.tld
```

Assuming that you have installed Struts at **c:\java\jakarta-struts-1.1**, installed
Tomcat at **c:\java\jakarta-tomcat-4.1.27**, and placed the Mini HR application files at
c:\java\MiniHR, the following command line will compile the Mini HR application
when run from the **c:\java\MiniHR** directory:

```
javac -classpath WEB-INF\lib\commons-beanutils.jar;
               WEB-INF\lib\commons-collections.jar;
               WEB-INF\lib\commons-lang.jar;
               WEB-INF\lib\commons-logging.jar;
               WEB-INF\lib\commons-validator.jar;
               WEB-INF\lib\digester.jar;
               WEB-INF\lib\fileupload.jar;
               WEB-INF\lib\jakarta-oro.jar;
               WEB-INF\lib\struts.jar;
               C:\java\jakarta-tomcat-4.1.27\common\lib\servlet.jar
```

```
WEB-INF\src\com\jamesholmes\minihr\*.java
-d WEB-INF\classes
```

Notice that you must specify the path to each **.jar** file explicitly. Of course, if you update CLASSPATH, this explicit specification is not needed. You should also notice that the compiled code will be placed into the **WEB-INF\classes** directory, as specified by the **-d WEB-INF\classes** section of the command line. Remember from the earlier discussion that this is the standard Web Archive directory that J2EE servlet containers will look in for compiled Web application code.

Packaging the Application

Because Struts applications are standard J2EE Web applications, this application will be packaged using the standard J2EE Web Archive format. Packaging the application as a **.war** file allows the application to be easily deployed on any J2EE-compliant servlet engine with ease. Because you arranged the files for the Mini HR application in the standard Web Archive directory structure, packaging them into a **.war** file is straightforward.

Following is the command line for creating a **MiniHR.war** file, assuming that you run the command from the Mini HR application directory (**c:\java\MiniHR**):

```
jar cf MiniHR.war *
```

After you run the command, a **MiniHR.war** file will be created and ready for deployment.

Running the Application

Once you have packaged your application, running it is as simple as placing the Web Archive file into Tomcat's **webapps** directory and then starting up Tomcat. By default, Tomcat starts up on port 8080, thus the server can be accessed at **http://localhost:8080/**. To access the Mini HR application, point your browser to **http://localhost:8080/MiniHR/**. You'll notice that the name of your Web Archive file is used for the URL of your application. Because you packaged the Mini HR application in a file called **MiniHR.war**, **/MiniHR/** is used for the application's URL.

When you first access the **http://localhost:8080/MiniHR/** URL, **index.jsp** will be run, because it was specified as the Welcome File in the **web.xml** deployment descriptor. From the opening page, select the Search for Employees link. The Search page allows you to search for employees by name or social security number. If you do not enter any search criteria, an error message will be shown on the page. Similarly, if you enter an invalid social security number, an error message will be shown on the page after you click the Search button.

Figures 2-2 through 2-5 show Mini HR in action.

FIGURE 2-2 The opening screen

FIGURE 2-3 The Employee Search screen

FIGURE 2-4   The Employee Search screen with a validation error

FIGURE 2-5   The Employee Search screen with search results

Understanding the Flow of Execution

Before leaving the Mini HR example, it is necessary to describe the way that execution takes place. As explained in Chapter 1, Struts uses the Model-View-Controller design pattern. The MVC architecture defines a specific flow of execution. An understanding of this flow of execution is crucial to an overall understanding of Struts.

For Mini HR, execution proceeds in the following way:

1. The browser makes a request to Mini HR for an employee lookup. This request is processed by **ActionServlet** (Controller).

2. **ActionServlet** populates the **SearchForm** object (View) with the search criteria entered on the **search.jsp** page.

3. **ActionServlet** delegates request-specific processing to the **SearchAction** object (Controller).

4. **SearchAction** (Controller) interfaces with the **EmployeeSearchService** object (Model) to perform the employee search. **EmployeeSearchService** returns an **ArrayList** of **Employee** objects (Model).

5. **SearchAction** (Controller) forwards control to **search.jsp** (View).

6. **search.jsp** (View) uses the **ArrayList** of **Employee** objects (Model) to generate a response to the browser.

The flow of execution for Mini HR can be generalized for any Struts application as shown here. Figure 2-6 shows the flow execution in graphic form.

1. The browser makes a request to the Struts application that is processed by **ActionServlet** (Controller).

2. **ActionServlet** (Controller) populates the **ActionForm** (View) object with HTML form data and invokes its **validate( )** method.

3. **ActionServlet** (Controller) executes the **Action** object (Controller).

4. **Action** (Controller) interfaces with model components and prepares data for view.

5. **Action** (Controller) forwards control to the JSP (View).

6. JSP (View) uses model data to generate a response to the browser.

Remember, the same basic pattern of execution applies to any Struts application.

Now that you understand the basic structure of a Struts application and how its components work together, its time to move on to an in-depth examination of Struts. As mentioned at the start, all of the topics presented in this chapter are examined in detail in the chapters that follow.

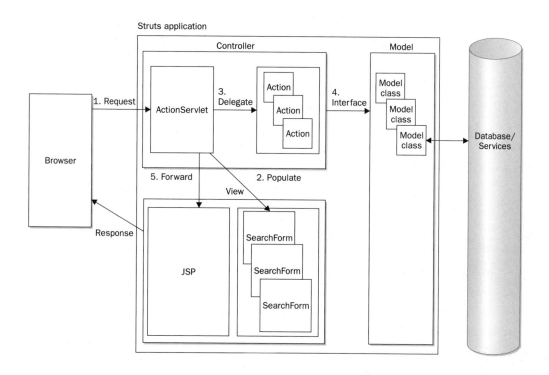

FIGURE 2-6   Flow of execution

CHAPTER 3

The Model Layer

A s you know, Struts is a framework that is used to build applications based on the Model-View-Controller (MVC) architecture. Because the MVC organization is at the foundation of Struts, it is not possible to fully utilize Struts without a clear understanding of each part of the MVC architecture. Therefore, this and the following two chapters examine in depth the Model, View, and Controller portions of a Struts application, beginning in this chapter with the Model.

What Is the Model?

In an MVC application, the Model layer is typically the largest and most important piece. The Model is designed to house the business logic and data access code; in other words, the Model consists of the core of the application. For example, if an application computes the average sell-through rate of a product, the Model layer performs that computation. For an application that maintains a database of employees, complete with salary and tax information, the Model handles the maintenance task. Thus, it is the Model that defines what the application does. The View and Controller interact with the Model and provide a user interface to it.

The MVC architecture dictates that the Model layer should be self contained and function independently from the View and Control layers. That way, the core application code can be used over and over again with multiple user interfaces. For example, you could have a Web interface for the application as well as a stand-alone or wireless interface. Each interface (Web, stand-alone, and so on) would have its own code for the user interface (View), but would reuse the core application (Model) code. This is the basis for the MVC architecture: having a clean separation of responsibilities and reducing coupling between application layers.

Model Layer Breakdown

The typical Model layer of a correctly designed MVC application can be broken down into three conceptual sublayers. Each sublayer can be thought of as a component or responsibility of the Model. Figure 3-1 illustrates this breakdown.

FIGURE 3-1
Model layer
breakdown

Each sublayer does not necessarily represent a separate set of classes, but rather the Model's set of responsibilities. You may choose to house a specific function's code for all layers in one large class, or you may break down each sublayer into fine-grained objects. The level of object granularity is up to you and what's best and/or necessary really depends on the size and complexity of your application. The following are the three sublayers:

- **External interface**   Composed of code that provides an interface that external code uses to interact with the Model.

- **Business logic**   Encompasses the bulk of the Model code and provides the business functionality for an application.

- **Data access**   Composed of code for communicating with an application's data sources such as a database.

Struts and the Model

The Struts framework does not provide any specific features or constraints for developing the Model layer of your application. At first glance this may seem odd, or even a shortcoming, given that Struts is designed for building MVC applications. However, it's actually a key design feature of Struts and is a great benefit. By not dictating how the Model layer should be built, Struts gives your application the flexibility to use any approach or technology for building the Model layer code. Whether it be Enterprise JavaBeans (EJB), Java Data Objects (JDO), or the Data Access Objects (DAO) pattern, Struts will accommodate.

Because the Model defines the business logic, the Model is where Struts ends and your application code begins. Your Model code will be accessed from subclasses of Struts' **Action** object that are part of the Controller layer of the Struts framework. **Action** subclasses interact with the Model via **Action**'s interfaces and use its Data Transfer Objects to pass and retrieve data.

You should not place any business logic or data access code in **Action** objects. Doing so would bypass the separation of the Model and the Controller. Similarly, your Model code should not have any references to Struts code or objects. Violating this rule unnecessarily couples your core application code to Struts.

Reviewing the Model Layer of the Mini HR Application

Because Struts has little to do with the Model layer, there is little more to say about it. However, before moving on, it will be helpful to review the Model layer of the Mini HR application developed in Chapter 2. Doing so clearly illustrates how the Model code is separate from the rest of the application.

Mini HR's Model layer consists of two classes: **EmployeeSearchService** and **Employee**. The **EmployeeSearchService** class is shown next:

```
package com.jamesholmes.struts;

import java.util.ArrayList;

public class EmployeeSearchService
{
  /* Hard-coded sample data. Normally this would come from a real data
     source such as a database. */
  private static Employee[] employees =
  {
    new Employee("Bob Davidson", "123-45-6789"),
    new Employee("Mary Williams", "987-65-4321"),
    new Employee("Jim Smith", "111-11-1111"),
    new Employee("Beverly Harris", "222-22-2222"),
    new Employee("Thomas Frank", "333-33-3333"),
    new Employee("Jim Davidson", "444-44-4444")
  };

  // Search for employees by name.
  public ArrayList searchByName(String name) {
    ArrayList resultList = new ArrayList();

    for (int i = 0; i < employees.length; i++) {
      if(employees[i].getName().toUpperCase().indexOf(name.toUpperCase())
         != -1)
      {
        resultList.add(employees[i]);
      }
    }

    return resultList;
  }
```

```
// Search for employee by social security number.
public ArrayList searchBySsNum(String ssNum) {
  ArrayList resultList = new ArrayList();

  for (int i = 0; i < employees.length; i++) {
    if (employees[i].getSsNum().equals(ssNum)) {
      resultList.add(employees[i]);
    }
  }

  return resultList;
  }
}
```

EmployeeSearchService fulfills all three of the model's sublayers: external interface, business logic, and data access. The external interface is defined by the methods **searchByName( )** and **searchBySsNum( )**. The business logic is contained in the implementation to those methods, which finds an employee based on either his or her name or social security number. Data access occurs each time the hard-coded **Employee** array is used.

In a small, sample application such as Mini HR, there is nothing wrong with implementing the entire Model within **EmployeeSearchService**. However, in a more complicated application, a class such as this would normally be used as only the external interface to the Model. In this approach, it would house only skeletal **searchByName( )** and **searchBySsNum( )** methods, which would pass through (or *delegate*) requests to the business logic sublayer where their actual implementation would exist. For example, the business logic sublayer code could be implemented in a class named **EmployeeSearchImpl**. Furthermore, **EmployeeSearchImpl** would then communicate with data access sublayer classes to actually query employee data from a database or such, rather than containing the data access code itself.

The **Employee** class, shown next, is used as a conduit for transferring data to and from the Model. As such, it can be thought of as being part of the Model layer.

```
package com.jamesholmes.struts;

public class Employee
{
  private String name;
  private String ssNum;

  public Employee(String name, String ssNum) {
    this.name = name;
    this.ssNum = ssNum;
  }
```

```
public void setName(String name) {
    this.name = name;
}

public String getName() {
    return name;
}

public void setSsNum(String ssNum) {
    this.ssNum = ssNum;
}

public String getSsNum() {
    return ssNum;
}
}
```

Typically, an instance of this type is referred to as a Data Transfer Object (DTO) or Value Object (VO) and is part of the external interface sublayer. The Model uses DTOs to send data back through its external interface and to accept data through its external interface. You can think of these classes as interfaces themselves because they specify the format and packaging of the data expected by the Model.

4

CHAPTER

The View Layer

In an MVC application, the View layer provides an interface to your application, be it for users with a browser or for another application using something like Web services. Basically the View layer is the conduit for getting data in and out of the application. It does not contain business logic, such as calculating interest for a banking application or storing items in a shopping cart for an online catalog. The View layer also does not contain any code for persisting data to or retrieving data from a data source. Rather, it is the Model layer that manages business logic and data access. The View layer simply concentrates on the interface.

Keeping the Model and View layers separate from one another allows an application's interface to change independent of the Model layer and vice versa. This separation also allows the application to have multiple interfaces (or views). For instance, an application could have a Web interface and a wireless interface. In this case, each interface is separate, but both use the same Model layer code without the Model layer being tied to either interface or either interface having to know about the other interface.

Struts and the View Layer

Struts provides a rich set of functionality and features for developing the View layer of MVC applications. There are several forms that the View layer of a Struts application can take. It can be HTML/JSP (the most common case) or it can be XML/XSLT, Velocity, Swing, or whatever your application requires. This is the power of Struts and MVC. Because HTML/JSP is the typical View technology used for Java-based Web applications, Struts provides the most functionality and features for developing your application this way. The remainder of this chapter focuses on Struts' support for creating the View layer using HTML/JSP.

Struts' HTML/JSP View layer support can be broken down into the following major components:

- JSP pages
- Form Beans

- JSP tag libraries
- Resource bundles

Each of these components is examined in detail in this chapter, but first it is helpful to understand how they fit together in the View layer.

JSP pages are at the center of the View components; they contain the HTML that is sent to browsers for users to see and they contain JSP library tags. The library tags are used to retrieve data from Form Beans and to generate HTML forms that, when submitted, will populate Form Beans. Additionally, library tags are used to retrieve content from resource bundles. Together, all of Struts' View layer components are used to generate HTML that browsers render. This is what the user sees.

On the back side, the View layer populates Form Beans with data coming from the HTML interface. The Controller layer then takes the Form Beans and manages getting their data and putting it into the Model layer. Additionally, the Controller layer takes data from the Model layer and populates Form Beans so that the data can be presented in the View layer.

The following sections explain each of these major View components in detail.

JSP Pages

JSPs are the centerpiece of the Struts View layer. They contain the static HTML and JSP library tags that generate dynamic HTML. Together the static and dynamically generated HTML gets sent to the user's browser for rendering. That is, the JSPs contain the code for the user interface with which a user interacts.

JSPs in Struts applications are like JSPs in any other Java-based Web application. However, to adhere to the MVC paradigm, the JSPs should not contain any code for performing business logic or code for directly accessing data sources. Instead, the JSPs are intended to be used solely for displaying data and capturing data. Struts provides a set of tag libraries that supports displaying data and creating HTML forms that capture data. Additionally, the tags support displaying content stored in resource bundles. Therefore, JSPs (coupled with Form Beans) provide the bulk of the Struts View layer. The JSP tag libraries glue those two together and the resource bundles provide a means of content management.

Form Beans

Form Beans provide the conduit for transferring data between the View and Controller layers of Struts applications. When HTML forms are submitted to a Struts application, Struts takes the incoming form data and uses it to populate the form's corresponding Form Bean. The Struts Controller layer then uses the Form Beans to access data that must be sent to the Model layer. On the flip side, the Controller layer populates Form Beans with Model layer data so that it can be displayed with the View layer. Essentially, Form Beans are simple data containers. They either contain data from an HTML form that is headed to the Model via the Controller or contain data from the Model headed to the View via the Controller.

   Form Beans are basic Java beans with getter and setter methods for each of their properties, allowing their data to be set and retrieved easily. The **org.apache.struts .action.ActionForm** class is the base abstract class that all Form Beans must subclass. Because Form Beans are simple data containers, they are principally comprised of fields, and setter and getter methods for those fields. Business logic and data access code should not be placed in these classes. That code goes in Model layer classes. The only other methods that should be in these classes are helper methods or methods that override **ActionForm**'s base **reset( )** and **validate( )** methods.

   The **ActionForm** class has a **reset( )** method and a **validate( )** method that are intended to be overridden by subclasses where necessary. The **reset( )** method is a hook that Struts calls before the Form Bean is populated from an HTML form submission. The **validate( )** method is a hook that Struts calls after the Form Bean has been populated from an HTML form submission. Both of these methods are described in detail later in this section.

   Following is an example Form Bean:

```java
import org.apache.struts.action.ActionForm;

public class EmployeeForm extends ActionForm
{
  private String firstName;
  private String lastName;
  private String department;

  public void setFirstName(String firstName) {
    this.firstName = firstName;
  }

  public String getFirstName() {
    return firstName;
  }

  public void setLastName(String lastName) {
    this.lastName = lastName;
  }

  public String getLastName() {
    return lastName;
  }

  public void setDepartment(String department) {
    this.department = department;
  }
```

```
public String getDepartment() {
  return department;
}
}
```

Form Bean properties can be of any object type, be it a built-in class like **String** or a complex application-specific class such as an **Address** object that has fields for street address, city, state, and ZIP. Struts uses reflection to populate the Form Beans and can traverse object hierarchies to any level so long as the getter and setter methods are public. For example, if your Form Bean had an **Address** object field named **address**, to access the **city** field on the **Address** object the Form Bean would need a public **getAddress( )** method that returned an **Address** object. The **Address** object would need a public **getCity( )** method that would return a **String**.

Often, it's best to have Form Bean fields be **String**s instead of other types. For example, instead of having an **Integer**-type field for storing a number, it's best to use a **String**-type field. This is because all HTML form data comes in the form of strings. If a letter rather than a number is entered in a numeric field, it's better to store the value in a **String** so that the original data can be returned to the form for correcting. If instead the data is stored in a **Long**, when Struts attempts to convert the string value to a number, it will throw a **NumberFormatException** if the value is a letter. Then, when the form is redisplayed showing the invalid data, it will show 0 instead of the originally entered value, because letters cannot be stored in numeric-type fields.

Configuring Form Beans

To use Form Beans, you have to configure them in the Struts configuration file. Following is a basic Form Bean definition:

```
<!-- Form Beans Configuration -->
<form-beans>
  <form-bean name="searchForm"
             type="com.jamesholmes.minihr.SearchForm"/>
</form-beans>
```

Form Bean definitions specify a logical name and the class type for a Form Bean. Once defined, Form Beans are associated with actions by action mapping definitions, as shown next:

```
<!-- Action Mappings Configuration -->
<action-mappings>
  <action path="/search"
          type="com.jamesholmes.minihr.SearchAction"
          name="searchForm"
          scope="request"
          validate="true"
          input="/search.jsp">
```

```
   </action>
</action-mappings>
```

Actions specify their associated Form Bean with the **name** attribute of the **action** tag, as shown in the preceding snippet. The value specified for the **name** attribute is the logical name of a Form Bean defined with the **form-bean** tag. The **action** tag also has a **scope** attribute to specify the scope that the Form Bean will be stored in and a **validate** attribute to specify whether or not the Form Bean's **validate( )** method should be invoked after the Form Bean is populated.

The reset( ) Method

As previously stated, the abstract **ActionForm** class has a **reset( )** method that subclasses can override. The **reset( )** method is a hook that gets called before a Form Bean is populated with request data from an HTML form. This method hook was designed to account for a shortcoming in the way browsers handle check boxes. Browsers send the value of a check box only if it is checked when the HTML form is submitted. For example, consider an HTML form with a check box for whether or not a file is read-only:

```
<input type="checkbox" name="readonly" value="true">
```

When the form containing this check box is submitted, the value of "true" is sent to the server only if the check box is checked. If the check box is not checked, no value is sent.

For most cases, this behavior is fine; however, it is problematic when Form Bean **boolean** properties have a default value of "true." For example, consider the read-only file scenario again. If your application has a Form Bean with a read-only property set to true and the Form Bean is used to populate a form with default settings, the read-only property will set the read-only check box's state to checked when it is rendered. If a user decides to uncheck the check box and then submits the form, no value will be sent to the server to indicate that the check box has been unchecked (i.e., set to false). By using the **reset( )** method, this can be solved by setting all properties tied to check boxes to false before the Form Bean is populated. Following is an example implementation of a Form Bean with a **reset( )** method that accounts for unchecked check boxes:

```
import org.apache.struts.action.ActionForm;

public class FileForm extends ActionForm
{
  private boolean readOnly;

  public void setReadOnly(boolean readOnly) {
    this.readOnly = readOnly;
  }

  public boolean getReadOnly() {
    return readOnly;
```

```
    }

    public void reset() {
      readOnly = false;
    }
}
```

The **reset( )** method in this example class ensures that the **readOnly** property is set to false before the form is populated. Having the **reset( )** method hook is equivalent to having the HTML form actually send a value for unchecked check boxes.

A side benefit of the **reset( )** method hook is that it offers a convenient place to reset data between requests when using Form Beans that are stored in session scope. When Form Beans are stored in session scope, they persist across multiple requests. This solution is most often used for wizard-style process flows. Sometimes it's necessary to reset data between requests, and the **reset( )** method provides a convenient hook for doing this.

The validate( ) Method

In addition to the **reset( )** method hook, the **ActionForm** class provides a **validate( )** method hook that can be overridden by subclasses to perform validations on incoming form data. The **validate( )** method hook gets called after a Form Bean has been populated with incoming form data. Following is the method signature for the **validate( )** method:

```
public ActionErrors validate(ActionMapping mapping,
                             HttpServletRequest request)
```

Notice that the **validate( )** method has a return type of **ActionErrors**. The **org.apache.struts.action.ActionErrors** class is a Struts class that is used for storing validation errors that have occurred in the **validate( )** method. If all validations in the **validate( )** method pass, a return value of null indicates to Struts that no errors occurred.

NOTE   *Form Bean data validations could be performed in action classes; however, having them in Form Beans allows them to be reused across multiple actions where more than one action uses the same Form Bean. Having the validation code in each action would be redundant.*

Following is an example Form Bean with a **validate( )** method:

```
import javax.servlet.http.HttpServletRequest;

import org.apache.struts.action.ActionError;
import org.apache.struts.action.ActionErrors;
import org.apache.struts.action.ActionForm;
import org.apache.struts.action.ActionMapping;

public class NameForm extends ActionForm
{
```

```
private String name;

public void setName(String name) {
  this.name = name;
}

public String getName() {
  return name;
}

public ActionErrors validate(ActionMapping mapping,
  HttpServletRequest request)
{
  if (name == null || name.length() < 1) {
    ActionErrors errors = new ActionErrors();
    errors.add("name",
      new ActionError("error.name.required"));
    return errors;
  }

  return null;
}
}
```

This example Form Bean has one field, **name**, that is validated in the **validate( )** method. The **validate( )** method checks whether or not the **name** field is empty. If it is empty, it returns an error indicating that fact. The **ActionErrors** object is basically a collection class for storing **org.apache.struts.action.ActionError** instances. Each validation inside the **validate( )** method creates an **ActionError** instance that gets stored in the **ActionErrors** object. The **ActionError** class takes a key to an error message stored in the Struts resource bundle. Struts uses the key to look up the corresponding error message. The **ActionError** class also has constructors that take additional arguments that contain replacement values for the error message associated with the specified key.

Struts also has a built-in Validator framework that greatly simplifies performing data validations. The Validator framework allows you to declaratively configure in an XML file the validations that should be applied to Form Beans. For more information on the Validator framework, see Chapter 6.

NOTE   *The **validate( )** method will be called only if the Form Bean has been configured for validation in the Struts configuration file.*

The Lifecycle of Form Beans

Form Beans have a defined lifecycle in Struts applications. To fully understand how Form Beans work, it's necessary to understand this lifecycle. The Form Bean lifecycle is shown in Figure 4-1.

FIGURE 4-1
The Form Bean
lifecycle

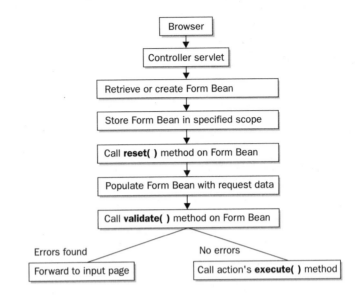

Following is an explanation of the Form Bean lifecycle. When a request is received by the Struts controller servlet, Struts maps the request to an action class that is delegated to process the request. If the action being delegated to has an associated Form Bean, Struts attempts to look up the specified Form Bean in request or session scope, based on how the action is configured in the Struts configuration file. If an instance of the Form Bean is not found in the specified scope, an instance is created and placed in the specified scope. Next, Struts calls the **reset( )** method on the Form Bean so that any processing is executed that needs to occur before the Form Bean is populated. After that, Struts populates the Form Bean with data from the incoming request. Next, the Form Bean's **validate( )** method is called. The next step in the process is based on the return value from the **validate( )** method. If the **validate( )** method records any errors and subsequently returns a non-null **ActionErrors** object, Struts forwards back to the action's input page. If, however, the return value from the **validate( )** method is null, Struts continues processing the request by calling the action's **execute( )** method.

DynaActionForms

A useful addition to the 1.1 release of Struts was the introduction of Dynamic Form Beans. Dynamic Form Beans are an extension of Form Beans that allows you to specify their properties inside the Struts configuration file instead of having to create a concrete class, with a getter and setter method for each property. The concept of Dynamic Form Beans originated because many developers found it tedious to create for every page a Form Bean that had a getter and setter method for each of the fields on the page's HTML form. Using Dynamic Form Beans allows the properties to be specified in a Struts configuration file. To change a property, simply update the configuration file. No code has to be recompiled.

The following snippet illustrates how Dynamic Form Beans are configured in the Struts configuration file:

```
<!-- Form Beans Configuration -->
<form-beans>
  <form-bean name="employeeForm"
           type="org.apache.struts.action.DynaActionForm">
    <form-property name="firstName"
                 type="java.lang.String"/>
    <form-property name="lastName"
                 type="java.lang.String"/>
    <form-property name="department"
                 type="java.lang.String"/>
  </form-bean>
</form-beans>
```

Dynamic Form Beans are declared in the same way as standard Form Beans, by using the **form-bean** tag. The difference is that the type of the Form Bean specified with the **form-bean** tag's **type** attribute must be **org.apache.struts.action.DynaActionForm** or a subclass thereof. Additionally, the properties for Dynamic Form Beans are specified by nesting **form-property** tags beneath the **form-bean** tag. Each property specifies its name and class type. Additionally, an initial value for the property can be specified using the **form-property** tag's **initial** attribute, as shown next:

```
<form-property name="department"
             type="java.lang.String"
             initial="Engineering"/>
```

If an initial value is not supplied for a property, Struts sets the initial value using Java's initialization conventions. That is, numbers are set to zero and objects are set to null.

Because you declare Dynamic Form Beans in the Struts configuration file instead of creating concrete classes that extend **ActionForm**, you do not define **reset( )** or **validate( )** methods for the Dynamic Form Beans. The **reset( )** method is no longer necessary for setting default values because the **initial** attribute on the **form-property** tag achieves the same effect. The **DynaActionForm** class's implementation of the **reset( )** method resets all properties to their initial value when it is called. You can either code the functionality of the **validate( )** method inside action classes or use the Validator framework for validation. These two options eliminate the need to create a **validate( )** method on the Form Bean. If, however, you have a special case where you need to have an implementation of the **reset( )** and/or **validate( )** method for your Dynamic Form Bean, you can subclass **DynaActionForm** and create the methods there. Simply specify your **DynaActionForm** subclass as the type of the Form Bean in the Struts configuration file to use it.

JSP Tag Libraries

Struts comes packaged with a set of its own custom JSP tag libraries that aids in the development of JSPs. The tag libraries are fundamental building blocks in Struts applications because they provide a convenient mechanism for creating HTML forms whose data will be captured in Form Beans and for displaying data stored in Form Beans. Additionally, Struts' tag libraries provide several utility tags to accomplish things such as conditional logic, iterating over collections, and so on. With the advent of the JSP Standard Tag Library (JSTL), many of the utility tags have been superceded. (Using JSTL with Struts is covered in Chapter 15.)

Following is a list of the Struts tag libraries and their purpose:

- **HTML**   Used to generate HTML forms that interact with the Struts APIs.
- **Bean**   Used to work with Java bean objects in JSPs, such as to access bean values.
- **Logic**   Used to cleanly implement simple conditional logic in JSPs.
- **Nested**   Used to allow arbitrary levels of nesting of the HTML, Bean, and Logic tags that otherwise do not work.

Later in this book, each of these libraries has an entire chapter dedicated to its use, but this section provides a brief introduction to using the tag libraries, focusing on Struts' core JSP tag library, the HTML Tag Library, as an example. This library is used to generate HTML forms that, when submitted, populate Form Beans. Additionally, the HTML Tag Library tags can create HTML forms populated with data from Form Beans. To use the HTML Tag Library in a Struts application, you need to include a snippet like the following in your application's Web Archive (**.war**) deployment descriptor, **web.xml**:

```
<taglib>
  <taglib-uri>/WEB-INF/tlds/struts-html.tld</taglib-uri>
  <taglib-location>/WEB-INF/tlds/struts-html.tld</taglib-location>
</taglib>
```

This snippet sets up the HTML Tag Library. For information on setting up the other tag libraries, see their respective chapters.

Recall from the overview of the **web.xml** file in Chapter 2 that the **<taglib-uri>** tag is used to declare the URI (or alias) that will be referenced in each of your JSPs with a **taglib** directive. The **<taglib-location>** tag is used to declare the actual location of the Tag Library Descriptor (**.tld**) file in your Web Archive.

The following snippet illustrates how your JSPs declare their use of the HTML Tag Library with a JSP **taglib** directive:

```
<%@ taglib uri="/WEB-INF/tlds/struts-html.tld" prefix="html" %>
```

Notice that the **uri** attribute specified here is the same as that declared with the **<taglib-uri>** tag in the **web.xml** file. Also, notice that the **prefix** attribute is set to **html**. This attribute can be set to whatever you want; however, **html** is the accepted default for the HTML Tag Library. The **prefix** attribute declares the prefix that each tag must have when it is used in the JSP, as shown here:

```
<html:form action="/Search">
```

Because **html** is defined as the prefix, the **form** tag is used as shown. However, if you were to choose to use a prefix of **struts-html**, the tag would be used as follows:

```
<struts-html:insert attribute="header"/>
```

Resource Bundles

Resource bundles allow Java applications to be easily internationalized by having application content placed into bundles. This content can then be read by the application at run time. Therefore, instead of having content hard-coded in the application, the application reads its content from the bundle. A side benefit of using resource bundles to store application content (whether for internationalization or not) is that the content can be changed without having to recompile the application. Additionally, bundles serve as a central repository for content that is common to multiple uses (i.e., multiple applications). Having content in a central repository reduces unnecessary duplication.

Struts has built-in support for working with Java's resource bundle mechanism. Having this support allows the Struts framework to seamlessly support application internationalization as well as have a mechanism for externalizing content so that it can be easily changed without having to modify JSPs or application code. Struts uses resource bundle resources throughout the framework. For example, resource bundle resources can be accessed from JSPs to populate them with content. Similarly, action objects can access content stored in resource bundles to do such things as generate error or informational messages that get displayed onscreen. Struts' Form Bean validation mechanism is also tied to resource bundles for managing error messages. Actually, there are several uses for resource bundles throughout Struts.

The rest of this section explains how to create a resource bundle properties file and configure Struts to use it. An example of accessing resource bundle content from a JSP is also shown. Later chapters provide specific information about how to use resource bundles in the context of those chapters' topics.

Using resource bundles in Struts is as easy as creating a properties file to store the resources in, and then configuring Struts to use the properties file. Once this is done, accessing the resources is straightforward. Following is a very simple resource bundle properties file containing a few properties:

```
page.title=Employee Search
link.employeeSearch=Search for Employees
link.addEmployee=Add a New Employee
```

Resource bundle properties files simply contain key/value pairs. The resources are accessed by their key. The standard name for the resource bundle properties file in Struts is **ApplicationResources.properties**. In order for Struts to be able to load this file, it must be stored on your application's classpath somewhere.

The following snippet configures the resource bundle with Struts:

```
<!-- Message Resources Configuration -->
<message-resources
  parameter="com.jamesholmes.minihr.ApplicationResources"/>
```

The **parameter** attribute of the **message-resources** tag specifies the fully qualified classpath for the resource bundle properties file minus the **.properties** file extension.

Once a properties file has been created and configured in the Struts configuration file, the resources in the bundle can be accessed from several places in the Struts framework. The most common place is in JSPs. The following snippet illustrates how to use the Bean Tag Library's **message** tag to load a message from the resource bundle:

```
<%@ taglib uri="/WEB-INF/tlds/struts-bean.tld" prefix="bean" %>

<html>
<head>
<title><bean:message key="page.title"/></title>
</head>
<body>

...
```

The value specified with the **message** tag's **key** attribute is the key for a message in the resource bundle. At run time, Struts retrieves the message and places it in the JSP.

NOTE   *Detailed information on internationalizing Struts applications is found in Chapter 10.*

Reviewing the View Layer of the Mini HR Application

To solidify your understanding of the View layer of Struts applications, it will be helpful to review the View layer of the Mini HR application developed in Chapter 2. Doing so clearly illustrates the core components involved in creating the View layer.

Mini HR's View layer consists of a Form Bean, two JSPs, and a resource bundle properties file. The **SearchForm** Form Bean is shown next:

```
package com.jamesholmes.struts;

import java.util.List;
```

```
import javax.servlet.http.HttpServletRequest;

import org.apache.struts.action.ActionError;
import org.apache.struts.action.ActionErrors;
import org.apache.struts.action.ActionForm;
import org.apache.struts.action.ActionMapping;

public class SearchForm extends ActionForm
{
  private String name = null;
  private String ssNum = null;
  private List results = null;

  public void setName(String name) {
    this.name = name;
  }

  public String getName() {
    return name;
  }

  public void setSsNum(String ssNum) {
    this.ssNum = ssNum;
  }

  public String getSsNum() {
    return ssNum;
  }

  public void setResults(List results) {
    this.results = results;
  }

  public List getResults() {
    return results;
  }

  // Reset form fields.
  public void reset(ActionMapping mapping, HttpServletRequest request)
  {
    name = null;
    ssNum = null;
    results = null;
  }

  // Validate form data.
  public ActionErrors validate(ActionMapping mapping,
    HttpServletRequest request)
```

```
{
  ActionErrors errors = new ActionErrors();

  boolean nameEntered = false;
  boolean ssNumEntered = false;

  // Determine if name has been entered.
  if (name != null && name.length() > 0) {
    nameEntered = true;
  }

  // Determine if social security number has been entered.
  if (ssNum != null && ssNum.length() > 0) {
    ssNumEntered = true;
  }

  /* Validate that either name or social security number
     has been entered. */
  if (!nameEntered && !ssNumEntered) {
    errors.add(null,
      new ActionError("error.search.criteria.missing"));
  }

  /* Validate format of social security number if
     it has been entered. */
  if (ssNumEntered && !isValidSsNum(ssNum.trim())) {
    errors.add("ssNum",
      new ActionError("error.search.ssNum.invalid"));
  }

  return errors;
}

// Validate format of social security number.
private static boolean isValidSsNum(String ssNum) {
  if (ssNum.length() < 11) {
    return false;
  }

  for (int i = 0; i < 11; i++) {
    if (i == 3 || i == 6) {
      if (ssNum.charAt(i) != '-') {
        return false;
      }
    } else if ("0123456789".indexOf(ssNum.charAt(i)) == -1) {
      return false;
    }
  }
```

```
    return true;
  }
}
```

The **SearchForm** class is a basic Form Bean with a few properties and implementations for the **reset( )** and **validate( )** method hooks. Mini HR uses this Form Bean to capture search criteria from the search page using the **name** and **ssNum** fields. The **results** field is used to transfer search results back to the search page after a search has been performed.

The **index.jsp** page, shown next, is a simple JSP used as an example menu page for linking to Mini HR's functions:

```
<%@ taglib uri="/WEB-INF/tlds/struts-html.tld" prefix="html" %>

<html>
<head>
<title>ABC, Inc. Human Resources Portal</title>
</head>
<body>

<font size="+1">ABC, Inc. Human Resources Portal</font><br>
<hr width="100%" noshade="true">

&#149; Add an Employee<br>
&#149; <html:link forward="search">Search for Employees</html:link><br>

</body>
</html>
```

This page is the opening page for the Mini HR application and provides a link to the Mini HR search page.

The **search.jsp** page shown here provides the core interface to the Mini HR search functionality. It serves as the search criteria page as well as the search results page.

```
<%@ taglib uri="/WEB-INF/tlds/struts-bean.tld" prefix="bean" %>
<%@ taglib uri="/WEB-INF/tlds/struts-html.tld" prefix="html" %>
<%@ taglib uri="/WEB-INF/tlds/struts-logic.tld" prefix="logic" %>

<html>
<head>
<title>ABC, Inc. Human Resources Portal - Employee Search</title>
</head>
<body>

<font size="+1">
ABC, Inc. Human Resources Portal - Employee Search
</font><br>
<hr width="100%" noshade="true">
```

```
<html:errors/>

<html:form action="/search">

<table>
<tr>
<td align="right"><bean:message key="label.search.name"/>:</td>
<td><html:text property="name"/></td>
</tr>
<tr>
<td></td>
<td>-- or --</td>
</tr>
<tr>
<td align="right"><bean:message key="label.search.ssNum"/>:</td>
<td><html:text property="ssNum"/> (xxx-xx-xxxx)</td>
</tr>
<tr>
<td></td>
<td><html:submit/></td>
</tr>
</table>

</html:form>

<logic:present name="searchForm" property="results">

<hr width="100%" size="1" noshade="true">

<bean:size id="size" name="searchForm" property="results"/>
<logic:equal name="size" value="0">
<center><font color="red"><b>No Employees Found</b></font></center>
</logic:equal>

<logic:greaterThan name="size" value="0">
<table border="1">
<tr>
<th>Name</th>
<th>Social Security Number</th>
</tr>
<logic:iterate id="result" name="searchForm" property="results">
<tr>
<td><bean:write name="result" property="name"/></td>
<td><bean:write name="result" property="ssNum"/></td>
</tr>
</logic:iterate>
</table>
</logic:greaterThan>
```

```
</logic:present>

</body>
</html>
```

This page uses Struts tag library tags to determine whether or not it is being executed before or after a search has been submitted. If the page is being displayed before a search, it simply displays the search criteria form. However, if the page is being displayed after a search, it displays the search criteria form in addition to the search results.

The **ApplicationResources.properties** resource bundle file, shown next, is used by the **SearchForm** Form Bean and the JSPs to retrieve externalized content from a central repository:

```
# Label Resources
label.search.name=Name
label.search.ssNum=Social Security Number

# Error Resources
error.search.criteria.missing=<li>Search Criteria Missing</li>
error.search.ssNum.invalid=<li>Invalid Social Security Number</li>
errors.header=<font color="red"><b>Validation Error(s)</b></font><ul>
errors.footer=</ul><hr width="100%" size="1" noshade="true">
```

The **SearchForm** Form Bean uses this file to store validation error messages. The JSPs use this file to store field labels. Together they are able to leverage Struts' built-in resource bundle mechanism for externalizing content. Doing so allows for easy updates to the content and provides a simple interface for internationalizing the content if necessary.

Alternative View Technologies

Before concluding this chapter, it's important to point out again that Struts is an extensible Web framework that allows you to use any technology you desire to develop the View layer of your Struts application. While this chapter has focused primarily on the built-in JSP-related support, there are several alternatives available. The following table lists a few of the options and a brief description, including a URL for each option.

Technology	Description and URL
Cocoon	The Apache Cocoon project is an XML-based Web application publishing engine for generating, transforming, processing, and outputting data. Don Brown created a Struts plugin, Cocoon Plugin, which integrates the Cocoon framework with the Struts framework. http://struts.sf.net/struts-cocoon/

Technology	Description and URL
stxx	Struts for transforming XML with XSL (stxx) is a third-party extension of the Struts framework that supports using XSLT (XML Style Language Templates) for the View layer. http://stxx.sourceforge.net/
Swing	Java's Swing library can be used to create rich GUI front ends for Struts applications. The following article illustrates how to do this. http://javaboutique.internet.com/tutorials/Swing/
Velocity	The Jakarta Velocity project is a Java-based templating engine that can be used as an alternative to JSPs. VelocityStruts is a Velocity subproject that integrates Velocity with the Struts framework. http://jakarta.apache.org/velocity/tools/struts/

The Controller Layer

The Controller layer of an MVC application is responsible for creating the abstraction between the Model and View layers. That is, the Controller layer acts as a liaison between the Model and View layers, separating one from the other. This abstraction is the foundation of the MVC design pattern. Recall that the Model contains the application's core, including the business logic and data access code, and the View contains the interface to the application. The Controller layer stands between these two layers, allowing them to change independently of one another. With this architecture, the Model (or core application code) is not limited to a singular use. This is a key advantage of MVC.

In MVC Web applications, the Controller layer serves as the central point of access to the application. All requests to an MVC Web application flow through the controller. By doing so, the Controller layer provides processing common to all requests, such as security, caching, logging, and so on. Most importantly, though, having all requests flow through the Controller allows the Controller to have complete autonomy over how requests are mapped to business processing and how the proper View is selected, based on the outcome of the business processing.

Struts and the Controller Layer

Struts provides a robust Controller layer implementation that has been designed from the ground up to be extensible. At its core is the Controller servlet, **ActionServlet**, which is responsible for initializing a Struts application's configuration from the Struts configuration file and for receiving all incoming requests to the application. Upon receiving a request, **ActionServlet** delegates its processing to the **RequestProcessor** class. The **RequestProcessor** class processes all aspects of the request, including selecting the Form Bean associated with the request, populating the Form Bean with data, validating the Form Bean, and then selecting the correct **Action** class to execute for the request. The **Action** class is where the Struts framework ends and your application code begins. **Action** classes provide the glue between the View and Model layers. Figure 5-1 illustrates the Controller layer lifecycle.

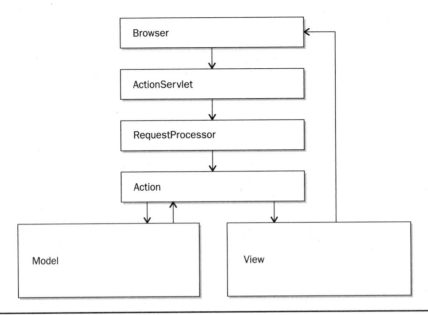

FIGURE 5-1   The Controller layer lifecycle

The following sections explain each of the major Controller layer components in detail.

The ActionServlet Class

The **ActionServlet** class is the main controller class that receives all incoming HTTP requests for the application. Additionally, **ActionServlet** is responsible for initializing the Struts framework for your application. Like any other servlet, **ActionServlet** must be configured in your application's Web application deployment descriptor: **web.xml**. The configuration settings in **web.xml** specify how to map requests to your Web application to the **ActionServlet**. There are two ways that **ActionServlet** can be configured to receive requests in **web.xml**. First, **ActionServlet** can be configured using path mapping, as shown here:

```
<?xml version="1.0"?>

<!DOCTYPE web-app PUBLIC
    "-//Sun Microsystems, Inc.//DTD Web Application 2.3//EN"
    "http://java.sun.com/dtd/web-app_2_3.dtd">

<web-app>
```

```
<!-- Action Servlet Configuration -->
<servlet>
  <servlet-name>action</servlet-name>
  <servlet-class>org.apache.struts.action.ActionServlet</servlet-class>
  <init-param>
    <param-name>config</param-name>
    <param-value>/WEB-INF/struts-config.xml</param-value>
  </init-param>
  <load-on-startup>1</load-on-startup>
</servlet>

<!-- Action Servlet Mapping -->
<servlet-mapping>
  <servlet-name>action</servlet-name>
  <url-pattern>/do/*</url-pattern>
</servlet-mapping>

</web-app>
```

Path mapping routes to **ActionServlet** all requests that match a specified path. The default path is **/do/***, as shown in the preceding **web.xml** file; however, you can use any path that you like.

The second way to map requests to **ActionServlet** is to use extension mapping, as shown next:

```
<?xml version="1.0"?>

<!DOCTYPE web-app PUBLIC
  "-//Sun Microsystems, Inc.//DTD Web Application 2.3//EN"
  "http://java.sun.com/dtd/web-app_2_3.dtd">

<web-app>

  <!-- Action Servlet Configuration -->
  <servlet>
    <servlet-name>action</servlet-name>
    <servlet-class>org.apache.struts.action.ActionServlet</servlet-class>
    <init-param>
      <param-name>config</param-name>
      <param-value>/WEB-INF/struts-config.xml</param-value>
    </init-param>
    <load-on-startup>1</load-on-startup>
  </servlet>

  <!-- Action Servlet Mapping -->
```

```
<servlet-mapping>
  <servlet-name>action</servlet-name>
  <url-pattern>*.do</url-pattern>
</servlet-mapping>

</web-app>
```

Extension mapping maps to **ActionServlet** all requests with the specified extension. The default extension to use is **.do**; however, you can use any extension you like.

NOTE   *Extension mapping is required if you are using Struts' module feature. For more information on modules, see Chapter 9.*

The RequestProcessor Class

Struts uses the **RequestProcessor** class to perform the processing for all requests received by the **ActionServlet**. The **RequestProcessor** class takes each request and breaks its processing down into several small tasks. Each task is carried out by a separate method. This approach lets you customize the way each individual part of the request is processed. Each of these methods is aptly named with a prefix of *process*; for example, **processMultipart( )** and **processPath( )**.

Table 5-1 lists and describes briefly each of the **process*( )** methods from the **RequestProcessor** class (in the order they are executed).

Method	Description
processMultipart( )	Wraps multipart requests with a special wrapper class.
processPath( )	Determines the path that will be used to select an action to which processing is delegated.
processLocale( )	Saves the user's locale in session scope.
processContent( )	Sets the default content type for the response.
processNoCache( )	Sets no-cache HTTP headers for the response if necessary.
processPreprocess( )	Provides a hook for subclasses to override. It is used to tell the request processor whether or not to continue processing the request after this method has been called.
processCachedMessages( )	Removes cached **ActionMessage** objects from the session so that they are available only for one request.
processMapping( )	Selects the action mapping to use for the request.
processRoles( )	Checks if the current user has a role that is allowed to access the requested resource.

TABLE 5-1   The **process*( )** Methods of the **RequestProcessor** Class

Method	Description
processActionForm( )	Creates a new Form Bean or retrieves one from the session for the request.
processPopulate( )	Populates the Form Bean returned from **processActionForm( )** with data from the incoming request.
processValidate( )	Invokes the **validate( )** method on the Form Bean returned from **processActionForm( )** if necessary.
processForward( )	Processes the forward for the action mapping matching the current request path, if the matching mapping is specified to be a forward.
processInclude( )	Processes the include for the action mapping matching the current request path, if the matching mapping is specified to be an include.
processActionCreate( )	Creates or recycles an existing action to process the current request.
processActionPerform( )	Invokes the **execute( )** method on the action returned from **processActionCreate( )**.
processForwardConfig( )	Forwards to the forward returned from **processActionPerform( )**.

TABLE 5-1   The **process*( )** Methods of the **RequestProcessor** Class *(continued)*

By having each phase of the request processing cycle take place in a separate method, request processing can easily be customized. Simply create a custom request processor that extends the base **RequestProcessor** class and override the methods that need to be customized. For example, a custom request processor can apply a logged-in security check before any action is executed. The **RequestProcessor** class provides the **processPreprocess( )** method hook expressly for this. The **processPreprocess( )** method is called before actions are executed. The following example shows how to do this:

```
package com.jamesholmes.example;

import javax.servlet.http.HttpServletRequest;
import javax.servlet.http.HttpServletResponse;

import org.apache.struts.action.RequestProcessor;

public class LoggedInRequestProcessor extends RequestProcessor
{
  protected boolean processPreprocess(
    HttpServletRequest request,
    HttpServletResponse response)
  {
```

```
    // Check if user is logged in.
    // If so return true to continue processing,
    // otherwise return false to not continue processing.
    return (true);
  }
}
```

To use a custom request processor, you have to configure Struts to use it in the Struts configuration file:

```
<controller processorClass="com.jamesholmes.example.LoggedInRequestProcessor"/>
```

NOTE *When using Struts' module feature, each module has its own request processor. Thus, if you want to apply a custom request processor to all modules, you must configure it in each module's Struts configuration file.*

The Action Class

The **Action** class is where the Struts framework ends and your application code begins. As previously mentioned, **Action** classes provide the glue between the View and Model layers and are responsible for processing specific requests. **Action** classes are intended to transfer data from the View layer to a specific business process in the Model layer, and then to return data from the business process to the View layer. Business logic should not be embedded in actions, because that violates the principles of MVC.

Each action is mapped to a path in the Struts configuration file. When a request with the specified path is made to the **ActionServlet**, the action is invoked to process the request. The following snippet illustrates how to configure an action in the Struts configuration file:

```
<action-mappings>
  <action path="/UpdateUser"
          type="com.jamesholmes.example.UpdateUserAction"/>
</action-mappings>
```

Which URL is used to access the action depends on how **ActionServlet** is configured in **web.xml**. If **ActionServlet** is configured to use path mapping, the action defined in the preceding example is accessed as **http://localhost:8080/MiniHR/do/UpdateUser**, assuming a server of **localhost** running on port **8080** and an application deployed as **MiniHR**. If extension mapping were used to configure **ActionServlet**, the URL would be **http://localhost:8080/MiniHR/UpdateUser.do**.

When an action is called to process a request, its **execute( )** method is invoked. The **execute( )** method is analogous to the **service( )** method in servlets. It handles all processing. Following is an example **Action** subclass and its **execute( )** method:

```
import javax.servlet.http.HttpServletRequest;
import javax.servlet.http.HttpServletResponse;

import org.apache.struts.action.Action;
import org.apache.struts.action.ActionForm;
import org.apache.struts.action.ActionForward;
import org.apache.struts.action.ActionMapping;

public class UpdateUserAction extends Action
{
  public ActionForward execute(ActionMapping mapping,
    ActionForm form,
    HttpServletRequest request,
    HttpServletResponse response)
    throws Exception
  {
    // Perform request processing here.
  }
}
```

Struts' Built-In Actions

Struts comes packaged with several built-in utility actions that provide functionality that is useful to many applications. Table 5-2 lists each of the built-in actions and their purpose.

The following sections describe each of the built-in actions in detail.

The org.apache.struts.actions.DispatchAction Class

The **DispatchAction** class provides a mechanism for modularizing a set of related functions into a single action, and thus eliminates the need to create separate, independent actions for each function. For example, consider a set of related functions for adding a user, updating a user, and removing a user. Instead of creating an **AddUserAction** class, an **UpdateUserAction** class, and a **RemoveUserAction** class, by extending **DispatchAction**, you can create one **UserAction** class that has three methods: **add( )**, **update( )**, and **remove( )**. At run time, **DispatchAction** manages routing requests to the appropriate method in its subclass. **DispatchAction** determines which method to call based on the value of a request parameter that is passed to it from the incoming request.

Action	Description
org.apache.struts.actions.DispatchAction	Provides a mechanism for modularizing a set of related functions into a single action instead of having to create separate, independent actions for each function.
org.apache.struts.actions.ForwardAction	Provides a mechanism for forwarding to a specified URL.
org.apache.struts.actions.IncludeAction	Provides a mechanism for including the contents of a specified URL.
org.apache.struts.actions.LocaleAction	Provides a mechanism for setting a user's locale and then forwarding to a specified page.
org.apache.struts.actions.LookupDispatchAction	Provides a mechanism for modularizing a set of related functions into a single action instead of having to create separate, independent actions for each function.
org.apache.struts.actions.MappingDispatchAction	Provides a mechanism for modularizing a set of related functions into a single action instead of having to create separate, independent actions for each function.
org.apache.struts.actions.SwitchAction	Provides a mechanism for switching between modules in a modularized Struts application.

TABLE 5-2   Struts' Built-in Utility Actions

To use **DispatchAction**, you must create a subclass from it and provide a set of methods that will be called to process requests. Additionally, you have to set up for the action an action mapping that specifies the name of a request parameter that will be used to select which method should be called for each request. Following is an example **UserAction** class that extends **DispatchAction**:

```
package com.jamesholmes.example;

import javax.servlet.http.HttpServletRequest;
import javax.servlet.http.HttpServletResponse;

import org.apache.struts.action.ActionForm;
import org.apache.struts.action.ActionForward;
import org.apache.struts.action.ActionMapping;
import org.apache.struts.actions.DispatchAction;
```

```
public class UserAction extends DispatchAction
{
  public ActionForward add(ActionMapping mapping,
    ActionForm form,
    HttpServletRequest request,
    HttpServletResponse response)
    throws Exception
  {
    // Add user.
    ...

    return new ActionForward("success");
  }

  public ActionForward update(ActionMapping mapping,
    ActionForm form,
    HttpServletRequest request,
    HttpServletResponse response)
    throws Exception
  {
    // Update user.
    ...

    return new ActionForward("success");
  }

  public ActionForward remove(ActionMapping mapping,
    ActionForm form,
    HttpServletRequest request,
    HttpServletResponse response)
    throws Exception
  {
    // Remove user.
    ...

    return new ActionForward("success");
  }
}
```

Notice that this class does not provide an implementation for the **execute( )** method the way typical **Action** classes do. This is because **DispatchAction** provides to you an implementation of this method that manages delegating to the individual methods. In order for your **DispatchAction** subclass to work, you must create in the Struts configuration file an action mapping that specifies the name of a request parameter that will be used to select the method that will be called for specific requests. Following is a sample snippet that illustrates how to do this:

```
<action-mappings>
  <action path="/User"
          type="com.jamesholmes.example.UserAction"
     parameter="function"/>
</action-mappings>
```

The value specified with the **parameter** attribute of the **action** tag will be used as the name of a request parameter that will contain the name of a method to invoke for handling the request. Given the preceding mapping of **/User** to **UserAction**, the following URL will invoke the **add( )** method (assuming the application was run on your **localhost** at port **8080** and the application was deployed as **/MiniHR/**):

http://localhost:8080/MiniHR/User.do?function=add

To invoke the **remove( )** method, use the following URL:

http://localhost:8080/MiniHR/User.do?function=remove

The org.apache.struts.actions.ForwardAction Class

The **ForwardAction** class provides a mechanism for forwarding to a specified URL. As explained earlier, in an MVC Web application, all requests to the application are supposed to flow through the Controller servlet. This ensures that the Controller layer of the application has an opportunity to prepare any resources that may be needed to handle the request (i.e., selecting the correct module and so on). **ForwardAction** is provided as a simple utility action that can be used for scenarios in which you simply want to link to a JSP page. Of course, linking directly to the JSP would be a violation of the MVC principles because all requests are supposed to be routed through the Controller. **ForwardAction** can be used to create links to JSPs so that you don't have to create an action whose only responsibility is to forward a request every time you want to link to a JSP. With **ForwardAction**, you simply create an action mapping in the Struts configuration file and specify the location to which the action will forward.

To use **ForwardAction**, simply create action mapping entries in the Struts configuration file, as shown next:

```
<action-mappings>
  <action path="/menu"
          type="org.apache.struts.actions.ForwardAction"
     parameter="/menu.jsp/>
</action-mappings>
```

For each page to which you want to link, you must create an action mapping. Each action mapping uses **ForwardAction**, but specifies a different path for the action. The **parameter** attribute specifies the URL that will be forwarded to when the specified path is accessed.

The org.apache.struts.actions.IncludeAction Class

The **IncludeAction** class provides a mechanism for including the contents of a specified URL. This action behaves similarly to **ForwardAction**, but instead of forwarding to the specified URL, the specified URL is included. This action is useful when you want to include the contents of one page in another.

Using **IncludeAction** is quite easy. Just create action mapping entries in the Struts configuration file:

```
<action-mappings>
  <action path="/menu"
          type="org.apache.struts.actions.IncludeAction"
      parameter="/menu.jsp/>
</action-mappings>
```

For each page you want to include, you must create an action mapping. Each action mapping uses **IncludeAction**, but specifies a different path for the action. The **parameter** attribute specifies the URL that will be included when the specified path is accessed.

The org.apache.struts.actions.LocaleAction Class

The **LocaleAction** class provides a mechanism for setting a user's locale and then forwarding to a specified page. This action provides a convenient mechanism for changing a user's locale. For example, consider a site that is offered in English and Spanish versions. **LocaleAction** can be used to offer users a way to switch between the two languages without having to change their browser settings. With **LocaleAction** you simply create an action mapping and then link to the action, specifying request parameters for which locale to switch to and a page to forward after the locale has been switched.

To use **LocaleAction**, you must create an action mapping entry for it in the Struts configuration file and then link to the action, specifying locale information and a page to forward to after the locale has been set. Following is an example of how to configure **LocaleAction** in the Struts configuration file:

```
<action-mappings>
  <action path="/SwitchLocale"
          type="org.apache.struts.actions.LocaleAction"/>
</action-mappings>
```

Once configured in the Struts configuration file, **LocaleAction** can be put to use. Simply create a link to the action and specify the locale settings that will be set and a page to forward to. Locale settings are specified with two request parameters: **language** and **country**. The page to forward to after setting the locale is specified with the **page** request parameter. The following URL illustrates how to use the request parameters:

http://localhost:8080/MiniHR/SwitchLocale.do?country=MX&language=es&page=/Menu.do

This example URL sets the country to **MX** and the language to **es**. The **/Menu.do** page will be forwarded to after the new locale has been set.

The org.apache.struts.actions.LookupDispatchAction Class

LookupDispatchAction is a subclass of **DispatchAction**. The **LookupDispatchAction** class provides a mechanism for modularizing a set of related functions into a single action, thus eliminating the need to create separate, independent actions for each function. For example, consider a set of related functions for adding a user, updating a user, and removing a user. Instead of creating an **AddUserAction** class, an **UpdateUserAction** class, and a **RemoveUserAction** class, by extending **MappingDispatchAction**, you can create one **UserAction** class that has three methods: **add( )**, **update( )**, and **remove( )**.

At run time, **LookupDispatchAction** manages routing requests to the appropriate method in its subclass. **LookupDispatchAction** determines which method to route to based on the value of a request parameter being passed to it from the incoming request. **LookupDispatchAction** uses the value of the request parameter to reverse-map to a property in the Struts resource bundle file, **ApplicationResources.properties**. That is, the value of the request parameter is compared against the values of properties in the resource bundle until a match is found. The key for the matching property is then used as a key to another map that maps to a method in your **LookupDispatchAction** subclass that will be executed.

To use **LookupDispatchAction**, you must create a subclass from it and provide a set of methods that will be called to process requests. The subclass must also include a **getKeyMethodMap( )** method that maps methods in the class to keys in the Struts resource bundle file. Additionally, you have to set up for the action an action mapping that specifies the name of a request parameter that will be used to select which method will be called for each request. Following is an example **UserAction** class that extends **DispatchAction**:

```
package com.jamesholmes.example;

import javax.servlet.http.HttpServletRequest;
import javax.servlet.http.HttpServletResponse;
```

```java
import org.apache.struts.action.ActionForm;
import org.apache.struts.action.ActionForward;
import org.apache.struts.action.ActionMapping;
import org.apache.struts.actions.DispatchAction;

public class UserAction extends LookupDispatchAction
{
  protected Map getKeyMethodMap()
  {
    HashMap map = new HashMap();
    map.put("button.add", "add");
    map.put("button.update", "update");
    map.put("button.remove", "remove");

    return map;
  }

  public ActionForward add(ActionMapping mapping,
    ActionForm form,
    HttpServletRequest request,
    HttpServletResponse response)
    throws Exception
  {
    // Add user.
    ...

    return new ActionForward("success");
  }

  public ActionForward update(ActionMapping mapping,
    ActionForm form,
    HttpServletRequest request,
    HttpServletResponse response)
    throws Exception
  {
    // Update user.
    ...

    return new ActionForward("success");
  }

  public ActionForward remove(ActionMapping mapping,
    ActionForm form,
    HttpServletRequest request,
    HttpServletResponse response)
    throws Exception
```

```
     {
        // Remove user.
        ...

        return new ActionForward("success");
     }
  }
```

Notice that this class does not provide an implementation for the **execute( )** method as other **Action** classes do. This is because **DispatchAction** provides to you an implementation of this method that manages delegating to the individual methods. Notice also the implementation of the **getKeyMethodMap( )** method. This method is required by **LookupDispatchAction** subclasses and is used to map the names of keys in the Struts resource bundle file to methods in the class. The keys' values in the bundle file are used to match against the value of the incoming request parameter specified by the **parameter** attribute of the **action** tag in the Struts configuration file.

In order for your **LookupDispatchAction** subclass to work, you must create in the Struts configuration file an action mapping that specifies the name of a request parameter that will be used to select the method that will be called for a specific request. Following is a sample snippet that illustrates how to do this:

```
<action-mappings>
  <action path="/User"
          type="com.jamesholmes.example.UserAction"
     parameter="function"/>
</action-mappings>
```

The value specified with the **parameter** attribute of the **action** tag will be used as the name of a request parameter that will contain the value of a key in the Struts resource bundle shown here:

```
button.add=Add User
button.update=Update User
button.remove=Remove User
```

LookupDispatchAction will use the value of the incoming request parameter to perform a reverse lookup for a key in the resource bundle. The matching key is then mapped to the appropriate method to execute based on the key-to-method mapping specified by the **getKeyMethodMap( )** method.

Given the preceding mapping of **/User** to **UserAction**, the following URL will invoke the **add( )** method (assuming the application was run on your **localhost** at port **8080** and the application was deployed as **/MiniHR/**):

http://localhost:8080/MiniHR/User.do?function=Add%20User

To invoke the **remove( )** method, use the following URL:

http://localhost:8080/MiniHR/User.do?function=Remove%20User

The org.apache.struts.actions.MappingDispatchAction Class

MappingDispatchAction is a subclass of **DispatchAction**. The **MappingDispatch Action** class provides a mechanism for modularizing a set of related functions into a single action, eliminating the need to create separate, independent actions for each function. For example, consider a set of related functions for adding a user, updating a user, and removing a user. Instead of creating an **AddUserAction** class, an **Update UserAction** class, and a **RemoveUserAction** class, by extending **MappingDispatch Action**, you can create one **UserAction** class that has three methods: **add( )**, **update( )**, and **remove( )**. At run time, **MappingDispatchAction** manages routing requests to the appropriate method in its subclass. **MappingDispatchAction** determines which method to route to based on the value of a parameter being passed to it from an action mapping in the Struts configuration file.

To use **MappingDispatchAction**, you must create a subclass from it and provide a set of methods that will be called to process requests. Additionally, you must set up action mappings that specify which method will be called for each request. Following is an example **UserAction** class that extends **MappingDispatchAction**:

```
package com.jamesholmes.example;

import javax.servlet.http.HttpServletRequest;
import javax.servlet.http.HttpServletResponse;

import org.apache.struts.action.ActionForm;
import org.apache.struts.action.ActionForward;
import org.apache.struts.action.ActionMapping;
import org.apache.struts.actions.MappingDispatchAction;

public class UserAction extends MappingDispatchAction
{
  public ActionForward add(ActionMapping mapping,
    ActionForm form,
    HttpServletRequest request,
    HttpServletResponse response)
    throws Exception
  {
    // Add user.
    ...

    return new ActionForward("success");
  }
```

```
public ActionForward update(ActionMapping mapping,
  ActionForm form,
  HttpServletRequest request,
  HttpServletResponse response)
  throws Exception
{
  // Update user.
  ...

  return new ActionForward("success");
}

public ActionForward remove(ActionMapping mapping,
  ActionForm form,
  HttpServletRequest request,
  HttpServletResponse response)
  throws Exception
{
  // Remove user.
  ...

  return new ActionForward("success");
}
}
```

Notice that this class does not provide an implementation for the **execute( )** method
as other **Action** classes do. This is because **MappingDispatchAction** provides to you
an implementation of this method that manages delegating to the individual function
methods.

In order for your **MappingDispatchAction** subclass to work, you must create in the
Struts configuration file action mappings that specify the method that will be called for
specific requests. Following is a sample snippet that illustrates how to do this:

```
<action-mappings>
  <action path="/AddUser"
          type="com.jamesholmes.example.UserAction"
     parameter="add"/>
  <action path="/UpdateUser"
          type="com.jamesholmes.example.UserAction"
     parameter="update"/>
  <action path="/RemoveUser"
          type="com.jamesholmes.example.UserAction"
     parameter="remove"/>
</action-mappings>
```

Notice that each action mapping uses the **UserAction** class, but specifies a different path for the action. Each of the unique paths will be processed by the same action, but a different method will be called based on the value specified with the **parameter** attribute. The value specified with the **parameter** attribute must match the name of a method in your **MappingDispatchAction** subclass.

The org.apache.struts.actions.SwitchAction Class

The **SwitchAction** class provides a mechanism for switching between modules in a modularized Struts application. As you'll see in Chapter 9, Struts enables you to modularize your Struts application. Each module has its own set of configuration data as well as its own request processor. **SwitchAction** works similarly to **ForwardAction**, except that before forwarding to a specified resource, the action changes the currently selected module. This is useful for forwarding to JSPs outside of the current module.

NOTE   Detailed information on using Struts' modules feature is found in Chapter 9.

To use **SwitchAction**, you must create an action mapping entry for it in the Struts configuration file and then link to the action, specifying the module to switch to and a page to forward to after the module has been switched. Following is an example of how to configure **SwitchAction** in the Struts configuration file:

```
<action-mappings>
  <action path="/SwitchModule"
          type="org.apache.struts.actions.SwitchAction"/>
</action-mappings>
```

Once configured in the Struts configuration file, **SwitchAction** can be put to use. Simply create a link to the action and specify the module to switch to and a page to forward to afterward. The module to switch to is specified with the **prefix** parameter and the page to forward to afterward is specified with the **page** parameter. The following URL illustrates how to use the request parameters:

http://localhost:8080/MiniHR/SwitchModule.do?prefix=/Corporate&page=/
Menu.do

This example URL switches to the **/Corporate** module, and the **/Menu.do** page will be forwarded to after the module has been switched.

The ActionForward Class

The **ActionForward** class encapsulates a *forward*. Forwards were introduced in Chapter 2, but this section takes a closer look at them because they are used by the **ActionForward** class.

Struts provides the forward as an alternative to hard-coding URLs inside your application. Forwards allow you to define logical names for URLs and then to use the names to reference the URLs. If you reference a URL by its logical name instead of referencing it directly, when the URL changes, you don't have to update each reference to the URL. For example, with forwards you can define a forward for a search page with a logical name of "search" that points to the **/search.jsp** page. Instead of hard-coding the search page's **/search.jsp** URL throughout your application, you use the forward's logical name. If the location of the search page changes, you need to make only one change to the forward definition and all places in the application that point to that forward will receive the change. Essentially, forwards are URL aliases. They shield you from changes and abstract URLs. The application knows only the alias. Where the alias points does not matter.

Forwards are defined declaratively in the Struts configuration file. There are two types of forwards that can be defined, a global forward and an action-specific forward. Global forwards are available throughout an application, whereas action-specific forwards are available only to their respective action. Following is an example of how to define a global forward in the Struts configuration file:

```
<global-forwards>
  <forward name="searchPage" path="/search.jsp"/>
</global-forwards>
```

Action-specific forwards are defined by nesting the **forward** tag inside an **action** tag, as shown next:

```
<action-mappings>
  <action path="/updateUser"
          type="com.jamesholmes.example.UpdateUserAction">
    <forward name="success" path="/updateSuccess.jsp"/>
  </action>
</action-mappings>
```

Struts' **ActionForward** class encapsulates a forward inside an application. For example, the **Action** class's **execute( )** method has a return type of **ActionForward**. After an action executes, it must return an **ActionForward** or null (to indicate processing is complete). **ActionForward**s returned from actions are used to forward to the View layer. The following snippet illustrates how the **ActionForward** class is used in an action:

```
package com.jamesholmes.struts;

import javax.servlet.http.HttpServletRequest;
import javax.servlet.http.HttpServletResponse;
```

```
import org.apache.struts.action.Action;
import org.apache.struts.action.ActionForm;
import org.apache.struts.action.ActionForward;
import org.apache.struts.action.ActionMapping;

public class UpdateUserAction extends Action
{
  public ActionForward execute(ActionMapping mapping,
    ActionForm form,
    HttpServletRequest request,
    HttpServletResponse response)
    throws Exception
  {
    // Perform action processing.

    return new ActionForward("updateSuccess");
  }
}
```

The value passed to the **ActionForward** class's constructor corresponds to the logical name of a forward defined in the Struts configuration file.

Reviewing the Controller Layer of the Mini HR Application

To solidify your understanding of the Controller layer of Struts applications, this section reviews the Controller layer of the Mini HR application developed in Chapter 2. Doing so clearly illustrates the core components involved in creating the Controller layer.

Mini HR's Controller layer consists of a single class: **SearchAction**. The **SearchAction** class, shown next, is responsible for processing requests from the **search.jsp** page:

```
package com.jamesholmes.struts;

import java.util.ArrayList;

import javax.servlet.http.HttpServletRequest;
import javax.servlet.http.HttpServletResponse;

import org.apache.struts.action.Action;
import org.apache.struts.action.ActionForm;
import org.apache.struts.action.ActionForward;
import org.apache.struts.action.ActionMapping;

public final class SearchAction extends Action
{
```

```
public ActionForward execute(ActionMapping mapping,
  ActionForm form,
  HttpServletRequest request,
  HttpServletResponse response)
  throws Exception
{
  EmployeeSearchService service = new EmployeeSearchService();
  ArrayList results;

  SearchForm searchForm = (SearchForm) form;

  // Perform employee search based on what criteria was entered.
  String name = searchForm.getName();
  if (name != null && name.trim().length() > 0) {
    results = service.searchByName(name);
  } else {
    results = service.searchBySsNum(searchForm.getSsNum().trim());
  }

  // Place search results in SearchForm for access by JSP.
  searchForm.setResults(results);

  // Forward control to this Action's input page.
  return mapping.getInputForward();
  }
}
```

When a search is initiated, Struts' **ActionServlet** Controller servlet delegates processing to this **Action** class. This class acts as the liaison between the Model layer and the View layer. Based on the search criteria entered from the View layer, **SearchAction** determines which search method to invoke on the **EmployeeSearchService** Model class and passes in the data from the View layer. **EmployeeSearchService** returns the results of the search and **SearchAction** manages getting the data back to the View layer.

Validator

One of the major benefits of using the Struts framework is its built-in interface for performing data validations on incoming form data. As discussed in Chapter 4, upon submitting an HTML form, Struts captures the form data and uses it to populate one of your application's **ActionForm** subclasses (Form Bean) assigned to the form. The Form Bean's **validate( )** method is then called to perform any necessary validation of the incoming data. If any validations fail, the HTML form is redisplayed so that the invalid data can be corrected. Otherwise, processing continues. This simple interface alleviates much of the headache associated with handling data validation, allowing you to focus on validation code and not the mechanics of capturing data and redisplaying incomplete or invalid data.

Struts' built-in validation interface, however, still has its shortcomings. Often, for example, validation code is heavily duplicated throughout an application because many fields require the same validation logic. Any change in the validation logic for similar fields requires code changes in several places, as well as recompilation of the affected code. To solve this problem and to enhance Struts' validation interface, David Winterfeldt created the Validator framework as a third-party add-on to Struts. Validator was later integrated into the core Struts code base and has since been detached from Struts and is now a stand-alone Jakarta Commons project that can be used with or without Struts. Although Validator is an independent framework again, Struts still comes packaged with it and it is seamlessly integrated.

The Validator framework comes prepackaged with several validation routines, making the transition from hard-coded validation logic painless. Instead of coding validation logic in each Form Bean's **validate( )** method, with Validator you use an XML configuration file to declare the validations that should be applied to each Form Bean. If you need a validation not provided by Validator, you can plug your own custom validations into Validator. Additionally, Validator supports both server-side and client-side (JavaScript) validations whereas Form Beans only provide a server-side validation interface.

Validator Overview

Before getting into the details of using the Validator framework, it's necessary to give an overview of how Validator works. Recall that without Validator, you have to code all of your form data validations into the **validate( )** methods of your Form Bean objects. Each Form Bean field that you want to perform a validation on requires you to code logic to do so. Additionally, you have to write code that will store error messages for validations that fail. With Validator, you don't have to write any code in your Form Beans for validations or storing error messages. Instead, your Form Beans extend one of Validator's **ActionForm** subclasses that provide this functionality for you.

The Validator framework is set up as a pluggable system of validation routines that can be applied to Form Beans. Each validation routine is simply a Java method that is responsible for performing a specific type of validation and can either pass or fail. By default, Validator comes packaged with several useful validation routines that will satisfy most validation scenarios. However, if you need a validation that is not provided by the framework, you can create your own custom validation routine and plug it into the framework.

Validator uses two XML configuration files to tell it which validation routines should be "installed" and how they should be applied for a given application, respectively. The first configuration file, **validator-rules.xml**, declares the validation routines that are plugged into the framework and assigns logical names to each of the validations. Additionally, the **validator-rules.xml** file is used to define client-side JavaScript code for each validation routine. If configured to do so, Validator will emit this JavaScript code to the browser so that validations are performed on the client side as well as the server side. The second configuration file, **validation.xml**, defines which validation routines are applied to which Form Beans. The definitions in this file use the logical names of Form Beans from the **struts-config.xml** file along with the logical names of validation routines from the **validator-rules.xml** file to tie the two together.

Using Validator

Using the Validator framework involves enabling the Validator plugin, configuring Validator's two configuration files, and creating Form Beans that extend Validator's **ActionForm** subclasses. The following sections explain how to configure and use the Validator in detail.

Enabling the Validator Plugin

Although the Validator framework comes packaged with Struts, by default Validator is not enabled. In order to enable and use Validator, you have to add to your application's **struts-config.xml** file the following definition for the **plug-in** tag:

```
<!-- Validator Configuration -->
<plug-in className="org.apache.struts.validator.ValidatorPlugIn">
  <set-property property="pathnames"
```

```
            value="/WEB-INF/validator-rules.xml,
                    /WEB-INF/validation.xml"/>
</plug-in>
```

This definition causes Struts to load and initialize the Validator plugin for your application. Upon initialization, the plugin loads the comma-delimited list of Validator configuration files specified by the **pathnames** property. Each configuration file's path should be specified using a Web application-relative path, as shown in the preceding example.

Note that your application's **struts-config.xml** file must conform to the Struts Configuration DTD, which specifies the order in which elements are to appear in the file. Because of this, you must place the Validator **plug-in** tag definition in the proper place in the file. The easiest way to ensure that you are properly ordering elements in the file is to use a tool like Struts Console that automatically formats your configuration file so that it conforms to the DTD.

Configuring validator-rules.xml

The Validator framework is set up as a pluggable system whereby each of its validation routines is simply a Java method that is plugged into the system to perform a specific validation. The **validator-rules.xml** file is used to declaratively plug in the validation routines that Validator will use for performing validations. Struts' example applications come packaged with preconfigured copies of this file. Under most circumstances, you will use these preconfigured copies and will not need to modify them unless you are adding your own custom validations to the framework.

Following is a sample **validator-rules.xml** file that illustrates how validation routines are plugged into Validator:

```
<!DOCTYPE form-validation PUBLIC
          "-//Apache Software Foundation//DTD Commons
           Validator Rules Configuration 1.0//EN"
          "http://jakarta.apache.org/commons/dtds/validator_1_0.dtd">

<form-validation>
  <global>
    <validator name="required"
        classname="org.apache.struts.validator.FieldChecks"
           method="validateRequired"
      methodParams="java.lang.Object,
                    org.apache.commons.validator.ValidatorAction,
                    org.apache.commons.validator.Field,
                    org.apache.struts.action.ActionErrors,
                    javax.servlet.http.HttpServletRequest"
              msg="errors.required">
      <javascript>
        <![CDATA[
```

```
function validateRequired(form) {
  var isValid = true;
  var focusField = null;
  var i = 0;
  var fields = new Array();
  oRequired = new required();
  for (x in oRequired) {
    var field = form[oRequired[x][0]];

    if (field.type == 'text' ||
        field.type == 'textarea' ||
        field.type == 'file' ||
        field.type == 'select-one' ||
        field.type == 'radio' ||
        field.type == 'password') {

      var value = '';

      // get field's value
      if (field.type == "select-one") {
        var si = field.selectedIndex;
        if (si >= 0) {
          value = field.options[si].value;
        }
      } else {
        value = field.value;
      }

      if (trim(value).length == 0) {
        if (i == 0) {
          focusField = field;
        }
        fields[i++] = oRequired[x][1];
        isValid = false;
      }
    }
  }

  if (fields.length > 0) {
    focusField.focus();
    alert(fields.join('\n'));
  }

  return isValid;
}

// Trim whitespace from left and right sides of s.
function trim(s) {
```

```
            return s.replace( /^\s*/, "" ).replace( /\s*$/, "" );
        }

        ]]>
      </javascript>
    </validator>
  </global>
</form-validation>
```

Each validation routine in the **validator-rules.xml** file has its own definition that is declared with a **validator** tag. The **validator** tag is used to assign a logical name to the routine, with the **name** attribute, and to specify the class and method for the routine. The logical name given to the routine will be used to refer to the routine by other routines in this file as well as by validation definitions in the **validation.xml** file.

Notice that the **validator** tag encapsulates a **javascript** tag. The **javascript** tag is used to define client-side JavaScript code for performing the same validation on the client side as is performed on the server side.

Included Validations

By default, Validator comes packaged with several basic validation routines that you can use to solve most validation scenarios. As mentioned, the sample applications provided by Struts come packaged with preconfigured **validator-rules.xml** files that define these routines. Table 6-1 lists each of the preconfigured validations by logical name and states its purpose.

NOTE *Detailed information on configuring the **validator-rules.xml** file is found in Chapter 18.*

Validation	Description
byte	Validates that the specified field contains a valid byte.
creditCard	Validates that the specified field contains a valid credit card number.
date	Validates that the specified field contains a valid date.
double	Validates that the specified field contains a valid double.
email	Validates that the specified field contains a valid e-mail address.
float	Validates that the specified field contains a valid float.
floatRange	Validates that the specified field contains a valid float and falls within the specified range.
integer	Validates that the specified field contains a valid integer.
intRange	Validates that the specified field contains a valid integer and falls within the specified range.
long	Validates that the specified field contains a valid long.

TABLE 6-1 Validator's Preconfigured Validations

Validation	Description
mask	Validates that the specified field conforms to a given regular expression (or "mask").
maxlength	Validates that the string in the specified field's length is less than or equal to the specified maximum length.
minlength	Validates that the string in the specified field's length is greater than or equal to the specified minimum length.
range	Deprecated Use the intRange validation instead.
required	Validates that the specified field contains characters other than white space (i.e., space, tab, and newline characters).
requiredif	Performs the required validation on the specified field if a specified rule is met.
short	Validates that the specified field contains a valid short.

TABLE 6-1   Validator's Preconfigured Validations *(continued)*

Creating Form Beans

In order to use Validator, your application's Form Beans have to subclass one of Validator's **ActionForm** subclasses instead of **ActionForm** itself. Validator's **ActionForm** subclasses provide an implementation for **ActionForm**'s **validate( )** method that hooks into the Validator framework. Instead of hard-coding validations into the **validate( )** method, as you would normally do, you simply omit the method altogether because Validator provides the validation code for you.

Parallel to the core functionality provided by Struts, Validator gives you two paths to choose from when creating Form Beans. The first path you can choose is to create a concrete Form Bean object like the one shown here:

```
package com.jamesholmes.minihr;

import org.apache.struts.validator.ValidatorForm;

public class LogonForm extends ValidatorForm {
  private String username;
  private String password;

  public String getUsername() {
    return username;
  }

  public void setUsername(String username) {
    this.username = username;
  }

  public String getPassword() {
```

```
    return password;
  }

  public void setPassword(String password) {
    this.password = password;
  }
}
```

This class is similar to one that you would create if you were not using Validator; however, this class extends **ValidatorForm** instead of **ActionForm**. This class also does not provide an implementation for **ActionForm**'s empty **reset( )** and **validate( )** methods, because **ValidatorForm** does.

You configure this Form Bean in the **struts-config.xml** file the same way you would a regular Form Bean, as shown here:

```
<form-beans>
  <form-bean name="logonForm"
             type="com.jamesholmes.minihr.LogonForm"/>
</form-beans>
```

The logical name given to the Form Bean with the **form-bean** tag's **name** attribute is the name that you will use when defining validations in the **validation.xml** file, as shown here:

```
<!DOCTYPE form-validation PUBLIC
          "-//Apache Software Foundation//DTD Commons
           Validator Rules Configuration 1.0//EN"
          "http://jakarta.apache.org/commons/dtds/validator_1_0.dtd">

<form-validation>
  <formset>
    <form name="logonForm">
      <field property="username" depends="required">
        <arg0 key="prompt.username"/>
      </field>
    </form>
  </formset>
</form-validation>
```

Validator uses the value of the **form** tag's **name** attribute to match validation definitions to the name of the Form Bean to which they are applied.

The second path you can choose when creating your Form Bean is to define a Dynamic Form Bean in the **struts-config.xml** file, as shown here:

```
<form-beans>
  <form-bean name="logonForm"
```

```
                    type="org.apache.struts.validator.DynaValidatorForm">
      <form-property name="username" type="java.lang.String"/>
      <form-property name="password" type="java.lang.String"/>
   </form-bean>
</form-beans>
```

Dynamic Form Beans do not require you to create concrete Form Bean objects; instead, you define the properties that your Form Bean should have and their types, and Struts will dynamically create the Form Bean for you. Validator allows you to use this concept just as you would with core Struts. The only difference for Validator is that you specify that your Form Bean is of type **org.apache.struts.validator.DynaValidatorForm** instead of **org.apache.struts.action.DynaActionForm**.

Identical to the way concrete Form Beans work with Validator, the logical name given to Dynamic Form Beans is the name that you will use when defining validations in the **validation.xml** file. Validator uses the matching names to tie the validations to the Form Bean.

In addition to the two standard options for creating Form Beans, Validator provides an advanced feature for tying multiple validation definitions to one Form Bean definition. When using **ValidatorForm-** or **DynaValidatorForm**-based Form Beans, Validator uses the logical name for the Form Bean from the **struts-config.xml** file to map the Form Bean to validation definitions in the **validation.xml** file. This mechanism is ideal for most cases; however, there are scenarios where Form Beans are shared among multiple actions. One action may use all the Form Bean's fields and another action may use only a subset of the fields. Because validation definitions are tied to the Form Bean, the action that uses only a subset of the fields has no way of bypassing validations for the unused fields. When the Form Bean is validated, it will generate error messages for the unused fields because Validator has no way of knowing not to validate the unused fields; it simply sees them as missing or invalid.

To solve this problem, Validator provides two additional **ActionForm** subclasses that allow you to tie validations to actions instead of Form Beans. That way you can specify which validations to apply to the Form Bean based on which action is using the Form Bean. For concrete Form Beans, you subclass **org.apache.struts.validator .ValidatorActionForm**, as shown here:

```
public class AddressForm extends ValidatorActionForm {
   ...
}
```

For Dynamic Form Beans, you specify a type of **org.apache.struts.validator .DynaValidatorActionForm** for your Form Bean definition in the **struts-config.xml** file:

```
<form-bean name="addressForm"
           type="org.apache.struts.validator.DynaValidatorActionForm">
   ...
</form-bean>
```

Inside your **validation.xml** file, you map a set of validations to an action path instead of a Form Bean name, because if you have two actions defined, Create Address and Edit Address, which use the same Form Bean, as shown here, each has a unique action path:

```
<action-mappings>
  <action path="/createAddress"
          type="com.jamesholmes.minihr.CreateAddressAction"
          name="addressForm"/>
  <action path="/editAddress"
          type="com.jamesholmes.minihr.EditAddressAction"
          name="addressForm"/>
</action-mappings>
```

The following **validation.xml** file snippet shows two sets of validations that are intended for the same Form Bean, but are distinguished by different action paths:

```
<formset>
  <form name="/createAddress">
    <field property="city" depends="required">
      <arg0 key="prompt.city"/>
    </field>
  </form>
  <form name="/editAddress">
    <field property="state" depends="required">
      <arg0 key="prompt.state"/>
    </field>
  </form>
</formset>
```

Because your Form Bean subclasses either **ValidatorActionForm** or **DynaValidatorActionForm**, Validator knows to use an action path to find validations instead of the Form Bean's logical name.

Configuring validation.xml

The **validation.xml** file is used to declare sets of validations that should be applied to Form Beans. Each Form Bean that you want to validate has its own definition in this file. Inside that definition you specify the validations that you want to apply to the Form Bean's fields. Following is a sample **validation.xml** file that illustrates how validations are defined:

```
<!DOCTYPE form-validation PUBLIC
        "-//Apache Software Foundation//DTD Commons
         Validator Rules Configuration 1.0//EN"
        "http://jakarta.apache.org/commons/dtds/validator_1_0.dtd">
```

```
<form-validation>
  <formset>
    <form name="logonForm">
      <field property="username" depends="required">
        <arg0 key="prompt.username"/>
      </field>
      <field property="password" depends="required">
        <arg0 key="prompt.password"/>
      </field>
    </form>
  </formset>
</form-validation>
```

The first element in the **validation.xml** file is the **<form-validation>** element. This element is the master element for the file and is defined only once. Inside the **<form-validation>** element you define **<form-set>** elements that encapsulate multiple **<form>** elements. Generally, you will define only one **<form-set>** element in your file; however, you would use a separate one for each locale if you were internationalizing validations.

Each **<form>** element uses the **name** attribute to associate a name to the set of field validations it encompasses. Validator uses this logical name to map the validations to a Form Bean defined in the **struts-config.xml** file. Based on the type of Form Bean being validated, Validator will attempt to match the name either against a Form Bean's logical name or against an action's path. Inside the **<form>** element, **<field>** elements are used to define the validations that will be applied to specified Form Bean fields. The **<field>** element's **property** attribute corresponds to the name of a field in the specified Form Bean. The **depends** attribute specifies the logical names of validation routines from the **validator-rules.xml** file that should be applied to the field. The validations specified with the **depends** attribute will be performed in the order specified and they all must pass.

NOTE *Detailed information on configuring the* **validation.xml** *file is found in Chapter 18.*

Configuring ApplicationResources.properties

Validator uses Struts' Resource Bundle mechanism for externalizing error messages. Instead of having hard-coded error messages in the framework, Validator allows you to specify a key to a message in the **ApplicationResources.properties** file that is returned if a validation fails. Each validation routine in the **validator-rules.xml** file specifies an error message key with the **validator** tag's **msg** attribute, as shown here:

```
<validator name="required"
      classname="org.apache.struts.validator.FieldChecks"
         method="validateRequired"
   methodParams="java.lang.Object,
```

```
    org.apache.commons.validator.ValidatorAction,
    org.apache.commons.validator.Field,
    org.apache.struts.action.ActionErrors,
    javax.servlet.http.HttpServletRequest"
msg="errors.required">
```

If the validation fails when it is run, the message corresponding to the key specified by the **msg** attribute will be returned.

The following snippet shows the default set of validation error messages from the **ApplicationResources.properties** file that comes prepackaged with Struts' example applications. Each message key corresponds to those specified by the validation routines in the **validator-rules.xml** file that also comes prepackaged with Struts' example applications:

```
# Error messages for Validator framework validations
errors.required={0} is required.
errors.minlength={0} cannot be less than {1} characters.
errors.maxlength={0} cannot be greater than {2} characters.
errors.invalid={0} is invalid.
errors.byte={0} must be a byte.
errors.short={0} must be a short.
errors.integer={0} must be an integer.
errors.long={0} must be a long.
errors.float={0} must be a float.
errors.double={0} must be a double.
errors.date={0} is not a date.
errors.range={0} is not in the range {1} through {2}.
errors.creditcard={0} is not a valid credit card number.
errors.email={0} is an invalid e-mail address.
```

Notice that each message has placeholders in the form of {0}, {1}, or {2}. At run time, the placeholders will be substituted for another value such as the name of the field being validated. This feature is especially useful in allowing you to create generic validation error messages that can be reused for several different fields of the same type.

Take for example the **required** validation's error message, **errors.required**:

```
errors.required={0} is required.
```

When you use the **required** validation in the **validation.xml** file, you have to define the value that should be used to substitute {0} in the error message:

```
<form name="auctionForm">
  <field property="bid" depends="required">
    <arg0 key="prompt.bid"/>
  </field>
</form>
```

Error messages can have up to four placeholders: {0} – {3}. These placeholders are known as *arg0 – arg3*, respectively, and can be specified using the **arg0 – arg3** tags. In the preceding example, the **arg0** tag specifies the value that should be used to replace the {0} placeholder. This tag's **key** attribute specifies a message key from the **ApplicationResources.properties** file, such as the one shown next, whose value will be used as the replacement for the placeholder:

```
prompt.bid=Auction Bid
```

Using a message key for the placeholder value frees you from having to hard-code the replacement value over and over in the **validation.xml** file. However, if you don't want to use the Resource Bundle key/value mechanism to specify placeholder values, you can explicitly specify the placeholder value by using the following syntax for the **arg0** tag:

```
<arg0 key="Auction Bid" resource="false"/>
```

In this example, the **resource** attribute is set to "false", telling Validator that the value specified with the **key** attribute should be taken as the literal placeholder value and not as a key for a message in the **ApplicationResources.properties** file.

NOTE *Detailed information on the ApplicationResources.properties file is found in Chapter 10.*

Enabling Client-Side Validations

In addition to providing a framework for simplifying server-side form data validations, Validator provides an easy-to-use mechanism for performing client-side validations. Each validation routine defined in the **validator-rules.xml** file optionally specifies JavaScript code that can be run in the browser (client side) to perform the same validations that take place on the server side. When run on the client side, the validations will not allow the form to be submitted until they have all passed.

To enable client-side validation, you have to place the HTML Tag Library's **javascript** tag in each JSP for which you want validation performed, as shown here:

```
<html:javascript formName="logonForm"/>
```

The **javascript** tag requires that you use the **formName** attribute to specify the name of a **<form>** definition from the **validation.xml** file, as shown here, for which you want validations performed:

```
<form name="logonForm">
  <field property="username" depends="required">
    <arg0 key="prompt.username"/>
```

```
    </field>
    <field property="password" depends="required">
      <arg0 key="prompt.password"/>
    </field>
</form>
```

All the validations that you have specified for the **<form>** definition to run on the server side will be run on the client side.

Creating Custom Validations

Validator comes packaged with several useful validations that will suit most validation scenarios; however, your application may require a specific validation that is not provided by the framework. For this situation, Validator provides a simple interface for creating your own custom validations that can easily be plugged into the framework. Following is a list of the steps you need to take to create your own custom validation:

1. Create a new validation method.
2. Add a new validation rule to the **validator-rules.xml** file.
3. Add new validation definitions to the **validation.xml** file.
4. Add messages to the **ApplicationResources.properties** file.

The following sections walk through each step of the process in detail, enabling you to create a custom validation based on the Social Security Number validation used in the example Mini HR application in Chapter 2. Remember that the Social Security Number validation in Chapter 2 was defined inside of the **SearchForm** Form Bean class. Creating a custom validation for social security numbers enables the validation code to be reused and to be used declaratively instead of being hard-coded in each Form Bean that wants to use it.

Creating a Validation Method

The first step in creating a custom validation is to create a validation method that can be called by the Validator framework. Typically, all of an application's methods for custom validations are grouped into a class of their own, as is the case for the example in this section. However, you can place the method in any class. Your validation method needs to have the following signature:

```
public static boolean validateSsNum(java.lang.Object,
  org.apache.commons.validator.ValidatorAction,
  org.apache.commons.validator.Field,
  org.apache.struts.action.ActionErrors,
  javax.servlet.http.HttpServletRequest);
```

Of course, the name of your method will vary, but its arguments should match the types shown in the preceding example. Table 6-2 explains each of the validation method's arguments.

Following is the custom validation code for validating social security numbers. Notice that the **validateSsNum( )** method conforms to the proper method signature for custom validations.

```
package com.jamesholmes.minihr;

import javax.servlet.http.HttpServletRequest;
import org.apache.commons.validator.Field;
import org.apache.commons.validator.ValidatorAction;
import org.apache.commons.validator.ValidatorUtil;
import org.apache.struts.action.ActionErrors;
import org.apache.struts.validator.Resources;

public class MiniHrValidator
{
  public static boolean validateSsNum(Object bean,
    ValidatorAction action,
    Field field,
    ActionErrors errors,
    HttpServletRequest request)
  {
    String value =
      ValidatorUtil.getValueAsString(bean, field.getProperty());

    if (value == null || value.length() < 11) {
      errors.add(field.getKey(),
        Resources.getActionError(request, action, field));
      return false;
    }

    for (int i = 0; i < 11; i++) {
      if (i == 3 || i == 6) {
        if (value.charAt(i) != '-') {
          errors.add(field.getKey(),
            Resources.getActionError(request, action, field));
          return false;
        }
      } else if ("0123456789".indexOf(value.charAt(i)) == -1) {
        errors.add(field.getKey(),
          Resources.getActionError(request, action, field));
        return false;
      }
    }

    return true;
  }
}
```

Argument	Description
java.lang.Object	The Form Bean object (down casted to **Object**) contains the field to be validated.
org.apache.commons.validator.ValidatorAction	The **ValidatorAction** object encapsulates the **<validator>** definition from the **validator-rules.xml** file for this validation routine.
org.apache.commons.validator.Field	The **Field** object encapsulates the **<field>** definition from the **validation.xml** file for the field that is currently being validated.
org.apache.struts.action.ActionErrors	The **ActionErrors** object stores validation error messages for the field that is currently being validated.
javax.servlet.http.HttpServletRequest	The **HTTPServletRequest** object encapsulates the current HTTP request.

TABLE 6-2 The Validation Method Arguments

The **validateSsNum( )** method begins by retrieving the value for the field being validated. The value is retrieved by determining the field's name with a call to **field.getProperty( )** and then looking up that field in the Form Bean with a call to **ValidatorUtil.getValueAsString( )**. The **getValueAsString( )** method matches the name of the field with the name of one of the Form Bean fields and then gets that field's value. The rest of the **validateSsNum( )** method performs the actual validation logic. If the validation fails for any reason, an error message will be stored in the **errors ActionErrors** object.

Adding a New Validation Rule

After the custom validation code has been created, a new validation rule needs to be added to the **validator-rules.xml** file. As discussed earlier in this chapter, validation rules "plug" validation methods into the Validator. Once defined in **validator-rules.xml**, as shown here, the validation rule can be referenced in the **validation.xml** file:

```
<validator name="ssNum"
      classname="com.jamesholmes.minihr.MiniHrValidator"
         method="validateSsNum"
   methodParams="java.lang.Object,
               org.apache.commons.validator.ValidatorAction,
               org.apache.commons.validator.Field,
               org.apache.struts.action.ActionErrors,
               javax.servlet.http.HttpServletRequest"
            msg="errors.ssNum">
  <javascript>
    <![CDATA[
```

```
function validateSsNum(form) {
  var bValid = true;
  var focusField = null;
  var i = 0;
  var fields = new Array();
  oSsNum = new ssNum();

  for (x in oSsNum) {
    if ((form[oSsNum[x][0]].type == 'text' ||
         form[oSsNum[x][0]].type == 'textarea') &&
        (form[oSsNum[x][0]].value.length > 0))
    {
      var value = form[oSsNum[x][0]].value;
      var bRightFormat = true;

      if (value.length != 11) {
        bRightFormat = false;
      }

      for (var n = 0; n < 11; n++) {
        if (n == 3 || n == 6) {
          if (value.substring(n, n+1) != '-') {
            bRightFormat = false;
          }
        } else if ("0123456789".indexOf(
                      value.substring(n, n+1)) == -1) {
          bRightFormat = false;
        }
      }

      if (!bRightFormat) {
        if (i == 0) {
          focusField = form[oSsNum[x][0]];
        }
        fields[i++] = oSsNum[x][1];
        bValid = false;
      }
    }
  }
  if (fields.length > 0) {
    focusField.focus();
    alert(fields.join('\n'));
  }
  return bValid;
}
]]>
</javascript>
</validator>
```

As you can see, the validation rule applies a name to the validation with the **name** attribute; specifies the class that the validation method is housed in with the **classname** attribute; and specifies the validation method's arguments with the **methodParams** attribute. The **msg** attribute specifies a key that will be used to look up an error message in the **ApplicationResources.properties** file if the validation fails. Note that the name applied with the **name** attribute is the logical name for the rule and will be used to apply the rule to definitions in the **validation.xml** file.

The preceding custom validation rule also defines JavaScript code, inside the opening and closing **<javascript>** elements, which will be used if client-side validation is enabled when using the rule. The JavaScript code simply performs the same validation on the client side as is performed on the server side. If the JavaScript validation fails, it will alert the user and prevent the HTML form from being submitted.

Note that validation rules must be placed underneath the **<global>** element in the **validator-rules.xml** file, as shown here:

```
<form-validation>
  <global>
    <validator name="ssnum" …/>
    …
    …
  </global>
</form-validation>
```

Of course, the order of the **<validator>** elements underneath the **<global>** element is arbitrary, so you can place the new "ssnum" validation rule anywhere.

Adding New Validation Definitions

Once you have defined your custom validation rule in the **validator-rules.xml** file, you can make use of it by referencing its logical name in the **validation.xml** file:

```
<!DOCTYPE form-validation PUBLIC
          "-//Apache Software Foundation//DTD Commons
           Validator Rules Configuration 1.0//EN"
          "http://jakarta.apache.org/commons/dtds/validator_1_0.dtd">

<form-validation>
  <formset>
    <form name="searchForm">
      <field property="ssNum" depends="required,ssNum">
        <arg0 key="prompt.ssNum"/>
      </field>
    </form>
  </formset>
</form-validation>
```

In the preceding validation definition, each of the comma-delimited values of the **field** tag's **depends** attribute corresponds to the logical name of a validation rule defined in the **validation-rules.xml** file. The use of "ssNum" instructs Validator to use the custom Social Security Number validation. Each time you want to use the new Social Security Number validation, you simply have to add its logical name to the **depends** attribute of a **field** tag.

Adding Messages to the ApplicationResources.properties File

The final step in creating a custom validation is to add messages to the **ApplicationResources.properties** file:

```
prompt.ssNum=Social Security Number
errors.ssNum={0} is not a valid Social Security Number
```

Remember that the **errors.ssNum** message key was specified by the **msg** attribute of the **validator** tag for the custom validation rule in the **validator-rules.xml** file. The key's corresponding message will be used if the validation fails. The **prompt.ssNum** message key was specified by the **arg0** tag of the validation definition in the **validation.xml** file. Its corresponding message will be used as the parametric replacement for the **errors.ssNum** message's {0} parameter. Thus, if the Social Security Number custom validation fails, the following error message will be generated by substituting the **prompt.ssNum** message for {0} in the **errors.ssNum** message:

```
Social Security Number is not a valid Social Security Number
```

Internationalizing Validations

Similar to other areas of Struts, Validator fully supports internationalization. Remember that internationalization is the process of tailoring content to a specific locale or region. In Validator's case, internationalization means tailoring validation error messages to a specific locale and/or tailoring actual validation routines to a specific locale. This way, the U.S. and French versions of a Web site can each have their own language-specific validation error messages. Similarly, internationalization enables the U.S. and French versions of a Web site to validate entries in monetary fields differently. The U.S. version requires commas to separate dollar values and a period to demarcate cents (i.e., 123,456.78), whereas the French (Euro monetary system) version requires periods to separate dollar amounts and a comma to demarcate cents (i.e., 123.456,78).

Tailoring validation error messages to a specific locale is built into Struts by way of its Resource Bundle mechanism for externalizing application strings, messages, and labels. You simply create an **ApplicationResources.properties** file for each locale you want to support. Each locale-specific properties file will have a locale identifier at the end of the filename that denotes which locale it is for, such as **ApplicationResources_ ja.properties** for Japan. (For detailed information on internationalizing a Struts application, see Chapter 10.)

Thus, when Validator goes to load an error message, it will use the locale for the current request to determine which properties file to load the message from. Remember that each validation rule in the **validator-rules.xml** file specifies a key for a validation error message stored in the **ApplicationResources.properties** files. This key is the same across each locale's properties file, thus allowing Validator to load the appropriate message based on only a locale and a key.

Tailoring validation routines to specific locales is similar to tailoring error messages; you have to define validation definitions in the **validation.xml** file for each locale. The **validation.xml** file contains a **form-validation** tag that contains one or more **formset** tags, which in turn contain one or more **form** tags, and so on:

```
<!DOCTYPE form-validation PUBLIC
        "-//Apache Software Foundation//DTD Commons
         Validator Rules Configuration 1.0//EN"
        "http://jakarta.apache.org/commons/dtds/validator_1_0.dtd">

<form-validation>
  <formset>
    <form name="auctionForm">
      <field property="bid" depends="mask">
        <var>
          <var-name>mask</var-name>
          <var-value>^\d{1,3}(,?\d{3})*\.?(\d{1,2})?$</var-value>
        </var>
      </field>
    </form>
  </formset>
</form-validation>
```

The **form-set** tag takes optional attributes, **country** and **language**, to tailor its nested forms to a specific locale. In the preceding example, all locales use the same currency validation to validate the "bid" property, because neither the **country** attribute nor the **language** attribute was specified for the **form-set** tag.

In order to have a generic currency validation for all users of the Web site and a Euro-specific currency validation for users from France, you'd create an additional **form-set** definition specifically for the French users, as shown here:

```
<!DOCTYPE form-validation PUBLIC
        "-//Apache Software Foundation//DTD Commons
         Validator Rules Configuration 1.0//EN"
        "http://jakarta.apache.org/commons/dtds/validator_1_0.dtd">

<form-validation>
  <formset>
    <form name="auctionForm">
      <field property="bid" depends="required,mask">
```

```
        <var>
          <var-name>mask</var-name>
          <var-value>^\d{1,3}(,?\d{3})*\.?(\d{1,2})?$</var-value>
        </var>
      </field>
    </form>
  </formset>
  <formset country="fr">
    <form name="auctionForm">
      <field property="bid" depends="required,mask">
        <var>
          <var-name>mask</var-name>
          <var-value>^\d{1,3}(\.?\d{3})*,?(\d{1,2})?$</var-value>
        </var>
      </field>
    </form>
  </formset>
</form-validation>
```

In this listing, the second **<formset>** definition specifies a **country** attribute set to "fr".
That instructs Validator to use the enclosed validation definitions for users with a
French locale. Notice that the bid validation in the second **<formset>** definition is
different from the first definition, as the period and comma are transposed in the mask
value. Thus, the first **<formset>** definition validates that bids are in U.S. currency
format and the second definition validates that bids are in Euro currency format.

A powerful feature of using internationalized **<formset>** definitions is that you can
define only the validations that are locale-specific, and all other validations are taken
from the default **<formset>** definition.

Adding Validator to the Mini HR Application

Now that you've seen the benefits of using the Validator framework and how it works,
you are ready to revisit the Mini HR application and replace the hard-coded validation
logic with Validator. Following is the list of steps involved in adding the Validator to
the Mini HR application:

1. Change **SearchForm** to extend **ValidatorForm**.

2. Add a **validator-rules.xml** file.

3. Create a **validation.xml** file.

4. Add the Validator plugin to the **struts-config.xml** file.

5. Add Validation error messages to the **ApplicationResources.properties** file.

6. Recompile, repackage, and run the updated application.

The following sections walk through each step of the process in detail.

Change SearchForm to Extend ValidatorForm

The first step in converting the Mini HR application to use Validator is to change
SearchForm to extend Validator's **ValidatorForm** class instead of extending Struts'
basic **ActionForm** class. Recall that **ValidatorForm** extends **ActionForm** and provides
an implementation for its **reset( )** and **validate( )** methods that hook into the Validator
framework; thus, those methods should be removed from the **SearchForm** class.
Additionally, the **isValidSsNum( )** method should be removed from the **SearchForm**
class because its functionality is being replaced by Validator as well.

Following is the updated **SearchForm.java** file:

```
package com.jamesholmes.minihr;

import java.util.List;
import org.apache.struts.validator.ValidatorForm;

public class SearchForm extends ValidatorForm
{
  private String name = null;
  private String ssNum = null;
  private List results = null;

  public void setName(String name) {
    this.name = name;
  }

  public String getName() {
    return name;
  }

  public void setSsNum(String ssNum) {
    this.ssNum = ssNum;
  }

  public String getSsNum() {
    return ssNum;
  }

  public void setResults(List results) {
    this.results = results;
  }

  public List getResults() {
    return results;
  }
}
```

Notice that this file no longer has the **reset( )**, **validate( )**, and **validateSsNum( )** methods
and that the class been updated to extend **ValidatorForm**.

Add a validator-rules.xml File

As mentioned earlier in this chapter, the sample applications that come packaged in Struts distributions contain a **validator-rules.xml** file underneath their **WEB-INF** directories that are preconfigured for all of Validator's basic validations. You will need to copy one of the preconfigured copies of the file to Mini HR's **WEB-INF** directory (e.g., **c:\java\MiniHR\WEB-INF**). Because this file is so large, its contents will not be shown here.

Create a validation.xml File

After removing the hard-coded validation logic from **SearchForm** and adding a **validator-rules.xml** file, you must create a **validation.xml** file. This file will inform Validator which validations from the **validator-rules.xml** file should be applied to **SearchForm**. Following is a basic **validation.xml** file that validates that social security numbers have the proper format if entered:

```
<!DOCTYPE form-validation PUBLIC
          "-//Apache Software Foundation//DTD Commons
            Validator Rules Configuration 1.0//EN"
          "http://jakarta.apache.org/commons/dtds/validator_1_0.dtd">

<form-validation>
  <formset>
    <form name="searchForm">
      <field property="ssNum" depends="mask">
        <arg0 key="label.search.ssNum"/>
        <var>
          <var-name>mask</var-name>
          <var-value>^\d{3}-\d{2}-\d{4}$</var-value>
        </var>
      </field>
    </form>
  </formset>
</form-validation>
```

Notice that this file does not contain any validation definitions to ensure that either a name or a social security number was entered, the way the original hard-coded logic did. This is because such logic is complicated to implement with Validator and thus should be implemented using Struts' basic validation mechanism.

Add the Validator Plugin to the struts-config.xml File

After setting up Validator's configuration files, the following snippet must be added to the Struts configuration file to cause Struts to load the Validator plugin:

```
<!-- Validator Configuration -->
<plug-in className="org.apache.struts.validator.ValidatorPlugIn">
```

```
        <set-property property="pathnames"
                   value="/WEB-INF/validator-rules.xml,
                        /WEB-INF/validation.xml"/>
</plug-in>
```

Notice that each of the configuration files is specified with the **set-property** tag. The following snippet lists the updated Struts configuration file for Mini HR in its entirety.

```
<!DOCTYPE struts-config PUBLIC
    "-//Apache Software Foundation//DTD Struts Configuration 1.1//EN"
    "http://jakarta.apache.org/struts/dtds/struts-config_1_1.dtd">

<struts-config>

    <!-- Form Beans Configuration -->
    <form-beans>
        <form-bean name="searchForm"
                   type="com.jamesholmes.minihr.SearchForm"/>
    </form-beans>

    <!-- Global Forwards Configuration -->
    <global-forwards>
        <forward name="search" path="/search.jsp"/>
    </global-forwards>

    <!-- Action Mappings Configuration -->
    <action-mappings>
        <action path="/search"
                type="com.jamesholmes.minihr.SearchAction"
                name="searchForm"
                scope="request"
                validate="true"
                input="/search.jsp">
        </action>
    </action-mappings>

    <!-- Message Resources Configuration -->
    <message-resources
        parameter="com.jamesholmes.minihr.ApplicationResources"/>

    <!-- Validator Configuration -->
    <plug-in className="org.apache.struts.validator.ValidatorPlugIn">
        <set-property property="pathnames"
                   value="/WEB-INF/validator-rules.xml,
                        /WEB-INF/validation.xml"/>
    </plug-in>

</struts-config>
```

Add Validation Error Messages to the ApplicationResources.properties File

Recall from earlier in this chapter that each validation routine defined in the **validator-rules.xml** file declares a key for an error message in Struts' resource bundle file: **ApplicationResources.properties**. At run time, Validator uses the keys to look up error messages to return when validations fail. Because you are using the "mask" validation defined in the **validator-rules.xml** file, you must add the following error message for its declared key to the **ApplicationResources.properties** file:

```
errors.invalid=<li>{0} is not valid</li>
```

The following code shows the updated **ApplicationResources.properties** file in its entirety:

```
# Label Resources
label.search.name=Name
label.search.ssNum=Social Security Number

# Error Resources
error.search.criteria.missing=<li>Search Criteria Missing</li>
error.search.ssNum.invalid=<li>Invalid Social Security Number</li>
errors.header=<font color="red"><b>Validation Error(s)</b></font><ul>
errors.footer=</ul><hr width="100%" size="1" noshade="true">

errors.invalid=<li>{0} is not valid</li>
```

Compile, Package, and Run the Updated Application

Because you removed the **reset( )**, **validate( )**, and **validateSsNum( )** methods from **SearchForm** and changed it to extend **ValidatorForm** instead of **ActionForm**, you need to recompile and repackage the Mini HR application before you run it. Assuming that you've made modifications to the original Mini HR application and it was set up in the **c:\java\MiniHR** directory (as described in Chapter 2), the following command line will recompile the application:

```
javac -classpath WEB-INF\lib\commons-beanutils.jar;
               WEB-INF\lib\commons-collections.jar;
               WEB-INF\lib\commons-lang.jar;
               WEB-INF\lib\commons-logging.jar;
               WEB-INF\lib\commons-validator.jar;
               WEB-INF\lib\digester.jar;
               WEB-INF\lib\fileupload.jar;
               WEB-INF\lib\jakarta-oro.jar;
```

```
WEB-INF\lib\struts.jar;
C:\java\jakarta-tomcat-4.1.27\common\lib\servlet.jar
    WEB-INF\src\com\jamesholmes\minihr\*.java
    -d WEB-INF\classes
```

After recompiling Mini HR, you need to repackage it using the following command line:

```
jar cf MiniHR.war *
```

This command should also be run from the directory where you have set up the Mini HR application (e.g., **c:\java\MiniHR**).

Similar to the way you ran Mini HR the first time, you now need to place the new **MiniHR.war** file that you just created into Tomcat's **webapps** directory and start Tomcat. As before, to access the Mini HR application, point your browser to **http://localhost: 8080/MiniHR/**. Once you have the updated Mini HR running, try entering valid and invalid social security numbers. As you will see, they are now verified using the new Validator code.

Tiles

Two of the foremost principles that underpin the Struts framework are the *separation of concerns* and *reuse*. These principles can be seen at work throughout the framework. For example, the separation of business logic into a Model layer applies separation of concerns, and the use of a configuration file for declarative coupling of components applies reuse. These principles are not, however, unique to the server side (Model and Controller) of applications.

Client-side (View) development has also been evolving to support the principles of separation of concerns and reuse. For example, cascading style sheets (CSS) allows common style elements to be defined in an external file that can be *sourced in* (that is, its contents included) by several pages. That way, each page does not have to define the same styles over and over. Instead, the pages simply use the common definitions defined in a style sheet. If a style needs to be changed, that change can be made in one file rather than in each page individually. This reduces the amount of time and overhead needed to make global changes, and reduces errors. This is the essence of reuse.

JSP technology supports a similar feature for reuse called *includes.* JSP includes allow other files (JSPs or otherwise) to be sourced in to a JSP, either at compile time or dynamically at run time. This feature is useful for abstracting common sections of pages, such as headers, footers, and menus, into reusable chunks that can be used by several files. If a change needs to be made to a common section, the change can be made once and each of the pages that includes that section will automatically receive the updates.

JSP includes offer both convenience and time savings. They are, however, somewhat limited insofar as the potential for a great deal of duplication still exists. Each JSP that sources in common sections duplicates the include definitions. If the name of one or more files being included change, each of the files including them would have to be updated. For example, assume that you have a set of JSPs called **a.jsp**, **b.jsp**, **c.jsp**, and **d.jsp** that all include **header.jsp**. If you rename **header.jsp** to **mainHeader.jsp**, then you would have to update **a.jsp**, **b.jsp**, **c.jsp**, and **d.jsp** to include **mainHeader.jsp** instead of **header.jsp**. This can be tedious, time consuming, and error prone. To solve this problem, and to enhance Struts, Cedric Dumoulin created the Tiles framework as a third-party add-on to Struts. Tiles has since been integrated into the core Struts code base and is now packaged with Struts as of version 1.1.

Tiles expands the concept of reuse via includes by allowing you to define layouts (or templates) and then specify how the layouts are populated with content. To understand the value of Tiles, first consider how the JSP include paradigm works. Each JSP specifies its layout and explicitly populates that layout through includes. Most JSP layouts are identical, sourcing in the same files in the same places and then having a section of unique content, which is usually body content. Thus, there is significant duplication. Tiles takes the reverse approach.

With Tiles, you define a master layout JSP that specifies each of the includes that fill in the layout and then you define which content should fill in the layout in an external configuration file. The same layout can be used over and over by simply specifying different filler content for the layout in the configuration file.

For example, consider a typical Web site layout that has a header at the top of the page, a menu on the left, body content in the middle, and a footer on the bottom, as shown in Figure 7-1. If you were to implement this page using only JSP includes, each JSP that has this layout would have to explicitly include the header, menu, and footer sections of the page, and the body content would be in the JSP itself. Essentially, the only unique part of the page is the body content.

Alternatively, if you were to implement this layout with Tiles, you'd create one JSP that includes the header, menu, and footer and then dynamically include the body based on a parameter passed to the layout that indicates which JSP to use for the body content. This Tiles layout could then be reused for as many pages as you'd like and the only thing your content JSPs would have to contain is the body content that goes in the middle of the page. Tiles takes care of wrapping the body content JSP with the layout. As you can see, Tiles significantly enhances JSP development and allows for an even greater amount of reuse than JSP includes offer.

FIGURE 7-1   Typical Web site layout

Tiles Overview

Before getting into the details of using the Tiles framework, it's necessary to give an overview of how Tiles works. Tiles allows you to exploit the concept of JSP includes by providing a framework for defining and dynamically populating page layouts. Each page layout is simply a JSP that defines a template frame (or outline) with placeholders for where content should go. At run time, Tiles replaces the placeholders with their associated content, creating a complete page and unique instance of the layout. To accomplish this, Tiles uses its concepts of *definitions* and *attributes.*

A Tiles definition creates a piece of content that Tiles can insert into a JSP using that definition's name. Each definition consists of a name (or identifier), a layout JSP, and a set of attributes associated with the definition. Once defined, a definition can be included in a page or, as is most often the case, be used as the target of a Struts forward. In both cases, when the definition is encountered, Tiles passes to the layout JSP specified by the definition the set of attributes that were declared for that definition. An attribute value can be the path to a JSP, a literal string, or a list of either.

To facilitate the use of definitions and attributes, Tiles uses an XML configuration file (**tiles-defs.xml**) for storing their definitions. Tiles also provides a JSP tag library for defining definitions and attributes. Additionally, the Tiles Tag Library is used for inserting attributes into JSPs.

Using Tiles

Using the Tiles framework involves these five steps:

1. Enable the Tiles plugin.
2. Create Tiles definitions.
3. Create layout JSPs and use the Tiles Tag Library.
4. Create content JSPs to fill in the layout JSPs.
5. Use the Tiles definitions.

The following sections explain how to configure and use Tiles in detail.

Enabling the Tiles Plugin

Although Tiles comes packaged with Struts, by default Tiles is not enabled. To enable and use Tiles, you have to add the following **<plug-in>** definition to your application's **struts-config.xml** file:

```
<!-- Tiles Configuration -->
<plug-in className="org.apache.struts.tiles.TilesPlugin">
  <set-property property="definitions-config"
                value="/WEB-INF/tiles-defs.xml"/>
</plug-in>
```

This definition causes Struts to load and initialize the Tiles plugin for your application. Upon initialization, the plugin loads the comma-delimited list of Tiles configuration files specified by the **definitions-config** property. Each configuration file's path should be specified using a Web application-relative path, as shown in the preceding example.

Note that your application's **struts-config.xml** file must conform to the Struts Configuration DTD, which specifies the order in which elements are to appear in the file. Because of this, you must place the Tiles **<plug-in>** definition in the proper place in the file. The easiest way to ensure that you are properly ordering elements in the file is to use a tool like Struts Console that automatically formats your configuration file so that it conforms to the DTD.

Creating Tiles Definitions

There are two ways that you can create Tiles definitions and specify their attributes for your application. First, you can define them in an XML configuration file. Second, you can define them inside JSPs using the Tiles Tag Library. Each approach is described here, along with information on extending definitions, and information on how to use definitions as attribute values.

XML Configuration File–Based Definitions and Attributes

The first, and most often used, way that you can define Tiles definitions and attributes is by placing them in an XML configuration file named **tiles-defs.xml**. Of course, you can use another name for the file, but that is the standard name. Upon application startup, Tiles loads this file and places its definitions into memory. Following is a basic example of how to define a definition in a Tiles configuration file:

```
<?xml version="1.0"?>

<!DOCTYPE tiles-definitions PUBLIC
    "-//Apache Software Foundation//DTD Tiles Configuration 1.1//EN"
    "http://jakarta.apache.org/struts/dtds/tiles-config_1_1.dtd">

<tiles-definitions>
  <definition name="search.page" path="/mainLayout.jsp">
    <put name="header" value="/header.jsp"/>
    <put name="body"   value="/search.jsp"/>
    <put name="footer" value="/footer.jsp" />
  </definition>
</tiles-definitions>
```

Each definition in the **tiles-defs.xml** file has its own definition that is declared with a **definition** tag. The **definition** tag assigns a logical name to the definition, with the **name** attribute, and specifies the path to a layout JSP for the definition, with the **path** attribute. The logical name given to the definition will be used to refer to the definition inside JSPs and the Struts configuration file. Nested inside the **definition** tag, **put** tags are used to specify the definition's list of attributes.

NOTE *Detailed information on the Tiles configuration file is found in Chapter 17.*

JSP-Based Definitions and Attributes

The second way that you can define a Tiles definition and its attributes is by specifying them with Tiles Tag Library tags inside JSPs. Following is a basic definition defined in a JSP:

```
<%@ taglib uri="/WEB-INF/struts-tiles.tld" prefix="tiles" %>

<tiles:definition id="search.page" template="/mainLayout.jsp" >
  <tiles:put name="header" value="/header.jsp" />
  <tiles:put name="body"   value="/search.jsp" />
  <tiles:put name="footer" value="/footer.jsp" />
</tiles:definition>
```

This definition will be stored in a page scope JSP variable named **search.page** (as specified by the **id** attribute of the **definition** tag) so that it can be accessed from other tags. To use this JSP-based definition, you must use Tiles' **insert** tag, as shown next:

```
<tiles:insert beanName="search.page" flush="true"/>
```

Because the **definition** tag stores the definition in a JSP scripting variable, you must use the **beanName** attribute of the **insert** tag to specify the definition. This differs from the way in which you would insert a definition defined in a Tiles configuration file.

The idea behind defining Tiles definitions inside JSPs is that you can define several definitions in a "layout configuration" JSP and then include that JSP in every JSP that uses the definitions. Thus, a layout configuration JSP is similar in purpose to a Tiles configuration file.

Extending Definitions

A powerful and often-used feature of definitions is the ability to have one definition extend another. This functionality is similar to the way inheritance works in Java. When defining a definition, you can specify that the definition extends another definition, instead of specifying a layout JSP for the definition. The child (or sub-) definition inherits the layout JSP and attributes of the parent and can override any of the parent attributes as well as add its own attributes. For example, you may want to have a master layout definition for your site that all other definitions extend from. The master definition can specify values for the attributes that are common across all pages. The child definitions can then specify values for just the attributes that are unique to that page. Additionally, child definitions can override any of the master definitions' common attribute values when necessary, such as for a page that needs a unique header or footer. Following is an example Tiles configuration file that illustrates a few definition-extending scenarios:

```
<?xml version="1.0"?>
```

```
<!DOCTYPE tiles-definitions PUBLIC
  "-//Apache Software Foundation//DTD Tiles Configuration 1.1//EN"
  "http://jakarta.apache.org/struts/dtds/tiles-config_1_1.dtd">

<tiles-definitions>

  <!-- Main Layout -->
  <definition name="main.layout" path="/mainLayout.jsp">
    <put name="title"  value=""/>
    <put name="header" value="/header.jsp"/>
    <put name="menu"    value="/menu.jsp"/>
    <put name="body"    value=""/>
    <put name="footer" value="/footer.jsp" />
  </definition>

  <!-- Search Page -->
  <definition name="search.page" extends="main.layout">
    <put name="title"  value="Search Page"/>
    <put name="body"    value="/search.jsp"/>
  </definition>

  <!-- Employee Layout -->
  <definition name="employee.layout" extends="main.layout">
    <put name="menu"    value="/employee/menu.jsp"/>
  </definition>

  <!-- Employee Edit Page -->
  <definition name="employeeEdit.page" extends="employee.layout">
    <put name="title"  value="Employee Edit Page"/>
    <put name="body"    value="/employee/edit.jsp"/>
  </definition>

</tiles-definitions>
```

As stated, this file contains a few different extension scenarios. First, the file declares the main layout from which the other definitions will extend. This layout specifies values for the attributes that will be common across most pages. However, it purposefully leaves the page-specific attributes' values blank, because they will be overridden by extending definitions. The first extending definition, **search.page**, extends the main layout definition and provides values for the **title** and **body** attributes. The rest of the attributes that are necessary to fill in the main layout will be inherited from the main layout definition. At run time, when the **search.page** definition is used, Tiles will use the **mainLayout.jsp** file and populate it with content from the child and parent definitions, as appropriate.

The second definition-extension scenario represented in the preceding configuration file creates a specific layout by extending the generic main layout and customizing it. The **employee.layout** definition extends the main layout and overrides the **menu** attribute's value to create a new employee-specific layout. Note that the **menu** attribute points to an employee-specific menu JSP. The **employeeEdit.page** definition extends the **employee.layout** layout definition. This final definition, like the **search.page** definition, specifies values for the **title** and **body** attributes. The rest of the attribute values that are necessary to populate the layout JSP are inherited from the parent definition.

Note that Tiles supports an essentially unlimited number of definition extensions. Thus, you could create a generic master definition followed by several more specific definitions that extend it. Then, you could add yet another level of definitions that extend the extended definitions to create even more specific page definitions. This is a very powerful feature and is the key advantage that Tiles has over JSP includes.

Using Tiles Definitions as Attribute Values

Another feature of the Tiles framework is the ability to use definitions as the value for an attribute. This feature allows pages to be constructed in a hierarchical fashion. For instance, you can define a master layout that has a **menu** attribute and, instead of specifying the URL to a JSP as the value for the attribute, specify the name of another definition. A sample configuration file for this scenario is shown next:

```xml
<?xml version="1.0"?>

<!DOCTYPE tiles-definitions PUBLIC
    "-//Apache Software Foundation//DTD Tiles Configuration 1.1//EN"
    "http://jakarta.apache.org/struts/dtds/tiles-config_1_1.dtd">

<tiles-definitions>

  <!-- Menu Layout -->
  <definition name="menu.layout" paths="/menu/layout.jsp">
    <put name="menuItem1" value="/meanu/menuItem1.jsp"/>
    <put name="menuItem2" value="/meanu/menuItem2.jsp"/>
    <put name="menuItem3" value="/meanu/menuItem3.jsp"/>
  </definition>

  <!-- Main Layout -->
  <definition name="main.layout" path="/mainLayout.jsp">
    <put name="title"  value=""/>
    <put name="header" value="/header.jsp"/>
    <put name="menu"   value="menu.layout"/>
    <put name="body"   value=""/>
    <put name="footer" value="/footer.jsp" />
  </definition>

  <!-- Search Page -->
  <definition name="search.page" extends="main.layout">
    <put name="title"  value="Search Page"/>
    <put name="body"   value="/search.jsp"/>
  </definition>

</tiles-definitions>
```

In this scenario, the **main.layout** definition has a **menu** attribute whose value points to the name of another definition, **menu.layout**. Tiles intelligently determines the type of value each attribute has and processes its content accordingly. Thus, if an attribute is set to a JSP, then Tiles will use a JSP. If the attribute is set to the name of a definition, Tiles will recognize that and use the definition. This feature allows you to create sophisticated layouts that maximize content reuse.

Creating Layout JSPs and Using the Tiles Tag Library

Creating layout JSPs with the Tiles Tag Library is similar to the way you would go about creating JSPs that leverage JSP's include mechanism. Simply place your layout page's HTML in the JSP and then use Tiles Tag Library tags to source in content. The HTML creates a template (or frame) for a page and the Tiles tags act as placeholders for content that will be inserted into the template at run time. Following is a basic layout JSP that illustrates how this works:

```
<%@ taglib uri="/WEB-INF/tlds/struts-tiles.tld" prefix="tiles" %>

<html>
<head>
<title><tiles:getAsString name="title"/></title>
</head>
<body>

<tiles:insert attribute="header"/>

<table>
<tr>
<td width="20%"><tiles:insert attribute="menu"/></td>
<td width="80%"><tiles:insert attribute="body"/></td>
</tr>
</table>

<tiles:insert attribute="footer"/>

</body>
</html>
```

At run time, when a definition uses this layout, it will make a set of attributes available to the page to be inserted with the Tiles Tag Library's **insert** tag.

NOTE   *A complete overview of the Tiles Tag Library is given later in this chapter, beginning in the "Using the Tiles Tag Library" section.*

Creating Content JSPs

Content JSPs are used to fill in the placeholders created by layouts. These JSPs simply contain the HTML necessary to fill in a specific section of a layout. You create these JSPs the same way you would create JSPs that are used for includes. You don't, however, specifically source in any of these JSPs into the layout JSPs, as you would if you were using includes. Instead, layout JSPs use Tiles tags to insert attributes whose values point to these content JSPs.

Using the Tiles Definitions

Once you have created Tiles layout JSPs and have defined definitions that use them, you can put the definitions to use. There are two different ways to use definitions: you can insert the definition's content into a JSP, or you can use definitions as the targets of Struts forwards.

The following example illustrates how to insert a Tiles definition into a JSP:

```
<%@ taglib uri="/WEB-INF/tlds/struts-tiles.tld" prefix="tiles" %>

<html>
<head>
<title>Employee Search</title>
</head>
<body>

<font size="+1">ABC, Inc. Human Resources Portal</font><br>
<hr width="100%" noshade="true">

<tiles:insert definition="search.page"/>

<hr width="100%" noshade="true">

</body>
</html>
```

As you can see, to insert a definition, you just use the Tiles Tag Library's **insert** tag. The content specified by the definition will be processed and inserted in its final state (i.e., all levels of layouts will be collapsed into one). This way of using definitions is very powerful because you can insert definitions that comprise a page's whole content, as shown next. Or you could insert definitions that are only intended to fill a portion of a page with content, as was shown in the first example.

```
<%@ taglib uri="/WEB-INF/tlds/struts-tiles.tld" prefix="tiles" %>

<tiles:insert definition="search.page"/>
```

The second way to use Tiles definitions is to have them be used as the target of Struts forwards. This way works by having the names of definitions be used as forwards. Instead of a forward pointing to a JSP or another URL, it points to the name of a Tiles definition. At run time, when the Tiles plugin is enabled, Tiles intercepts all requests being made through the Struts controller servlet. Tiles does this by having its own request processor that extends the behavior of the base Struts request processor. If the Tiles request processor sees a forward whose value is the name of a definition, it will handle the request and return the contents of the definition. Following is an example of how to define a forward in the Struts configuration file that uses a Tiles definition:

```
<global-forwards>
  <forward name="search" path="search.page"/>
</global-forwards>
```

Notice that the **path** attribute specifies the name of a Tiles definition. The Tiles request processor will recognize this and handle processing for this forward.

Internationalizing Tiles

Similar to other areas of Struts, Tiles fully supports internationalization. Remember that internationalization is the process of tailoring content to a specific locale or region. For Tiles, internationalization means tailoring Tiles definitions and attributes to a specific locale. That way, the U.S. and French versions of a Web site can each have their own language-specific definitions and attributes, for example.

Although Tiles' internationalization support is similar to the core internationalization support in Struts, it's intended to allow you to provide locale-specific layout differences, not to internationalize text or messages. That should be done with the core Struts internationalization features. Tiles internationalization support is for such things as the differences in the size of internationalized images or the length of internationalized text. For example, using Tiles' internationalization support, you can define one version of a definition that handles the appropriate sizing for images and text for the United States and a second version designed for France, which accommodates the larger images and longer text necessary for the French content. Tiles simply provides the mechanism to define the layout appropriately for each locale.

> **NOTE** *Internationalizing text and images should be left to the core Struts internationalization functionality.*

To tailor Tiles definitions and attributes to a specific locale, you have to create a Tiles XML configuration file for each locale. Each locale-specific configuration file is distinguished by its filename using the same naming scheme that is used for Java Resource Bundles. Thus, to create English and French versions of a set of definitions and their attributes, you would create a file named **tiles-defs_en.xml** for the English version and a file named **tiles-defs_fr.xml** for the French version. The suffix portion of each filename contains the language code for the locale that the file is intended for. At run time, Tiles uses the locale from the current request to determine which configuration file it should use definitions from to process the current request. Each configuration file should have the same definitions with the same attributes. All of the names of definitions and attributes must be the same (that is, line up) in each file. The values of the definitions and attributes, however, will be specific to the locale of the particular file.

Parallel to the way Java Resource Bundles function, Tiles will attempt to find definitions and attributes for the current request's locale in a configuration file specific to that locale. If the definitions and attributes are not found in the locale-specific configuration file, Tiles will attempt to load them from the default configuration file whose filename does not contain any locale information (e.g., **tiles-defs.xml**). This is especially helpful when you want to tailor only a few definitions to a specific locale. To accomplish this, create a default configuration file (**tiles-defs.xml**) that contains all the "master" Tiles definitions and attributes. Then, create locale-specific configuration files (e.g., **tiles-defs_fr.xml** or **tiles-defs_es.xml**) that override definitions in the default configuration file. You can choose to override as few or as many definitions as you like. At run time, if Tiles cannot find a locale-specific version of a definition, it will automatically use the definition from the default configuration file.

To illustrate how Tiles' internationalization support works, let's step through an example scenario. Assume that you have a Web site that is available in English (default), French, and Spanish versions. This requires three Tiles configuration files.

The first file, **tiles-defs.xml**, which is shown next, houses the master Tiles definitions for the Web site. Because the default language for the site is English, the English definitions will reside in this file and serve as the default definitions for the other languages when the other languages are not overriding the definitions in this file.

```
<?xml version="1.0"?>

<!DOCTYPE tiles-definitions PUBLIC
   "-//Apache Software Foundation//DTD Tiles Configuration 1.1//EN"
   "http://jakarta.apache.org/struts/dtds/tiles-config_1_1.dtd">

<tiles-definitions>

  <!-- Search Page -->
  <definition name="search.page" path="/mainLayout.jsp">
    <put name="header" value="/header.jsp"/>
    <put name="body"   value="/search.jsp"/>
    <put name="footer" value="/footer.jsp" />
  </definition>

  <!-- View Employee Page -->
  <definition name="viewEmployee.page" path="/mainLayout.jsp"">
    <put name="header" value="/header.jsp"/>
    <put name="body"   value="/viewEmployee.jsp"/>
```

```
    <put name="footer" value="/footer.jsp" />
  </definition>

</tiles-definitions>
```

This configuration file contains two basic page definitions that utilize the same page layout and simply provide different values for the **body** attribute.

The second file, **tiles-defs_fr.xml,** provides French-specific definitions and attributes:

```
<?xml version="1.0"?>

<!DOCTYPE tiles-definitions PUBLIC
  "-//Apache Software Foundation//DTD Tiles Configuration 1.1//EN"
  "http://jakarta.apache.org/struts/dtds/tiles-config_1_1.dtd">

<tiles-definitions>

  <!-- Search Page -->
  <definition name="search.page" path="/mainLayout_fr.jsp">
    <put name="header" value="/header_fr.jsp"/>
    <put name="body"   value="/search_fr.jsp"/>
    <put name="footer" value="/footer_fr.jsp" />
  </definition>

  <!-- View Employee Page -->
  <definition name="viewEmployee.page" path="/mainLayout_fr.jsp"">
    <put name="header" value="/header_fr.jsp"/>
    <put name="body"   value="/viewEmployee_fr.jsp"/>
    <put name="footer" value="/footer_fr.jsp" />
  </definition>

</tiles-definitions>
```

The definitions in this file mirror those of the default configuration file, with the exception that the values for the definitions and attributes are different. The definition and attribute names are the same so that they match up with those in the default file. Notice that the values for the definition paths are set to a JSP named **mainLayout _fr.jsp.** That is a French-specific version of **mainLayout.jsp.** If the layout JSP itself did not need to change to accommodate the French version, you would leave the path set to **/mainLayout.jsp** and specify only French-specific versions of the attributes inside the definitions. It's up to you to determine how much customization you need or want for each locale.

The third file, **tiles-defs_es.xml,** includes the Spanish-specific definitions and attributes. This file, shown next, includes only a Spanish-specific version of the **search.page** definition.

```
<?xml version="1.0"?>

<!DOCTYPE tiles-definitions PUBLIC
    "-//Apache Software Foundation//DTD Tiles Configuration 1.1//EN"
    "http://jakarta.apache.org/struts/dtds/tiles-config_1_1.dtd">

<tiles-definitions>

  <!-- Search Page -->
  <definition name="search.page" path="/es/mainLayout.jsp">
    <put name="header" value="/es/header.jsp"/>
    <put name="body"   value="/es/search.jsp"/>
    <put name="footer" value="/es/footer.jsp" />
  </definition>

</tiles-definitions>
```

Because this file contains only a Spanish version of the **search.page** definition, if a
request is made for the Spanish version of the **viewEmployee.page** definition, Tiles
will (after not finding it in **tiles-defs_es.xml**) look for it in the default configuration
file, **tiles-defs.xml**. Notice that the attributes in this file point to JSPs underneath an
es directory. There are many ways you can organize your application's content to
support internationalization. This example places the locale-specific files in a directory
dedicated to that locale. The French configuration file points to files whose locale is
part of the filename. Which approach you take to organizing content is up to you.

NOTE   *Detailed information on internationalizing a Struts application is found in Chapter 10.*

Using the Tiles Tag Library

The Tiles Tag Library provides a set of tags that you can use to create Tiles-based page
layouts. Also, as mentioned earlier in this chapter, with the Tiles tags, you can define
Tiles definitions inside JSPs instead of (or in addition to) defining them in a Tiles XML
configuration file.

To use the Tiles Tag Library in a Struts application, you need to include the
following snippet in your application's Web Archive (**.war**) deployment descriptor,
web.xml:

```
<taglib>
  <taglib-uri>/WEB-INF/tlds/struts-tiles.tld</taglib-uri>
  <taglib-location>/WEB-INF/tlds/struts-tiles.tld</taglib-location>
</taglib>
```

Recall from the overview of the **web.xml** file in Chapter 2 that the **<taglib-uri>** tag is used to declare the URI (or alias) that will be referenced in each of your JSPs with a **taglib** directive. The **<taglib-location>** tag is used to declare the actual location of the Tag Library Descriptor (**.tld**) file in your Web Archive.

The following snippet illustrates how your JSPs will declare their use of the Tiles Tag Library with a JSP **taglib** directive:

```
<%@ taglib uri="/WEB-INF/tlds/struts-tiles.tld" prefix="tiles" %>
```

Notice that the **uri** attribute specified here is the same as that declared with the **<taglib-uri>** tag in the **web.xml** file. Also, notice that the **prefix** attribute is set to **tiles**. This attribute can be set to whatever you want; however, **tiles** is the accepted default for the Tiles Tag Library. The **prefix** attribute declares the prefix that each tag must have when it is used in the JSP, as shown here:

```
<tiles:insert attribute="header"/>
```

Because **tiles** was defined as the prefix, the **insert** tag was used as shown. However, if you were to choose to use a prefix of **strutstiles**, the tag would be used as follows:

```
<strutstiles:insert attribute="header"/>
```

The Tiles Tag Library Tags

Table 7-1 lists each of the tags in the Tiles Tag Library and provides a short description of each tag's purpose.

The remainder of this section discusses each tag in detail, including a complete description of the tag, a table listing each of the tag's attributes, and a usage example for the tag. In the tables that describe each tag's attributes, pay special attention to the Required and Accepts Scriptlet columns.

The Required column simply denotes whether or not the given attribute is required when using the tag. If an attribute is required and you do not specify it when using the tag, the tag will throw a **javax.servlet.jsp.JspException** at run time. Note that you can declare an error page in your JSP with a **page** directive to capture any **JspExceptions** that might be thrown, as shown here:

```
<%@ page errorPage="error.jsp" %>
```

If an exception occurs, the page specified by the **errorPage** attribute will be internally redirected to display an error page.

Tag	Description
add	Defines an entry for a list created with the **putList** tag.
definition	Defines a tile (which is a region within a page) and stores it in a JSP scripting variable.
get	Deprecated Originally for compatibility with the now defunct Template Tag Library. Use the **insert** tag instead.
getAsString	Renders the value of a Tiles attribute to the JSP's output stream.
importAttribute	Stores the values of all defined Tiles attributes in JSP scripting variables.
initComponentDefinitions	Initializes Tiles' definition factory with definitions from a Tiles XML configuration file.
insert	Inserts a Tiles definition or attribute into a JSP page.
put	Defines an attribute (or parameter) for a definition.
putList	Defines a list attribute (of **java.util.List** type) containing an ordered collection of individual attributes.
useAttribute	Stores the value of a Tiles attribute in a JSP scripting variable.

TABLE 7-1   The Tiles Tag Library Tags

The Accepts Scriptlet column denotes whether or not the given attribute's value can be specified with a JSP scriptlet. If a JSP scriptlet is used to specify an attribute value, the scriptlet must comprise the complete value, quote (") to quote ("), as shown here.

Correct:

```
<tiles:put name="<%=title%>">
```

Incorrect:

```
<tiles:put name="<%=title%>-title">
```

Notice in the incorrect example that "-title" is used as part of the value for the **name** attribute following the scriptlet. This is invalid because there are extra characters between the end of the scriptlet and the ending quote.

A corrected version of the incorrect example follows:

```
<tiles:put name="<%=title + "-title"%>"/>
```

The concatenation of "-title" is now part of the scriptlet and the scriptlet comprises the complete value for the attribute.

The add Tag

The **add** tag is used to define an entry for a list created with the **putList** tag. There are two ways that the value for the entry can be specified. The value can be specified with the **value** attribute, or the value can be placed between opening and closing **add** tags, as shown next:

```
<tiles:add>value goes here</tiles:add>
```

Attributes

Attribute	Description	Accepts Scriptlet	Required
beanName	Specifies the name of an object whose value will be used for this entry. If the **property** attribute is also specified, one of the fields of the object defined by this attribute will have its getter method called to return the object whose value will be used for this entry.	Yes	No
beanProperty	Specifies the field of the object specified by the **name** attribute whose value will be used for this entry.	Yes	No
beanScope	Specifies the scope (application, page, request, or session) to look in for the object specified by the **name** attribute. If not specified, each scope will be searched, in this order: page, request, session, and then application.	No	No
content	Deprecated Originally for compatibility with the now defunct Template Tag Library. Use the **value** attribute instead.	Yes	No
direct	Deprecated Originally for compatibility with the now defunct Template Tag Library. Use the **type** attribute set to "string" instead.	No	No
role	Specifies the role the currently authenticated user must have for this entry to be added to the enclosing list. If the user is not in the specified role, the entry will not be added to the list.	Yes	No
type	Specifies the type (string, page, or definition) of the value. If present, it indicates how the value specified with the **value** attribute is treated.	No	No
value	Specifies the value for this entry.	No	No

Example Usage
The following example illustrates the basic usage of the **add** tag:

```
<tiles:insert page="/mainLayout.jsp">
  <tiles:putList name="menu">
    <tiles:add value="Home"/>
    <tiles:add value="Products"/>
    <tiles:add value="Search"/>
  </tiles:putList>
</tiles:insert>
```

Each **add** definition is added to the enclosing list in the order specified.

The definition Tag
The **definition** tag is used to define a tile (which is a region within a page) and store it in a JSP scripting variable. Additionally, this tag allows you to specify the scope in which the JSP scripting variable should be placed. Once this definition is defined it can be inserted into JSPs by using the **insert** tag.

Attributes

Attribute	Description	Accepts Scriptlet	Required
extends	Specifies the name of another definition that this definition extends.	Yes	No
id	Specifies the name of the JSP variable that will hold this definition.	No	Yes
page	Specifies the URL for the tile.	Yes	No
role	Specifies the role the currently authenticated user must have for this definition to be created. If the user is not in the specified role, the definition will not be created.	Yes	No
scope	Specifies the scope (application, page, request, or session) in which the JSP scripting variable defined by the **id** attribute will be stored. If not specified, the JSP scripting variable will be stored in page scope.	No	No
template	Deprecated. Originally for compatibility with the now defunct Template Tag Library. Use the **page** attribute instead.	Yes	No

Example Usage

The following example illustrates the basic usage of the **definition** tag:

```
<tiles:definition name="mainLayout"
                  page="/layouts/main.jsp">
  <tiles:put name="header" value="/layouts/header.jsp"/>
  <tiles:put name="footer" value="/layouts/footer.jsp"/>
</tilesdefinition>
```

Each of the attributes nested underneath the **definition** tag can be accessed by the JSP specified with the **page** attribute.

The getAsString Tag

The **getAsString** tag is used to render the value of a Tiles attribute to the JSP's output stream.

Attributes

Attribute	Description	Accepts Scriptlet	Required
ignore	Accepts "true" or "false" to denote whether or not this tag should return without error if the specified Tiles attribute does not exist. Defaults to false, which will cause a run-time exception to be thrown if the attribute does not exist.	Yes	No
name	Specifies the name of a Tiles attribute whose value should be rendered.	Yes	Yes
role	Specifies the role the currently authenticated user must have for the specified Tiles attribute to be rendered.	Yes	No

Example Usage

The following example illustrates how to use the **getAsString** tag:

```
<tiles:getAsString name="title"/>
```

This example renders the value of the **title** attribute to the JSP's output stream.

The importAttribute Tag

The **importAttribute** tag is used to store the values of all defined Tiles attributes in JSP scripting variables. Additionally, this tag allows you to specify the scope in which the JSP scripting variables should be placed. This tag functions similarly to the **useAttribute** tag in that it can store the value of a specific attribute in a JSP scripting variable. However, it differs in that it can import all attributes at once and that it does not have an **id** attribute to specify the name of the JSP scripting variable in which values will be stored.

Attributes

Attribute	Description	Accepts Scriptlet	Required
ignore	Accepts "true" or "false" to denote whether or not this tag should return without error if the specified Tiles attribute does not exist. Defaults to false, which will cause a run-time exception to be thrown if the attribute does not exist.	Yes	No
name	Specifies the name of a Tiles attribute that should be imported.	Yes	No
scope	Specifies the scope (application, page, request, or session) that attribute values should be stored in. If not specified, JSP scripting variables will be stored in page scope.	No	No

Example Usage

The following example illustrates how to use the **importAttribute** tag:

```
<tiles:importAttribute/>
```

This example stores the values of all defined Tiles attributes in JSP scripting variables. Alternatively, you could import just one attribute by specifying its name with the **name** attribute, as shown here:

```
<tiles:importAttribute name="title"/>
```

The initComponentDefinitions Tag

The **initComponentDefinitions** tag is used to initialize Tiles' definition factory with definitions from a Tiles XML configuration file. This tag was created when Tiles was initially a third-party add-on to Struts. At that time, Tiles required you to use a special subclass of **ActionServlet** to initialize the definition factory. Alternatively, you could use this tag to initialize the factory. However, now that Tiles has been integrated into the core of Struts, this tag is no longer relevant. The Tiles plugin takes care of initializing the definition factory now.

Attributes

Attribute	Description	Accepts Scriptlet	Required
classname	Specifies the fully qualified class name of the Tiles definition factory to use.	No	No
file	Specifies the Tiles configuration file containing the definitions for the factory.	No	Yes

Example Usage

The following example illustrates how to use the **initComponentDefinitions** tag:

```
<tiles:initComponentDefinitions file="tiles-defs.xml"/>
```

As you can see, using this tag is straightforward.

The insert Tag

The **insert** tag is used to insert a Tiles definition or attribute into a JSP page. Additionally, this tag can be used to create and insert a definition at the same time by specifying a layout JSP with the **page** attribute and optionally nesting **put** tags inside this tag.

Attributes

Attribute	Description	Accepts Scriptlet	Required
attribute	Specifies the name of an attribute to insert.	No	No
beanName	Specifies the name of an object whose value will be inserted into the JSP. If the **property** attribute is also specified, one of the fields of the object defined by this attribute will have its getter method called to return the object whose value will be inserted into the JSP.	Yes	No
beanProperty	Specifies the field of the object specified by the **name** attribute whose value will be inserted into the JSP.	Yes	No
beanScope	Specifies the scope (application, page, request, or session) to look in for the object specified by the **name** attribute. If not specified, each scope will be searched, in this order: page, request, session, and then application.	No	No
component	Deprecated Use the **page** attribute instead.	Yes	No

Attribute	Description	Accepts Scriptlet	Required
controllerClass	Specifies the fully qualified class name of a controller object that is executed before this definition is inserted.	Yes	No
controllerUrl	Specifies the URL for a controller that is executed before this definition is inserted.	Yes	No
definition	Specifies the name of a definition to insert.	Yes	No
flush	Accepts "true" to denote that the JSP's output stream should be flushed before this definition is inserted.	No	No
ignore	Accepts "true" or "false" to denote whether or not this tag should return without error if the specified Tiles attribute does not exist. Defaults to false, which will cause a run-time exception to be thrown if the attribute does not exist.	Yes	No
name	Specifies the name of an entity (definition or attribute) to insert.	Yes	No
page	Specifies the URL to a page to insert into the JSP.	Yes	No
role	Specifies the role the currently authenticated user must have for the specified attribute to be inserted. If the user is not in the specified role, the attribute will not be inserted.	Yes	No
template	Deprecated Originally for compatibility with the now defunct Template Tag Library. Use the **page** attribute instead.	Yes	No

Example Usage

The following example illustrates the basic usage of the **insert** tag:

```
<tiles:insert attribute="header"/>
```

This example inserts an attribute named "header" into a JSP.
   To insert a definition, you use the **definition** attribute, as shown next:

```
<tiles:insert definition="tabLayout"/>
```

This example inserts an entire definition into a JSP.
   As mentioned, you can also use the **insert** tag to create and insert a definition:

```
<tiles:insert page="/layouts/tabLayout.jsp">
  <tiles:put name="header" value="/tabHeader.jsp"/>
```

```
    <tiles:put name="body" value="/search.jsp"/>
    <tiles:put name="footer" value="/tabFooter.jsp"/>
</tiles:insert>
```

This type of insertion is useful for declaring the attributes that get passed to a layout JSP from inside the JSP instead of in a Tiles configuration file.

The put Tag

The **put** tag is used to define an attribute (or parameter) for a definition. There are two ways that the value for the attribute can be specified. The value can be specified with the **value** attribute, or the value can be placed between opening and closing **put** tags, as shown next:

```
<tiles:put name="header">value goes here</tiles:put>
```

Attributes

Attribute	Description	Accepts Scriptlet	Required
beanName	Specifies the name of an object whose value will be used for this attribute. If the **property** attribute is also specified, one of the fields of the object defined by this attribute will have its getter method called to return the object whose value will be used for this attribute.	Yes	No
beanProperty	Specifies the field of the object specified by the **name** attribute whose value will be used for this attribute.	Yes	No
beanScope	Specifies the scope (application, page, request, or session) to look in for the object specified by the **name** attribute. If not specified, each scope will be searched, in this order: page, request, session, and then application.	No	No
content	Deprecated Originally for compatibility with the now defunct Template Tag Library. Use the **value** attribute instead.	Yes	No
direct	Deprecated Originally for compatibility with the now defunct Template Tag Library. Use the **value** attribute instead.	No	No
name	Specifies the name for the attribute.	No	No

Attribute	Description	Accepts Scriptlet	Required
role	Specifies the role the currently authenticated user must have for this attribute to be created. If the user is not in the role, this attribute will not be created.	Yes	No
type	Specifies the type (string, page, or definition) of the value. If present, it indicates how the value specified with the **value** attribute is treated.	No	No
value	Specifies the value for the attribute.	Yes	No

Example Usage

The following example illustrates the basic usage of the **put** tag:

```
<tiles:definition name="mainLayout"
                  page="/layouts/main.jsp">
  <tiles:put name="header" value="/layouts/header.jsp"/>
  <tiles:put name="footer" value="/layouts/footer.jsp"/>
</tiles:definition>
```

Defining attributes with the **put** tag is as simple as specifying their names and values.

The putList Tag

The **putList** tag is used to define a list attribute (of **java.util.List** type) containing an ordered collection of individual attributes. The elements of the list are set by nesting instances of the **add** tag or instances of this tag. This tag must be nested inside either the **definition** tag or the **insert** tag.

Attribute

Attribute	Description	Accepts Scriptlet	Required
name	Specifies the name of the attribute.	No	Yes

Example Usage

The following example illustrates how to use the **putList** tag:

```
<tiles:insert page="/mainLayout.jsp">
  <tiles:putList name="menu">
    <tiles:add value="Home"/>
    <tiles:add value="Products"/>
    <tiles:add value="Search"/>
  </tiles:putList>
</tiles:insert>
```

This example creates a **java.util.List**-based Tiles attribute named **menu** containing the values specified with the nested **add** tags.

You can also create hierarchical structures with the **putList** tag by nesting instances of the **putList** tag inside itself, as shown next:

```
<tiles:putList name="menu">
  <tiles:add value="Home"/>
  <tiles:putList name="Products">
    <tiles:add value="Products Menu Item 1"/>
    <tiles:add value="Products Menu Item 2"/>
  </tiles:putList>
  <tiles:add value="Search"/>
</tiles:putList>
```

Tiles allows you to nest the **putList** tags to any level for whatever hierarchal structure you need.

The useAttribute Tag

The **useAttribute** tag is used to store the value of a Tiles attribute in a JSP scripting variable. Additionally, this tag allows you to specify what scope the JSP scripting variable should be placed in.

Attributes

Attribute	Description	Accepts Scriptlet	Required
classname	Deprecated This attribute is no longer used.	No	No
id	Specifies the name of the JSP variable that will hold the specified attribute's value.	No	No
ignore	Accepts "true" or "false" to denote whether or not this tag should return without error if the specified Tiles attribute does not exist. Defaults to false, which will cause a run-time exception to be thrown if the attribute does not exist.	Yes	No
name	Specifies the name of a Tiles attribute whose value should be stored.	Yes	Yes
scope	Specifies the scope (application, page, request, or session) in which the JSP scripting variable defined by the **id** attribute will be stored. If not specified, the JSP scripting variable will be stored in page scope.	No	No

Example Usage

The following example illustrates how to use the **useAttribute** tag:

```
<tiles:useAttribute name="title"/>
```

This example stores the value of the Tiles attribute named **title** in a JSP scripting variable with the same name.

If you want to store the value in a JSP scripting variable with a different name, you must use the **id** attribute, as shown next:

```
<tiles:useAttribute id="pageTitle" name="title"/>
```

Additionally, you can specify the scope of the JSP scripting variable that the attribute value will be stored in with the **scope** attribute:

```
<tiles:useAttribute id="pageTitle" name="title" scope="session"/>
```

Adding Tiles to the Mini HR Application

Now that you've reviewed the benefits of using the Tiles framework and how it works, you are ready to update the Mini HR application to use Tiles. Following is the list of steps that you follow to add Tiles to the Mini HR application:

1. Add the Tiles TLD file to the application.
2. Create layout JSPs.
3. Update existing JSPs to work with layouts.
4. Create a **tiles-defs.xml** file.
5. Update forward definitions in, and add the Tiles plugin to, the **struts-config.xml** file.
6. Repackage and run the updated application.

The following sections walk through each step of the process in detail.

Add the Tiles TLD File to the Application

Adding the Tiles TLD file to the application is necessary so that JSPs can use the Tiles Tag Library. The Tiles Tag Library allows you to work with Tiles layouts in JSPs. To do this, copy the **struts-tiles.tld** file from the Struts distribution's **lib** directory (e.g., **c:\java\jakarta-struts-1.1\lib**) to Mini HR's **/WEB-INF/tlds** directory. Next, you have to add an entry for the TLD in the Web application deployment descriptor, **web.xml**, as shown next:

```
<taglib>
  <taglib-uri>/WEB-INF/tlds/struts-tiles.tld</taglib-uri>
  <taglib-location>/WEB-INF/tlds/struts-tiles.tld</taglib-location>
</taglib>
```

After adding this entry, the TLD can be referenced from JSPs using the following snippet:

```
<%@ taglib uri="/WEB-INF/tlds/struts-tiles.tld" prefix="tiles" %>
```

Create Layout JSPs

Now that you have registered the Tiles TLD, you can create the layout JSPs. This section demonstrates how to create one layout, to illustrate the basic concepts of Tiles. This layout will be based on the structure of the application's existing pages. Following is the original **search.jsp** page that will be used to extract the common template:

```
<%@ taglib uri="/WEB-INF/tlds/struts-bean.tld" prefix="bean" %>
<%@ taglib uri="/WEB-INF/tlds/struts-html.tld" prefix="html" %>
<%@ taglib uri="/WEB-INF/tlds/struts-logic.tld" prefix="logic" %>

<html>
<head>
<title>ABC, Inc. Human Resources Portal - Employee Search</title>
</head>
<body>

<font size="+1">
ABC, Inc. Human Resources Portal - Employee Search
</font><br>
<hr width="100%" noshade="true">

<html:errors/>

<html:form action="/search">

<table>
<tr>
<td align="right"><bean:message key="label.search.name"/>:</td>
<td><html:text property="name"/></td>
</tr>
<tr>
```

```
<td></td>
<td>-- or --</td>
</tr>
<tr>
<td align="right"><bean:message key="label.search.ssNum"/>:</td>
<td><html:text property="ssNum"/> (xxx-xx-xxxx)</td>
</tr>
<tr>
<td></td>
<td><html:submit/></td>
</tr>
</table>

</html:form>

<logic:present name="searchForm" property="results">

<hr width="100%" size="1" noshade="true">

<bean:size id="size" name="searchForm" property="results"/>
<logic:equal name="size" value="0">
<center><font color="red"><b>No Employees Found</b></font></center>
</logic:equal>

<logic:greaterThan name="size" value="0">
<table border="1">
<tr>
<th>Name</th>
<th>Social Security Number</th>
</tr>
<logic:iterate id="result" name="searchForm" property="results">
<tr>
<td><bean:write name="result" property="name"/></td>
<td><bean:write name="result" property="ssNum"/></td>
</tr>
</logic:iterate>
</table>
</logic:greaterThan>

</logic:present>

</body>
<html>
```

The body content of the page is shown in bold. This section will be different for each distinct page. The rest of the page, however, will be consistent across several pages, thus allowing for it to be abstracted into a general-purpose layout.

There are three JSP files that make up the layout: **mainLayout.jsp**, **header.jsp**, and **footer.jsp**. The **mainLayout.jsp** file is shown here:

```
<%@ taglib uri="/WEB-INF/tlds/struts-tiles.tld" prefix="tiles" %>

<html>
<head>
<title><tiles:getAsString name="title"/></title>
</head>
<body>

<tiles:insert attribute="header"/>

<tiles:insert attribute="body"/>

<tiles:insert attribute="footer"/>

</body>
</html>
```

This JSP defines the layout's template and is used to source in the other layout JSPs as well as the body content that will be defined by pages utilizing the layout. The body content and other layout JSPs are sourced in with **<tiles:insert>** tags. These tags specify the names of attributes defined in the Tiles configuration file whose values are the names of the JSPs that should be inserted into the JSP at run time. Notice the use of the **<tiles:getAsString>** tag. This tag works similarly to the **<tiles:insert>** tag, but instead of using the specified attribute's value as the name of a page to include, it is used as a literal string. This is useful for defining variables that can be customized by page definitions that extend layout definitions in the Tiles configuration file.

Following are the header and footer layout JSPs.

header.jsp:

```
<font size="+1">ABC, Inc. Human Resources Portal</font><br>
<hr width="100%" noshade="true">
```

footer.jsp:

```
<hr width="100%" noshade="true">
Copyright &copy; ABC, Inc.
```

As you can see, the header and footer JSPs are quite simple and do not contain much HTML. The content of these JSPs could have been placed directly in the **mainLayout.jsp** file instead of here and content pages would still only have to contain the body content of the page. However, breaking the pages up into smaller chunks allows for more flexibility in how layouts are used. For example, if you wanted all pages to have the standard header and footer, you wouldn't have to worry about changing anything. On the other hand, if you needed some pages to have a custom header and footer and others to use the standard ones, separating the header and footer into discreet chunks would allow you to do that. You would simply define values for the header and footer attributes at the layout level, and each page that wanted a custom header, footer, or both would override the necessary attributes with new values at the page level. This will make more sense after you see the Tiles configuration file, which is discussed shortly.

Update Existing JSPs to Work with Layouts

Once you have created the layout JSPs, the next step is to update the application's original JSPs to contain only the body content of their pages. To do this, you must remove each of the pieces of the original page that were used to craft the common layout. Following is the updated **search.jsp** page containing only body content:

```
<%@ taglib uri="/WEB-INF/tlds/struts-bean.tld" prefix="bean" %>
<%@ taglib uri="/WEB-INF/tlds/struts-html.tld" prefix="html" %>
<%@ taglib uri="/WEB-INF/tlds/struts-logic.tld" prefix="logic" %>

<html:errors/>

<html:form action="/search">

<table>
<tr>
<td align="right"><bean:message key="label.search.name"/>:</td>
<td><html:text property="name"/></td>
</tr>
<tr>
<td></td>
<td>-- or --</td>
</tr>
<tr>
<td align="right"><bean:message key="label.search.ssNum"/>:</td>
<td><html:text property="ssNum"/> (xxx-xx-xxxx)</td>
</tr>
<tr>
<td></td>
<td><html:submit/></td>
</tr>
</table>

</html:form>

<logic:present name="searchForm" property="results">
```

```
<hr width="100%" size="1" noshade="true">

<bean:size id="size" name="searchForm" property="results"/>
<logic:equal name="size" value="0">
<center><font color="red"><b>No Employees Found</b></font></center>
</logic:equal>

<logic:greaterThan name="size" value="0">
<table border="1">
<tr>
<th>Name</th>
<th>Social Security Number</th>
</tr>
<logic:iterate id="result" name="searchForm" property="results">
<tr>
<td><bean:write name="result" property="name"/></td>
<td><bean:write name="result" property="ssNum"/></td>
</tr>
</logic:iterate>
</table>
</logic:greaterThan>

</logic:present>
```

As you can see, the updated page no longer contains the header or footer portions of the content. At run time, the layout JSPs will surround the contents of this updated page with the common layout content to create the complete page.

Create a tiles-defs.xml File

As mentioned, there are two ways to declare Tiles layouts: with Tiles tags in a master JSP that gets included into each of the layout JSPs or by declaring them in an XML configuration file. This example uses the configuration file option because it is the most flexible and easy to maintain approach. Following is the **tiles-defs.xml** file that declares the layouts. This file should be placed inside Mini HR's **/WEB-INF/** folder.

```
<?xml version="1.0"?>

<!DOCTYPE tiles-definitions PUBLIC
   "-//Apache Software Foundation//DTD Tiles Configuration 1.1//EN"
   "http://jakarta.apache.org/struts/dtds/tiles-config_1_1.dtd">

<tiles-definitions>

  <!-- Main Layout -->
  <definition name="main.layout" path="/mainLayout.jsp">
       <put name="title"  value=""/>
```

```
        <put name="header"  value="/header.jsp"/>
        <put name="body"    value=""/>
        <put name="footer"  value="/footer.jsp" />
    </definition>

    <!-- Search Page -->
    <definition name="search.page" extends="main.layout">
        <put name="title"   value="Search Page"/>
        <put name="body"    value="/search.jsp"/>
    </definition>

</tiles-definitions>
```

There are two Tiles definitions in this file. The first definition in the file declares a
layout named **main.layout**. The **.layout** extension given to the definition's name is
used to denote that it is a *layout* definition. This is not a formal naming scheme; however,
it is a simple way to distinguish the types of definitions. Generally speaking, layout
definitions specify the template for a page and the list of attributes whose values will
be used to fill in the template. *Page* definitions extend layout definitions and provide
values for the attributes defined in the extended layout. So, essentially, page definitions
are instances of a layout with attributes set to the content for a specific page.

Notice that the first definition defines four attributes with **put** tags. These attributes
will be available for use by the layout JSP specified by the **path** attribute. The layout JSP
uses these attributes to supply it with the locations of its content. Additionally, attributes
can be used to supply literal strings, as is the case with the **title** attribute. This attribute
will be used by **mainLayout.jsp** to enable a dynamic title based on the value set by
page definitions that extend the layout definition.

The second definition in the file declares a page definition named **search.page**.
This definition extends the **main.layout** layout definition and supplies values for the
attributes that don't have values in the layout definition. This definition can override
any of the attributes in the layout definition if so desired; however, only the **title** and
body attributes are overridden in this case.

Update Forward Definitions in, and Add the Tiles Plugin to, the struts-config.xml File

After you have created the Tiles configuration file, you must update Mini HR's
struts-config.xml file to point to Tiles definitions instead of pointing directly to JSPs
for each page that has been converted to use Tiles. Additionally, the Tiles plugin must
be added to the file. Without Tiles, forward and action definitions point directly to
JSPs. With Tiles, they point to the page's definition in the Tiles configuration file. For
example, before, the **search** action pointed directly to **search.jsp**, as shown here:

```
<action path="/search"
        type="com.jamesholmes.minihr.SearchAction"
```

```
        name="searchForm"
       scope="request"
    validate="true"
       input="/search.jsp"/>
```

However, now the action will point to the search page's Tiles definition, as shown here:

```
<action path="/search"
        type="com.jamesholmes.minihr.SearchAction"
        name="searchForm"
        scope="request"
     validate="true"
        input="search.page"/>
```

At run time, the Tiles plugin will determine if a specified page is the name of a Tiles definition or an actual path to a page. If a Tiles definition is specified, then Tiles will process the page accordingly; otherwise, normal Struts processing will take place.

To add the Tiles plugin to the application, you must add the following snippet to **struts-config.xml**:

```
<!-- Tiles Configuration -->
<plug-in className="org.apache.struts.tiles.TilesPlugin">
  <set-property property="definitions-config"
                    value="/WEB-INF/tiles-defs.xml"/>
</plug-in>
```

This causes Struts to load the Tiles plugin at application startup. Notice that the Tiles configuration file is specified with the **set-property** tag. You can specify multiple configuration files by providing a comma-delimited list of files.

The following code shows the updated Struts configuration file for Mini HR in its entirety. The sections that have changed or that have been added are shown in bold.

```
<?xml version="1.0"?>

<!DOCTYPE struts-config PUBLIC
   "-//Apache Software Foundation//DTD Struts Configuration 1.1//EN"
   "http://jakarta.apache.org/struts/dtds/struts-config_1_1.dtd">

<struts-config>

  <!-- Form Beans Configuration -->
  <form-beans>
    <form-bean name="searchForm"
               type="com.jamesholmes.minihr.SearchForm"/>
```

```
    </form-beans>

    <!-- Action Mappings Configuration -->
    <action-mappings>
      <action path="/viewSearch"
              type="org.apache.struts.actions.ForwardAction"
          parameter="search.page"/>
      <action path="/search"
              type="com.jamesholmes.minihr.SearchAction"
              name="searchForm"
             scope="request"
          validate="true"
             input="search.page"/>
    </action-mappings>

    <!-- Message Resources Configuration -->
    <message-resources
      parameter="com.jamesholmes.minihr.ApplicationResources"/>

    <!-- Tiles Configuration -->
    <plug-in className="org.apache.struts.tiles.TilesPlugin">
      <set-property property="definitions-config"
                        value="/WEB-INF/tiles-defs.xml"/>
    </plug-in>

</struts-config>
```

Repackage and Run the Updated Application

Because no Java code was modified during this process, it's not necessary to recompile the Mini HR application. However, several files have been added and a few have been modified, so the application needs to be repackaged and redeployed before it is run. Assuming you've made modifications to the original Mini HR application and it was set up in the **c:\java\MiniHR** directory (as described in Chapter 2), the following command line will repackage the application when run from **c:\java\MiniHR**:

```
jar cf MiniHR.war *
```

Similar to the way you ran Mini HR the first time, you now need to place the new **MiniHR.war** file that you just created into Tomcat's **webapps** directory and start Tomcat. As before, to access the Mini HR application, point your browser to **http://localhost:8080/MiniHR/**. Once you have the updated Mini HR running, everything should work as it did before. However, now you can add new pages and make global changes to the application with minimal effort.

Declarative Exception Handling

A major part of developing Java applications is handling error conditions, and Struts applications are no exception to that rule. Like most other applications, Struts' error handling is based around Java's exception-handling mechanism. However, as of version 1.1, Struts supports a powerful exception-handling mechanism called *declarative exception handling*. Declarative exception handling is a mechanism that lets you specify how an exception should be handled, but without having to include the handler within your application's Java code. Instead, the exception handler is declared in Struts' XML-based configuration file, **struts-config.xml**. Declarative exception handling enables you to change how exceptions are handled without having to recompile your application's code. You simply update the **struts-config.xml** file and restart the application. This is a significant advantage.

Prior to version 1.1, exception handling in Struts applications functioned much the same way as it does in most other applications. Inside your code, you had to have several **try-catch** blocks to handle each of the exceptions that could be thrown. While this solution works and is effective, there is often a great deal of overlap between different parts (i.e., **Action** classes) of a Struts application that have to implement the same exception processing logic. For instance, if two **Action** classes interface with the same business service and that service throws a custom business exception, then when something goes awry, each class would have to implement logic to handle the exception being thrown. Now, imagine that you have 20 or 30 **Action** classes that use a service (or set of services) that could throw a custom business exception. There would be a great deal of exception-handling logic duplicated across those **Action** classes. Struts' new declarative exception-handling mechanism allows you to create a common exception handler that can be reused by all of those actions. This centralizes all of the exception-handling logic in one place and reduces the duplication of code.

This chapter illustrates how to configure and use Struts' built-in exception handler and provides instructions for creating your own custom exception handler. Finally, this chapter steps through the process of updating the Mini HR application to take advantage of declarative exception handling.

Configuring Struts' Exception Handler

Using Struts' declarative exception-handling mechanism is very simple. All you have to do is add exception-handler definitions to the **struts-config.xml** file. Exception-handler definitions work in much the same way as forward definitions. You can create global exception-handler definitions and/or create action-specific handlers. Each exception-handler definition specifies the exception that it is to handle, a key to an error message in the **ApplicationResources.properties** resource bundle, and the path to a page to forward to when the exception is caught by the handler. Following is an example global exception-handler definition:

```
<global-exceptions>
  <exception
    type="com.jamesholmes.minihr.NoResultsFoundException"
     key="error.NoResultsFoundException"
    path="/exception.jsp"/>
</global-exceptions>
```

The **type** attribute specifies the fully qualified class name of the exception that the handler is for. When an exception of this type is thrown, the exception handler will take control and process the exception. The **key** attribute specifies the name of a key in the **ApplicationResources.properties** file that will be used to populate an **ActionError** object that will be passed to the page specified by the **path** attribute. The **path** attribute specifies the path to a page that will be forwarded to by the exception handler when the specified exception type is thrown. The page can then display the error message placed in the **ActionError** object, if so desired.

The second way you can define exception handlers is by nesting them inside action definitions, as shown next:

```
<!-- Action Mappings Configuration -->
<action-mappings>
  <action path="/search"
          type="com.jamesholmes.minihr.SearchAction"
          name="searchForm"
          scope="request"
          validate="true"
          input="/search.jsp">
```

```
    <exception
      type="com.jamesholmes.minihr.NoResultsFoundException"
       key="error.NoResultsFoundException"
      path="/exception.jsp"/>
  </action>
</action-mappings>
```

Action-nested exception handlers handle the specified exception only if it is thrown by
the enclosing action. If the exception is thrown by another action, it will not be handled.

You don't have to modify your **Action** classes in any way to take advantage of
declarative exception handling. However, if you already have **try-catch** blocks for
exceptions that you want handled by the exception handler, you need to remove them
so that the exception gets propagated up the chain for the exception handler to process.

Creating a Custom Exception Handler

Strut's built-in exception handler will suit most exception-handling scenarios; however,
your application may require a specialized exception handler. For this situation, Struts
provides a simple interface for creating your own custom exception handler that can
easily be plugged into the framework. Following are the two steps you need to take to
create your own custom exception handler:

1. Create a new exception-handler class.

2. Add new exception-handler definitions to the **struts-config.xml** file.

The following sections walk through each step of the process in detail, illustrating
how to create a custom exception handler that can send an e-mail when an exception
is caught. The example is designed to be generic so that it can be used with any type
of exception and can be easily enhanced.

Create a New Exception-Handler Class

The first step in creating a custom exception handler is to create an exception-handler
class that can be plugged into Struts. Custom exception-handler classes must extend
Struts' base **org.apache.struts.action.ExceptionHandler** class and override its **execute( )**
method. The **execute( )** method of the **ExceptionHandler** class that gets overridden is
very similar to the **execute( )** method of the **Action** class and behaves almost identically.
However, **ExceptionHandler.execute( )** takes two additional arguments, **java.lang
.Exception** and **org.apache.struts.config.ExceptionConfig**. Table 8-1 explains each of
the **ExceptionHandler.execute( )** method's arguments.

Argument	Description
java.lang.Exception	The exception that has been thrown and is to be handled.
org.apache.struts.config.ExceptionConfig	The **ExceptionConfig** object encapsulates the **<exception>** definition from the **struts-config.xml** file for this exception handler.
org.apache.struts.action.ActionMapping	The **ActionMapping** object encapsulates the **<action>** definition from the **struts-config.xml** file for the action that threw the exception that this exception handler is configured to handle.
org.apache.struts.action.ActionForm	The **ActionForm** object encapsulates the Form Bean associated with the action that threw the exception that this exception handler is configured to handle.
javax.servlet.http.HttpServletRequest	The **HttpServletRequest** object encapsulates the current HTTP request.
javax.servlet.http.HttpServletResponse	The **HttpServletResponse** object encapsulates the current HTTP response.

TABLE 8-1   The **execute( )** Method Arguments

To illustrate how to create a custom exception handler, we'll examine a sample exception handler that can be used to send an e-mail with a stack trace for the exception when the handler is triggered. Following is the example **EmailExceptionHandler** class:

```
package com.jamesholmes.minihr.EmailExceptionHandler;

import java.io.*;
import java.util.*;
import javax.mail.*;
import javax.mail.internet.*;
import javax.servlet.*;
import javax.servlet.http.*;
import org.apache.struts.action.*;
import org.apache.struts.config.*;

public class EmailExceptionHandler extends ExceptionHandler
{
  private static final String EMAIL_SERVER = "smtp.company.com";
  private static final String EMAIL_SENDER = "sender@company.com";
  private static final String EMAIL_RECIPIENT = "receiver@company.com";
  private static final String EMAIL_SUBJECT = "Exception Thrown";
```

```java
public ActionForward execute(Exception ex,
  ExceptionConfig config, ActionMapping mapping, ActionForm form,
  HttpServletRequest request, HttpServletResponse response)
    throws ServletException
{
  // Send email with exception.
  try {
    sendEmail(ex);
  } catch (Exception e) {
    throw new ServletException(e);
  }

  // Forward processing to the default exception handler.
  return
    super.execute(ex, config, mapping, form, request, response);
}

private void sendEmail(Exception ex)
  throws Exception
{
  // Set the host SMTP address.
  Properties props = new Properties();
  props.put("mail.smtp.host", EMAIL_SERVER);

  // Get the default mail session.
  Session session = Session.getDefaultInstance(props, null);

  // Store exception stack trace as message text string.
  ByteArrayOutputStream stream = new ByteArrayOutputStream();
  ex.printStackTrace(new PrintStream(stream));
  String messageText = stream.toString();

  // Create a message.
  Message message = new MimeMessage(session);
  message.setFrom(new InternetAddress(EMAIL_SENDER));
  message.setRecipient(Message.RecipientType.TO,
    new InternetAddress(EMAIL_RECIPIENT));
  message.setSubject(EMAIL_SUBJECT);
  message.setSentDate(new Date());
  message.setText(messageText);

  // Send the message.
  Transport.send(message);
}
}
```

Instead of completely overriding the functionality of the base **ExceptionHandler** class, the **EmailExceptionHandler** class augments its functionality. The **EmailExceptionHandler** class takes the exception passed to it and uses JavaMail to send the exception's stack trace in an e-mail. After sending the e-mail, **EmailExceptionHandler** calls **super.execute( )**, which invokes the default exception handler. This example illustrates how you can jump into the exception-handling process and add processing of your own. Alternatively, you could create an exception handler that completely overrides the behavior of the base handler.

Add New Exception-Handler Definitions to the struts-config.xml File

After you have created the custom exception handler, you put it to use by adding exception-handler definitions to the **struts-config.xml** configuration file. Using a custom exception handler is not much different from using the default handler. All you have to add to the standard definition is the fully qualified class name of the handler with the **exception** tag's **handler** attribute, as shown next:

```
<exception type="com.jamesholmes.minihr.NoResultsFoundException"
        handler="com.jamesholmes.minihr.EmailExceptionHandler"
          key="error.NoResultsFoundException"
          path="/exception.jsp"/>
```

Because the **EmailExceptionHandler** handler simply extends the base handler and does not completely override it, you must specify a path, by using the **path** attribute, for the handler to forward to. However, if you were to create a custom handler that completely overrides the base handler, you would not have to specify a value for the **path** attribute unless your handler wanted to use it. The **type** and **key** attributes are required regardless of what handler you use.

Adding Declarative Exception Handling to the Mini HR Application

Now that you've seen the benefits of using declarative exception handling and how it works, you are ready to revisit the Mini HR application and add declarative exception handling to it. Following is the list of steps involved in adding declarative exception handling to the Mini HR application:

1. Create an application exception class.
2. Update **SearchAction** to throw an application exception.
3. Set up an exception handler in the **struts-config.xml** file.
4. Create an exception-handler JSP.
5. Add an exception error message to the **ApplicationResources.properties** file.
6. Recompile, repackage, and run the updated application.

The following sections walk through each step of the process in detail.

Create an Application Exception Class

The first step in updating the Mini HR application to use declarative exception handling is to create an application exception class. Application exceptions are useful for distinguishing between specific error conditions. For example, an application could have a **ConfigurationFileNotFoundException** class and use it to indicate that a configuration file was not found, instead of simply throwing the more general **java.io.FileNotFoundException**. Application exceptions are also useful for distinguishing business logic–based exceptions, as is the case for the following **NoResultsFoundException** exception, which you will add to the Mini HR application:

```
package com.jamesholmes.minihr;

public class NoResultsFoundException extends Exception
{
}
```

As you can see, this exception is very basic; it simply extends **Exception** and does not provide any other functionality. This approach uniquely identifies the exception and is useful when no additional functionality is needed beyond the base functionality provided by the **Exception** class.

Update SearchAction to Throw an Application Exception

Once you have created the application exception, **NoResultsFoundException**, you can put it to use in the **SearchAction** class. To use the exception, you'll add a check that determines whether or not any search results were returned from the **EmployeeSearchService** class. If no results are found, a **NoResultsFoundException** exception will be thrown. Following is the code that implements this logic:

```
// Throw an application exception if results were not found.
if (results.size() < 1) {
  throw new NoResultsFoundException();
}
```

When this exception is thrown, Struts will catch it and process it accordingly.
    Following is the updated **SearchAction** class in its entirety:

```
package com.jamesholmes.minihr;

import java.util.ArrayList;

import javax.servlet.http.HttpServletRequest;
import javax.servlet.http.HttpServletResponse;

import org.apache.struts.action.Action;
```

```
import org.apache.struts.action.ActionForm;
import org.apache.struts.action.ActionForward;
import org.apache.struts.action.ActionMapping;

public final class SearchAction extends Action
{
  public ActionForward execute(ActionMapping mapping,
    ActionForm form,
    HttpServletRequest request,
    HttpServletResponse response)
    throws Exception
  {
    EmployeeSearchService service = new EmployeeSearchService();
    ArrayList results;

    SearchForm searchForm = (SearchForm) form;

    // Perform employee search based on what criteria was entered.
    String name = searchForm.getName();
    if (name != null && name.trim().length() > 0) {
      results = service.searchByName(name);
    } else {
      results = service.searchBySsNum(searchForm.getSsNum().trim());
    }

    // Throw an application exception if results were not found.
    if (results.size() < 1) {
      throw new NoResultsFoundException();
    }

    // Place search results in SearchForm for access by JSP.
    searchForm.setResults(results);

    // Forward control to this Action's input page.
    return mapping.getInputForward();
  }
}
```

Set Up an Exception Handler in the struts-config.xml File

After you create an application exception and put it to use in an action, you must
set up an exception handler for it in the **struts-config.xml** file. For Mini HR, the
NoResultsFoundException exception will be thrown only by the **SearchAction**
class, thus you'll define the action-specific exception handler shown next rather
than a global exception handler:

```
<!-- Action Mappings Configuration -->
<action-mappings>
```

```
<action path="/search"
        type="com.jamesholmes.minihr.SearchAction"
        name="searchForm"
        scope="request"
        validate="true"
        input="/search.jsp">
  <exception
    type="com.jamesholmes.minihr.NoResultsFoundException"
     key="error.NoResultsFoundException"
    path="/exception.jsp"/>
</action>
</action-mappings>
```

Because this exception handler is nested inside the action definition for
SearchAction, it will only handle **NoResultsFoundException** exceptions
that are thrown from that action. Alternatively, if you wanted to handle
NoResultsFoundExceptions being thrown from *any* action, you would have
to define a global exception handler, as shown next:

```
<global-exceptions>
  <exception
    type="com.jamesholmes.minihr.NoResultsFoundException"
     key="error.NoResultsFoundException"
    path="/exception.jsp"/>
</global-exceptions>
```

Following is the updated **struts-config.xml** file in its entirety:

```
<?xml version="1.0"?>

<!DOCTYPE struts-config PUBLIC
  "-//Apache Software Foundation//DTD Struts Configuration 1.1//EN"
  "http://jakarta.apache.org/struts/dtds/struts-config_1_1.dtd">

<struts-config>

  <!-- Form Beans Configuration -->
  <form-beans>
    <form-bean name="searchForm"
               type="com.jamesholmes.minihr.SearchForm"/>
  </form-beans>

  <!-- Global Forwards Configuration -->
  <global-forwards>
    <forward name="search" path="/search.jsp"/>
  </global-forwards>
```

```
<!-- Action Mappings Configuration -->
<action-mappings>
  <action path="/search"
          type="com.jamesholmes.minihr.SearchAction"
          name="searchForm"
          scope="request"
          validate="true"
          input="/search.jsp">
    <exception
      type="com.jamesholmes.minihr.NoResultsFoundException"
       key="error.NoResultsFoundException"
      path="/exception.jsp"/>
  </action>
</action-mappings>

<!-- Message Resources Configuration -->
<message-resources
   parameter="com.jamesholmes.minihr.ApplicationResources"/>

</struts-config>
```

Create an Exception-Handler JSP

When using exception handlers, you have to specify the URL to the page that will
be forwarded to if the specified exception is caught by the handler. Following is
the **exception.jsp** file specified for the **NoResultsFoundException** exception in the
struts-config.xml file:

```
<%@ taglib uri="/WEB-INF/tlds/struts-html.tld" prefix="html" %>

<html>
<head>
<title>ABC, Inc. Human Resources Portal</title>
</head>
<body>

<font size="+1">ABC, Inc. Human Resources Portal</font><br>
<hr width="100%" noshade="true">

<html:errors/>

</body>
</html>
```

As stated earlier in this chapter, when an exception is processed by Struts' built-in
exception handler, it creates an **ActionError** object and stores it in request or session
scope so that it can be accessed by the page being forwarded to. This page uses the
HTML Tag Library's **errors** tag to output the error message.

One other point: Although this JSP is intended to be used by the exception handler for **NoResultsFoundException**, it is generic enough that you could use it as a general-purpose exception-handler page.

Add an Exception Error Message to the ApplicationResources.properties File

Recall from earlier in this chapter that each exception handler defined in the **struts-config.xml** file declares a key for an error message in Struts' resource bundle file: **ApplicationResources.properties**. At run time, the key is used to look up an error message to pass to the exception-handler page when the exception handler is triggered. Following is the error message that you must add to the **ApplicationResources .properties** file for the exception handler that was defined in the **struts-config.xml** file:

```
# Exception Error Resources
error.NoResultsFoundException=<li>No Search Results Found</li>
```

The following code shows the updated **ApplicationResources.properties** file in its entirety:

```
# Label Resources
label.search.name=Name
label.search.ssNum=Social Security Number


# Error Resources
error.search.criteria.missing=<li>Search Criteria Missing</li>
error.search.ssNum.invalid=<li>Invalid Social Security Number</li>
errors.header=<font color="red"><b>Error(s)</b></font><ul>
errors.footer=</ul><hr width="100%" size="1" noshade="true">

# Exception Error Resources
error.NoResultsFoundException=<li>No Search Results Found</li>
```

Recompile, Repackage, and Run the Updated Application

Because you created a new application exception class and updated the **SearchAction** class, you need to recompile and repackage the Mini HR application before you run it. Assuming that you've made modifications to the original Mini HR application and it was set up in the **c:\java\MiniHR** directory (as described in Chapter 2), the following command line will recompile the application:

```
javac -classpath WEB-INF\lib\commons-beanutils.jar;
               WEB-INF\lib\commons-collections.jar;
               WEB-INF\lib\commons-lang.jar;
               WEB-INF\lib\commons-logging.jar;
               WEB-INF\lib\commons-validator.jar;
```

```
WEB-INF\lib\digester.jar;
WEB-INF\lib\fileupload.jar;
WEB-INF\lib\jakarta-oro.jar;
WEB-INF\lib\struts.jar;
C:\java\jakarta-tomcat-4.1.27\common\lib\servlet.jar
    WEB-INF\src\com\jamesholmes\minihr\*.java
    -d WEB-INF\classes
```

After recompiling Mini HR, you need to repackage it using the following command line:

```
jar cf MiniHR.war *
```

This command must also be run from the directory where you have set up the Mini HR application (e.g., **c:\java\MiniHR**).

Similar to the way you ran Mini HR the first time, you now need to place the new **MiniHR.war** file that you just created into Tomcat's **webapps** directory and start Tomcat. As before, access the Mini HR application at **http://localhost:8080/MiniHR/**. Once you have the updated Mini HR application running, try entering a name or social security number that will not be found when searched for. When this happens, the **SearchAction** class will throw the **NoResultsFoundException** exception and then the **exception.jsp** page will be displayed, as shown in Figure 8-1.

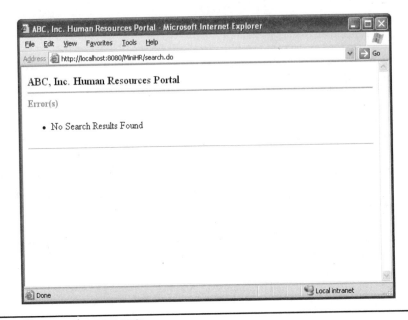

FIGURE 8-1 The exception error page

Struts Modules

During the 1.1 release cycle of Struts, a significant number of new features were added to the framework. Each of these features greatly improved the framework, and each is important in its own right. However, one feature stands out because of its profound impact on the framework: support for *modules*.

Support for modules solves a problem commonly encountered when using earlier versions of Struts. In all versions of Struts, including version 1.1, you can run only one instance of the **ActionServlet** controller servlet per Web application (i.e., **.war** file). This is because **ActionServlet** stores several details of the framework's configuration in variables within the Web application scope, which is the scope shared by all parts of the application. Thus, attempting to run multiple instances of **ActionServlet** in the same Web application causes a problem, because the data associated with one instance overwrites the data associated with another instance. Prior to version 1.1 and its introduction of modules, this was a major limitation of Struts, because your entire application's configuration had to reside in a single Struts configuration file. For large applications, where the configuration file gets very large and several developers are involved, that proved to be a problematic point of contention.

Today, you still can have only one instance of **ActionServlet** for the same reasons as before; however, you can *simulate* the functionality of having multiple instances by subdividing your application into discreet units by using modules. Each module has its own Struts configuration file, its own set of actions and forwards, a separate URL namespace, and so on. Essentially, modules are like mini-Struts applications inside a master Struts application and are analogous to the way Web applications reside in a servlet container. Each module has its own URL namespace, just as Web applications do. Modules also solve the problems of parallel development that are commonly experienced when using versions of Struts prior to 1.1.

Before moving on, it is necessary to mention another feature added by Struts 1.1 that, in some cases, offers an alternative to modules: support for multiple configuration files. Although added in the same release (1.1) as modules, multiple configuration files can be used independently, without having to convert your application for use with modules. Support for multiple configuration files alleviates some of the problems associated with large, team-based development with Struts. However, multiple configuration files do not partition your Struts application the way that modules do. When using multiple configuration files, the information in the files is combined to create one large set of configuration data. This can cause a problem, however. For example, if you define an action with a certain name in one file and another configuration file defines another action with the same name, the configuration file last read will override the first file's data. Basically, last one in wins. Modules do not have this problem, because Struts stores each module's configuration data separately. Thus, modules offer the best solution when you need the functionality of multiple instances of **ActionServlet**.

This chapter describes how to set up and use modules in your application, including details on how to use Tiles and Validator with modules. It also shows how to apply modules to the Mini HR application.

Using Modules

As stated, using modules allows you to partition your Struts application into discreet functional areas, almost like having wholly separate applications. Each module has its own Struts configuration file, actions, forwards, and JSPs, which allows it to function independently of other modules. Using modules in a Struts application involves these three steps:

1. Create a Struts configuration file for each module.
2. Configure the **web.xml** deployment descriptor for modules.
3. Configure links to access module-specific JSPs.

The following sections explain how to configure and use modules in detail.

Creating a Struts Configuration File for Each Module

In order to separate each module's configuration details, you must create a separate Struts configuration file for each module. Having a separate configuration file for each module allows all of a module's actions, forwards, and so on to be grouped into one module-specific file that is independent of other modules' configuration data. You configure actions, forwards, and so on inside the file, just as you would with a nonmodularized application. The only difference with module configuration files is in the way the Tiles and Validator plugin definitions are set up, which is described later in this chapter.

The typical naming convention for module configuration files is **struts-config-** *module***.xml**, where *module* is the name of the module that the file is for. Note, however, that there are no restrictions on the names of module configuration files and thus any name can be used so long as it is unique. Alternatively, if your application is using Tiles and/or Validator, you may want to create a module-specific directory under **/WEB-INF/** for each module to store its configuration files. For example, if your application is using modules, Tiles, and Validator, you could arrange the files as shown next:

```
/WEB-INF/moduleA/struts-config.xml
/WEB-INF/moduleA/tiles-defs.xml
/WEB-INF/moduleA/validation.xml
/WEB-INF/moduleB/struts-config.xml
/WEB-INF/moduleB/tiles-defs.xml
/WEB-INF/moduleB/validation.xml
```

With this arrangement you wouldn't have to use the module name in the names of the configuration files, because they are under a module-specific directory.

NOTE   *Detailed information on the Struts configuration file is found in Chapter 16.*

Configuring the web.xml Deployment Descriptor for Modules

Each module's Struts configuration file has to be specified in the **web.xml** deployment descriptor, just as is done for nonmodularized Struts applications; however, the way they are configured is slightly different. Recall that with a nonmodularized application, you specify the path to Struts' configuration file with the **config** initialization parameter for the **ActionServlet** controller servlet, as shown next:

```
<!-- Action Servlet Configuration -->
<servlet>
  <servlet-name>action</servlet-name>
  <servlet-class>org.apache.struts.action.ActionServlet</servlet-class>
  <init-param>
    <param-name>config</param-name>
    <param-value>/WEB-INF/struts-config.xml</param-value>
  </init-param>
  <load-on-startup>1</load-on-startup>
</servlet>
```

The **config** parameter is set to the location of your application's Struts configuration file.

   To specify module configuration files, you need an initialization parameter for each module and it must be named **config/***moduleName*, where *moduleName* is the name you want to assign to the module. For example, to specify two modules named **moduleA** and **moduleB**, your **ActionServlet** definition must look like this:

```
<!-- Action Servlet Configuration -->
<servlet>
  <servlet-name>action</servlet-name>
  <servlet-class>org.apache.struts.action.ActionServlet</servlet-class>
  <init-param>
    <param-name>config/moduleA</param-name>
    <param-value>/WEB-INF/struts-config-moduleA.xml</param-value>
  </init-param>
  <init-param>
```

```
    <param-name>config/moduleB</param-name>
    <param-value>/WEB-INF/struts-config-moduleB.xml</param-value>
  </init-param>
  <load-on-startup>1</load-on-startup>
</servlet>
```

In this file, two configuration files are specified: **struts-config-moduleA.xml** and **struts-config-moduleB.xml**.

The name given to the module through the **param-name** tag is known as the *module prefix* and is very important. Struts uses the module prefix to distinguish and route requests to the module. The module name becomes part of the URL that must be used to access the module's actions.

It is important to understand that all of a module's action paths are relative to the module. For example, the modularized version of the Mini HR application developed later in this chapter is deployed at **/MiniHR/** on the server (i.e., **http://localhost:8080/MiniHR/**). It has a module named **employee**, which has an action mapped to **/search**. Therefore, the URL to access the action is **/MiniHR/employee/search.do**. Figure 9-1 shows a breakdown of what each piece of the URL is.

When using modules, the standard **config** parameter (that is, the one without any module name appended to it) is used to specify a configuration file for a *default* module. The default module has no module prefix, thus any URL whose path does not include a module name will be routed to the default module. Thus, using the Mini HR example developed later in this chapter, if a request were made to **/MiniHR/admin/viewAppUsers.do**, Struts would execute the action mapped to **/admin/viewAppUsers** in the default module's configuration file, because the URL does not contain a module prefix in it.

NOTE   *A side effect of using modules is that you cannot use path mapping (e.g., /do/*) for the ActionServlet controller servlet. Instead, you must use extension mapping (e.g., *.do) because Struts uses the URL path to determine which module a request is being made for; using path mapping would interfere with that mechanism. For more information on setting up ActionServlet's mapping, refer to Chapter 5.*

Configuring Links to Access Module-Specific JSPs

Modules fundamentally change the way JSPs are linked to and accessed in a Struts application. Recall that in nonmodularized Struts applications, you link to and access JSPs just as you would in any Web application. With modules, the rules change because

FIGURE 9-1
The module URL
breakdown

Struts requires that URLs that are used to access a module must have a module prefix that designates which module is being accessed. This is necessary to enable Struts to select the correct module configuration data to use for each request.

When using modules, Struts needs some way to know how to select the correct module configuration data to use for a JSP. Here's why: When you access JSPs, the request for the JSP does not go through Struts' controller servlet, like requests for actions do. Because of this, Struts does not have the opportunity to select the correct module configuration data to use for the JSP. Thus, if the JSP is using any Struts tag library tags that reference a Struts action, Struts will not know how to determine what action the JSP is trying to reference because no module has been selected.

To solve this problem, all requests for module JSPs must be routed through Struts' controller servlet. Struts provides a built-in action called **org.apache.struts.actions .SwitchAction** to help with this. **SwitchAction** allows you to create module-specific JSP links that preserve the module name so that Struts can properly select the right module configuration data. **SwitchAction** does this by taking a module name and a JSP as request parameters. When executed, it takes care of selecting the module specified and then forwarding to the specified JSP. This way the module configuration data is set up for the JSP. To use **SwitchAction**, you must add an action definition for it in your Struts configuration file. Typically this is added to the default module configuration file, but you can add it to module-specific configuration files, too. Following is a sample **SwitchAction** definition:

```
<action path="/switchMod"
        type="org.apache.struts.actions.SwitchAction"/>
```

You can put this definition to use with the following example link:

```
<html:link action="/switchMod?prefix=/moduleA&page=/moduleA/main.jsp">
ModuleA main JSP
</html:link>
```

This example usage creates a link that will route the Struts request processor to the JSP at **/moduleA/main.jsp** and select the configuration data for **moduleA**.

Using Validator with Modules

Using Validator with modules works the same way as it does with a nonmodularized application. You simply add the Validator plugin to each module's Struts configuration file. Doing so allows each module to specify its own module-specific Validator configuration file, as shown next:

```
<!-- Validator Configuration -->
<plug-in className="org.apache.struts.validator.ValidatorPlugIn">
  <set-property property="pathnames"
```

```
           value="/WEB-INF/validator-rules.xml,
             /WEB-INF/validation-moduleA.xml"/>
</plug-in>
```

In this example, the first configuration file specified with the **pathnames** property is the **validator-rules.xml** file. Recall from Chapter 6 that this file is used to declaratively plug in the validation routines that Validator will use to perform validations. Because validation routines are typically the same across all modules, you do not have to create a **validator-rules.xml** file for each module. Instead, you simply point each module's Validator plugin to the one common file. However, using modules does allow you to specify a unique Validator rules configuration file for each module.

The second configuration file specified with the **pathnames** property is the module-specific Validator configuration file. This file should include all of the validation definitions specific to the given module.

Using Tiles with Modules

Like Validator, in order to use Tiles with modules, you have to add the Tiles plugin to each module's Struts configuration file that you want to use Tiles with. For example, if your application has two modules, **moduleA** and **moduleB**, you have to add a Tiles plugin definition to **moduleA**'s Struts configuration file and a definition to **moduleB**'s Struts configuration file. This is necessary because Struts uses a separate request processor for each module, and the Tiles plugin adds its own custom request processor that extends the base Struts request processor (per module). If you don't add the Tiles plugin to each module's Struts configuration file, not all modules will have the Tiles request processor that is necessary for processing forwards to Tiles definitions.

Following is the standard Tiles plugin definition that you would have in your Struts configuration file for a nonmodularized Struts application:

```
<!-- Tiles Configuration -->
<plug-in className="org.apache.struts.tiles.TilesPlugin">
  <set-property property="definitions-config"
                value="/WEB-INF/tiles-defs.xml"/>
</plug-in>
```

You would use this exact same definition in each module's Struts configuration file for a modularized application. Of course, the name of the Tiles configuration file specified with the **definitions-config** property would change with each module, unless they all shared the same configuration file.

If you want each of your modules to have its own Tiles configuration file and don't want each module's Tiles definitions to be shared across modules, you can indicate this intent with the Tiles plugin **moduleAware** parameter. Following is a sample Tiles plugin definition for the Struts configuration file that illustrates this:

```
<!-- Tiles Configuration -->
<plug-in className="org.apache.struts.tiles.TilesPlugin">
  <set-property property="definitions-config"
                value="/WEB-INF/tiles-defs.xml"/>
  <set-property property="moduleAware" value="true"/>
</plug-in>
```

By default, Tiles stores each module's configuration file settings in the same internal configuration structure. Thus, **moduleA** can see all of the Tiles definitions from **moduleB**'s Tiles configuration file and vice versa. Tiles does this by default to save memory in case each module uses the same configuration file. However, in most cases each module has its own module-specific definitions that other modules shouldn't be able to access. For this scenario, you set the **moduleAware** property to true. This informs Tiles to create a separate configuration structure for each module's Tiles definitions.

As explained earlier, module prefixes apply only to actions. Thus, any URLs to JSPs specified in your Tiles configuration files are not relative to a module prefix, but rather are relative to the root of the application, just as they are in nonmodularized Struts applications.

Converting the Mini HR Application to Use Modules

Now that you've seen the benefits of using Strut's module mechanism and how it works, you are ready to update the Mini HR application to use modules. Here are the steps that you will follow:

1. Set up module directories and files.
2. Create a Struts configuration file for each module.
3. Update the application's **web.xml** deployment descriptor file.
4. Repackage and run the updated application.

The following sections walk you through each step of the process in detail.

Set Up Module Directories and Files

The first step in updating the Mini HR application is to set up a directory for each module that will store its JSPs. This example will have two modules, an **employee** module and a **reports** module. The **employee** module will contain functionality previously existing in Mini HR. The **reports** module adds new functionality. You need to create a directory for each of these modules beneath the main Mini HR application directory (e.g., **c:\java\MiniHR**). Thus, you will have the following directories:

```
c:\java\MiniHR\employee
c:\java\MiniHR\reports
```

After you have created the directories, you need to put the corresponding JSPs into them. Because the original Mini HR application already has **employee** functionality, you can simply move the employee search JSP (**search.jsp**) from the root application directory (e.g., **c:\java\MiniHR**) to the new **employee** module directory you just created. The **reports** module contains new functionality, which is provided by the **menu.jsp** file, shown here. Store this file in the **reports** module directory.

```html
<html>
<head>
<title>ABC, Inc. Human Resources Portal - Reports Menu</title>
</head>
<body>

<font size="+1">
ABC, Inc. Human Resources Portal - Reports Menu
</font><br>
<hr width="100%" noshade="true">

&#149; New Employee Report<br>
&#149; 5-Year Employee Report<br>
&#149; 10-Year Employee Report<br>
&#149; 20-Year Employee Report<br>

</body>
<html>
```

After you move the **search.jsp** file and create the **menu.jsp** file, your main application directory should look like this:

```
C:\java\MiniHR\employee\search.jsp
c:\java\MiniHR\reports\menu.jsp
c:\java\MiniHR\index.jsp
```

Before moving on, a short, but important, digression is in order. The general idea behind the directory structure just described can be extended to configuration files, if you like. For example, you could create a directory for each module beneath **/WEB-INF/** that would hold the module's Struts, Tiles, and Validator configuration files. Following is an example directory layout illustrating this:

```
MiniHR/WEB-INF/moduleA/struts-config.xml
MiniHR/WEB-INF/moduleA/tiles-defs.xml
MiniHR/WEB-INF/moduleA/validation.xml
MiniHR/WEB-INF/moduleB/struts-config.xml
```

```
MiniHR/WEB-INF/moduleB/tiles-defs.xml
MiniHR/WEB-INF/moduleB/validation.xml
```

Create a Struts Configuration File for Each Module

After you have set up the module directories and files, the next step is to create a Struts configuration file for each of the modules. The application's current **struts-config.xml** file will be used as the configuration file for the **employee** module, and thus must be renamed to **struts-config-employee.xml**. Following is the renamed and updated **struts-config-employee.xml** file:

```
<?xml version="1.0"?>

<!DOCTYPE struts-config PUBLIC
  "-//Apache Software Foundation//DTD Struts Configuration 1.1//EN"
  "http://jakarta.apache.org/struts/dtds/struts-config_1_1.dtd">

<struts-config>

  <!-- Form Beans Configuration -->
  <form-beans>
    <form-bean name="searchForm"
               type="com.jamesholmes.minihr.SearchForm"/>
  </form-beans>

  <!-- Action Mappings Configuration -->
  <action-mappings>
    <action path="/viewSearch" forward="/search.jsp"/>
    <action path="/search"
            type="com.jamesholmes.minihr.SearchAction"
            name="searchForm"
            scope="request"
            validate="true"
            input="/search.jsp">
    </action>
  </action-mappings>

  <!-- Message Resources Configuration -->
  <message-resources
    parameter="com.jamesholmes.minihr.ApplicationResources"/>

</struts-config>
```

In addition to being renamed, this file has also been updated. Notice that the Global Forwards Configuration section has been removed and the **/viewSearch** action has been added.

As mentioned earlier in this chapter, Struts incorporates the concept of a default module. The default module's configuration file is named **struts-config.xml** and is shown next:

```
<?xml version="1.0"?>

<!DOCTYPE struts-config PUBLIC
  "-//Apache Software Foundation//DTD Struts Configuration 1.1//EN"
  "http://jakarta.apache.org/struts/dtds/struts-config_1_1.dtd">

<struts-config>

  <!-- Global Forwards Configuration -->
  <global-forwards>
    <forward name="viewSearch" path="/employee/viewSearch.do"/>
  </global-forwards>

  <!-- Message Resources Configuration -->
  <message-resources
    parameter="com.jamesholmes.minihr.ApplicationResources"/>

</struts-config>
```

You will need to create this new file and place it under the **/WEB-INF/** directory (e.g., **c:\java\MiniHR\WEB-INF**). This configuration file simply has a forward pointing to the Search page that is used by **index.jsp** for its Search for Employees link.

The **reports** module's configuration file, **struts-config-reports.xml**, is shown next:

```
<?xml version="1.0"?>

<!DOCTYPE struts-config PUBLIC
  "-//Apache Software Foundation//DTD Struts Configuration 1.1//EN"
  "http://jakarta.apache.org/struts/dtds/struts-config_1_1.dtd">

<struts-config>

  <!-- Action Mappings Configuration -->
  <action-mappings>
    <action path="/viewMenu" forward="/menu.jsp"/>
  </action-mappings>

  <!-- Message Resources Configuration -->
  <message-resources
    parameter="com.jamesholmes.minihr.ApplicationResources"/>

</struts-config>
```

You will also need to create this new file and place it under the **/WEB-INF/** directory (e.g., **c:\java\MiniHR\WEB-INF**). This configuration file simply has a forward action pointing to the Reports Menu page that is used by **index.jsp** for its Reports Menu link.

Update the Application's web.xml Deployment Descriptor File

Once you have created the Struts configuration files for each module, you must update Mini HR's **web.xml** deployment descriptor file. Each module's configuration file will be passed to Strut's **ActionServlet** controller servlet as an initialization parameter, as shown next:

```
<!-- Action Servlet Configuration -->
<servlet>
  <servlet-name>action</servlet-name>
  <servlet-class>org.apache.struts.action.ActionServlet</servlet-class>
  <init-param>
    <param-name>config</param-name>
    <param-value>/WEB-INF/struts-config.xml</param-value>
  </init-param>
  <init-param>
    <param-name>config/employee</param-name>
    <param-value>/WEB-INF/struts-config-employee.xml</param-value>
  </init-param>
  <init-param>
    <param-name>config/reports</param-name>
    <param-value>/WEB-INF/struts-config-reports.xml</param-value>
  </init-param>
  <load-on-startup>1</load-on-startup>
</servlet>
```

Each initialization parameter specifies a name and a value for the parameter with the **param-name** and **param-value** tags, respectively. The default module's configuration file is specified with a parameter named **config**. Each of the module-specific configuration files is specified with a parameter named **config/***moduleName*, where *moduleName* is the name of the module the configuration file is for.

Following is the updated **web.xml** file in its entirety:

```
<?xml version="1.0"?>

<!DOCTYPE web-app PUBLIC
  "-//Sun Microsystems, Inc.//DTD Web Application 2.3//EN"
  "http://java.sun.com/dtd/web-app_2_3.dtd">

<web-app>
```

```xml
<!-- Action Servlet Configuration -->
<servlet>
  <servlet-name>action</servlet-name>
  <servlet-class>org.apache.struts.action.ActionServlet</servlet-class>
  <init-param>
    <param-name>config</param-name>
    <param-value>/WEB-INF/struts-config.xml</param-value>
  </init-param>
  <init-param>
    <param-name>config/employee</param-name>
    <param-value>/WEB-INF/struts-config-employee.xml</param-value>
  </init-param>
  <init-param>
    <param-name>config/reports</param-name>
    <param-value>/WEB-INF/struts-config-reports.xml</param-value>
  </init-param>
  <load-on-startup>1</load-on-startup>
</servlet>

<!-- Action Servlet Mapping -->
<servlet-mapping>
  <servlet-name>action</servlet-name>
  <url-pattern>*.do</url-pattern>
</servlet-mapping>

<!-- The Welcome File List -->
<welcome-file-list>
  <welcome-file>/index.jsp</welcome-file>
</welcome-file-list>

<!-- Struts Tag Library Descriptors -->
<taglib>
  <taglib-uri>/WEB-INF/tlds/struts-bean.tld</taglib-uri>
  <taglib-location>/WEB-INF/tlds/struts-bean.tld</taglib-location>
</taglib>
<taglib>
  <taglib-uri>/WEB-INF/tlds/struts-html.tld</taglib-uri>
  <taglib-location>/WEB-INF/tlds/struts-html.tld</taglib-location>
</taglib>
<taglib>
  <taglib-uri>/WEB-INF/tlds/struts-logic.tld</taglib-uri>
  <taglib-location>/WEB-INF/tlds/struts-logic.tld</taglib-location>
</taglib>

</web-app>
```

Repackage and Run the Updated Application

Because no Java source code files had to be modified to update the Mini HR application to use modules, you do not have to recompile the application. All you have to do is repackage the application and redeploy it before running it again. Assuming that you have made modifications to the original Mini HR application and it was set up in the **c:\java\MiniHR** directory (as described in Chapter 2), the following command line will repackage the application:

```
jar cf MiniHR.war *
```

This command should be run from the directory where you have set up the Mini HR application (e.g., **c:\java\MiniHR**).

Similar to the way you ran Mini HR the first time, you now need to place the new **MiniHR.war** file that you just created into Tomcat's **webapps** directory and start Tomcat. As before, to access the Mini HR application, point your browser to **http://localhost:8080/MiniHR/**. Once you have the updated Mini HR application running, you will see the screen shown in Figure 9-2.

Clicking the Search for Employees link takes you to the same employee search page that you were taken to by clicking the same link in the original application. The Reports Menu link takes you to the new **menu.jsp** page created for the **reports** module.

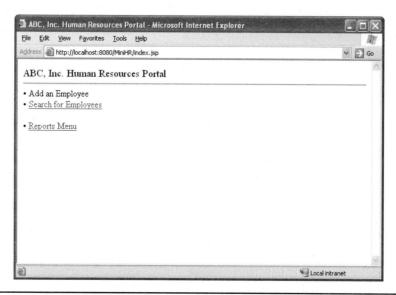

FIGURE 9-2   The opening Mini HR application screen

Internationalizing Struts Applications

The Internet has created a global, electronic shopping mall. Whereas businesses once catered only to customers in their same geographic region, today business is transacted with customers worldwide. A product of this globalization is the need for software that can adapt to the conventions and languages used by customers in different countries. To achieve this, applications must provide content in multiple languages. This is called *internationalization*.

From the start, Java was designed with internationalization in mind. For example, it offers support for Unicode character sets and provides built-in classes that manage locale-specific content. Struts builds upon Java's support, making development of internationalized Struts applications straightforward. This chapter presents an overview of Java's built-in internationalization support and then explains how Struts' internationalization builds upon it.

Understanding Java's Internationalization Support

Java's built-in internationalization support is centered on three main classes. The following table lists each class and its description.

Class	Description
java.util.Locale	Encapsulates the language, country, and variant for a specific locale.
java.util.ResourceBundle	Encapsulates locale-specific resources.
java.text.MessageFormat	Provides methods for creating locale-specific formatted messages.

The following three sections provide a brief introduction to each class.

The java.util.Locale Class

At the core of Java's internationalization API is the **Locale** class. The **Locale** class encapsulates the language, country, and variant for a specific locale. That is, the **Locale** class is used to uniquely represent a specific locale. All other locale-oriented classes use instances of this class to tailor their behavior and output to a specific locale.

When you create a **Locale** object you specify the locale's language; language and country; or language, country, and variant. Thus, **Locale** lets you represent as specific a locale as needed. The constructors for the **Locale** class are shown here:

```
Locale(String language)
Locale(String language, String country)
Locale(String language, String country, String variant)
```

The following snippet illustrates each of these uses in order:

```
Locale locale1 = new Locale("en");
Locale locale2 = new Locale("en", "US");
Locale locale3 = new Locale("en", "US", "WIN");
```

The first example creates an English language–specific locale; the second example creates a United States English language–specific locale; and the third example creates a United States English language Windows–specific locale. The more attributes you specify, the more specific the locale is. For example, if you create a Spanish language **Locale** object, as shown next, it will serve all users whose language is Spanish, independent of what country they are from:

```
Locale spanishLocale = new Locale("es");
```

Alternatively, to create a Spanish language locale specific to Mexico, you can use this declaration:

```
Locale mexicoSpanishLocale = new Locale("es", "MX");
```

Using combinations of language, country, and variant together narrows the scope of **Locale** objects.

The **Locale** object's **language** argument must be specified using a valid two-letter ISO-639 language code (e.g., "en" for English or "es" for Spanish). The **country** argument must be specified using a valid uppercase two-letter ISO-3166 country code (e.g., "US" for United States or "CA" for Canada"). The **variant** argument is for a vendor- or browser-specific code (e.g., "WIN" for Windows or "MAC" for Macintosh). For a listing of each of the ISO language and country codes, visit their respective specification Web sites listed here:

http://www.unicode.org/unicode/onlinedat/languages.html

http://www.unicode.org/unicode/onlinedat/countries.html

Here are a couple important notes about **Locale** objects that you should know. First, **Locale** objects are immutable; thus, once you have created an instance, you cannot change any of its attributes (i.e., language, country, or variant). Because of this, if you need to change a locale for some reason, you must create a new locale instance. Second, the **Locale** class provides several static locale constants as a convenience. For example, **Locale.US** and **Locale.FRANCE** are country code constants and **Locale.ENGLISH** and **Locale.FRENCH** are language code constants. Following is an example use of the constants:

```
Locale us = Locale.US;
Locale french = Locale.FRENCH;
```

The java.util.ResourceBundle Class

The **ResourceBundle** class encapsulates locale-specific resources for an application. Essentially, the **ResourceBundle** class is a central repository that applications use to hold resources. Applications simply provide the name of a resource and a locale, and the bundle returns the application resource for the specified locale. The resource names are the same across all locales, enabling an application to know only the name of a resource and how it should be handled. For example, assume that a label is displayed beside a field on an HTML form. Using a resource bundle, an application can obtain the text for the label by requesting the label from the resource bundle by name. When requesting the label, the application passes a locale that specifies what version of the label's text to obtain, such as English, Spanish, and so on. The resource bundle returns to the application the proper version of the text, which it can then display beside the field. The application does not need to have separate logic for each translation. It just needs to know how to get the text and display it. This is the premise and power of internationalization.

Resource bundles most often contain locale-specific text (e.g., error messages, field and button labels, and so on) for applications, but can also be used to manage any locale-specific resources. The **ResourceBundle** class provides the core interface for working with resource bundles, but is not intended to be used directly because it is an abstract class. Java provides two subclasses of **ResourceBundle**: **java.util.ListResourceBundle** and **java.util.PropertyResourceBundle**. The **ListResourceBundle** class is an abstract class that provides a mechanism for using lists to store resources; because it's abstract you must provide a concrete subclass implementation to make use of it. The **PropertyResourceBundle** class is a concrete subclass that provides a mechanism for using properties files to store resources. This class is the most commonly used for working with resource bundles in Java and is the default mechanism used by the **ResourceBundle** class's static **getBundle( )** methods.

Because the **PropertyResourceBundle** class is the default (and the most commonly used) implementation, it's important to know how it works. The **PropertyResourceBundle** class provides an interface to access resources stored in properties files. Internally, it uses the **java.util.Properties** class. The **PropertyResourceBundle** class requires that resource bundle properties files be named using a special scheme, which takes the following format:

bundlename_language_country_variant.properties

For example, if you had a bundle named ApplicationResources for the English language in the United States for the Windows platform, the properties file would be **ApplicationResources_en_US_WIN.properties**. Of course, not all locale components are required, so the name for a simple English file would be **ApplicationResources_en.properties**. Resource bundles also support the concept of a default resource bundle, which in this case is simply **ApplicationResources.properties**.

The default resource bundle is used when there is not a bundle for a locale or if a locale-specific bundle does not have an entry for a certain resource. For example, if you have a French bundle and it does not contain an entry for a requested resource, the **ResourceBundle** classes will attempt to find an entry for that resource in the default bundle. Typically, applications use the default bundle to store the English version of resources and then create language-specific bundles for other languages. However, if a language-specific bundle does not have an entry for a resource, the English version will be used from the default bundle.

The java.text.MessageFormat Class

The **MessageFormat** class provides methods for creating locale-specific, formatted messages. As you saw in the previous section, resource bundles can be used to retrieve locale-specific static messages from properties files. Although that is quite useful, there will be times when a message needs to be constructed dynamically, at run time. The **MessageFormat** class provides the means for creating locale-specific dynamic messages. To understand what dynamic messages are, it helps to first review properties file–based static messages. An example snippet from a properties file is shown next:

```
error.firstName.required=First Name is required.
error.lastName.required=Last Name is required.
```

This snippet shows two properties whose values are very similar. The main difference between them is simply the subject of what is required. Using this model, a property would have to be created for every required field, with each property being almost identical to the next. Thus, significant duplication would exist.

With the **MessageFormat** class, you can create a dynamic message to solve the problem of duplication. Instead of creating a separate static property for each required field, you create one dynamic property that can be used to generate specific messages. Following is an example of a dynamic message:

```
error.required={0} is required.
```

This property specifies a placeholder with {0}. The **MessageFormat** class takes a dynamic message and a list of substitution data and replaces the dynamic message's placeholders with the substitution data. To illustrate how this works, consider the following example code:

```
ResourceBundle bundle = ResourceBundle.getBundle("ApplicationResources");
String requiredMessage = bundle.getString("error.required");

String[] substituteData1 = {"First Name"};
String firstNameMessage =
  MessageFormat.format(requiredMessage, substituteData1);

String[] substituteData2 = {"Last Name"};
String lastNameMessage =
  MessageFormat.format(requiredMessage, substituteData2);
```

In this example, the dynamic message is used twice, with different substitution data to create unique messages. This is a powerful and often used technique in internationalized applications. Of course, the **MessageFormat** class accepts a locale in its constructor so that dynamic messages can be tailored to specific locales.

Understanding Struts' Internationalization Support

Now that you have reviewed Java's built-in support for internationalization, you are ready to see how internationalization works in Struts. Struts is similar to Java in that internationalization support was a base requirement and not an afterthought. Struts was designed from the ground up to provide strong support for internationalizing an application. This is one of its most valuable features. For the most part, Struts' internationalization support is built on top of Java's. However, Struts uses some of its own facilities for internationalization where necessary.

Like Java, Struts' internationalization support is centered on the **Locale** class and resource bundles. However, Struts differs in that it uses its own custom set of classes for managing and accessing resource bundles. The Struts **org.apache.struts .util.MessageResources** class and its descendant class, **org.apache.struts.util .PropertyMessageResources**, provide functionality parallel to the **ResourceBundle** and **PropertyResourceBundle** classes built into Java. Struts uses these custom classes to manage resource bundles because the built-in Java classes are not serializable. Because Struts applications can be deployed in distributed (i.e., clustered) application server environments, Struts requires that any objects it manages be serializable (that is, they must implement the **java.io.Serializable** interface). Because Java's **ResourceBundle** classes are not serializable, Struts has created its own classes that duplicate their functionality and are serializable.

The following three sections cover the specifics of how internationalization works in Struts, starting with an overview of how Struts handles locale, followed by an overview of Struts' message resources, and concluding with a section on how Struts' tag libraries support internationalization.

Locale

Like other Java applications, Struts applications use **Locale** objects to store users' locale settings and to customize content based on those settings. Struts determines a user's locale from the HTTP requests made to the application. When making a request to a Web server, browsers pass along an HTTP header (**Accept-Language**) that indicates the user's locale. Java's **javax.servlet.http.HttpServletRequest** request object makes this locale setting available to servlets via a **getLocale( )** method, which returns a **Locale** object containing the settings from the request.

When a user first accesses a Struts application, Struts captures the user's locale and stores it in the user's session. Storing the locale in the session allows it to be easily accessed throughout the Struts framework from one convenient place. A side benefit of placing the **Locale** object in a user's session (instead of simply requesting it each time from a request) is that applications can update the locale settings for a user independent of the browser settings. For example, assume that a user accesses an application from a browser with English set as its locale. You can change the user's locale (say to French) without making the user change the browser settings by simply placing another **Locale** object into the user's session. Struts would then operate based on the new locale because Struts determines locale settings from the object stored in the session, not the settings passed in on each request.

Conversely, sometimes it's necessary to override Struts' default behavior of storing locale settings in the session. For example, your application may want to always use the locale settings specified in the request. That way if the user changes their browser settings, Struts will pick up the change. To do this, you have to configure Struts not to store locales in the session by setting the **controller** element's **locale** attribute to **false** in your application's Struts configuration file, as shown here:

```
<controller locale="false"/>
```

Message Resources

As you saw in the example application in Chapter 2, message resources are a fundamental building block in Struts applications whether you're intending to internationalize your application or not. Struts uses message resources as a means of dynamically inserting text into JSPs as well as for storing error messages that get returned from data validations. By using message resources in this way, it's easy to internationalize an application, whether it is an initial requirement for your application or an enhancement. You simply store all of your application's text in resource bundles. Then, when it comes time to internationalize the application, all you have to do is create locale-specific versions of the resource bundle. Struts transparently handles selecting the right resource bundle from which to obtain resources based on the users' locales.

To use message resources, you must create a properties file for your resources to be stored in. The standard name that Struts applications use for this file is **ApplicationResources .properties**; however, you can use any filename with an extension of **.properties**. Like

Java's built-in **PropertyResourceBundle** class, **PropertyMessageResources** requires that locale-specific versions of the file specify the locale information in the filename. For example, to create a French version of the **ApplicationResources.properties** file, you would create a file named **ApplicationResources_fr.properties**. Also in parallel with Java's version, **PropertyMessageResources** will attempt to load resources for a locale from the corresponding locale-specific resource bundle. If the resource bundle does not exist or the resource does not exist in the bundle, Struts will attempt to load the resource from the default resource bundle.

Once you have created a properties file, it has to be placed somewhere on your application's classpath (i.e., somewhere beneath the **/WEB-INF/classes/** directory or inside a **.jar** file underneath the **/WEB-INF/lib** directory). This is necessary because Struts uses Java's class loader to load the properties file. This is very important. If the file is not in your application's classpath, Struts will not be able to access the file. Next, you have to configure Struts to know where the file is located. This is done by placing a **message-resources** element in your application's Struts configuration file, as shown next:

```
<!-- Message Resources Configuration -->
<message-resources
  parameter="com.jamesholmes.minihr.ApplicationResources"/>
```

The **parameter** attribute of the **message-resources** element informs Struts of the location of your application's resource bundle. Notice that the directory of the file is specified using Java's package notation with dots. Thus, the resource bundle in the preceding example is in a directory named **com/jamesholmes/minihr** that is somewhere in the classpath, and the resource bundle filename is **ApplicationResources**. Struts automatically appends **.properties** to the filename specified with the **parameter** attribute. If you mistakenly specify the **.properties** extension, Struts will not be able to locate your file.

You can define multiple resource bundles in the Struts configuration files by using multiple **message-resources** elements. Each additional resource bundle beyond the main, default bundle has to specify a bundle name using the **key** attribute, as shown next:

```
<!-- Message Resources Configuration -->
<message-resources
  parameter="com.jamesholmes.minihr.ApplicationResources"/>
<message-resources
      key="alternate"
  parameter="com.jamesholmes.minihr.AlternateResources"/>
```

The main resource bundle does not specify a name because it is the default bundle. Additional bundles have to specify a name so that they can be explicitly used by name by the application.

After you have created a resource bundle and configured Struts to use it, you can make use of it in your application a couple ways. First, you can dynamically insert text into JSPs by using the Bean Tag Library's **message** tag, as shown here:

```
...
<head>
<title><bean:message key="searchPage.title"/></title>
</head>
...
```

This example dynamically inserts the value of the **searchPage.title** resource into the JSP at run time. Second, you can also return a set of messages from an action to a JSP by using Struts' **ActionMessages** class.

When your application first accesses a resource bundle, Struts loads the bundle into memory and caches it so that it can be quickly accessed again. Because of this, if you modify your resource bundles while your application is running, you will have to restart your application server before you can see the changes.

Struts' Tag Library Support for Internationalization

Several of Struts' tag library tags support internationalization by way of allowing certain attributes' values to be specified as keys to properties in a message resources bundle. At run time, Struts uses the keys to look up a corresponding value and then uses the value for the given attribute. The following table lists each of the tags and their attributes that support internationalization.

Library	Tag	Attribute
Bean	message	key
Bean	write	formatKey
HTML	button	altKey
HTML	button	titleKey
HTML	cancel	altKey
HTML	cancel	titleKey
HTML	checkbox	altKey
HTML	checkbox	titleKey
HTML	file	altKey
HTML	file	titleKey
HTML	frame	titleKey
HTML	hidden	altKey
HTML	hidden	titleKey
HTML	image	altKey
HTML	image	pageKey

Library	Tag	Attribute
HTML	image	srcKey
HTML	image	titleKey
HTML	img	altKey
HTML	img	pageKey
HTML	img	srcKey
HTML	img	titleKey
HTML	link	titleKey
HTML	multibox	altKey
HTML	multibox	titleKey
HTML	option	key
HTML	password	altKey
HTML	password	titleKey
HTML	radio	altKey
HTML	radio	titleKey
HTML	reset	altKey
HTML	reset	titleKey
HTML	select	altKey
HTML	select	titleKey
HTML	submit	altKey
HTML	submit	titleKey
HTML	text	altKey
HTML	text	titleKey
HTML	textarea	altKey
HTML	textarea	titleKey

NOTE: *Several of Struts' tags have a **bundle** attribute that allows you to specify the name of a bundle from which values are loaded. That way you're not limited to putting all of your internationalized properties into a single resource bundle.*

Internationalizing the Mini HR Application

Now that you've seen how Struts' internationalization support works, you are ready to revisit the Mini HR application and update it to support internationalization. Following is the list of steps involved in adding internationalization support to Mini HR:

1. Add entries for all application text to the **ApplicationResources.properties** file.

2. Create a Spanish version of the **ApplicationResources.properties** file.

3. Update JSPs to retrieve all application text from the
   ApplicationResources.properties file.

4. Repackage and run the updated application.

The following sections walk through each step of the process in detail.

Add Entries for All Application Text to the ApplicationResources.properties File

The first step in updating Mini HR to support internationalization is to add entries
for all application text to the **ApplicationResources.properties** file. As you'll see,
having all application text in this file allows it to be easily translated into other
languages. The **ApplicationResources.properties** file from the original Mini HR
application in Chapter 2 already contains some of the application's text; however,
all text needs to be placed in this file for internationalization to work.

Following is the updated **ApplicationResources.properties** file in its entirety:

```
# Title Resources
title.application=ABC, Inc. Human Resources Portal
title.employee.search=Employee Search

# Link Resources
link.employee.add=Add an Employee
link.employee.search=Search for Employees

# Label Resources
label.search.name=Name
label.search.ssNum=Social Security Number

# Error Resources
error.search.criteria.missing=<li>Search Criteria Missing</li>
error.search.ssNum.invalid=<li>Invalid Social Security Number</li>
error.search.not.found=No Employees Found
errors.header=<font color="red"><b>Validation Error(s)</b></font><ul>
errors.footer=</ul><hr width="100%" size="1" noshade="true">
```

Notice that there are several new entries. All of the text from the JSPs has been moved
into this file so that the application can have both an English and a Spanish version.

Create a Spanish Version of the ApplicationResources.properties File

Once entries for all of the application text have been put in the **ApplicationsResources
.properties** file, you have to create a Spanish version of the file to support Spanish
users. Do this by creating the **ApplicationResources_es.properties** file, shown here:

```
# Title Resources
title.application=ABC, Inc. Recursos Humanos Porta
title.employee.search=Búsqueda Del Empleado

# Link Resources
link.employee.add=Agregue a empleado
link.employee.search=Búsqueda para los empleados

# Label Resources
label.search.name=Nombre
label.search.ssNum=Número De la Seguridad Social

# Error Resources
error.search.criteria.missing=<li>El Faltar De los Criterios De la Búsqueda</li>
error.search.ssNum.invalid=<li>Número Inválido De la Seguridad Social</li>
error.search.not.found=Ningunos Empleados Encontraron
errors.header=<font color="red"><b>Error De la Validación(s)</b></font><ul>
errors.footer=</ul><hr width="100%" size="1" noshade="true">
```

Notice that this file's name is only slightly different from **ApplicationResources
.properties** in that it has **_es** appended to the **ApplicationResources** part of the original
filename. The **_es** denotes which locale the file is for—in this case, the Spanish language.
You could, of course, include a country code along with the language code to make the
file specific to a certain country/language combination. This file contains all the same
entries as the **ApplicationResources.properties** file, but the property values are in
Spanish. The property names are universal across all locales' files. That's how applications
reference the text.

NOTE: *The translations in this section were performed using Google's translation service and
are for demonstration purposes only.*

Update JSPs to Retrieve All Application Text
from the ApplicationResources.properties File

After you have updated **ApplicationResources.properties** and created an
ApplicationResources_es.properties file, you have to update Mini HR's JSPs.
The original JSPs have a mix of hard-coded text and text that is dynamically inserted
into the page from the **ApplicationResources.properties** file. In order to support
internationalization, all of the hard-coded text has to be moved into the
ApplicationResources.properties file so that it can be obtained dynamically,
based on locale. Following are the updated JSPs, **index.jsp** and **search.jsp**, with
all the hard-coded text replaced with **<bean:message>** tags that dynamically
insert the text into the page.

index.jsp:

```
<%@ taglib uri="/WEB-INF/tlds/struts-bean.tld" prefix="bean" %>
<%@ taglib uri="/WEB-INF/tlds/struts-html.tld" prefix="html" %>

<html>
<head>
<title><bean:message key="title.application"/></title>
</head>
<body>

<font size="+1"><bean:message key="title.application"/></font><br>

<hr width="100%" noshade="true">

&#149; <bean:message key="link.employee.add"/><br>
&#149; <html:link forward="search">
<bean:message key="link.employee.search"/></html:link><br>

</body>
</html>
```

search.jsp:

```
<%@ taglib uri="/WEB-INF/tlds/struts-bean.tld" prefix="bean" %>
<%@ taglib uri="/WEB-INF/tlds/struts-html.tld" prefix="html" %>
<%@ taglib uri="/WEB-INF/tlds/struts-logic.tld" prefix="logic" %>

<html>
<head>
<title>
<bean:message key="title.application"/> -
<bean:message key="title.employee.search"/>
</title>
</head>
<body>

<font size="+1">
<bean:message key="title.application"/> -
<bean:message key="title.employee.search"/>
</font><br>
<hr width="100%" noshade="true">

<html:errors/>

<html:form action="/search">
```

```
<table>
<tr>
<td align="right"><bean:message key="label.search.name"/>:</td>
<td><html:text property="name"/></td>
</tr>
<tr>
<td></td>
<td>-- or --</td>
</tr>
<tr>
<td align="right"><bean:message key="label.search.ssNum"/>:</td>
<td><html:text property="ssNum"/> (xxx-xx-xxxx)</td>
</tr>
<tr>
<td></td>
<td><html:submit/></td>
</tr>
</table>

</html:form>

<logic:present name="searchForm" property="results">

<hr width="100%" size="1" noshade="true">

<bean:size id="size" name="searchForm" property="results"/>
<logic:equal name="size" value="0">
<center><font color="red"><b>
<bean:message key="error.search.not.found"/>
</b></font></center>
</logic:equal>

<logic:greaterThan name="size" value="0">
<table border="1">
<tr>
<th><bean:message key="label.search.name"/></th>
<th><bean:message key="label.search.ssNum"/></th>
</tr>
<logic:iterate id="result" name="searchForm" property="results">
<tr>
<td><bean:write name="result" property="name"/></td>
<td><bean:write name="result" property="ssNum"/></td>
</tr>
</logic:iterate>
</table>
</logic:greaterThan>
```

```
</logic:present>

</body>
<html>
```

Note that the Bean Tag Library definition had to be added to **index.jsp** so that it could use the **<bean:message>** tag to source in text.

Repackage and Run the Updated Application

Because no Java source code files had to be modified to update the Mini HR application to support internationalization, you do not have to recompile the application. All you have to do is repackage the application and redeploy it before running it again. Assuming that you've made modifications to the original Mini HR application and it was set up in the **c:\java\MiniHR** directory (as described in Chapter 2), the following command line will repackage the application:

```
jar cf MiniHR.war *
```

This command should be run from the directory where you have set up the Mini HR application (e.g., **c:\java\MiniHR**).

To test the Spanish version of the application, you have to change your browser's language settings to Spanish. Following are the instructions for doing this with Microsoft Internet Explorer 6:

1. Open Internet Explorer's Internet Options dialog box by selecting Tools | Internet Options.

2. Click the Languages button on the General tab of the Internet Options dialog box, as shown here:

3. Click the Add button in the Language Preference dialog box.

4. Add the Spanish (United States) [es-us] language preference by selecting it in the list, as shown here, and then clicking OK.

5. Select the Spanish (United States) [es-us] language preference and click Move Up so that it is the first preference in the list, like this:

Once you have added the Spanish language setting for your browser, you need to place the new **MiniHR.war** file that you just created into Tomcat's **webapps** directory and start Tomcat. As before, to access the Mini HR application, point your browser to **http://localhost:8080/MiniHR/**. When you run the updated Mini HR application with your browser set to Spanish, it should detect that you are accessing it from a Spanish-language browser and automatically serve the Spanish version of the application. Figure 10-1 shows the search page in Spanish.

FIGURE 10-1   The Spanish version of the search page.

PART

II

The Struts Tag Libraries

The HTML Tag Library

The HTML Tag Library provides a set of tags that parallels HTML's set of tags for creating forms. Instead of using HTML tags to create forms, you can use their corresponding HTML Tag Library tags to create forms that tie into the Struts framework. The tags in this library can automatically populate form controls with data from Form Beans, thereby saving you time and several lines of code. Additionally, the HTML Tag Library provides a few other tags that parallel HTML tags, such as the **base**, **frame**, and **img** tags.

Understanding Variables and Scope in JSP Pages

Before the tags in this library are discussed, it's necessary to review how variables and scope work in JSPs. First, remember that JSPs get converted into servlets and then compiled before they are executed. All of the HTML and code inside the JSP gets placed into the generated servlet's **service( )** method. Because of this, any variables that get defined inside the JSP with a scriptlet, as shown here, are local to the **service( )** method:

```
<%
String test = "test value";
%>
```

Similarly, any variables that are defined with a JSP declaration are local to the **service( )** method:

```
<%! String test = "test value"; %>
```

Also, all of the implicit JSP objects, such as **application**, **request**, and **session**, are local to the resulting servlet's **service( )** method.

JSPs and servlets also have the notion of "scope" for variables, because some variables need to persist longer than the lifespan of a page request and some variables need to be accessible outside of a servlet's **service( )** method. There are four scopes that

195

JSP variables can be placed in: application, page, request, and session. The following table explains each scope.

Scope	Description
application	Variables placed in this scope persist for the life of an application.
page	Variables placed in this scope persist until the current JSP's **service( )** method completes. Included JSPs cannot see page scope variables from the page including them. Also, this scope is exclusive to JSPs.
request	Variables placed in this scope persist until processing for the current request is completed. This scope differs from page scope because multiple servlets may be executed during the lifespan of a request. Page scope variables persist only for the execution of one servlet.
session	Variables placed in this scope persist until the current user's session is invalidated or expires. This scope is valid only if the JSP or servlet in question is participating in a session.

Note that variables must be explicitly placed into a scope, as shown here:

```
<%
request.setAttribute("reqScopeVar", "test");
%>
```

This snippet uses JSP's implicit **request** object to place a variable into request scope. Similarly, the following snippet uses JSP's implicit **session** object to place a variable into session scope:

```
<%
session.setAttribute("sesScopeVar", "test");
%>
```

Of course, variables can also be put into each of the scopes by JSP library tags as many of the tags in the Logic Tag Library do.

Using the HTML Tag Library

To use the HTML Tag Library in a Struts application, you need to include the following snippet in your Web Archive (**.war**) deployment descriptor, **web.xml**:

```
<taglib>
  <taglib-uri>/WEB-INF/tlds/struts-html.tld</taglib-uri>
  <taglib-location>/WEB-INF/tlds/struts-html.tld</taglib-location>
</taglib>
```

Remember from the overview of the **web.xml** file in Chapter 2 that the **<taglib-uri>** tag declares the URI (or alias) that will be referenced in each of your JSPs with a **taglib** directive. The **<taglib-location>** tag declares the actual location of the Tag Library Descriptor (**.tld**) file in your Web Archive.

The following snippet illustrates how your JSPs will declare their use of the HTML Tag Library with a JSP **taglib** directive:

```
<%@ taglib uri="/WEB-INF/tlds/struts-html.tld" prefix="html" %>
```

Notice that the **uri** attribute specified here is the same as that declared with the **<taglib-uri>** tag in the **web.xml** file. Also, notice that the **prefix** attribute is set to "html". This attribute can be set to whatever you want; however, "html" is the accepted default for the HTML Tag Library. The **prefix** attribute declares the prefix that each tag must have when it is used in the JSP, as shown here:

```
<html:html action="/logon">
```

Because "html" was defined as the prefix, the **form** tag was used as shown. However, if you chose to use a prefix of "strutshtml", the tag would be used the following way:

```
<strutshtml:form action="/logon">
```

The HTML Tag Library Tags

The following table lists each of the tags in the HTML Tag Library and a short description of each tag's purpose.

Tag	Description
base	Generates an HTML **<base>** tag with its **href** attribute set to the absolute URL of the enclosing JSP.
button	Generates an HTML **<input type="button">** tag.
cancel	Generates an HTML **<input type="submit">** tag that, when executed, causes Struts' Cancel feature to be triggered.
checkbox	Generates an HTML **<input type="checkbox">** tag populated with data from a specified object.
errors	Displays a set of error messages stored as an **org.apache.struts.action.ActionErrors** object, a **String**, or a **String** array in request scope.
file	Generates an HTML **<input type="file">** tag populated with data from a specified object.
form	Generates an HTML **<form>** tag tied to an **Action** object and its corresponding Form Bean from the **struts-config.xml** file.
frame	Generates an HTML **<frame>** tag.

Tag	Description
hidden	Generates an HTML **<input type="hidden">** tag populated with data from a specified object.
html	Generates an HTML **<html>** tag with language attributes set to the current user's locale.
image	Generates an HTML **<input type="image">** tag.
img	Generates an HTML **<img>** tag
javascript	Generates client-side JavaScript validation code for validations defined in the Validator framework's **validation.xml** file.
link	Generates an HTML hyperlink **<a>** tag whose URL is composed by specifying a base URL and optionally specifying an anchor and/or query string parameters to add to the URL.
messages	Displays a set of messages stored as an **org.apache.struts.action.ActionErrors** object, an **org.apache.struts.action.ActionMessages** object, a **String**, or a **String** array in request scope.
multibox	Generates an HTML **<input type="checkbox">** tag whose checked status is based on whether or not a specified value matches one of the values in a specified array of values.
option	Generates an HTML **<option>** tag.
options	Generates a set of HTML **<option>** tags for each element in a collection.
optionsCollection	Generates a set of HTML **<option>** tags for each element in a collection.
password	Generates an HTML **<input type="password">** tag populated with data from a specified object.
radio	Generates an HTML **<input type="radio">** tag populated with data from a specified object.
reset	Generates an HTML **<input type="reset">** tag.
rewrite	Generates a URL by specifying a base URL and optionally specifying an anchor and/or query string parameters to add to the URL.
select	Generates an HTML **<select>** tag.
submit	Generates an HTML **<input type="submit">** tag.
text	Generates an HTML **<input type="text">** tag populated with data from a specified object.
textarea	Generates an HTML **<textarea>** tag populated with data from a specified object.
xhtml	Instructs the rest of the tags in the HTML Tag Library to generate their output as XHTML instead of HTML.

The remainder of this chapter discusses each tag in detail, including a complete description of the tag, a table listing each of the tag's attributes, and a usage example for the tag. In the tables that describe each tag's attributes, pay special attention to the Required and Accepts Scriptlet columns.

The Required column denotes whether or not the given attribute is required when using the tag. If an attribute is required and you do not specify it when using the tag, the tag will throw a **javax.servlet.jsp.JspException** at run time. Note that you can declare an error page in your JSP with a **page** directive to capture any **JspExceptions** that might be thrown, as shown here:

```
<%@ page errorPage="error.jsp" %>
```

If an exception occurs, the page specified by the **errorPage** attribute will be internally redirected to display an error page.

The Accepts Scriptlet column denotes whether or not the given attribute's value can be specified with a JSP scriptlet. If a JSP scriptlet is used to specify an attribute value, the scriptlet must comprise the complete value, quote (") to quote ("), as shown here.

Correct:

```
<html:checkbox property="<%=prop%>">
```

Incorrect:

```
<html:checkbox property="<%=result%>-checked">
```

Notice in the incorrect example that "-checked" is used as part of the value for the **property** attribute following the scriptlet. This is invalid because there are extra characters between the end of the scriptlet and the ending quote.

A corrected version of the incorrect example follows:

```
<html:checkbox property="<%=result + "-checked"%>"/>
```

The concatenation of "-checked" is now part of the scriptlet and the scriptlet comprises the complete value for the attribute.

One other point: Several of the tags have a set of tag attributes in common, such as **onclick**, **onmousedown**, and **onkeypress**. Rather than repeat the description for these common attributes numerous times, they are described once, at the end of this chapter in the "Common Tag Attributes" section. The Description column in each tag's table of attributes refers you to the "Common Tag Attributes" section for any of the common tag attributes that the tag has in its set of tag attributes.

The base Tag

The **base** tag is used to generate an HTML **<base>** tag with its **href** attribute set to the absolute URL of the enclosing JSP. Note that this tag must be nested inside of an HTML **<head>** tag.

Attributes

Attribute	Description	Accepts Scriptlet	Required
server	Specifies the server name to use when generating the corresponding HTML tag's **href** attribute.	Yes	No
target	Same as the corresponding HTML tag's attribute with the same name. Specifies the frame or window target in which links will be opened.	Yes	No

Example Usage

The following snippet shows the basic usage of the **base** tag:

```
<html:html>
<head>
  <title></title>
  <html:base/>
</head>
```

Remember that this tag must be enclosed by opening and closing HTML **<head>** tags.

The button Tag

The **button** tag is used to generate an HTML **<input type="button">** tag. Note that this tag must be nested inside of this library's **form** tag.

Attributes

Attribute	Description	Accepts Scriptlet	Required
accesskey	See the "Common Tag Attributes" section at the end of this chapter.	Yes	No
alt	See "Common Tag Attributes."	Yes	No
altKey	See "Common Tag Attributes."	Yes	No
disabled	See "Common Tag Attributes."	Yes	No
indexed	Accepts "true" to denote that the value assigned to the corresponding HTML tag's **name** attribute will have an index (e.g., "property[x]").This attribute is applicable only when this tag is nested inside the Logic Tag Library's **iterate** tag.	Yes	No

Attribute	Description	Accepts Scriptlet	Required
onblur	See "Common Tag Attributes."	Yes	No
onchange	See "Common Tag Attributes."	Yes	No
onclick	See "Common Tag Attributes."	Yes	No
ondblclick	See "Common Tag Attributes."	Yes	No
onfocus	See "Common Tag Attributes."	Yes	No
onkeydown	See "Common Tag Attributes."	Yes	No
onkeypress	See "Common Tag Attributes."	Yes	No
onkeyup	See "Common Tag Attributes."	Yes	No
onmousedown	See "Common Tag Attributes."	Yes	No
onmousemove	See "Common Tag Attributes."	Yes	No
onmouseout	See "Common Tag Attributes."	Yes	No
onmouseover	See "Common Tag Attributes."	Yes	No
onmouseup	See "Common Tag Attributes."	Yes	No
property	Same as the corresponding HTML tag's **name** attribute. Specifies the name that will be associated with this control.	Yes	Yes
style	See "Common Tag Attributes."	Yes	No
styleClass	See "Common Tag Attributes."	Yes	No
styleId	See "Common Tag Attributes."	Yes	No
tabindex	See "Common Tag Attributes."	Yes	No
title	See "Common Tag Attributes."	Yes	No
titleKey	See "Common Tag Attributes."	Yes	No
value	Specifies a constant value that this control will be populated with. This value will be used for the button's label. If not specified, this tag will attempt to use its body content as the value for the button's label.	Yes	No

Example Usage

The following snippet illustrates the basic usage of the **button** tag:

```
<html:button property="direction" value="Next Page"/>
```

The value specified with the **value** attribute will be used for the button's label. Alternatively, you can specify the button's label value by nesting a string between opening and closing **button** tags, as shown here:

```
<html:button>Next Page</html:button>
```

The cancel Tag

Struts has a built-in Cancel feature that will cause it to bypass calling a Form Bean's **validate( )** method if a request parameter named "org.apache.struts.taglib.html.CANCEL" is present in an incoming request. Additionally, **Action** objects can call an **isCancelled( )** method to determine whether or not a request was cancelled. The **cancel** tag generates an HTML **<input type="submit">** tag with its **name** attribute set to "org.apache.struts.taglib.html.CANCEL" so that, when executed, Struts' Cancel feature will be triggered. Note that this tag must be nested inside of the **form** tag.

Attributes

Attribute	Description	Accepts Scriptlet	Required
accesskey	See the "Common Tag Attributes" section at the end of this chapter.	Yes	No
alt	See "Common Tag Attributes."	Yes	No
altKey	See "Common Tag Attributes."	Yes	No
disabled	See "Common Tag Attributes."	Yes	No
onblur	See "Common Tag Attributes."	Yes	No
onchange	See "Common Tag Attributes."	Yes	No
onclick	See "Common Tag Attributes."	Yes	No
ondblclick	See "Common Tag Attributes."	Yes	No
onfocus	See "Common Tag Attributes."	Yes	No
onkeydown	See "Common Tag Attributes."	Yes	No
onkeypress	See "Common Tag Attributes."	Yes	No
onkeyup	See "Common Tag Attributes."	Yes	No
onmousedown	See "Common Tag Attributes."	Yes	No
onmousemove	See "Common Tag Attributes."	Yes	No
onmouseout	See "Common Tag Attributes."	Yes	No
onmouseover	See "Common Tag Attributes."	Yes	No
onmouseup	See "Common Tag Attributes."	Yes	No

Attribute	Description	Accepts Scriptlet	Required
property	Same as the corresponding HTML tag's **name** attribute. Specifies the name that will be associated with this control. *Caution: If you set this attribute to a value other than its default, Struts' Cancel feature will not be triggered.*	Yes	No
style	See "Common Tag Attributes."	Yes	No
styleClass	See "Common Tag Attributes."	Yes	No
styleId	See "Common Tag Attributes."	Yes	No
tabindex	See "Common Tag Attributes."	Yes	No
title	See "Common Tag Attributes."	Yes	No
titleKey	See "Common Tag Attributes."	Yes	No
value	Specifies a constant value that this control will be populated with. This value will be used for the button's label. If not specified, this tag will attempt to use its body content as the value for the button's label.	Yes	No

Example Usage

The following snippet illustrates the basic usage of the **cancel** tag:

```
<html:cancel value="Cancel Update"/>
```

The value specified with the **value** attribute will be used for the button's label. Alternatively, you can specify the button's label value by nesting a string between opening and closing **cancel** tags, as shown here:

```
<html:cancel>Cancel Update</html:cancel>
```

The checkbox Tag

The **checkbox** tag is used to generate an HTML **<input type="checkbox">** tag populated with data from a specified object. Note that this tag must be nested inside of this library's **form** tag. Additionally, the underlying Form Bean field associated with this control must be of primitive type **boolean** or of type **Boolean** and the Form Bean's **reset( )** method must include a statement that resets the field to **false**.

Attributes

Attribute	Description	Accepts Scriptlet	Required
accesskey	See the "Common Tag Attributes" section at the end of this chapter.	Yes	No
alt	See "Common Tag Attributes."	Yes	No
altKey	See "Common Tag Attributes."	Yes	No
disabled	See "Common Tag Attributes."	Yes	No
indexed	Accepts "true" to denote that the value assigned to the corresponding HTML tag's **name** attribute will have an index. (e.g., "name[x].property"). This attribute is applicable only when this tag is nested inside the Logic Tag Library's **iterate** tag.	Yes	No
name	Specifies the name of an object (in any scope) whose field, specified by the **property** attribute, will be used to populate this control with data.	Yes	No
onblur	See "Common Tag Attributes."	Yes	No
onchange	See "Common Tag Attributes."	Yes	No
onclick	See "Common Tag Attributes."	Yes	No
ondblclick	See "Common Tag Attributes."	Yes	No
onfocus	See "Common Tag Attributes."	Yes	No
onkeydown	See "Common Tag Attributes."	Yes	No
onkeypress	See "Common Tag Attributes."	Yes	No
onkeyup	See "Common Tag Attributes."	Yes	No
onmousedown	See "Common Tag Attributes."	Yes	No
onmousemove	See "Common Tag Attributes."	Yes	No
onmouseout	See "Common Tag Attributes."	Yes	No
onmouseover	See "Common Tag Attributes."	Yes	No
onmouseup	See "Common Tag Attributes."	Yes	No

Attribute	Description	Accepts Scriptlet	Required
property	Specifies the value to set the corresponding HTML tag's **name** attribute to. Additionally, this attribute is used to specify the field of the object specified by the **name** attribute whose getter method will be called to return an object whose value will be used to populate this control. If no object is specified with the **name** attribute, the Form Bean object associated with the enclosing **form** tag will be used to retrieve the property specified by this attribute.	Yes	Yes
style	See "Common Tag Attributes."	Yes	No
styleClass	See "Common Tag Attributes."	Yes	No
styleId	See "Common Tag Attributes."	Yes	No
tabindex	See "Common Tag Attributes."	Yes	No
title	See "Common Tag Attributes."	Yes	No
titleKey	See "Common Tag Attributes."	Yes	No
value	Specifies a constant value that the control will be populated with.	Yes	No

Example Usage

The following snippet illustrates the basic usage of the **checkbox** tag:

```
<html:form action="/register">
Subscribe to mailing list: <html:checkbox property="subscribe"/><br>
<html:submit/>
</html:form>
```

This tag will look up the Form Bean associated with the **Action** specified by the **form** tag's **action** attribute and then call the getter method for the field specified by this tag's **property** attribute. The field's value will then be used to populate the HTML control with data.

The errors Tag

The **errors** tag is used to display a set of error messages stored as an **org.apache.struts.action.ActionErrors** object, a **String**, or a **String** array in request scope. This tag will take the stored error messages and iterate over them, displaying them in succession. Additionally, this tag uses the values for the following table of keys from Strut's **ApplicationResources.properties** file to format the messages.

Key	Purpose
errors.header	Text that will be output before the list of error messages.
errors.footer	Text that will be output after the list of error messages.
errors.prefix	Text that will be output before each error message.
errors.suffix	Text that will be output after each error message.

Attributes

Attribute	Description	Accepts Scriptlet	Required
bundle	Specifies the logical name of a resource bundle that will be used when looking up error keys.	Yes	No
locale	Specifies the key for a **java.util.Locale** instance stored as a session attribute that will be used when looking up error keys.	Yes	No
name	Specifies the key (in any scope) under which the errors to be displayed are stored. If not specified, the default **org.apache.struts.Globals.ERROR_KEY** key will be used.	Yes	No
property	Specifies the field for which errors will be displayed. If not specified, all errors will be displayed.	Yes	No

Example Usage

The following snippet illustrates the basic usage of the **errors** tag:

```
<html:errors/>
```

This example will display all the errors currently stored. If you want to limit the errors that are displayed to a specific property, you can specify that property when using the **errors** tag, as shown here:

```
<html:errors property="username"/>
```

In this case, only the errors associated with the property specified by the **property** attribute will be displayed.

The file Tag

The **file** tag is used to generate an HTML **<input type="file">** tag populated with data from a specified object. Note that this tag must be nested inside of the **form** tag. Additionally, the enclosing **form** tag must specify its HTTP method as being POST and its encoding type as being multipart/form-data, as shown here:

```
<html:form method="POST" enctype="multipart/form-data">
...
</html:form>
```

Attributes

Attribute	Description	Accepts Scriptlet	Required
accept	Same as the corresponding HTML tag's attribute with the same name. Specifies a comma-delimited list of content types that the server you submit the enclosing form to knows how to process. Browsers can use this list to limit the set of files made available for selection.	Yes	No
accesskey	See the "Common Tag Attributes" section at the end of this chapter.	Yes	No
alt	See "Common Tag Attributes."	Yes	No
altKey	See "Common Tag Attributes."	Yes	No
disabled	See "Common Tag Attributes."	Yes	No
indexed	Accepts "true" to denote that the value assigned to the corresponding HTML tag's **name** attribute will have an index (e.g., "name[x].property"). This attribute is applicable only when this tag is nested inside the Logic Tag Library's **iterate** tag.	Yes	No
maxlength	Same as the corresponding HTML tag's attribute with the same name. Specifies the maximum number of characters that this control will accept.	Yes	No
name	Specifies the name of an object (in any scope) whose field, specified by the **property** attribute, will be used to populate this control with data.	Yes	No
onblur	See "Common Tag Attributes."	Yes	No
onchange	See "Common Tag Attributes."	Yes	No
onclick	See "Common Tag Attributes."	Yes	No

Attribute	Description	Accepts Scriptlet	Required
ondblclick	See "Common Tag Attributes."	Yes	No
onfocus	See "Common Tag Attributes."	Yes	No
onkeydown	See "Common Tag Attributes."	Yes	No
onkeypress	See "Common Tag Attributes."	Yes	No
onkeyup	See "Common Tag Attributes."	Yes	No
onmousedown	See "Common Tag Attributes."	Yes	No
onmousemove	See "Common Tag Attributes."	Yes	No
onmouseout	See "Common Tag Attributes."	Yes	No
onmouseover	See "Common Tag Attributes."	Yes	No
onmouseup	See "Common Tag Attributes."	Yes	No
property	Specifies the value to which the corresponding HTML tag's **name** attribute is set. Additionally, this attribute is used to specify the field of the object specified by the **name** attribute whose getter method will be called to return an object whose value will be used to populate this control. If no object is specified with the **name** attribute, the Form Bean object associated with the enclosing **form** tag will be used to retrieve the property specified by this attribute.	Yes	Yes
size	Same as the corresponding HTML tag's attribute with the same name. Specifies the number of characters that will be visible in the control.	Yes	No
style	See "Common Tag Attributes."	Yes	No
styleClass	See "Common Tag Attributes."	Yes	No
styleId	See "Common Tag Attributes."	Yes	No
tabindex	See "Common Tag Attributes."	Yes	No
title	See "Common Tag Attributes."	Yes	No
titleKey	See "Common Tag Attributes."	Yes	No
value	Specifies a constant value that is used to populate the control.	Yes	No

Example Usage

The following snippet illustrates the basic usage of the **file** tag:

```
<html:form method="POST"
        enctype="multipart/form-data"
        action="/attachFile">
```

```
Upload File: <html:file property="uploadFile"/><br>
<html:submit/>
</html:form>
```

This tag will look up the Form Bean associated with the **Action** specified by the **form** tag's **action** attribute and then call the getter method for the field specified by this tag's **property** attribute. The field's value will then be used to populate the HTML control with data.

The form Tag

The **form** tag is used to generate an HTML **<form>** tag tied to an **Action** and its corresponding Form Bean from the **struts-config.xml** file. The **Action**'s Form Bean will be used by other tags from this library to populate them with data when they are nested inside this tag.

Attributes

Attribute	Description	Accepts Scriptlet	Required
action	Specifies the logical name of an **Action**, defined in the **struts-config.xml** file, whose path will be used to define the corresponding HTML tag's attribute with the same name.	Yes	Yes
enctype	Same as the corresponding HTML tag's attribute with the same name. Specifies the encoding to be used when submitting this form if the POST method is used. This must be set to "multipart/form-data" if you are using the **file** tag to upload files.	Yes	No
focus	Specifies the name of a field inside this form that initial focus will be assigned to using JavaScript.	Yes	No
focusIndex	Specifies an index to be used if the field specified with the **focus** attribute is a field array such as a radio button group.	Yes	No
method	Same as the corresponding HTML tag's attribute with the same name. Specifies the HTTP method that will be used when submitting this form (i.e., GET or POST).	Yes	No
name	Deprecated Use the **action** attribute instead.	Yes	No

Attribute	Description	Accepts Scriptlet	Required
onreset	Same as the corresponding HTML tag's attribute with the same name. Specifies the JavaScript code to execute when this form is reset.	Yes	No
onsubmit	Same as the corresponding HTML tag's attribute with the same name. Specifies the JavaScript code to execute when this form is submitted.	Yes	No
scope	Deprecated Use the **action** attribute instead.	Yes	No
scriptLanguage	Accepts "false" to denote that the **language** attribute of the **\<focus\>** tag generated by this tag's **focus** attribute should be omitted. Note that the generated **\<focus\>** tag's **language** attribute is omitted regardless when the tags in this library are in XHTML mode.	Yes	No
style	See the "Common Tag Attributes" section at the end of this chapter.	Yes	No
styleClass	See "Common Tag Attributes."	Yes	No
styleId	See "Common Tag Attributes."	Yes	No
target	Same as the corresponding HTML tag's attribute with the same name. Specifies the frame or window target in which this form will be submitted.	Yes	No
type	Deprecated Use the **action** attribute instead.	Yes	No

Example Usage

The following snippet illustrates the basic usage of the **form** tag:

```
<html:form action="/logon">
UserName: <html:text property="username"/><br>
Password: <html:password property="password"/><br>
<html:submit/>
</html:form>
```

The Form Bean associated with the **Action** specified by the **action** attribute will be used for populating the nested HTML controls inside the opening and closing **form** tags.

The frame Tag

The **frame** tag is used to generate an HTML **<frame>** tag. The frame's URL is composed by specifying a base URL and optionally specifying an anchor and/or query string parameters to add to the URL.

There are four ways to specify the base URL:

- You can use the **action** attribute to specify the name of an **Action** from the Struts configuration file whose URL will be used.

- You can use the **forward** attribute to specify the name of a forward from the Struts configuration file whose URL will be used.

- You can use the **href** attribute to specify an absolute URL, including protocol (e.g., http://www.yahoo.com/).

- You can use the **page** attribute to specify an application-relative URL.

In addition to specifying the base URL, you have two options for specifying query string parameters to add to the base URL:

- You can use the **paramId** attribute in conjunction with the **paramName** attribute, and optionally the **paramProperty** attribute, to specify a single parameter.

- You can use the **name** attribute, either alone or in tandem with the **property** attribute, to specify a **java.util.Map** object that will be used to add several parameters.

Attributes

Attribute	Description	Accepts Scriptlet	Required
action	Specifies the name of an **Action**, from the Action Mappings section of the Struts configuration file, that contains the URL for this frame.	Yes	No
anchor	Specifies the anchor (e.g., "#bottom") to be added to the URL for this frame. This value must be specified without the leading hash (#) character.	Yes	No
forward	Specifies the name of a forward, from the Global Forwards Configuration section of the Struts configuration file, that contains the URL for this frame.	Yes	No
frameborder	Same as the corresponding HTML tag's attribute with the same name. Specifies the border size for this frame (0 for no border).	Yes	No

PART II

Attribute	Description	Accepts Scriptlet	Required
frameName	Same as the corresponding HTML tag's **name** attribute. Specifies the logical name to give the frame.	Yes	No
href	Specifies the absolute URL, including protocol (e.g., http://www.yahoo.com), for this frame.	Yes	No
longdesc	Same as the corresponding HTML tag's attribute with the same name. Specifies the URL for a long description of the frame that supplements the short description provided by the **title** attribute.	Yes	No
marginheight	Same as the corresponding HTML tag's attribute with the same name. Specifies the number of pixels that will be placed between this frame's contents and its top and bottom margins.	Yes	No
marginwidth	Same as the corresponding HTML tag's attribute with the same name. Specifies the number of pixels that will be placed between this frame's contents and its left and right margins.	Yes	No
name	Specifies the name of the **java.util.Map** object whose elements are added as query string parameters to the URL for this frame. If the **property** attribute is also specified, one of the fields of the object defined by this attribute will have its getter method called to return the **java.util.Map** object whose elements are added as query string parameters to the URL for this frame.	Yes	No
noresize	Same as the corresponding HTML tag's attribute with the same name. Accepts "true" to denote that this frame will not be resizable.	Yes	No
page	Specifies the application-relative URL (starts with a leading slash, /) for this frame.	Yes	No
paramId	Specifies the name of a single parameter to add to the URL for this frame.	Yes	No
paramName	Specifies the name of an object whose value will be used as the value for the parameter specified with the **paramId** attribute. If the **property** attribute is also specified, one of the fields of the object defined by this attribute will have its getter method called to return an object whose value will be used as the value for the parameter specified with the **paramId** attribute.	Yes	No

Attribute	Description	Accepts Scriptlet	Required
paramProperty	Specifies the field of the object specified by the **name** attribute whose getter method will be called to return an object whose value will be used as the value for the parameter specified with the **paramId** attribute.	Yes	No
paramScope	Specifies the scope (application, page, request, or session) to look in for the object specified by the **paramName** attribute. If not specified, each scope will be searched, in this order: page, request, session, and then application.	Yes	No
property	Specifies the field of the object specified by the **name** attribute whose getter method will be called to return the **java.util.Map** object whose elements are added as query string parameters to the URL for this frame.	Yes	No
scope	Specifies the scope (application, page, request, or session) to look in for the object specified by the **name** attribute. If not specified, each scope will be searched, in this order: page, request, session, and then application.	Yes	No
scrolling	Same as the corresponding HTML tag's attribute with the same name. Specifies whether or not this frame is scrollable. Specify "yes" to have scroll bars unconditionally, "no" to never have scroll bars, or "auto" to have scroll bars automatically based on how much content is in the frame.	Yes	No
style	See the "Common Tag Attributes" section at the end of this chapter.	Yes	No
styleClass	See "Common Tag Attributes."	Yes	No
styleId	See "Common Tag Attributes."	Yes	No
title	See "Common Tag Attributes."	Yes	No
titleKey	See "Common Tag Attributes."	Yes	No
transaction	Accepts "true" or "false" to denote whether or not the current transaction token is included in the URL for this frame.	Yes	No

Example Usage

There are a few different ways to use the **frame** tag. The first way, shown here, uses the **href** attribute to specify an absolute URL for the frame:

```
<html:frame href="http://www.yahoo.com/"/>
```

The following example adds to the first example by specifying a single query string parameter to add to the base URL specified by the **href** attribute:

```
<html:frame href="http://www.yahoo.com/"
        paramId="query"
        paramName="queryObj"/>
```

This example takes the base URL specified by the **href** attribute and appends the query string parameter specified by the **paramId** and **paramName** attributes and composes a URL for the frame.

Another way to use the **frame** tag is shown here:

```
<html:frame page="/search.jsp" name="params"/>
```

This example uses the **page** attribute to specify an application-relative base URL and uses the **name** attribute to specify a **java.util.Map** object whose entries are added to the URL as query string parameters.

The hidden Tag

The **hidden** tag is used to generate an HTML **<input type="hidden">** tag populated with data from a specified object. Note that this tag must be nested inside of the **form** tag.

Attributes

Attribute	Description	Accepts Scriptlet	Required
accesskey	See the "Common Tag Attributes" section at the end of this chapter.	Yes	No
alt	See "Common Tag Attributes."	Yes	No
altKey	See "Common Tag Attributes."	Yes	No
indexed	Accepts "true" to denote that the value assigned to the corresponding HTML tag's **name** attribute will have an index (e.g., "name[x].property"). This attribute is applicable only when this tag is nested inside the Logic Tag Library's **iterate** tag.	Yes	No
name	Specifies the name of an object (in any scope) whose field, specified by the **property** attribute, will be used to populate this control with data.	Yes	No
onblur	See "Common Tag Attributes."	Yes	No
onchange	See "Common Tag Attributes."	Yes	No
onclick	See "Common Tag Attributes."	Yes	No
ondblclick	See "Common Tag Attributes."	Yes	No

Attribute	Description	Accepts Scriptlet	Required
onfocus	See "Common Tag Attributes."	Yes	No
onkeydown	See "Common Tag Attributes."	Yes	No
onkeypress	See "Common Tag Attributes."	Yes	No
onkeyup	See "Common Tag Attributes."	Yes	No
onmousedown	See "Common Tag Attributes."	Yes	No
onmousemove	See "Common Tag Attributes."	Yes	No
onmouseout	See "Common Tag Attributes."	Yes	No
onmouseover	See "Common Tag Attributes."	Yes	No
onmouseup	See "Common Tag Attributes."	Yes	No
property	Specifies the value to which the corresponding HTML tag's **name** attribute is set. Additionally, this attribute is used to specify the field of the object specified by the **name** attribute whose getter method will be called to return an object whose value will be used to populate this control. If no object is specified with the **name** attribute, the Form Bean object associated with the enclosing **form** tag will be used to retrieve the property specified by this attribute.	Yes	Yes
style	See "Common Tag Attributes."	Yes	No
styleClass	See "Common Tag Attributes."	Yes	No
styleId	See "Common Tag Attributes."	Yes	No
title	See "Common Tag Attributes."	Yes	No
titleKey	See "Common Tag Attributes."	Yes	No
value	Specifies a constant value that this control will be populated with.	Yes	No
write	Accepts "true" to denote that this control's value will also be written out to the page so that it is visible.	Yes	No

Example Usage

The following snippet illustrates the basic usage of the **hidden** tag:

```
<html:form action="/search">
<html:hidden property="lastId"/>
<html:submit/>
</html:form>
```

This tag will look up the Form Bean associated with the **Action** specified by the **form** tag's **action** attribute and then call the getter method for the field specified by this tag's **property** attribute. The field's value will then be used to populate the HTML control with data.

The html Tag

The **html** tag is used to generate an HTML **<html>** tag with language attributes set to the current user's locale. Additionally, you can use this tag to instruct the rest of the tags in the HTML Tag Library to generate their output as XHTML instead of HTML. More information on XHTML can be found at **http://www.w3.org/TR/xhtml1/**.

Attributes

Attribute	Description	Accepts Scriptlet	Required
locale	Accepts "true" to denote that a **java.util.Locale** object, set to the current request's "AcceptLanguage" HTTP header, will be placed into the session. If a session does not exist, one will be created upon this tag storing the **Locale** object.	Yes	No
xhtml	Accepts "true" to denote that the rest of the tags in the HTML Tag Library will generate their output as XHTML instead of HTML.	Yes	No

Example Usage

The following snippet shows the basic usage of the **html** tag:

```
<html:html/>
```

If you want the HTML Tag Library's tags to generate XHTML instead of HTML, use the **html** tag as shown here:

```
<html:html xhtml="true"/>
```

The image Tag

The **image** tag is used to generate an HTML **<input type="image">** tag. Note that this tag must be nested inside of a **form** tag.

There are two ways you can use the **image** tag, as listed here and shown later in the "Example Usage" section:

- You can use the **page** or **pageKey** attribute to specify a module-relative URL that will be used as the generated HTML tag's **src** attribute.
- You can use the **src** or **srcKey** attribute to specify a URL that will be used as the generated HTML tag's **src** attribute.

Attributes

Attribute	Description	Accepts Scriptlet	Required
accesskey	See the "Common Tag Attributes" section at the end of this chapter.	Yes	No
align	Same as the corresponding HTML tag's attribute with the same name. Specifies how the image will be aligned (i.e., left, right, top, bottom, and so on).	Yes	No
alt	See "Common Tag Attributes."	Yes	No
altKey	See "Common Tag Attributes."	Yes	No
border	Same as the corresponding HTML tag's attribute with the same name. Specifies the width of the border surrounding the image.	Yes	No
bundle	Specifies the logical name of a resource bundle that will be used when looking up message keys specified by other attributes of this tag (i.e., **pageKey** and **srcKey**).	Yes	No
disabled	See "Common Tag Attributes."	Yes	No
indexed	Accepts "true" to denote that the value assigned to the corresponding HTML tag's **name** attribute will have an index (e.g., "property[x]"). This attribute is applicable only when this tag is nested inside the Logic Tag Library's **iterate** tag.	Yes	No
locale	Specifies the key for a **java.util.Locale** instance stored as a session attribute that will be used when looking up message keys specified by other attributes of this tag (i.e., **pageKey** and **srcKey**).	Yes	No
onblur	See "Common Tag Attributes."	Yes	No
onchange	See "Common Tag Attributes."	Yes	No
onclick	See "Common Tag Attributes."	Yes	No
ondblclick	See "Common Tag Attributes."	Yes	No
onfocus	See "Common Tag Attributes."	Yes	No
onkeydown	See "Common Tag Attributes."	Yes	No
onkeypress	See "Common Tag Attributes."	Yes	No
onkeyup	See "Common Tag Attributes."	Yes	No
onmousedown	See "Common Tag Attributes."	Yes	No
onmousemove	See "Common Tag Attributes."	Yes	No
onmouseout	See "Common Tag Attributes."	Yes	No
onmouseover	See "Common Tag Attributes."	Yes	No

Attribute	Description	Accepts Scriptlet	Required
onmouseup	See "Common Tag Attributes."	Yes	No
page	Specifies a module-relative URL for this button's image.	Yes	No
pageKey	Specifies a key from Struts' **ApplicationResources.properties** file whose value will be used to set the corresponding HTML tag's **src** attribute with a module-relative URL.	Yes	No
property	Same as the corresponding HTML tag's **name** attribute. Specifies the name that will be associated with this control.	Yes	No
src	Same as the corresponding HTML tag's attribute with the same name. Specifies the source URL for this button's image.	Yes	No
srcKey	Specifies a key from Struts' **ApplicationResources.properties** file whose value will be used to set the corresponding HTML tag's **src** attribute.	Yes	No
style	See "Common Tag Attributes."	Yes	No
styleClass	See "Common Tag Attributes."	Yes	No
styleId	See "Common Tag Attributes."	Yes	No
tabindex	See "Common Tag Attributes."	Yes	No
title	See "Common Tag Attributes."	Yes	No
titleKey	See "Common Tag Attributes."	Yes	No
value	Specifies a constant value that this control will be populated with. If not specified, this tag will attempt to use its body content as the value.	Yes	No

Example Usage

As mentioned, there are two ways you can use the **image** tag. The first way, shown here, uses the **page** attribute to specify a module-relative URL for the generated HTML tag's **src** attribute:

```
<html:image page="previous.gif"/>
```

The second way to use the **image** tag is shown here:

```
<html:image src="/images/next.gif"/>
```

This example uses the **src** attribute to specify a URL for the generated HTML tag's **src** attribute. The **image** tag will be used in this way for most applications; however, if you are taking advantage of Struts' module functionality, you will use the **page** or **pageKey** attribute.

The img Tag

The **img** tag is used to generate an HTML **<img>** tag. The image's URL is composed by specifying a base URL and optionally specifying query string parameters to add to the URL.

Attributes

Attribute	Description	Accepts Scriptlet	Required
action	Specifies the name of an action, from the Action Mappings Configuration section of the Struts configuration file, that contains the base URL for the image.	Yes	No
align	Same as the corresponding HTML tag's attribute with the same name. Specifies how the image will be aligned (i.e., left, right, top, bottom, and so on).	Yes	No
alt	See the "Common Tag Attributes" section at the end of this chapter.	Yes	No
altKey	See "Common Tag Attributes."	Yes	No
border	Same as the corresponding HTML tag's attribute with the same name. Specifies the width of the border surrounding the image.	Yes	No
bundle	Specifies the logical name of a resource bundle that will be used to look up messages for this tag.	Yes	No
height	Same as the corresponding HTML tag's attribute with the same name. Specifies the height of this image in pixels.	Yes	No
hspace	Same as the corresponding HTML tag's attribute with the same name. Specifies the number of pixels that will be placed between this image and text surrounding it from the top or bottom.	Yes	No
imageName	Same as the corresponding HTML tag's **name** attribute. Specifies the scriptable name for the image.	Yes	No

Attribute	Description	Accepts Scriptlet	Required
ismap	Same as the corresponding HTML tag's attribute with the same name. Specifies the name of a server-side image map to use to map different regions of the image to different URLs.	Yes	No
locale	Specifies the key for a **java.util.Locale** instance stored as a session attribute that will be used when looking up message keys specified by other attributes of this tag (i.e., **pageKey** and **srcKey**).	Yes	No
lowsrc	Deprecated This attribute has been removed from the HTML spec as of version 4.01 and will no longer be supported in future versions of Struts.	Yes	No
module	Specifies the name of a module that contains the action specified with the **action** attribute.	Yes	No
name	Specifies the name of the **java.util.Map** object whose elements are added as query string parameters to the URL for this image. If the **property** attribute is also specified, one of the fields of the object defined by this attribute will have its getter method called to return the **java.util.Map** object whose elements are added as query string parameters to the URL for this image.	Yes	No
onclick	See "Common Tag Attributes."	Yes	No
ondblclick	See "Common Tag Attributes."	Yes	No
onkeydown	See "Common Tag Attributes."	Yes	No
onkeypress	See "Common Tag Attributes."	Yes	No
onkeyup	See "Common Tag Attributes."	Yes	No
onmousedown	See "Common Tag Attributes."	Yes	No
onmousemove	See "Common Tag Attributes."	Yes	No
onmouseout	See "Common Tag Attributes."	Yes	No
onmouseover	See "Common Tag Attributes."	Yes	No
onmouseup	See "Common Tag Attributes."	Yes	No
page	Specifies a module-relative URL for this image.	Yes	No
pageKey	Specifies a key from Struts' **ApplicationResources.properties** file whose value will be used to set the corresponding HTML tag's **src** attribute with a module-relative URL.	Yes	No

Attribute	Description	Accepts Scriptlet	Required
paramId	Specifies the name of a single parameter to add to the URL for this image.	Yes	No
paramName	Specifies the name of an object whose value will be used as the value for the parameter specified with the **paramId** attribute. If the **property** attribute is also specified, one of the fields of the object defined by this attribute will have its getter method called to return an object whose value will be used as the value for the parameter specified with the **paramId** attribute.	Yes	No
paramProperty	Specifies the field of the object specified by the **name** attribute whose getter method will be called to return an object whose value will be used as the value for the parameter specified with the **paramId** attribute.	Yes	No
paramScope	Specifies the scope (application, page, request, or session) to look in for the object specified by the **paramName** attribute. If not specified, each scope will be searched, in this order: page, request, session, and then application.	Yes	No
property	Specifies the field of the object specified by the **name** attribute whose getter method will be called to return the **java.util.Map** object whose elements are added as query string parameters to the URL for this image.	Yes	No
scope	Specifies the scope (application, page, request, or session) to look in for the object specified by the **name** attribute. If not specified, each scope will be searched, in this order: page, request, session, and then application.	Yes	No
src	Same as the corresponding HTML tag's attribute with the same name. Specifies the source URL for this image.	Yes	No
srcKey	Specifies a key from Struts' **ApplicationResources.properties** file whose value will be used to set the corresponding HTML tag's **src** attribute.	Yes	No
style	See "Common Tag Attributes."	Yes	No
styleClass	See "Common Tag Attributes."	Yes	No
styleId	See "Common Tag Attributes."	Yes	No
title	See "Common Tag Attributes."	Yes	No
titleKey	See "Common Tag Attributes."	Yes	No

PART II

Attribute	Description	Accepts Scriptlet	Required
usemap	Same as the corresponding HTML tag's attribute with the same name. Specifies the name of a client-side image map to use for mapping different regions of the image to different URLs.	Yes	No
vspace	Same as the corresponding HTML tag's attribute with the same name. Specifies the number of pixels that will be placed between this image and text surrounding it from the left or right.	Yes	No
width	Same as the corresponding HTML tag's attribute with the same name. Specifies the width of this image in pixels.	Yes	No

Example Usage

There are a few different ways to use the **img** tag. The first way, shown here, uses the **src** attribute to specify an absolute URL for the image:

```
<html:img src="http://www.domain.com/image.gif"/>
```

The following example adds to the first example by specifying a single query string parameter to add to the base URL specified by the **src** attribute:

```
<html:img href=" http://www.domain.com/image.gif"
      paramId="image"
    paramName="imageObj"/>
```

This example takes the base URL specified by the **href** attribute and appends the query string parameter specified by the **paramId** and **paramName** attributes and composes a URL for the image.

The javascript Tag

The **javascript** tag is used to generate client-side JavaScript validation code for validations defined in the Validator framework's **validation.xml** file.

The JavaScript code generated by the **javascript** tag can be broken down into two pieces: static code and dynamic code. The static piece is composed of all the generic validation routine methods. The dynamic piece is composed of the code that is specific to a particular HTML form and that calls the static validation methods. Because the static piece of code is typically very large and is often repeated across several pages, it is advantageous to break that piece out and store it in its own file. That way it can simply be referenced by each page that makes use of it. The **javascript** tag allows you to break up the two pieces of code by specifying which code it generates with the **dynamicJavascript** and **staticJavascript** attributes.

Attributes

Attribute	Description	Accepts Scriptlet	Required
cdata	Accepts "false" to denote that the generated JavaScript code will not be enclosed in XML CDATA tags (i.e., **<![CDATA[ ]]>**). Note that CDATA tags are necessary to prevent JavaScript code from being parsed when used in conjunction with XHTML.	Yes	No
dynamicJavascript	Accepts "false" to denote that dynamic JavaScript will not be generated.	No	No
formName	Specifies the logical name of a Form Bean whose validation rules will be used to generate JavaScript validation code.	Yes	No
htmlComment	Accepts "false" to denote that the generated JavaScript code will not be enclosed in HTML comment tags (i.e., **<!-- -->**).	Yes	No
method	Specifies an alternate JavaScript method name to be used instead of the default.	Yes	No
page	Specifies the logical name of a page to use to filter which validations for the specified form will be generated. This logical name matches the logical name that can be applied to individual fields in the **validation.xml** file.	Yes	No
scriptLanguage	Accepts "false" to denote that the **language** attribute of the **<script>** tag generated by this tag should be omitted. Note that the generated **<script>** tag's **language** attribute is omitted regardless when the tags in this library are in XHTML mode.	Yes	No
src	Same as the corresponding JavaScript tag's attribute with the same name. Specifies the URL to a static JavaScript file to be included.	Yes	No
staticJavascript	Accepts "false" to denote that static JavaScript will not be generated.	No	No

Example Usage

The following snippet illustrates the basic usage of the **javascript** tag:

```
<html:javascript formName="logonForm"/>
```

This example will generate JavaScript code for all the validation rules in the **validation.xml** file that are tied to the Form Bean specified by the **formName** attribute.

If you want to separate the dynamic and static pieces of the generated JavaScript code, you can use the **javascript** tag as shown next:

```
<html:javascript formName="logonForm"
        staticJavascript="false"
                    src="staticJavascript.jsp"/>
```

This usage only generates the dynamic JavaScript for the specified form. The following example generates the generic static JavaScript code:

```
<html:javascript formName="logonForm" dynamicJavascript="false"/>
```

This snippet must be placed into a separate file named **staticJavascript.jsp** to match the file name specified by the **src** attribute of the previous example.

The link Tag

The **link** tag is used to generate an HTML hyperlink **<a>** tag whose URL is composed by specifying a base URL and optionally specifying an anchor and/or query string parameters to add to the URL.

There are four ways to specify the base URL:

- You can use the **action** attribute to specify the name of an **Action** from the Struts configuration file whose URL will be used.
- You can use the **forward** attribute to specify the name of a forward from the Struts configuration file whose URL will be used.
- You can use the **href** attribute to specify an absolute URL, including protocol (e.g., http://www.yahoo.com/).
- You can use the **page** attribute to specify an application-relative URL.

In addition to specifying the base URL, you have two options for specifying query string parameters to add to the base URL:

- You can use the **paramId** attribute in conjunction with the **paramName** attribute, and optionally the **paramProperty** attribute, to specify a single parameter.
- You can use the **name** attribute, either alone or in tandem with the **property** attribute, to specify a **java.util.Map** object that will be used to add several parameters.

Attributes

Attribute	Description	Accepts Scriptlet	Required
accesskey	See the "Common Tag Attributes" section at the end of this chapter.	Yes	No
action	Specifies the name of an **Action**, from the Action Mappings section of the Struts configuration file, that contains the URL for this link.	Yes	No
anchor	Specifies the anchor (e.g., "#bottom") to be added to the URL for this link. This value must be specified without the leading hash (#) character.	Yes	No
forward	Specifies the name of a forward, from the Global Forwards Configuration section of the Struts configuration file, that contains the URL for this link.	Yes	No
href	Specifies the absolute URL, including protocol (e.g., http://www.yahoo.com), for this link.	Yes	No
indexed	Accepts "true" to denote that an indexed parameter, whose name is specified by the **indexId** attribute, will be added to the URL for this link. This attribute is applicable only when this tag is nested inside the Logic Tag Library's **iterate** tag.	Yes	No
indexId	Specifies the name to use for an indexed parameter if the **indexed** attribute is used. This attribute is applicable only when this tag is nested inside the Logic Tag Library's **iterate** tag.	Yes	No
linkName	Same as the corresponding HTML tag's **name** attribute. Specifies the name of a page anchor for intra-page hyperlinks.	Yes	No
module	Specifies the name of a module that contains the action specified with the **action** attribute.	Yes	No
name	Specifies the name of the **java.util.Map** object whose elements are added as query string parameters to the URL for this link. If the **property** attribute is also specified, one of the fields of the object defined by this attribute will have its getter method called to return the **java.util.Map** object whose elements are added as query string parameters to the URL for this link.	Yes	No
onblur	See "Common Tag Attributes."	Yes	No

Attribute	Description	Accepts Scriptlet	Required
onclick	See "Common Tag Attributes."	Yes	No
ondblclick	See "Common Tag Attributes."	Yes	No
onfocus	See "Common Tag Attributes."	Yes	No
onkeydown	See "Common Tag Attributes."	Yes	No
onkeypress	See "Common Tag Attributes."	Yes	No
onkeyup	See "Common Tag Attributes."	Yes	No
onmousedown	See "Common Tag Attributes."	Yes	No
onmousemove	See "Common Tag Attributes."	Yes	No
onmouseout	See "Common Tag Attributes."	Yes	No
onmouseover	See "Common Tag Attributes."	Yes	No
onmouseup	See "Common Tag Attributes."	Yes	No
page	Specifies the application-relative URL (starts with a leading slash, /) for this link.	Yes	No
paramId	Specifies the name of a single parameter to add to the URL for this link.	Yes	No
paramName	Specifies the name of an object whose value will be used as the value for the parameter specified with the **paramId** attribute. If the **property** attribute is also specified, one of the fields of the object defined by this attribute will have its getter method called to return an object whose value will be used as the value for the parameter specified with the **paramId** attribute.	Yes	No
paramProperty	Specifies the field of the object specified by the **name** attribute whose getter method will be called to return an object whose value will be used as the value for the parameter specified with the **paramId** attribute.	Yes	No
paramScope	Specifies the scope (application, page, request, or session) to look in for the object specified by the **paramName** attribute. If not specified, each scope will be searched, in this order: page, request, session, and then application.	Yes	No
property	Specifies the field of the object specified by the **name** attribute whose getter method will be called to return the **java.util.Map** object whose elements are added as query string parameters to the URL for this link.	Yes	No

Attribute	Description	Accepts Scriptlet	Required
scope	Specifies the scope (application, page, request, or session) to look in for the object specified by the **name** attribute. If not specified, each scope will be searched, in this order: page, request, session, and then application.	Yes	No
style	See "Common Tag Attributes."	Yes	No
styleClass	See "Common Tag Attributes."	Yes	No
styleId	See "Common Tag Attributes."	Yes	No
tabindex	See "Common Tag Attributes."	Yes	No
title	See "Common Tag Attributes."	Yes	No
titleKey	See "Common Tag Attributes."	Yes	No
transaction	Accepts "true" or "false" to denote whether or not the current transaction token will be included in the URL for this link.	Yes	No

Example Usage

There are a few different ways to use the **link** tag. The first way, shown here, uses the **href** attribute to specify an absolute URL for the frame:

```
<html:link href="http://www.yahoo.com/"/>
```

The following example adds to the first example by specifying a single query string parameter to add to the base URL specified by the **href** attribute:

```
<html:link href="http://www.yahoo.com/"
        paramId="query"
      paramName="queryObj"/>
```

This example takes the base URL specified by the **href** attribute and appends the query string parameter specified by the **paramId** and **paramName** attributes and composes a URL that the tag then redirects to.

Another way to use the **link** tag is shown here:

```
<html:link page="/search.jsp" name="params"/>
```

This example uses the **page** attribute to specify an application-relative base URL and uses the **name** attribute to specify a **java.util.Map** object whose entries are added to the URL as query string parameters.

The messages Tag

The **messages** tag is used to display a set of messages stored as an **org.apache.struts .action.ActionErrors** object, an **org.apache.struts.action.ActionMessages** object, a **String**, or a **String** array in request scope. Similar to the **errors** tag, this tag will take the stored messages and iterate over them; however, instead of actually outputting the messages to the JSP, this tag behaves similar to the Logic Tag Library's **iterate** tag. On each iteration, it stores the current message in a page scope JSP variable.

Attributes

Attribute	Description	Accepts Scriptlet	Required
bundle	Specifies the logical name of a resource bundle that will be used when looking up message keys specified by other attributes of this tag (e.g., **footer** and **header**).	Yes	No
footer	Specifies a key from Struts' **ApplicationResources.properties** file whose value will be printed after the messages have been iterated through.	Yes	No
header	Specifies a key from Struts' **ApplicationResources.properties** file whose value will be printed before the messages have been iterated through.	Yes	No
id	Specifies the name for a page scope JSP variable that will hold a reference to the current message on each iteration.	No	Yes
locale	Specifies the key for a **java.util.Locale** instance stored as a session attribute that will be used when looking up message keys specified by other attributes of this tag (e.g., **footer** and **header**).	Yes	No
message	Accepts "true" to denote that the messages to be displayed are stored under the **org.apache.struts.Globals.MESSAGE_KEY** key instead of the **org.apache.struts.Globals.ERROR_KEY** key.	Yes	No
name	Specifies the key (in any scope) under which the messages to be displayed are stored. If not specified, the default **org.apache.struts.Globals.ERROR_KEY** key will be used.	Yes	No

Attribute	Description	Accepts Scriptlet	Required
property	Specifies the field for which messages will be displayed. If not specified, all messages will be displayed.	Yes	No

Example Usage

The following snippet illustrates the basic usage of the **messages** tag:

```
<html:messages id="msg">
<li><bean:write name="msg"/></li>
</html:messages>
```

This example will display all the messages currently stored. If you want to limit the messages that are displayed to a specific property, you can specify that property when using the **messages** tag, as shown here:

```
<html:messages id="msg" property="category">
<li><bean:write name="msg"/></li>
</html:messages>
```

In this case, only the messages associated with the property specified by the **property** attribute will be displayed.

The multibox Tag

The **multibox** tag is used to generate an HTML **<input type="checkbox">** tag whose checked status is based on whether or not a specified value matches one of the values in a specified array of values. This tag is useful when your JSP is displaying several check boxes at a time. Instead of using several instances of the **checkbox** tag, you can use this tag in conjunction with the Logic Tag Library's **iterate** tag to reduce the amount of code it takes to deal with several check boxes.

Attributes

Attribute	Description	Accepts Scriptlet	Required
accesskey	See the "Common Tag Attributes" section at the end of this chapter.	Yes	No
alt	See "Common Tag Attributes."	Yes	No
altKey	See "Common Tag Attributes."	Yes	No
disabled	See "Common Tag Attributes."	Yes	No

Attribute	Description	Accepts Scriptlet	Required
name	Specifies the name of an object (in any scope) whose field, specified by the **property** attribute, will be used to populate this control with data.	Yes	No
onblur	See "Common Tag Attributes."	Yes	No
onchange	See "Common Tag Attributes."	Yes	No
onclick	See "Common Tag Attributes."	Yes	No
ondblclick	See "Common Tag Attributes."	Yes	No
onfocus	See "Common Tag Attributes."	Yes	No
onkeydown	See "Common Tag Attributes."	Yes	No
onkeypress	See "Common Tag Attributes."	Yes	No
onkeyup	See "Common Tag Attributes."	Yes	No
onmousedown	See "Common Tag Attributes."	Yes	No
onmousemove	See "Common Tag Attributes."	Yes	No
onmouseout	See "Common Tag Attributes."	Yes	No
onmouseover	See "Common Tag Attributes."	Yes	No
onmouseup	See "Common Tag Attributes."	Yes	No
property	Specifies the value to set the corresponding HTML tag's **name** attribute to. Additionally, this attribute is used to specify the field of the object specified by the **name** attribute whose getter method will be called to return an object whose value will be used to populate this control. If no object is specified with the **name** attribute, the Form Bean object associated with the enclosing **form** tag will be used to retrieve the property specified by this attribute.	Yes	Yes
style	See "Common Tag Attributes."	Yes	No
styleClass	See "Common Tag Attributes."	Yes	No
styleId	See "Common Tag Attributes."	Yes	No
tabindex	See "Common Tag Attributes."	Yes	No
title	See "Common Tag Attributes."	Yes	No
titleKey	See "Common Tag Attributes."	Yes	No
value	Specifies a constant value that the control will be populated with.	Yes	No

Example Usage

The following snippet illustrates the basic usage of the **multibox** tag:

```
<logic:iterate id="item" property="items">
  <html:multibox property="selectedItems">
    <bean:write name="item"/>
  </html:multibox>
  <bean:write name="item"/>
</logic:iterate>
```

In this example, the **iterate** tag loops through each of the elements in the collection specified by its **property** attribute. Each iteration of the loop uses the **multibox** tag to generate an HTML **<input type="checkbox">** tag whose checked status is based on whether or not the loop's current element is present in the collection specified by the property attribute of the **multibox** tag.

The option Tag

The **option** tag is used to generate an HTML **<option>** tag. Note that this tag must be nested inside of the **select** tag. If an instance of this tag's value matches the value of the Form Bean field corresponding to the enclosing **select** tag, the instance will be marked as selected.

Attributes

Attribute	Description	Accepts Scriptlet	Required
bundle	Specifies the logical name of a resource bundle that will be used to look up the message specified by the **key** attribute.	Yes	No
disabled	See the "Common Tag Attributes" section at the end of this chapter.	Yes	No
key	Specifies a key from Struts' **ApplicationResources.properties** file whose value will be used to set the text that will be displayed for this option. If not specified, the text displayed for this option will be taken from this tag's body content.	Yes	No
locale	Specifies the key for a **java.util.Locale** instance stored as a session attribute that will be used when looking up the message specified by the **key** attribute.	Yes	No
style	See "Common Tag Attributes."	Yes	No
styleClass	See "Common Tag Attributes."	Yes	No
styleId	See "Common Tag Attributes."	Yes	No
value	Specifies a constant value that the control will be populated with.	Yes	Yes

Example Usage

The following snippet illustrates the basic usage of the **option** tag:

```
<html:select property="gender">
  <html:option value="male">Male</html:option>
  <html:option value="female">Female</html:option>
</html:select>
```

If the value specified by an **option** tag's **value** attribute matches the value of the Form Bean field specified by the **select** tag's property attribute, the HTML **<option>** tag will be marked as selected when it is generated.

The options Tag

The **options** tag is used to generate a set of HTML **<option>** tags for each element in a collection. Note that this tag must be nested inside of the **select** tag.

There are three ways you can specify which collection to generate options from, as listed here and shown later in the "Example Usage" section:

- You can use the **collection** attribute to specify a scriptlet that evaluates to a collection object.
- You can use the **name** attribute to specify the name of a collection object that can be in any scope.
- You can use the **name** and **property** attributes in tandem to specify the name of an object and its field whose getter method will be called to return a collection object.

Attributes

Attribute	Description	Accepts Scriptlet	Required
collection	Specifies the name of a collection object (in any scope) whose elements will be used to create a set of options.	Yes	No
filter	Accepts "false" to denote that option labels will not be filtered for sensitive HTML characters (e.g., > and <).	Yes	No
labelName	Specifies the name of an object (in any scope) whose field, specified by the **property** attribute, will have its getter method called to return a collection object whose elements will be used as labels for the created options.	Yes	No

Attribute	Description	Accepts Scriptlet	Required
labelProperty	Specifies the field of the object specified by the **name** attribute whose getter method will be called to return a collection object whose elements will be used as labels for the created options. If no object is specified with the **name** attribute, the Form Bean object associated with the enclosing **form** tag will be used to retrieve the property specified by this attribute.	Yes	No
name	Specifies the name of an object (in any scope) whose field, specified by the **property** attribute, will have its getter method called to return a collection object whose elements will be used to create a set of options.	Yes	No
property	Specifies the field of the object specified by the **name** attribute whose getter method will be called to return a collection object whose elements will be used to create a set of options. If no object is specified with the **name** attribute, the Form Bean object associated with the enclosing **form** tag will be used to retrieve the property specified by this attribute.	Yes	No
style	See the "Common Tag Attributes" section at the end of this chapter.	Yes	No
styleClass	See "Common Tag Attributes."	Yes	No

Example Usage

As mentioned there are three basic ways you can use the **options** tag. The first way, shown here, uses the **collection** attribute to specify the collection from which to create options:

```
<html:select property="category">
  <html:options collection="catOptions"/>
</html:select>
```

This example assumes you have defined a collection named "category" and then uses its elements to generate a set of options.

The second way to use the **options** tag is shown here:

```
<html:select property="category">
  <html:options name="catOptions"/>
</html:select>
```

This example is very similar to the first example; however, it differs in that the collection from which to generate options is specified with the **name** attribute.

The third way to use the **options** tag is shown here:

```
<html:select property="category">
  <html:options name="cat" property="options"/>
</html:select>
```

In this example, the **name** and **property** attributes are used in tandem to specify the name of an object and its field whose getter method will be called to return a collection for which to generate options.

The optionsCollection Tag

The **optionsCollection** tag is used to generate a set of HTML **<option>** tags for each element in a collection. This tag is very similar to the **options** tag, but differs in that it requires the objects in the specified collection to have fields for the generated options' labels and values. Note that this tag must be nested inside of the **select** tag.

Attributes

Attribute	Description	Accepts Scriptlet	Required
filter	Accepts "false" to denote that option labels will not be filtered for sensitive HTML characters (e.g., > and <).	Yes	No
label	Specifies the field of the object specified with the **name** and **property** attributes whose value will be used as the label for the generated options.	Yes	No
name	Specifies the name of an object (in any scope) whose field, specified by the **property** attribute, will have its getter method called to return a collection object whose elements will be used to create a set of options.	Yes	No
property	Specifies the field of the object specified by the **name** attribute whose getter method will be called to return a collection object whose elements will be used to create a set of options. If no object is specified with the **name** attribute, the Form Bean object associated with the enclosing **form** tag will be used to retrieve the property specified by this attribute.	Yes	No
style	See the "Common Tag Attributes" section at the end of this chapter.	Yes	No
styleClass	See "Common Tag Attributes."	Yes	No
value	Specifies the field of the object specified with the **name** and **property** attributes whose value will be used as the value for the generated options.	Yes	No

Example Usage

The following snippet illustrates the basic usage of the **optionsCollection** tag:

```
<html:select property="category">
  <html:optionsCollection name="cat" property="options"/>
</html:select>
```

In this example, the **name** and **property** attributes are used in tandem to specify the name of an object and its field whose getter method will be called to return a collection for which to generate options.

The password Tag

The **password** tag is used to generate an HTML **<input type="password">** tag populated with data from a specified object. Note that this tag must be nested inside of the **form** tag.

Attributes

Attribute	Description	Accepts Scriptlet	Required
accesskey	See the "Common Tag Attributes" section at the end of this chapter.	Yes	No
alt	See "Common Tag Attributes."	Yes	No
altKey	See "Common Tag Attributes."	Yes	No
disabled	See "Common Tag Attributes."	Yes	No
indexed	Accepts "true" to denote that the value assigned to the corresponding HTML tag's **name** attribute will have an index (e.g., "name[x].property"). This attribute is applicable only when this tag is nested inside the Logic Tag Library's **iterate** tag.	Yes	No
maxlength	Same as the corresponding HTML tag's attribute with the same name. Specifies the maximum number of characters that this control will accept.	Yes	No
name	Specifies the name of an object (in any scope) whose field, specified by the **property** attribute, will be used to populate this control with data.	Yes	No
onblur	See "Common Tag Attributes."	Yes	No
onchange	See "Common Tag Attributes."	Yes	No
onclick	See "Common Tag Attributes."	Yes	No
ondblclick	See "Common Tag Attributes."	Yes	No
onfocus	See "Common Tag Attributes."	Yes	No
onkeydown	See "Common Tag Attributes."	Yes	No

Attribute	Description	Accepts Scriptlet	Required
onkeypress	See "Common Tag Attributes."	Yes	No
onkeyup	See "Common Tag Attributes."	Yes	No
onmousedown	See "Common Tag Attributes."	Yes	No
onmousemove	See "Common Tag Attributes."	Yes	No
onmouseout	See "Common Tag Attributes."	Yes	No
onmouseover	See "Common Tag Attributes."	Yes	No
onmouseup	See "Common Tag Attributes."	Yes	No
property	Specifies the value to set the corresponding HTML tag's **name** attribute to. Additionally, this attribute is used to specify the field of the object specified by the **name** attribute whose getter method will be called to return an object whose value will be used to populate this control. If no object is specified with the **name** attribute, the Form Bean object associated with the enclosing **form** tag will be used to retrieve the property specified by this attribute.	Yes	Yes
readonly	Same as the corresponding HTML tag's attribute with the same name. Accepts "true" to denote that the control's value will be read-only, preventing it from being changed.	Yes	No
redisplay	Accepts "false" to denote that the value specified with the **name** and **property** attributes or specified with the **value** attribute will not be used to populate this control.	Yes	No
size	Same as the corresponding HTML tag's attribute with the same name. Specifies the number of characters that will be visible in the control.	Yes	No
style	See "Common Tag Attributes."	Yes	No
styleClass	See "Common Tag Attributes."	Yes	No
styleId	See "Common Tag Attributes."	Yes	No
tabindex	See "Common Tag Attributes."	Yes	No
title	See "Common Tag Attributes."	Yes	No
titleKey	See "Common Tag Attributes."	Yes	No
value	Specifies a constant value that the control will be populated with.	Yes	No

Example Usage

The following snippet illustrates the basic usage of the **password** tag:

```
<html:form action="/logon">
UserName: <html:text property="username"/><br>
Password: <html:password property="password"/><br>
<html:submit/>
</html:form>
```

This tag will look up the Form Bean associated with the **Action** specified by the **form** tag's **action** attribute and then call the getter method for the field specified by this tag's **property** attribute. The field's value will then be used to populate the HTML control with data.

The radio Tag

The **radio** tag is used to generate an HTML **<input type="radio">** tag populated with data from a specified object. Note that this tag must be nested inside of the **form** tag.

Attributes

Attribute	Description	Accepts Scriptlet	Required
accesskey	See the "Common Tag Attributes" section at the end of this chapter.	Yes	No
alt	See "Common Tag Attributes."	Yes	No
altKey	See "Common Tag Attributes."	Yes	No
disabled	See "Common Tag Attributes."	Yes	No
idName	If an iterator is used to generate a series of **radio** tags, this attribute can be used to specify a name for the object exposed by the iterator. In this case, the **value** attribute is used as the name of a field on the exposed object whose getter method will be called to return the value that the **radio** tag for this iteration will be populated with.	Yes	No
indexed	Accepts "true" to denote that the value assigned to the corresponding HTML tag's **name** attribute will have an index (e.g., "name[x].property"). This attribute is applicable only when this tag is nested inside the Logic Tag Library's **iterate** tag.	Yes	No
name	Specifies the name of an object (in any scope) whose field, specified by the **property** attribute, will be used to populate this control with data.	Yes	No
onblur	See "Common Tag Attributes."	Yes	No

Attribute	Description	Accepts Scriptlet	Required
onchange	See "Common Tag Attributes."	Yes	No
onclick	See "Common Tag Attributes."	Yes	No
ondblclick	See "Common Tag Attributes."	Yes	No
onfocus	See "Common Tag Attributes."	Yes	No
onkeydown	See "Common Tag Attributes."	Yes	No
onkeypress	See "Common Tag Attributes."	Yes	No
onkeyup	See "Common Tag Attributes."	Yes	No
onmousedown	See "Common Tag Attributes."	Yes	No
onmousemove	See "Common Tag Attributes."	Yes	No
onmouseout	See "Common Tag Attributes."	Yes	No
onmouseover	See "Common Tag Attributes."	Yes	No
onmouseup	See "Common Tag Attributes."	Yes	No
property	Specifies the value to set the corresponding HTML tag's **name** attribute to. Additionally, this attribute is used to specify the field of the object specified by the **name** attribute whose getter method will be called to return an object whose value will be used to populate this control. If no object is specified with the **name** attribute, the Form Bean object associated with the enclosing **form** tag will be used to retrieve the property specified by this attribute.	Yes	Yes
style	See "Common Tag Attributes."	Yes	No
styleClass	See "Common Tag Attributes."	Yes	No
styleId	See "Common Tag Attributes."	Yes	No
tabindex	See "Common Tag Attributes."	Yes	No
title	See "Common Tag Attributes."	Yes	No
titleKey	See "Common Tag Attributes."	Yes	No
value	Specifies a constant value that the control will be populated with.	Yes	Yes

Example Usage

The following snippet illustrates the basic usage of the **radio** tag:

```
<html:form action="/register"/>
Male: <html:radio property="gender" value="male"/><br>
Female: <html:radio property="gender" value="female"/><br>
<html:submit/>
</html:form>
```

This tag will look up the Form Bean associated with the **Action** specified by the **form** tag's **action** attribute and then call the getter method for the field specified by this tag's **property** attribute. If the field's value matches the value specified with the **value** attribute, the radio button will be selected.

The reset Tag

The **reset** tag is used to generate an HTML **<input type="reset">** tag. Note that this tag must be nested inside of the **form** tag.

Attributes

Attribute	Description	Accepts Scriptlet	Required
accesskey	See the "Common Tag Attributes" section at the end of this chapter.	Yes	No
alt	See "Common Tag Attributes."	Yes	No
altKey	See "Common Tag Attributes."	Yes	No
disabled	See "Common Tag Attributes."	Yes	No
onblur	See "Common Tag Attributes."	Yes	No
onchange	See "Common Tag Attributes."	Yes	No
onclick	See "Common Tag Attributes."	Yes	No
ondblclick	See "Common Tag Attributes."	Yes	No
onfocus	See "Common Tag Attributes."	Yes	No
onkeydown	See "Common Tag Attributes."	Yes	No
onkeypress	See "Common Tag Attributes."	Yes	No
onkeyup	See "Common Tag Attributes."	Yes	No
onmousedown	See "Common Tag Attributes."	Yes	No
onmousemove	See "Common Tag Attributes."	Yes	No
onmouseout	See "Common Tag Attributes."	Yes	No
onmouseover	See "Common Tag Attributes."	Yes	No
onmouseup	See "Common Tag Attributes."	Yes	No
property	Same as the corresponding HTML tag's **name** attribute. Specifies the name that will be associated with this control.	Yes	No
style	See "Common Tag Attributes."	Yes	No
styleClass	See "Common Tag Attributes."	Yes	No
styleId	See "Common Tag Attributes."	Yes	No
tabindex	See "Common Tag Attributes."	Yes	No
title	See "Common Tag Attributes."	Yes	No

Attribute	Description	Accepts Scriptlet	Required
titleKey	See "Common Tag Attributes."	Yes	No
value	Specifies a constant value that this control will be populated with. This value will be used for the button's label. If not specified, this tag will attempt to use its body content as the value for the button's label.	Yes	No

Example Usage

The following snippet illustrates the basic usage of the **reset** tag:

```
<html:reset value="Reset Form"/>
```

The value specified with the **value** attribute will be used for the button's label. Alternatively, you can specify the button's label value by nesting a string between opening and closing **reset** tags, as shown here:

```
<html:reset>Reset Form</html:reset>
```

The rewrite Tag

Similar to the **link** tag, the **rewrite** tag is used to generate a URL by specifying a base URL and optionally specifying an anchor and/or query string parameters to add to the URL. However, this tag does not create an HTML <a> tag for the generated URL. This tag is useful for creating URLs that are used as string constants in JavaScript code.

There are four ways to specify the base URL:

- You can use the **action** attribute to specify the name of an **Action** from the Struts configuration file whose URL will be used.

- You can use the **forward** attribute to specify the name of a forward from the Struts configuration file whose URL will be used.

- You can use the **href** attribute to specify an absolute URL, including protocol (e.g., http://www.yahoo.com/).

- You can use the **page** attribute to specify an application-relative URL.

In addition to specifying the base URL, you have two options for specifying query string parameters to add to the base URL:

- You can use the **paramId** attribute in conjunction with the **paramName** attribute, and optionally the **paramProperty** attribute, to specify a single parameter.

- You can use the **name** attribute, either alone or in tandem with the **property** attribute, to specify a **java.util.Map** object that will be used to add several parameters.

Attributes

Attribute	Description	Accepts Scriptlet	Required
action	Specifies the name of an action, from the Action Mappings Configuration section of the Struts configuration file, that contains the base URL for the generated URL.	Yes	No
anchor	Specifies the anchor (e.g., "#bottom") to be added to the generated URL. This value must be specified without the leading hash (#) character.	Yes	No
forward	Specifies the name of a forward, from the Global Forwards Configuration section of the Struts configuration file, that contains the base URL for the generated URL.	Yes	No
href	Specifies the absolute base URL, including protocol (e.g., http://www.yahoo.com), for the generated URL.	Yes	No
module	Specifies the name of a module that contains the action specified with the **action** attribute.	Yes	No
name	Specifies the name of the **java.util.Map** object whose elements are added as query string parameters to the generated URL. If the **property** attribute is also specified, one of the fields of the object defined by this attribute will have its getter method called to return the **java.util.Map** object whose elements are added as query string parameters to the generated URL.	Yes	No
page	Specifies the application-relative base URL (starts with a leading slash, /) for the generated URL.	Yes	No
paramId	Specifies the name of a single parameter to add to the generated URL.	Yes	No
paramName	Specifies the name of an object whose value will be used as the value for the parameter specified with the **paramId** attribute. If the **property** attribute is also specified, one of the fields of the object defined by this attribute will have its getter method called to return an object whose value will be used as the value for the parameter specified with the **paramId** attribute.	Yes	No

PART II

Attribute	Description	Accepts Scriptlet	Required
paramProperty	Specifies the field of the object specified by the **name** attribute whose getter method will be called to return an object whose value will be used as the value for the parameter specified with the **paramId** attribute.	Yes	No
paramScope	Specifies the scope (application, page, request, or session) to look in for the object specified by the **paramName** attribute. If not specified, each scope will be searched, in this order: page, request, session, and then application.	Yes	No
property	Specifies the field of the object specified by the **name** attribute whose getter method will be called to return the **java.util.Map** object whose elements are added as query string parameters to the generated URL.	Yes	No
scope	Specifies the scope (application, page, request, or session) to look in for the object specified by the **name** attribute. If not specified, each scope will be searched, in this order: page, request, session, and then application.	Yes	No
transaction	Accepts "true" or "false" to denote whether or not the current transaction token will be included in the generated URL.	Yes	No

Example Usage

There are a few different ways to use the **rewrite** tag. The first way, shown here, uses the **href** attribute to specify an absolute URL for the frame:

```
<html:rewrite href="http://www.yahoo.com/"/>
```

The following example adds to the first example by specifying a single query string parameter to add to the base URL specified by the **href** attribute:

```
<html:rewrite href="http://www.yahoo.com/"
        paramId="query"
        paramName="queryObj"/>
```

This example takes the base URL specified by the **href** attribute and appends the query string parameter specified by the **paramId** and **paramName** attributes and composes a URL that the tag then redirects to.

Another way to use the **rewrite** tag is shown here:

```
<html:rewrite page="/search.jsp" name="params"/>
```

This example uses the **page** attribute to specify an application-relative base URL and uses the **name** attribute to specify a **java.util.Map** object whose entries are added to the URL as query string parameters.

The select Tag

The **select** tag is used to generate an HTML **<select>** tag. Note that this tag must be nested inside of the **form** tag.

There are two ways you can use the **select** tag, as listed here and shown later in the "Example Usage" section:

- You can omit the **multiple** attribute so that only one selection can be made. If you take this route, the **property** attribute must evaluate to a scalar value for the nested option that is selected.

- You can assign an arbitrary value to the **multiple** attribute so that multiple selections can be made. If you take this route, the **property** attribute must evaluate to an array of scalar values for each nested option that is selected.

Attributes

Attribute	Description	Accepts Scriptlet	Required
alt	See the "Common Tag Attributes" section at the end of this chapter.	Yes	No
altKey	See "Common Tag Attributes."	Yes	No
disabled	See "Common Tag Attributes."	Yes	No
indexed	Accepts "true" to denote that the value assigned to the corresponding HTML tag's **name** attribute will have an index (e.g., "name[x].property"). This attribute is applicable only when this tag is nested inside the Logic Tag Library's **iterate** tag.	Yes	No
multiple	Same as the corresponding HTML tag's attribute with the same name. Accepts an arbitrary value to denote that multiple selections can be made on the control.	Yes	No
name	Specifies the name of an object (in any scope) whose field, specified by the **property** attribute, will be used to determine which nested **option** tag will be set as selected.	Yes	No
onblur	See "Common Tag Attributes."	Yes	No
onchange	See "Common Tag Attributes."	Yes	No
onclick	See "Common Tag Attributes."	Yes	No
ondblclick	See "Common Tag Attributes."	Yes	No

Attribute	Description	Accepts Scriptlet	Required
onfocus	See "Common Tag Attributes."	Yes	No
onkeydown	See "Common Tag Attributes."	Yes	No
onkeypress	See "Common Tag Attributes."	Yes	No
onkeyup	See "Common Tag Attributes."	Yes	No
onmousedown	See "Common Tag Attributes."	Yes	No
onmousemove	See "Common Tag Attributes."	Yes	No
onmouseout	See "Common Tag Attributes."	Yes	No
onmouseover	See "Common Tag Attributes."	Yes	No
onmouseup	See "Common Tag Attributes."	Yes	No
property	Specifies the value to set the corresponding HTML tag's **name** attribute to. Additionally, this attribute is used to specify the field of the object specified by the **name** attribute whose getter method will be called to return an object whose value will be used to determine which nested **option** tag will be set as selected. If no object is specified with the **name** attribute, the Form Bean object associated with the enclosing **form** tag will be used to retrieve the property specified by this attribute.	Yes	Yes
size	Same as the corresponding HTML tag's attribute with the same name. Specifies the number of options that will be visible at a time.	Yes	No
style	See "Common Tag Attributes."	Yes	No
styleClass	See "Common Tag Attributes."	Yes	No
styleId	See "Common Tag Attributes."	Yes	No
tabindex	See "Common Tag Attributes."	Yes	No
title	See "Common Tag Attributes."	Yes	No
titleKey	See "Common Tag Attributes."	Yes	No
value	Specifies the value to use when determining which nested **option** tag will be set as selected.	Yes	No

Example Usage

As mentioned, there are two ways you can use the **select** tag. The first way, shown here, omits the **multiple** attribute so that only one nested option will be selected:

```
<html:select property="gender">
  <html:option value="male">Male</html:option>
  <html:option value="female">Female</html:option>
</html:select>
```

The second way to use the **select** tag is shown here:

```
<html:select property="color" multiple="true" size="3">
  <html:option value="red">Red</html:option>
  <html:option value="green">Green</html:option>
  <html:option value="blue">Blue</html:option>
  <html:option value="black">Black</html:option>
  <html:option value="white">White</html:option>
</html:select>
```

This example uses the **multiple** attribute to denote that the object specified with the **property** attribute will be an array of values for each nested option that will be selected.

The submit Tag

The **submit** tag is used to generate an HTML **<input type="submit">** tag. Note that this tag must be nested inside of the **form** tag.

Attributes

Attribute	Description	Accepts Scriptlet	Required
accesskey	See the "Common Tag Attributes" section at the end of this chapter.	Yes	No
alt	See "Common Tag Attributes."	Yes	No
altKey	See "Common Tag Attributes."	Yes	No
disabled	See "Common Tag Attributes."	Yes	No
indexed	Accepts "true" to denote that the value assigned to the corresponding HTML tag's **name** attribute will have an index (e.g., "property[x]"). This attribute is applicable only when this tag is nested inside the Logic Tag Library's **iterate** tag.	Yes	No
onblur	See "Common Tag Attributes."	Yes	No
onchange	See "Common Tag Attributes."	Yes	No
onclick	See "Common Tag Attributes."	Yes	No
ondblclick	See "Common Tag Attributes."	Yes	No
onfocus	See "Common Tag Attributes."	Yes	No
onkeydown	See "Common Tag Attributes."	Yes	No
onkeypress	See "Common Tag Attributes."	Yes	No
onkeyup	See "Common Tag Attributes."	Yes	No
onmousedown	See "Common Tag Attributes."	Yes	No

Attribute	Description	Accepts Scriptlet	Required
onmousemove	See "Common Tag Attributes."	Yes	No
onmouseout	See "Common Tag Attributes."	Yes	No
onmouseover	See "Common Tag Attributes."	Yes	No
onmouseup	See "Common Tag Attributes."	Yes	No
property	Same as the corresponding HTML tag's **name** attribute. Specifies the name that will be associated with this control.	Yes	No
style	See "Common Tag Attributes."	Yes	No
styleClass	See "Common Tag Attributes."	Yes	No
styleId	See "Common Tag Attributes."	Yes	No
tabindex	See "Common Tag Attributes."	Yes	No
title	See "Common Tag Attributes."	Yes	No
titleKey	See "Common Tag Attributes."	Yes	No
value	Specifies a constant value that this control will be populated with. This value will be used as the button's label.	Yes	No

Example Usage

The following snippet illustrates the basic usage of the **submit** tag:

```
<html:submit value="Add Record"/>
```

The value specified with the **value** attribute will be used for the button's label. Alternatively, you can specify the button's label value by nesting a string between opening and closing **submit** tags, as shown here:

```
<html:submit>Next Page</html:submit>
```

The text Tag

The **text** tag is used to generate an HTML **<input type="text">** tag populated with data from a specified object. Note that this tag must be nested inside of the **form** tag.

Attributes

Attribute	Description	Accepts Scriptlet	Required
accesskey	See the "Common Tag Attributes" section at the end of this chapter.	Yes	No

Attribute	Description	Accepts Scriptlet	Required
alt	See "Common Tag Attributes."	Yes	No
altKey	See "Common Tag Attributes."	Yes	No
disabled	See "Common Tag Attributes."	Yes	No
indexed	Accepts "true" to denote that the value assigned to the corresponding HTML tag's **name** attribute must have an index (e.g., "name[x].property"). This attribute is applicable only when this tag is nested inside the Logic Tag Library's **iterate** tag.	Yes	No
maxlength	Same as the corresponding HTML tag's attribute with the same name. Specifies the maximum number of characters that this control will accept.	Yes	No
name	Specifies the name of an object (in any scope) whose field, specified by the **property** attribute, will be used to populate this control with data.	Yes	No
onblur	See "Common Tag Attributes."	Yes	No
onchange	See "Common Tag Attributes."	Yes	No
onclick	See "Common Tag Attributes."	Yes	No
ondblclick	See "Common Tag Attributes."	Yes	No
onfocus	See "Common Tag Attributes."	Yes	No
onkeydown	See "Common Tag Attributes."	Yes	No
onkeypress	See "Common Tag Attributes."	Yes	No
onkeyup	See "Common Tag Attributes."	Yes	No
onmousedown	See "Common Tag Attributes."	Yes	No
onmousemove	See "Common Tag Attributes."	Yes	No
onmouseout	See "Common Tag Attributes."	Yes	No
onmouseover	See "Common Tag Attributes."	Yes	No
onmouseup	See "Common Tag Attributes."	Yes	No
property	Specifies the value to set the corresponding HTML tag's **name** attribute to. Additionally, this attribute is used to specify the field of the object specified by the **name** attribute whose getter method will be called to return an object whose value will be used to populate this control. If no object is specified with the **name** attribute, the Form Bean object associated with the enclosing **form** tag will be used to retrieve the property specified by this attribute.	Yes	Yes

Attribute	Description	Accepts Scriptlet	Required
readonly	Same as the corresponding HTML tag's attribute with the same name. Accepts "true" to denote that the control's value will be read-only, preventing it from being changed.	Yes	No
size	Same as the corresponding HTML tag's attribute with the same name. Specifies the number of characters that will be visible in the control.	Yes	No
style	See "Common Tag Attributes."	Yes	No
styleClass	See "Common Tag Attributes."	Yes	No
styleId	See "Common Tag Attributes."	Yes	No
tabindex	See "Common Tag Attributes."	Yes	No
title	See "Common Tag Attributes."	Yes	No
titleKey	See "Common Tag Attributes."	Yes	No
value	Specifies a constant value that the control will be populated with.	Yes	No

Example Usage

The following snippet illustrates the basic usage of the **text** tag:

```
<html:form action="/search">
Search Query: <html:text property="query"/><br>
<html:submit/>
</html:form>
```

This tag will look up the Form Bean associated with the **Action** specified by the **form** tag's **action** attribute and then call the getter method for the field specified by this tag's **property** attribute. The field's value will then be used to populate the HTML control with data.

The textarea Tag

The **textarea** tag is used to generate an HTML **<textarea>** tag populated with data from a specified object. Note that this tag must be nested inside of the **form** tag.

Attributes

Attribute	Description	Accepts Scriptlet	Required
accesskey	See the "Common Tag Attributes" section at the end of this chapter.	Yes	No

Attribute	Description	Accepts Scriptlet	Required
alt	See "Common Tag Attributes."	Yes	No
altKey	See "Common Tag Attributes."	Yes	No
cols	Same as the corresponding HTML tag's attribute with the same name. Specifies the number of columns to display.	Yes	No
disabled	See "Common Tag Attributes."	Yes	No
indexed	Accepts "true" to denote that the value assigned to the corresponding HTML tag's **name** attribute will have an index (e.g., "name[x].property"). This attribute is applicable only when this tag is nested inside the Logic Tag Library's **iterate** tag.	Yes	No
name	Specifies the name of an object (in any scope) whose field, specified by the **property** attribute, will be used to populate this control with data.	Yes	No
onblur	See "Common Tag Attributes."	Yes	No
onchange	See "Common Tag Attributes."	Yes	No
onclick	See "Common Tag Attributes."	Yes	No
ondblclick	See "Common Tag Attributes."	Yes	No
onfocus	See "Common Tag Attributes."	Yes	No
onkeydown	See "Common Tag Attributes."	Yes	No
onkeypress	See "Common Tag Attributes."	Yes	No
onkeyup	See "Common Tag Attributes."	Yes	No
onmousedown	See "Common Tag Attributes."	Yes	No
onmousemove	See "Common Tag Attributes."	Yes	No
onmouseout	See "Common Tag Attributes."	Yes	No
onmouseover	See "Common Tag Attributes."	Yes	No
onmouseup	See "Common Tag Attributes."	Yes	No
property	Specifies the value to set the corresponding HTML tag's **name** attribute to. Additionally, this attribute is used to specify the field of the object specified by the **name** attribute whose getter method will be called to return an object whose value will be used to populate this control. If no object is specified with the **name** attribute, the Form Bean object associated with the enclosing **form** tag will be used to retrieve the property specified by this attribute.	Yes	Yes

Attribute	Description	Accepts Scriptlet	Required
readonly	Same as the corresponding HTML tag's attribute with the same name. Accepts "true" to denote that the control's value will be read-only, preventing it from being changed.	Yes	No
rows	Same as the corresponding HTML tag's attribute with the same name. Specifies the number of rows to display.	Yes	No
style	See "Common Tag Attributes."	Yes	No
styleClass	See "Common Tag Attributes."	Yes	No
styleId	See "Common Tag Attributes."	Yes	No
tabindex	See "Common Tag Attributes."	Yes	No
title	See "Common Tag Attributes."	Yes	No
titleKey	See "Common Tag Attributes."	Yes	No
value	Specifies a constant value that the control will be populated with.	Yes	No

Example Usage

The following snippet illustrates the basic usage of the **textarea** tag:

```
<html:form action="/feedback">
Comments: <html:textarea property="comments"/><br>
<html:submit/>
</html:form>
```

This tag will look up the Form Bean associated with the **Action** specified by the **form** tag's **action** attribute and then call the getter method for the field specified by this tag's **property** attribute. The field's value will then be used to populate the HTML control with data.

The xhtml Tag

The **xhtml** tag causes the rest of the tags in the HTML Tag Library to generate their output as XHTML instead of HTML. For more information on XHTML, see **http://www.w3.org/TR/xhtml1/**.

Using this tag is equivalent to using this library's **html** tag with the **xhtml** attribute set to "true", as shown here:

```
<html:html xhtml="true"/>
```

Attributes

This tag does not have any attributes.

Example Usage

Using the **xhtml** tag is very simple because it has no attributes that can or need to be set. You simply just use the tag as shown here:

```
<html:xhtml/>
```

You must place this tag before using any other tags from this library; otherwise, they will not know to generate XHTML. Note that using this tag will not guarantee that your JSP is 100 percent XHTML compliant; you must ensure that any direct usages of HTML tags also conform.

Common Tag Attributes

As mentioned earlier, many of the tags in this library have several attributes in common. They are described in the following table.

Attribute	Description	Accepts Scriptlet	Required
accesskey	Same as the corresponding HTML tag's attribute with the same name. Specifies the keyboard key that causes this control to immediately receive focus when the key is pressed.	Yes	No
alt	Same as the corresponding HTML tag's attribute with the same name. Specifies the alternate text for this control.	Yes	No
altKey	Specifies a key from Struts' **ApplicationResources.properties** file whose value will be used to set the corresponding HTML tag's **alt** attribute.	Yes	No
disabled	Same as the corresponding HTML tag's attribute with the same name. Accepts "true" to denote that the control will be disabled, preventing its use.	Yes	No
onblur	Same as the corresponding HTML tag's attribute with the same name. Specifies the JavaScript code to execute when this control loses input focus.	Yes	No
onchange	Same as the corresponding HTML tag's attribute with the same name. Specifies the JavaScript code to execute when this control loses input focus and its value has changed.	Yes	No

Attribute	Description	Accepts Scriptlet	Required
onclick	Same as the corresponding HTML tag's attribute with the same name. Specifies the JavaScript code to execute when this control receives a mouse click.	Yes	No
ondblclick	Same as the corresponding HTML tag's attribute with the same name. Specifies the JavaScript code to execute when this control receives a mouse double-click.	Yes	No
onfocus	Same as the corresponding HTML tag's attribute with the same name. Specifies the JavaScript code to execute when this control receives input focus.	Yes	No
onkeydown	Same as the corresponding HTML tag's attribute with the same name. Specifies the JavaScript code to execute when this control has focus and a key is pressed.	Yes	No
onkeypress	Same as the corresponding HTML tag's attribute with the same name. Specifies the JavaScript code to execute when this control has focus and a key is pressed and released.	Yes	No
onkeyup	Same as the corresponding HTML tag's attribute with the same name. Specifies the JavaScript code to execute when this control has focus and a key is released.	Yes	No
onmousedown	Same as the corresponding HTML tag's attribute with the same name. Specifies the JavaScript code to execute when this control is under the mouse pointer and a mouse button is pressed.	Yes	No
onmousemove	Same as the corresponding HTML tag's attribute with the same name. Specifies the JavaScript code to execute when this control is under the mouse pointer and the mouse is moved.	Yes	No
onmouseout	Same as the corresponding HTML tag's attribute with the same name. Specifies the JavaScript code to execute when this control is under the mouse pointer and is then moved away from the control.	Yes	No

Attribute	Description	Accepts Scriptlet	Required
onmouseover	Same as the corresponding HTML tag's attribute with the same name. Specifies the JavaScript code to execute when this control is not under the mouse pointer and is then moved to the control.	Yes	No
onmouseup	Same as the corresponding HTML tag's attribute with the same name. Specifies the JavaScript code to execute when this control is under the mouse pointer and a mouse button is released.	Yes	No
style	Same as the corresponding HTML tag's attribute with the same name. Specifies the CSS style to apply to this control.	Yes	No
styleClass	Same as the corresponding HTML tag's **class** attribute. Specifies the CSS class to apply to this control.	Yes	No
styleId	Same as the corresponding HTML tag's **id** attribute. Specifies the CSS id to apply to this control.	Yes	No
tabindex	Same as the corresponding HTML tag's attribute with the same name. Specifies the tab order for this control.	Yes	No
title	Same as the corresponding HTML tag's attribute with the same name. Specifies the title for this control.	Yes	No
titleKey	Specifies a key from Struts' **ApplicationResources.properties** file whose value will be used to set the corresponding HTML tag's **title** attribute.	Yes	No

The Bean Tag Library

The Bean Tag Library is a collection of utility tags that provides convenient access for interacting with Web application objects within a JSP. Most of the tags are used to capture references to specific objects and store them in JSP scripting variables so that other tags can access the objects. The remaining tags are used to render objects to the JSP output.

Understanding Variables and Scope in JSPs

Before discussing each of the tags in this library, it's necessary to review how variables and scope work in JSPs. First, remember that JSPs get converted into servlets and then compiled before they are executed. All of the HTML and code inside the JSP gets placed into the generated servlet's **service( )** method. Because of this, any variables that get defined inside the JSP with a scriptlet, as shown here, are local to the **service( )** method:

```
<%
String test = "test value";
%>
```

Similarly, any variables that are defined with a JSP declaration are local to the **service( )** method:

```
<%! String test = "test value"; %>
```

Also, all of the implicit JSP objects, such as **application**, **request**, and **session**, are local to the resulting servlet's **service( )** method.

JSPs and servlets also have the notion of "scope" for variables, because some variables need to persist longer than the lifespan of a page request and some variables need to be accessible outside of a servlet's **service( )** method. There are four scopes that JSP variables can be placed in: application, page, request, and session. The following table explains each scope.

Scope	Description
application	Variables placed in this scope persist for the life of an application.
page	Variables placed in this scope persist until the current JSP's **service( )** method completes. Included JSPs cannot see page scope variables from the page including them. Also, this scope is exclusive to JSPs.
request	Variables placed in this scope persist until processing for the current request is completed. This scope differs from page scope because multiple servlets may be executed during the lifespan of a request. Page scoped variables only persist for the execution of one servlet.
session	Variables placed in this scope persist until the current user's session is invalidated or expires. This scope is only valid if the JSP or servlet in question is participating in a session.

Note that variables must be explicitly placed into a scope, as shown here:

```
<%
request.setAttribute("reqScopeVar", "test");
%>
```

This snippet uses JSP's implicit **request** object to place a variable into request scope. Similarly, the following snippet uses JSP's implicit **session** object to place a variable into session scope:

```
<%
session.setAttribute("sesScopeVar", "test");
%>
```

Of course, variables can also be put into each of the scopes by JSP tag library tags as do many of the tags in the Bean Tag Library.

Using the Bean Tag Library

To use the Bean Tag Library in your Struts application, you need to include the following snippet in your Web Archive (**.war**) deployment descriptor, **web.xml**:

```
<taglib>
  <taglib-uri>/WEB-INF/tlds/struts-bean.tld</taglib-uri>
  <taglib-location>/WEB-INF/tlds/struts-bean.tld</taglib-location>
</taglib>
```

Remember from the review of the **web.xml** file in Chapter 2 that the **<taglib-uri>** tag is used to declare the URI (or alias) that will be referenced in each of your JSPs with a **taglib** directive. The **<taglib-location>** tag is used to declare the actual location of the Tag Library Descriptor (**.tld**) file in your Web Archive.

The following snippet illustrates how your JSPs will declare their use of the Bean Tag Library with a JSP **taglib** directive:

```
<%@ taglib uri="/WEB-INF/tlds/struts-bean.tld" prefix="bean" %>
```

Notice that the **uri** attribute specified here is the same as that declared with the **<taglib-uri>** tag in the **web.xml** file. Also, notice that the **prefix** attribute is set to "bean." This attribute can be set to whatever you want; however, "bean" is the accepted default for the Bean Library. The **prefix** attribute declares the prefix that each tag must have when it is used in the JSP, as shown here:

```
<bean:write name="result" property="ssNum"/>
```

Because "bean" was defined as the prefix, the **write** tag was used as shown. However, if you chose to use a prefix of "strutsbn", the tag would be used the following way:

```
<strutsbn:write name="result" property="ssNum"/>
```

The Bean Tag Library Tags

The following table lists each of the tags in the Bean Tag Library and a short description of each tag's purpose.

Tag	Description
cookie	Used to store a reference to an HTTP cookie (**javax.servlet.http.Cookie**) from the incoming request in a JSP scripting variable with page scope.
define	Used to store a reference to a new or existing object in a JSP scripting variable.
header	Used to store an HTTP header from the incoming request as a **String** object in a JSP scripting variable with page scope.
include	Used to perform a request to a page and store the contents as a **String** object in a JSP scripting variable with page scope.
message	Used to retrieve an internationalized message from Struts' **ApplicationResources.properties** file and render it to a JSP's output stream.

Tag	Description
page	Used to store one of a JSP's implicit objects in a JSP scripting variable with page scope.
parameter	Used to store a parameter from the incoming request as a **String** object in a JSP scripting variable with page scope.
resource	Used to load the contents of a Web application resource and store them as a **String** object in a JSP scripting variable with page scope.
size	Used to store the size (number of elements) of an array, **java.util.Collection**-based object, or **java.util.Map**-based object as a **java.lang.Integer** in a JSP scripting variable with page scope.
struts	Used to store a reference to a Struts configuration object in a JSP scripting variable with page scope.
write	Used to render the value of an object to a JSP's output stream.

Following is a dedicated section for each tag, including a complete description of the tag, a table listing each of the tag's attributes, and a usage example for the tag. In the tables that describe each tag's attributes, pay special attention to the Accepts Scriptlet and Required columns. The Required column simply denotes whether or not the given attribute is required when using the tag. If an attribute is required and you do not specify it when using the tag, the tag will throw a **javax.servlet.jsp.JspException** at run time. Note that you can declare an error page in your JSP with a **page** directive to capture any **JspException**s that might be thrown, as shown here:

```
<%@ page errorPage="error.jsp" %>
```

If an exception occurs, the page specified by the **errorPage** attribute will be internally redirected to display an error page.

The Accepts Scriptlet column denotes whether or not the given attribute's value can be specified with a JSP scriptlet. If a JSP scriptlet is used to specify an attribute value, the scriptlet must comprise the complete value, quote (") to quote ("), as shown here.

Correct:

```
<bean:cookie id="category" name="<%=catName%>"/>
```

Incorrect:

```
<bean:cookie id="category" name="<%=catName%>-cat"/>
```

Notice in the incorrect example that "-cat" is used as part of the value for the **name** attribute following the scriptlet. This is invalid because there are extra characters between the end of the scriptlet and the ending quote.

A corrected version of the incorrect example follows:

```
<bean:cookie id="category" name="<%=catName + "-cat"%>"/>
```

The concatenation of "-cat" is now part of the scriptlet and the scriptlet comprises the complete value for the attribute.

The cookie Tag

The **cookie** tag is used to store a reference to an HTTP cookie (**javax.servlet.http.Cookie**) from the incoming request in a JSP scripting variable with page scope. Additionally, the **cookie** tag can be used to store multiple cookies of the same name if the **multiple** attribute is specified. For example, if the incoming request has two cookies that are both named "category", a **Cookie[ ]** array would be used to capture each cookie value and then the array would be stored in the specified JSP variable.

If the incoming request does not include a cookie with the specified **name** attribute and the **value** attribute is not specified, a **JspException** will be thrown by this tag at run time.

Attributes

Attribute	Description	Accepts Scriptlet	Required
id	Specifies the name of the JSP variable that will hold the specified HTTP cookie(s).	No	Yes
multiple	Accepts an arbitrary value to denote that multiple cookies should be stored. If specified, cookies will be stored in a **Cookie[ ]** array. If not specified and multiple cookies have the same name, the first cookie with the name specified will be stored.	Yes	No
name	Specifies the name of the HTTP cookie(s) to store in the JSP variable.	Yes	Yes

Attribute	Description	Accepts Scriptlet	Required
value	If the cookie specified with the **name** attribute is not found and this attribute is specified, a new **Cookie** object will be created and assigned the value of this attribute.	Yes	No

Example Usage

The following snippet shows a basic usage of the **cookie** tag:

```
<bean:cookie id="category" name="cat" value="default"/>
```

This example attempts to find a cookie named "cat" in the incoming request and store a reference to it in a variable named "category". If the cookie is not in the request, a new cookie will be created and assigned the value of "default". This new cookie will then have a reference stored to it.

After you have used the **cookie** tag to store a cookie, you can access it with the following snippet:

```
Category Cookie: <%=category.getValue()%>
```

This snippet simply uses a JSP expression to render the value of the **Cookie** object stored in the **category** variable. Additionally, because the **cookie** tag places the **category** variable in page scope, it can be accessed by other tags, as shown here:

```
Category Cookie: <bean:write name="category" property="value"/>
```

The following snippet shows an example of using the **cookie** tag for multiple cookies with the same name:

```
<bean:cookie id="category" name="cat" multiple="true"/>
```

The **multiple** attribute accepts arbitrary values; thus, you could use "true" as shown in the example, or any other value. As long as a value is present, a **Cookie[ ]** array will be used to store the cookies. To access the first cookie stored when using the **multiple** attribute, use the following snippet:

```
Category Cookie: <%=category[0].getValue()%>
```

The define Tag

The **define** tag is used to store a reference to an existing object in a JSP scripting variable. This tag can also be used to create a new object (of type **String**), whose reference will be stored in a JSP scripting variable. Additionally, the **define** tag allows you to specify what scope the object reference should be placed in.

There are four ways you can use the **define** tag, as listed here and shown later in the "Example Usage" section:

- You can use the **name** attribute to specify the name of the object to which a reference will be stored. This object can be in any scope or limited to a specific scope with the **scope** attribute.

- You can use the **name** and **property** attributes in tandem to specify the name of an object and its field whose getter method will be called to return an object to which a reference will be stored. Again, the object specified by the **name** attribute can be in any scope or limited to a specific scope with the **scope** attribute.

- You can use the **value** attribute to specify a value that will be used to create a new **String** object whose reference will be stored.

- You can place text between opening and closing **define** tags that will be used to create a new **String** object whose reference will be stored.

If none of the aforementioned ways is used to specify the object whose reference should be stored, a **JspException** will be thrown by the tag at run time.

You may have noticed that this tag is similar to JSP's "built-in" **<jsp:useBean>** tag; however, it differs markedly, as described in this list:

- The **define** tag unconditionally creates (or replaces) a scripting variable with the specified **id** attribute.

- The **define** tag can create a scripting variable from one of an object's fields, as specified with the **property** attribute.

- The **define** tag can create a scripting variable from a literal string with use of the **value** attribute.

- The **define** tag does not support nested **<jsp:setProperty>** tags.

Attributes

Attribute	Description	Accepts Scriptlet	Required
id	Specifies the name of the JSP variable that will hold the specified object reference.	No	Yes
name	Specifies the name of the object to which a reference will be stored. If the **property** attribute is also specified, one of the fields of the object defined by this attribute will have its getter method called to return the object to which a reference will be stored.	Yes	No

Attribute	Description	Accepts Scriptlet	Required
property	Specifies the field of the object specified by the **name** attribute, whose getter method will be called to return the object to which a reference will be stored.	Yes	No
scope	Specifies the scope (application, page, request, or session) to look in for the object specified by the **name** attribute. If not specified, each scope will be searched, in this order: page, request, session, and then application.	Yes	No
toScope	Specifies the scope (application, page, request, or session) that the specified object reference should be stored in.	Yes	No
type	Specifies the fully qualified class type (e.g., **java.lang.Integer**) of the object being stored as a scripting variable. If not specified, defaults to **java.lang.String** if you specify a **value** attribute; otherwise, defaults to **java.lang.Object**.	Yes	No
value	Specifies a value that will be used to create a new **String** object whose reference will be stored.	Yes	No

Example Usage

As mentioned, there are four ways you can use the **define** tag. The first way, shown here, uses the **name** attribute to specify the name of the object to which a reference will be stored:

```
<bean:define id="name" name="nameObj"/>
```

Of course, this example assumes you have an object in some scope with the name "nameObj". Remember that you can explicitly specify the scope of the object with the **scope** attribute.

The second way to use the **define** tag is shown here:

```
<bean:define id="name" name="nameObj" property="nameField"/>
```

In this example, the **name** and **property** attributes are used in tandem to specify the name of an object and its field whose getter method will be called to return an object to which a reference will be stored. Again, you can explicitly specify the scope of the object with the **scope** attribute.

The third way to use the **define** tag is shown here:

```
<bean:define id="name" value="James"/>
```

In this example, the **value** attribute is used to specify the value for a new **String** object whose reference will be stored.

The following is the fourth and final way to use the **define** tag:

```
<bean:define id="name">James</bean:define>
```

This example uses the nested string between the opening and closing **define** tags to specify a value for a new **String** object whose reference will be stored.

After you have used the **define** tag to store a reference to an object, you can access it with the following snippet:

```
Name: <%=name%>
```

This snippet simply uses a JSP expression to render the value of the object stored in the **name** variable. Additionally, because the **define** tag places the **name** variable into a scope, it can be accessed by other tags, as shown here:

```
Name: <bean:write name="name"/>
```

The header Tag

The **header** tag is used to store a reference to an HTTP header from the incoming request as a **String** object in a JSP scripting variable with page scope. Additionally, the **header** tag can be used to store multiple headers of the same name if the **multiple** attribute is specified. For example, if the incoming request has two headers that are both named "Accept-Language", a **String[ ]** array would be used to capture each header value and then the array would be stored in the specified JSP variable.

For more information on the HTTP protocol and its headers, visit the World Wide Web Consortium (W3C) page located at **http://www.w3.org/Protocols/HTTP/**.

If the incoming request does not include a header with the specified **name** attribute and the **value** attribute is not specified, a **JspException** will be thrown by this tag at run time.

Attributes

Attribute	Description	Accepts Scriptlet	Required
id	Specifies the name of the JSP variable that will hold the specified HTTP header(s).	No	Yes

Attribute	Description	Accepts Scriptlet	Required
multiple	Accepts an arbitrary value to denote that multiple headers should be stored. If specified, headers will be stored in a **String[ ]** array. If not specified and multiple headers have the same name, the first header with the name specified will be stored.	Yes	No
name	Specifies the name of the HTTP header(s) to store in the JSP variable.	Yes	Yes
value	Specifies the default value to assign to the **String** object being placed in the JSP variable if the specified header is not present in the incoming request.	Yes	No

Example Usage

The following snippet shows a basic usage of the **header** tag:

```
<bean:header id="browser" name="User-Agent" value="unknown"/>
```

This example attempts to find an HTTP header named "User-Agent" in the incoming request and store a reference to it in a variable named "browser". If the header is not in the request, a new **String** object will be created and have the value of the **value** attribute assigned to it. A reference to the **String** will then be stored.

After you have used the **header** tag to store a header, you can access it with the following snippet:

```
This page was requested using: <%=browser%>
```

This snippet simply uses a JSP expression to render the value of the **browser** variable. Additionally, because the **header** tag places the **browser** variable in page scope, it can be accessed by other tags, as shown here:

```
This page was requested using: <bean:write name="browser"/>
```

The following snippet shows an example of using the **header** tag for multiple headers with the same name:

```
<bean:header id="languages" name="Accept-Language" multiple="true"/>
```

Remember that the **multiple** attribute accepts an arbitrary value; thus, you could use "true" as shown in the example, or any other value. As long as a value is present, a **String[ ]** array will be used to store the headers. To access the first header stored when using the **multiple** attribute, use the following snippet:

```
First Language: <%=languages[0]%>
```

The include Tag

The **include** tag is used to perform a request to a page and store the contents as a **String** object in a JSP scripting variable with page scope. This tag is similar to JSP's built-in **<jsp:include>** tag; however, it differs because it stores the contents of the included page in a scripting variable instead of writing the contents to the JSP output.

There are three ways you can use the **include** tag, as listed here and shown later in the "Example Usage" section:

- You can use the **forward** attribute to specify the name of a forward, from the Global Forwards Configuration section of the Struts configuration file, which contains the URL of the page whose contents should be stored.
- You can use the **href** attribute to specify the absolute URL of the page whose contents should be stored.
- You can use the **page** attribute to specify an application-relative URL whose contents should be stored.

Attributes

Attribute	Description	Accepts Scriptlet	Required
anchor	Specifies the anchor (e.g., "#bottom") to be added to the URL for this include. This value should be specified without the leading hash (#) character.	Yes	No
forward	Specifies the name of a forward, from the Global Forwards Configuration section of the Struts configuration file, which contains the URL of the page whose contents should be stored.	Yes	No

PART II

Attribute	Description	Accepts Scriptlet	Required
href	Specifies the absolute URL, including the protocol, of the page whose contents should be stored (e.g., http://www.yahoo.com).	Yes	No
id	Specifies the name of the JSP variable that will hold the contents of the specified page.	No	Yes
name	Deprecated Use the **page** attribute instead.	Yes	No
page	Specifies the application-relative URL (starts with a leading slash, /) of the page whose contents should be stored.	Yes	No
transaction	Accepts "true" or "false" to denote whether or not you want the current transaction token included in the URL for this include.	Yes	No

Example Usage

As mentioned, there are three ways you can use the **include** tag. The first way, shown here, uses the **forward** attribute to specify the name of a forward, from the Global Forwards Configuration section of the Struts configuration file, whose contents will be stored:

```
<bean:include id="searchPageContents" forward="search"/>
```

The following is the second way to use the **include** tag:

```
<bean:include id="yahooContents" href="http://www.yahoo.com/"/>
```

This example uses the **href** attribute to specify the absolute URL of a page whose contents will be stored.

The third way to use the **include** tag is shown here:

```
<bean:include id="searchPageContents" page="/search.jsp"/>
```

In this example, the **page** attribute is used to specify an application-relative URL whose contents will be stored.

The message Tag

The **message** tag is used to retrieve an internationalized message from Struts' **ApplicationResources.properties** file and render it to a JSP's output stream. Remember that Struts' **ApplicationResources.properties** file is based on Java's Resource Bundle functionality for externalizing and internationalizing application strings, messages, and labels. Following is a sample **ApplicationResources .properties** file:

```
# Label Resources
label.search.name=Name
label.search.ssNum=Social Security Number

# Error Resources
error.search.criteria.missing=<li>Search Criteria Missing</li>
error.search.ssNum.invalid=<li>Invalid Social Security Number</li>
errors.header=<font color="red"><b>Validation Error(s)</b></font><ul>
errors.footer=</ul><hr width="100%" size="1" noshade="true">
```

As you can see, the file is made up of key/value pairs. The **message** tag simply looks up a message with a given key and returns its matching value.

The **message** tag also allows you to insert content into messages at run time before they are rendered using *parametric replacement,* which is the substitution of an argument for a placeholder parameter at run time. Following is an example message that uses parametric replacement:

```
missing.field=The {0} field is missing.
```

Notice the {0} reference in the message. At run time, the {0} parameter will be replaced with another value. The **message** tag allows you to specify what the replacement values are by use of the **arg0** – **arg4** attributes. Thus, you can have up to five parametric replacements in a message with {0} – {4}.

There are three ways you can use the **message** tag, as listed here and shown later in the "Example Usage" section:

- You can specify a message's key with the **key** attribute.
- You can use the **name** attribute to specify the name of the object whose value will be used as the key for the message. This object can be in any scope or limited to a specific scope with the **scope** attribute.

- You can use the **name** and **property** attributes in tandem to specify the name of an object and its field whose getter method will be called to return an object whose value will be used as the key for the message. Again, the object specified by the **name** attribute can be in any scope or limited to a specific scope with the **scope** attribute.

If the specified message does not exist, a **JspException** will be thrown by this tag at run time.

Attributes

Attribute	Description	Accepts Scriptlet	Required
arg0	First parametric replacement value as specified by {0} in the message to be rendered.	Yes	No
arg1	Second parametric replacement value as specified by {1} in the message to be rendered.	Yes	No
arg2	Third parametric replacement value as specified by {2} in the message to be rendered.	Yes	No
arg3	Fourth parametric replacement value as specified by {3} in the message to be rendered.	Yes	No
arg4	Fifth parametric replacement value as specified by {4} in the message to be rendered.	Yes	No
bundle	Specifies the name of the application scoped **org.apache.struts.util .MessageResources** object that contains the messages to be rendered. Defaults to the value stored in the **org.apache.struts.Globals .MESSAGES_KEY** constant.	Yes	No
key	Specifies the name of the key whose corresponding value will be rendered.	Yes	No

Attribute	Description	Accepts Scriptlet	Required
locale	Specifies the name of the session scoped **java.util.Locale** object to use for selecting which message to render. Defaults to the value stored in the **org.apache.struts .Globals.LOCALE_KEY** constant.	Yes	No
name	Specifies the name of the object whose value will be used as the key for the message. If the **property** attribute is also specified, one of the fields of the object defined by this attribute will have its getter method called to return the object whose value will be used as the key for the message.	Yes	No
property	Specifies the field, of the object specified by the **name** attribute, whose getter method will be called to return the object whose value will be used as the key for the message.	Yes	No
scope	Specifies the scope (application, page, request, or session) to look in for the object specified by the **name** attribute. If not specified, each scope will be searched, in this order: page, request, session, and then application.	Yes	No

Example Usage

As mentioned, there are three ways you can use the **message** tag. The first way, shown here, uses the **key** attribute to specify the key for the message that will be rendered:

```
<bean:message key="label.search.name"/>
```

The following is the second way to use the **message** tag:

```
<bean:message name="keyObj"/>
```

This example uses the **name** attribute to specify the name of an object whose value will be used as the key for the message. Remember that you can explicitly specify the scope of the object with the **scope** attribute.

The third way to use the **message** tag is shown here:

```
<bean:message name="keyObj" property="keyField"/>
```

In this example, the **name** and **property** attributes are used in tandem to specify the name of an object and its field whose getter method will be called to return an object whose value will be used as the key for the message. Again, you can explicitly specify the scope of the object with the **scope** attribute.

The page Tag

The **page** tag is used to store one of a JSP's implicit objects in a JSP scripting variable with page scope. By default, a JSP's implicit objects cannot be "seen" by JSP tag library tags because they are not stored in a scope. Remember that JSPs get converted into a servlet and then compiled into a class file before they are run. JSP implicit objects are simply local variables in a servlet's **service( )** method. For this reason, JSP tag library tags cannot "see" the objects. However, JSP tag library tags can access objects that have been stored in a scope, thus the reason for the **page** tag.

The **page** tag works with the following implicit JSP objects:

- application
- config
- request
- response
- session

One of the aforementioned objects must be specified with the **property** attribute or this tag will throw a **JspException** at run time.

Attributes

Attribute	Description	Accepts Scriptlet	Required
id	Specifies the name of the JSP variable that will hold the specified JSP implicit object.	No	Yes
property	Specifies the name of the JSP implicit object to store in the JSP variable. Must be application, config, request, response, or session.	Yes	Yes

Example Usage

The following snippet shows a basic usage of the **page** tag:

```
<bean:page id="cfg" property="config"/>
```

This example simply stores a reference to the implicit **config** object in a page scope variable named "cfg".

After you have used the **page** tag to store a JSP implicit object, you can use it with a JSP tag library tag as shown here:

```
<bean:write name="cfg" property="servletName"/>
```

Remember that the **write** tag wouldn't be able to see the implicit **config** object without the use of the **page** tag.

The parameter Tag

The **parameter** tag is used to store a parameter from the incoming request as a **String** object in a JSP scripting variable with page scope. Additionally, the **parameter** tag can be used to store multiple parameters of the same name if the **multiple** attribute is specified. For example, if the incoming request has two parameters that are both named "color", a **String[ ]** array would be used to capture each parameter value and then the array would be stored in the specified JSP variable.

If the incoming request does not include a parameter with the specified **name** attribute and the **value** attribute is not specified, a **JspException** will be thrown by this tag at run time.

PART II

Attributes

Attribute	Description	Accepts Scriptlet	Required
id	Specifies the name of the JSP variable that will hold the specified parameter(s).	No	Yes
multiple	Accepts an arbitrary value to denote that multiple parameters should be stored. If specified, parameters will be stored in a **String[ ]** array. If not specified and multiple parameters have the same name, the first parameter with the name specified will be stored.	Yes	No
name	Specifies the name of the parameter(s) to store in the JSP variable.	Yes	Yes
value	Specifies the default value to assign to the **String** object being placed in the JSP variable if the specified parameter is not present in the incoming request.	Yes	No

Example Usage

The following snippet shows a basic usage of the **parameter** tag:

```
<bean:parameter id="color" name="clr" value="none"/>
```

This example attempts to find a parameter named "clr" in the incoming request and store a reference to it in a variable named "color". If the parameter is not in the request, a new **String** object will be created and have the value of the **value** attribute assigned to it. A reference to the **String** will then be stored.

After you have used the **parameter** tag to store a parameter, you can access it with the following snippet:

```
Color Request Parameter: <%=color%>
```

This snippet simply uses a JSP expression to render the value of the **color** variable. Additionally, because the **parameter** tag places the **color** variable in page scope, it can be accessed by JSP tag library tags, as shown here:

```
Color Request Parameter: <bean:write name="color"/>
```

The following snippet shows an example of using the **parameter** tag for multiple parameters with the same name:

```
<bean:parameter id="color" name="clr" multiple="true" value="none"/>
```

Remember that the **multiple** attribute accepts an arbitrary value; thus, you could use "true" as shown in the example, or any other value. As long as a value is present, a **String[ ]** array will be used to store the parameters. To access the first parameter stored when using the **multiple** attribute, use the following snippet:

```
First Color: <%=color[0]%>
```

The resource Tag

The **resource** tag is used to load the contents of a Web application resource and store them as a **String** object in a JSP scripting variable with page scope. Additionally, you have the option of specifying whether or not you simply want a **java.io.InputStream** reference for the resource instead of storing its contents in a **String**.

Web application resources are those files that are packaged as part of a Web application. For example, if your Web application is housed in a directory called **c:\java\MiniHR** and has the following files

- c:\java\MiniHR\index.jsp
- c:\java\MiniHR\WEB-INF\struts-config.xml
- c:\java\MiniHR\WEB-INF\web.xml

then you can access the **index.jsp** file as "/index.jsp." Similarly, you can access the **struts-config.xml** file as "/WEB-INF/struts-config.xml." Note that Web application resource paths are relative to the application and must begin with a leading slash (/).

A **JspException** will be thrown by the **resource** tag at run time if there is a problem loading the resource.

Attributes

Attribute	Description	Accepts Scriptlet	Required
id	Specifies the name of the JSP variable that will hold the contents of the specified resource.	No	Yes
input	Accepts an arbitrary value to denote that a **java.io.InputStream** reference for the resource should be stored in the JSP variable instead of storing the contents of the resource in a **String**.	Yes	No
name	Specifies the path of the Web application resource that will be loaded. The path must begin with a leading slash (/).	Yes	Yes

Example Usage

The following snippet shows how you could use the **resource** tag to load the contents of a **struts-config.xml** file:

```
<bean:resource id="strutsConfig" name="/WEB-INF/struts-config.xml"/>
```

After you have used the **resource** tag to load the contents of the Struts configuration file, you can access them with the following snippet:

```
Struts Config file contents: <%=strutsConfig%>
```

This snippet simply uses a JSP expression to render the value of the **String** object stored in the **strutsConfig** variable. Additionally, because the **resource** tag places the **strutsConfig** variable in page scope, it can be accessed by JSP tag library tags, as shown here:

```
Struts Config file: <bean:write name="strutsConfig"/>
```

The following snippet shows how to use the **resource** tag to obtain a **java.io. InputStream** reference for a Web application resource:

```
<bean:resource id="strutsConfig"
            input="true"
            name="/WEB-INF/struts-config.xml"/>
```

Remember that the **input** attribute accepts arbitrary values; thus, you could use "true" as shown in the example, or any other value. As long as a value is present, a **java.io.InputStream** reference will be stored in the JSP variable instead of a **String** containing the contents of the resource file.

As you can imagine, using the **resource** tag is significantly cleaner and less involved than using a scriptlet to load the contents of a Web application resource.

The size Tag

The **size** tag is used to store the size (number of elements) of an array, **java.util .Collection**-based object, or **java.util.Map**-based object as a **java.lang.Integer** in a JSP scripting variable with page scope. This tag is especially useful when used in conjunction with tags in the Logic Tag Library. For example, you could use this tag to determine the size of a collection and then use the Logic Library's **iterate** tag to iterate over each item in the collection.

There are three ways you can specify which collection's size to store, as listed here and shown later in the "Example Usage" section:

- You can use the **collection** attribute to specify a scriptlet that evaluates to a collection object.

- You can use the **name** attribute to specify the name of a collection object that can be in any scope or limited to a specific scope with the **scope** attribute.

- You can use the **name** and **property** attributes in tandem to specify the name of an object and its field whose getter method will be called to return a collection object. Again, the object specified by the **name** attribute can be in any scope or limited to a specific scope with the **scope** attribute.

Note that if none of the aforementioned ways is used to specify the collection whose size should be taken, a **JspException** will be thrown by this tag at run time.

Attributes

Attribute	Description	Accepts Scriptlet	Required
collection	Specifies a scriptlet that evaluates to an array, **java.util.Collection**-based object, or **java.util.Map**-based object.	Yes	No

Attribute	Description	Accepts Scriptlet	Required
id	Specifies the name of the JSP variable that will hold the size value (**java.lang.Integer**).	No	Yes
name	Specifies the name of the object that contains the collection whose size will be taken. If the **property** attribute is also specified, one of the fields of the object defined by this attribute will have its getter method called to return the collection whose size will be taken.	Yes	No
property	Specifies the field, of the object specified by the **name** attribute, whose getter method will be called to return the collection whose size will be taken.	Yes	No
scope	Specifies the scope (application, page, request, or session) to look in for the object specified by the **name** attribute. If not specified, each scope will be searched, in this order: page, request, session, and then application.	Yes	No

Example Usage

As mentioned, there are three basic ways you can use the **size** tag. The first way, shown here, uses the **collection** attribute to specify which collection's size to store:

```
<%
// Example array.
String[] genders = {"male", "female"};
%>

<bean:size id="genderCount" collection="<%=genders%>"/>
```

Remember that the **collection** attribute only accepts a scriptlet as a value. Because the **collection** attribute was used to specify the collection whose size will be taken, variables that are not in any particular scope can be accessed by the tag by way of a scriptlet. The following two ways of using the **size** tag require the collection whose size is being taken to be in a scope.

The second way to use the **size** tag is shown here:

```
<%
// Example Collection.
ArrayList genders = new ArrayList();
genders.add("male");
genders.add("female");
pageContext.setAttribute("genders", genders);
%>

<bean:size id="genderCount" name="genders"/>
```

In this example, the **name** attribute is used to specify the name of a JSP scripting variable that has a collection in it. Remember that all scopes will be searched in succession (page then request then session then application) to find the specified object. Optionally, you can use the **scope** attribute to explicitly tell the tag which scope to look in for the collection.

The third and final way to use the **size** tag is shown here:

```
<bean:size id="genderCount" name="employee" property="genders"/>
```

This example assumes you have an object named "employee" with a field called "genders". The object's **getGenders( )** method will be called to return a collection whose size will be taken.

After you have used the **size** tag to store a collection's size, you can access it with the following snippet:

```
Gender Count: <%=genderCount%>
```

This snippet simply uses a JSP expression to render the value of the **Integer** object stored in the **genderCount** variable. Additionally, because the **size** tag places the **genderCount** variable in page scope, it can be accessed by JSP tag library tags, as shown here:

```
Gender Count: <bean:write name="genderCount"/>
```

The struts Tag

The **struts** tag is used to store a reference to a Struts configuration object in a JSP scripting variable with page scope. When Strut's **ActionServlet** initializes, it loads in **struts-config.xml** files and creates an internal representation of the configuration settings with configuration objects. The **struts** tag provides convenient access to the three most prominent of these configuration objects: **FormBeanConfig, ForwardConfig,** and **ActionConfig.**

Note that one of the **formBean, forward,** or **mapping** attributes must be specified when using this tag or a **JspException** will be thrown at run time. Additionally, a **JspException** will be thrown at run time if the specified configuration object cannot be found.

Attributes

Attribute	Description	Accepts Scriptlet	Required
formBean	Specifies the name of a **FormBean** whose **org.apache.struts.config .FormBeanConfig** object reference will be stored in the specified JSP scripting variable.	Yes	No
forward	Specifies the name of a forward whose **org.apache.struts.config .ForwardConfig** object reference will be stored in the specified JSP scripting variable.	Yes	No
id	Specifies the name of the JSP variable that will hold the reference to the specified Struts configuration object.	No	Yes
mapping	Specifies the name of an **Action** whose **org.apache.struts.config .ActionConfig** object reference will be stored in the specified JSP scripting variable.	Yes	No

Example Usage

Before you examine the **struts** tag usage, review the following sample Struts configuration file. Each of the following examples is based on this configuration file.

```
<?xml version="1.0"?>

<!DOCTYPE struts-config PUBLIC
   "-//Apache Software Foundation//DTD Struts Configuration 1.1//EN"
```

```
    "http://jakarta.apache.org/struts/dtds/struts-config_1_1.dtd">

<struts-config>

  <!-- Form Beans Configuration -->
  <form-beans>
    <form-bean name="searchForm"
               type="com.jamesholmes.minihr.SearchForm"/>
  </form-beans>

  <!-- Global Forwards Configuration -->
  <global-forwards>
    <forward name="search" path="/search.jsp"/>
  </global-forwards>

  <!-- Action Mappings Configuration -->
  <action-mappings>
    <action path="/search"
            type="com.jamesholmes.minihr.SearchAction"
            name="searchForm"
            scope="request"
            validate="true"
            input="/search.jsp">
    </action>
  </action-mappings>

  <!-- Message Resources Configuration -->
  <message-resources
    parameter="com.jamesholmes.minihr.ApplicationResources"/>

</struts-config>
```

There are three ways to use the **struts** tag. The first way, shown here, is used to store a reference to a **FormBean** configuration object:

```
<bean:struts id="cfg" formBean="searchForm"/>
```

Notice that the value used for the **formBean** attribute matches the value given to the **name** attribute of the **<form-bean>** tag in the Struts configuration file shown earlier.

The second way to use the **struts** tag, shown next, stores a reference to a forward configuration object:

```
<bean:struts id="cfg" forward="search"/>
```

Again, notice in this example that the value used for the **forward** attribute matches the value given to the **name** attribute of the **<forward>** tag in the Struts configuration file shown earlier.

The third way to use the **struts** tag stores a reference to an **Action** configuration object, as shown here:

```
<bean:struts id="cfg" mapping="/search"/>
```

Similar to the previous two examples, the value used for the **mapping** attribute matches the value given to the **path** attribute of the **<action>** tag in the Struts configuration file shown earlier.

Because the **struts** tag stores configuration object references in page scope, the objects can be accessed both with scriptlets and JSP tag library tags.

The write Tag

The **write** tag is used to render the value of an object to a JSP's output stream. Additionally, this tag can optionally format the value of the object before it is rendered by use of the **format** attribute.

There are two ways you can use the **write** tag, as listed here and shown later in the "Example Usage" section:

- You can use the **name** attribute to specify the name of any object to render. This object can be in any scope or limited to a specific scope with the **scope** attribute.

- You can use the **name** and **property** attributes in tandem to specify the name of an object and its field whose getter method will be called to return an object to be rendered. Again, the object specified by the **name** attribute can be in any scope or limited to a specific scope with the **scope** attribute.

Attributes

Attribute	Description	Accepts Scriptlet	Required
bundle	Specifies the name of the application scoped **org.apache.struts.util .MessageResources** object that contains the format key/value pairs for the **formatKey** attribute. Defaults to the value stored in the **org.apache.struts.Globals .MESSAGES_KEY** constant.	Yes	No
filter	Accepts "true" or "false" to denote whether or not HTML-sensitive characters should be converted to their entity equivalents. For example, if this attribute is enabled, the less-than sign (<) would get converted to < before it is rendered. Defaults to "true."	Yes	No

Attribute	Description	Accepts Scriptlet	Required
format	Specifies the format string to use to convert the value being rendered. If not specified, **write** will try to use the **formatKey** attribute to look up the format string.	Yes	No
formatKey	Specifies the key for a format string to look up in Struts' **ApplicationResources.properties** file.	Yes	No
ignore	Accepts "true" or "false" to denote whether or not to skip throwing a **JspException**, similar to the other tags in this library, when the object specified by the **name** attribute is not found. Defaults to "false."	Yes	No
locale	Specifies the name of the session scoped **java.util.Locale** object to use when formatting values with the **format** attribute. Defaults to the value stored in the **org.apache.struts .Globals.LOCALE_KEY** constant.	Yes	No
name	Specifies the name of the object that will be rendered. If the **property** attribute is also specified, one of the fields of the object defined by this attribute will have its getter method called to return the object that will be rendered.	Yes	Yes
property	Specifies the field, of the object specified by the **name** attribute, whose getter method will be called to return the object that will be rendered.	Yes	No
scope	Specifies the scope (application, page, request, or session) to look in for the object specified by the **name** attribute. If not specified, each scope will be searched, in this order: page, request, session, and then application.	Yes	No

Example Usage

As mentioned, there are two ways you can use the **write** tag. The first way, shown here, uses the **name** attribute to specify the name of an object to be rendered. Remember that you can explicitly specify the scope of the object with the **scope** attribute.

```
<bean:write name="bizObj"/>
```

The following is the second way to use the **write** tag:

```
<bean:write name="bizObj" property="bizField"/>
```

In this example, the **name** and **property** attributes are used in tandem to specify the name of an object and its field whose getter method will be called to return an object to be rendered. Again, you can explicitly specify the scope of the object with the **scope** attribute.

The Logic Tag Library

The Logic Tag Library provides a rich set of tags for cleanly implementing simple conditional logic in JSPs. With these tags you can wrap content that will be processed only when a particular condition is true. For example, you can use the **equal** tag to wrap content that is conditionally processed based on whether two specified values are equal or not. The following snippet illustrates this:

```
<logic:equal name="resultCount" value="0">
Search returned no results.
</logic:equal>
```

If the object specified by the **name** attribute is equal to "0", as specified by the **value** attribute, then the content between the starting and ending **equal** tags will be processed. Otherwise, the content will be ignored.

Note that the Logic Library has two tags that are not used for conditional logic: the **iterate** tag and the **redirect** tag. The **iterate** tag is used to wrap content that should be processed for each element of a collection, and the **redirect** tag is used to send an HTTP redirect response to a browser, causing it to load another page.

Understanding Variables and Scope in JSPs

Before discussing each of the tags in this library, it's necessary to review how variables and scope work in JSPs. First, remember that JSPs get converted into servlets and then compiled before they are executed. All of the HTML and code inside the JSP gets placed into the generated servlet's **service( )** method. Because of this, any variables that get defined inside the JSP with a scriptlet, as shown here, are local to the **service( )** method:

```
<%
String test = "test value";
%>
```

Similarly, any variables that are defined with a JSP declaration are local to the **service( )** method:

```
<%! String test = "test value"; %>
```

Also, all of the implicit JSP objects, such as **application, request,** and **session,** are local to the resulting servlet's **service( )** method.

JSPs and servlets also have the notion of "scope" for variables, because some variables need to persist longer than the lifespan of a page request and some variables need to be accessible outside of a servlet's **service( )** method. There are four scopes that JSP variables can be placed in: application, page, request, and session. The following table explains each scope.

Scope	Description
application	Variables placed in this scope persist for the life of an application.
page	Variables placed in this scope persist until the current JSP's **service( )** method completes. Included JSPs cannot see page scope variables from the page including them. Also, this scope is exclusive to JSPs.
request	Variables placed in this scope persist until processing for the current request is completed. This scope differs from page scope because multiple servlets may be executed during the lifespan of a request. Page scope variables persist only for the execution of one servlet.
session	Variables placed in this scope persist until the current user's session is invalidated or expires. This scope is valid only if the JSP or servlet in question is participating in a session.

Note that variables must be explicitly placed into a scope, as shown here:

```
<%
request.setAttribute("reqScopeVar", "test");
%>
```

This snippet uses JSP's implicit **request** object to place a variable into request scope. Similarly, the following snippet uses JSP's implicit **session** object to place a variable into session scope:

```
<%
session.setAttribute("sesScopeVar", "test");
%>
```

Of course, variables can also be put into each of the scopes by JSP tag library tags as many of the tags in the Logic Tag Library do.

Using the Logic Tag Library

To use the Logic Tag Library in a Struts application, you need to include the following snippet in your Web Archive (**.war**) deployment descriptor, **web.xml**:

```
<taglib>
  <taglib-uri>/WEB-INF/tlds/struts-logic.tld</taglib-uri>
  <taglib-location>/WEB-INF/tlds/struts-logic.tld</taglib-location>
</taglib>
```

Recall from the overview of the **web.xml** file in Chapter 2 that the **<taglib-uri>** tag is used to declare the URI (or alias) that will be referenced in each of your JSPs with a **taglib** directive. The **<taglib-location>** tag is used to declare the actual location of the Tag Library Descriptor (**.tld**) file in your Web Archive.

The following snippet illustrates how your JSPs will declare their use of the Logic Tag Library with a JSP **taglib** directive:

```
<%@ taglib uri="/WEB-INF/tlds/struts-logic.tld" prefix="logic" %>
```

Notice that the **uri** attribute specified here is the same as that declared with the **<taglib-uri>** tag in the **web.xml** file. Also, notice that the **prefix** attribute is set to "logic". This attribute can be set to whatever you want; however, "logic" is the accepted default for the Logic Library. The **prefix** attribute declares the prefix that each tag must have when it is used in the JSP, as shown here:

```
<logic:present name="searchForm" property="results">
```

Because "logic" was defined as the prefix, the **present** tag was used as shown. However, if you chose to use a prefix of "strutslgc", the tag would be used the following way:

```
<strutslgc:present name="searchForm" property="results">
```

The Logic Tag Library Tags

The following table lists each of the tags in the Logic Tag Library and a short description of each tag's purpose.

Tag	Description
empty	Wraps content that is conditionally processed based on whether or not the specified object is **null** or contains an empty (zero length) **String**.
equal	Wraps content that is conditionally processed based on whether or not a specified object's value equals a specified constant value.

Tag	Description
forward	Looks up a forward from the Struts configuration file and redirects to it.
greaterEqual	Wraps content that is conditionally processed based on whether or not a specified object's value is greater than or equal to a specified constant value.
greaterThan	Wraps content that is conditionally processed based on whether or not a specified object's value is greater than a specified constant value.
iterate	Wraps content that is repeated for each element of a specified collection.
lessEqual	Wraps content that is conditionally processed based on whether or not a specified object's value is less than or equal to a specified constant value.
lessThan	Wraps content that is conditionally processed based on whether or not a specified object's value is less than a specified constant value.
match	Wraps content that is conditionally processed based on whether or not a specified object's value contains, starts with, or ends with a specified constant value.
messagesNotPresent	Wraps content that is conditionally processed based on whether or not Struts' **org.apache.struts.action.ActionErrors** or **org.apache.struts.action.ActionMessages** objects do not have any errors or messages in them, respectively.
messagesPresent	Wraps content that is conditionally processed based on whether or not Struts' **org.apache.struts.action.ActionErrors** or **org.apache.struts.action.ActionMessages** objects have any errors or messages in them, respectively.
notEmpty	Wraps content that is conditionally processed based on whether or not the specified object is non-**null** and does not contain an empty (zero length) **String**.
notEqual	Wraps content that is conditionally processed based on whether or not a specified object's value is not equal to a specified constant value.
notMatch	Wraps content that is conditionally processed based on whether or not a specified object's value does not contain, start with, or end with a specified constant value.
notPresent	Wraps content that is conditionally processed based on whether or not a specified object does not exist.
present	Wraps content that is conditionally processed based on whether or not a specified object exists.
redirect	Composes a URL to another page and then redirects to it.

The remainder of this chapter discusses each tag in detail, including a complete description of the tag, a table listing each of the tag's attributes, and a usage example for the tag. In the tables that describe each tag's attributes, pay special attention to the Required and Accepts Scriptlet columns.

The Required column simply denotes whether or not the given attribute is required when using the tag. If an attribute is required and you do not specify it when using the tag, the tag will throw a **javax.servlet.jsp.JspException** at run time. Note that you can declare an error page in your JSP with a **page** directive to capture any **JspException**s that might be thrown, as shown here:

```
<%@ page errorPage="error.jsp" %>
```

If an exception occurs, the page specified by the **errorPage** attribute will be internally redirected to display an error page.

The Accepts Scriptlet column denotes whether or not the given attribute's value can be specified with a JSP scriptlet. If a JSP scriptlet is used to specify an attribute value, the scriptlet must comprise the complete value, quote (") to quote ("), as shown here.

Correct:

```
<logic:present name="<%=result%>">
```

Incorrect:

```
<logic:present name="<%=result%>-result">
```

Notice in the incorrect example that "-result" is used as part of the value for the **name** attribute following the scriptlet. This is invalid because there are extra characters between the end of the scriptlet and the ending quote.

A corrected version of the incorrect example follows:

```
<logic:present name="<%=result + "-result"%>"/>
```

The concatenation of "-result" is now part of the scriptlet and the scriptlet comprises the complete value for the attribute.

The empty Tag

The **empty** tag wraps content that is conditionally processed based on whether or not the specified object is **null** or contains an empty (zero length) **String**. Additionally, if the object specified implements **java.util.Collection** or **java.util.Map**, this tag will call the object's **isEmpty( )** method to determine whether or not the object is empty. If the object is empty, then the wrapped content will be processed.

Attributes

Attribute	Description	Accepts Scriptlet	Required
name	Specifies the name of an object to check as being empty. If the **property** attribute is also specified, one of the fields of the object defined by this attribute will have its getter method called to return an object to check as being empty.	Yes	No
property	Specifies the field of the object specified by the **name** attribute whose getter method will be called to return an object to check as being empty.	Yes	No
scope	Specifies the scope (application, page, request, or session) to look in for the object specified by the **name** attribute. If not specified, each scope will be searched, in this order: page, request, session, and then application.	Yes	No

Example Usage

There are two ways you can use the **empty** tag. The first way, shown here, uses the **name** attribute to specify the name of an object to check as being empty:

```
<logic:empty name="results">
Your search yielded no results.
</logic:empty>
```

If the **results** object is **null**, contains a zero-length string, or contains a **Collection** or **Map** with zero elements, then the content between the starting and ending **empty** tags will be processed. Remember that you can explicitly specify the scope of the object with the **scope** attribute.

The second way to use the **empty** tag is shown here:

```
<logic:empty name="bizObj" property="results">
Your search yielded no results.
</logic:empty>
```

In this example, the **name** and **property** attributes are used in tandem to specify the name of an object and its field whose getter method will be called to return an object to check as being empty. Again, you can explicitly specify the scope of the object with the **scope** attribute.

The equal Tag

The **equal** tag wraps content that is conditionally processed based on whether or not a specified object's value equals a specified constant value. This tag works for both numeric and string comparisons.

There are five ways you can use the **equal** tag, as listed here and shown later in the "Example Usage" section:

- You can use the **cookie** attribute to specify the name of an HTTP cookie from the incoming request whose value will be used for the comparison.
- You can use the **header** attribute to specify the name of an HTTP header from the incoming request whose value will be used for the comparison.
- You can use the **parameter** attribute to specify the name of a parameter from the incoming request whose value will be used for the comparison.
- You can use the **name** attribute to specify the name of an object whose value will be used for the comparison. This object can be in any scope or limited to a specific scope with the **scope** attribute.
- You can use the **name** and **property** attributes in tandem to specify the name of an object and its field whose getter method will be called to return an object whose value will be used for the comparison. Again, the object specified by the **name** attribute can be in any scope or limited to a specific scope with the **scope** attribute.

Attributes

Attribute	Description	Accepts Scriptlet	Required
cookie	Specifies the name of the HTTP cookie from the incoming request whose value is used for comparison.	Yes	No
header	Specifies the name of the HTTP header from the incoming request whose value is used for comparison.	Yes	No
name	Specifies the name of an object whose value is used for comparison. If the **property** attribute is also specified, one of the fields of the object defined by this attribute will have its getter method called to return an object whose value is used for comparison.	Yes	No
parameter	Specifies the name of the parameter from the incoming request whose value is used for comparison.	Yes	No
property	Specifies the field of the object specified by the **name** attribute whose getter method will be called to return an object whose value is used for comparison.	Yes	No

Attribute	Description	Accepts Scriptlet	Required
scope	Specifies the scope (application, page, request, or session) to look in for the object specified by the **name** attribute. If not specified, each scope will be searched, in this order: page, request, session, and then application.	Yes	No
value	Specifies the constant value to which the value, specified by other attributes of this tag, will be compared.	Yes	Yes

Example Usage

As mentioned, there are five ways you can use the **equal** tag. The first way, shown here, uses the **cookie** attribute to specify the name of an HTTP cookie from the incoming request whose value is compared against the value specified with the **value** attribute:

```
<logic:equal cookie="role" value="Manager">
User is a Manager.
</logic:equal>
```

If the cookie's value and the **value** attribute's value are equal, the content between the starting and ending **equal** tags will be processed. Otherwise it will be ignored.

The second way to use the **equal** tag is shown here:

```
<logic:equal header="User-Agent" value="MSIE">
Browser is Internet Explorer.
</logic:equal>
```

This example compares the incoming request's User-Agent header against the **value** attribute to determine whether or not they are equal. If so, the content between the starting and ending **equal** tags will be processed.

The following is the third way to use the **equal** tag:

```
<logic:equal parameter="catId" value="10">
Category Id is 10.
</logic:equal>
```

This example compares a request parameter from the incoming request against the value of the **value** attribute. If the two values are equal, the content between the starting and ending **equal** tags will be processed.

The fourth way to use the **equal** tag is shown here:

```
<logic:equal name="resultCount" value="0">
Search returned no results.
</logic:equal>
```

This example compares the value of the **resultCount** object against the value of the **value** attribute. If the two values are equal, the content between the starting and ending **equal** tags will be processed. Remember that you can explicitly specify the scope of the **resultCount** object with the **scope** attribute.

The following is the fifth and final way to use the **equal** tag:

```
<logic:equal name="employee" property="name" value="Bob">
Hello, Bob!
</logic:equal>
```

In this example, the **name** and **property** attributes are used in tandem to specify the name of an object and its field whose getter method will be called to return an object whose value will be compared against that of the **value** attribute. Again, you can explicitly specify the scope of the object with the **scope** attribute.

The forward Tag

The **forward** tag looks up a forward from the Struts configuration file and redirects to it. Based on the way that the forward is defined in the configuration file, this tag will either forward to the URL specified by the forward or perform a redirect to it. If the forward has its **redirect** attribute set to "true", as shown in the following example, this tag will perform a redirect:

```
<forward name="google" path="http://www.google.com/" redirect="true"/>
```

A redirect sends a response to the user's browser instructing it to load another page. A forward, on the other hand, simply "forwards" control (on the server side) to another URL without having the browser make another request. Note that only URLs residing on the same server can be forwarded to, whereas any URL can be redirected to.

Attribute

Attribute	Description	Accepts Scriptlet	Required
name	Specifies the name of the forward to redirect to.	Yes	Yes

Example Usage

The following snippet shows how to use the **forward** tag:

```
<logic:forward name="search"/>
```

As you can see, this tag is very straightforward. All you have to do is specify the name of the forward to redirect to.

The greaterEqual Tag

The **greaterEqual** tag wraps content that is conditionally processed based on whether or not a specified object's value is greater than or equal to a specified constant value. Note that this tag works for both numeric and string comparisons.

There are five ways you can use the **greaterEqual** tag, as listed here and shown later in the "Example Usage" section:

- You can use the **cookie** attribute to specify the name of an HTTP cookie from the incoming request whose value will be used for the comparison.
- You can use the **header** attribute to specify the name of an HTTP header from the incoming request whose value will be used for the comparison.
- You can use the **parameter** attribute to specify the name of a parameter from the incoming request whose value will be used for the comparison.
- You can use the **name** attribute to specify the name of an object whose value will be used for the comparison. This object can be in any scope or limited to a specific scope with the **scope** attribute.
- You can use the **name** and **property** attributes in tandem to specify the name of an object and its field whose getter method will be called to return an object whose value will be used for the comparison. Again, the object specified by the **name** attribute can be in any scope or limited to a specific scope with the **scope** attribute.

Attributes

Attribute	Description	Accepts Scriptlet	Required
cookie	Specifies the name of the HTTP cookie from the incoming request whose value is used for comparison.	Yes	No
header	Specifies the name of the HTTP header from the incoming request whose value is used for comparison.	Yes	No
name	Specifies the name of an object whose value is used for comparison. If the **property** attribute is also specified, one of the fields of the object defined by this attribute will have its getter method called to return an object whose value is used for comparison.	Yes	No
parameter	Specifies the name of the parameter from the incoming request whose value is used for comparison.	Yes	No
property	Specifies the field of the object specified by the **name** attribute whose getter method will be called to return an object whose value is used for comparison.	Yes	No

Attribute	Description	Accepts Scriptlet	Required
scope	Specifies the scope (application, page, request, or session) to look in for the object specified by the **name** attribute. If not specified, each scope will be searched, in this order: page, request, session, and then application.	Yes	No
value	Specifies the constant value to which the value, specified by other attributes of this tag, will be compared.	Yes	Yes

Example Usage

As mentioned, there are five ways you can use the **greaterEqual** tag. The first way, shown here, uses the **cookie** attribute to specify the name of an HTTP cookie from the incoming request whose value is compared against the value specified with the **value** attribute:

```
<logic:greaterEqual cookie="size" value="0">
Size is valid.
</logic:greaterEqual>
```

If the cookie's value is greater than or equal to the **value** attribute's value, the content between the starting and ending **greaterEqual** tags will be processed. Otherwise it will be ignored.

The following is the second way to use the **greaterEqual** tag:

```
<logic:greaterEqual header="Content-Length" value="100000">
Page has large amount of content.
</logic:greaterEqual>
```

This example compares the incoming request's User-Agent header against the **value** attribute to determine whether or not it is greater than or equal to it. If so, the content between the starting and ending **greaterEqual** tags will be processed.

The third way to use the **greaterEqual** tag is shown here:

```
<logic:greaterEqual parameter="catId" value="10">
Category Id is greater than or equal to 10.
</logic:greaterEqual>
```

This example compares a request parameter from the incoming request against the value of the **value** attribute. If the parameter is greater than or equal to the value, the content between the starting and ending **greaterEqual** tags will be processed.

The fourth way to use the **greaterEqual** tag is shown here:

```
<logic:greaterEqual name="resultCount" value="1">
Search returned at least 1 result.
</logic:greaterEqual>
```

This example compares the value of the **resultCount** object against the value of the **value** attribute. If the **resultCount** object's value is greater than or equal to the value of the **value** attribute, the content between the starting and ending **greaterEqual** tags will be processed. Remember that you can explicitly specify the scope of the **resultCount** object with the **scope** attribute.

The following is the fifth and final way to use the **greaterEqual** tag:

```
<logic:greaterEqual name="employee" property="age" value="21">
Employee is old enough to drink.
</logic:greaterEqual>
```

In this example, the **name** and **property** attributes are used in tandem to specify the name of an object and its field whose getter method will be called to return an object whose value will be compared against that of the **value** attribute. Again, you can explicitly specify the scope of the object with the **scope** attribute.

The greaterThan Tag

The **greaterThan** tag wraps content that is conditionally processed based on whether or not a specified object's value is greater than a specified constant value. This tag works for both numeric and string comparisons.

There are five ways you can use the **greaterThan** tag, as listed here and shown later in the "Example Usage" section:

- You can use the **cookie** attribute to specify the name of an HTTP cookie from the incoming request whose value will be used for the comparison.

- You can use the **header** attribute to specify the name of an HTTP header from the incoming request whose value will be used for the comparison.

- You can use the **parameter** attribute to specify the name of a parameter from the incoming request whose value will be used for the comparison.

- You can use the **name** attribute to specify the name of an object whose value will be used for the comparison. This object can be in any scope or limited to a specific scope with the **scope** attribute.

- You can use the **name** and **property** attributes in tandem to specify the name of an object and its field whose getter method will be called to return an object whose value will be used for the comparison. Again, the object specified by the **name** attribute can be in any scope or limited to a specific scope with the **scope** attribute.

Attributes

Attribute	Description	Accepts Scriptlet	Required
cookie	Specifies the name of the HTTP cookie from the incoming request whose value is used for comparison.	Yes	No
header	Specifies the name of the HTTP header from the incoming request whose value is used for comparison.	Yes	No
name	Specifies the name of an object whose value is used for comparison. If the **property** attribute is also specified, one of the fields of the object defined by this attribute will have its getter method called to return an object whose value is used for comparison.	Yes	No
parameter	Specifies the name of the parameter from the incoming request whose value is used for comparison.	Yes	No
property	Specifies the field of the object specified by the **name** attribute whose getter method will be called to return an object whose value is used for comparison.	Yes	No
scope	Specifies the scope (application, page, request, or session) to look in for the object specified by the **name** attribute. If not specified, each scope will be searched, in this order: page, request, session, and then application.	Yes	No
value	Specifies the constant value to which the value, specified by other attributes of this tag, will be compared.	Yes	Yes

Example Usage

As mentioned, there are five ways you can use the **greaterThan** tag. The first way, shown here, uses the **cookie** attribute to specify the name of an HTTP cookie from the incoming request whose value is compared against the value specified with the **value** attribute:

```
<logic:greaterThan cookie="size" value="0">
Size is valid.
</logic:greaterThan>
```

If the cookie's value is greater than the **value** attribute's value, the content between the starting and ending **greaterThan** tags will be processed. Otherwise it will be ignored.

The second way to use the **greaterThan** tag is shown here:

```
<logic:greaterThan header="Content-Length" value="100000">
Page has large amount of content.
</logic:greaterThan>
```

This example compares the incoming request's User-Agent header against the **value** attribute to determine whether or not it is greater than it. If so, the content between the starting and ending **greaterThan** tags will be processed.

The following is the third way to use the **greaterThan** tag:

```
<logic:greaterThan parameter="catId" value="10">
Category Id is greater than 10.
</logic:greaterThan>
```

This example compares a request parameter from the incoming request against the value of the **value** attribute. If the parameter is greater than the value, the content between the starting and ending **greaterThan** tags will be processed.

The fourth way to use the **greaterThan** tag is shown here:

```
<logic:greaterThan name="resultCount" value="1">
Search returned at least 1 result.
</logic:greaterThan>
```

This example compares the value of the **resultCount** object against the value of the **value** attribute. If the **resultCount** object's value is greater than the value of the **value** attribute, the content between the starting and ending **greaterThan** tags will be processed. Remember that you can explicitly specify the scope of the **resultCount** object with the **scope** attribute.

The following is the fifth and final way to use the **greaterThan** tag:

```
<logic:greaterThan name="employee" property="age" value="21">
Employee is old enough to drink.
</logic:greaterThan>
```

In this example, the **name** and **property** attributes are used in tandem to specify the name of an object and its field whose getter method will be called to return an object whose value will be compared against that of the **value** attribute. Again, you can explicitly specify the scope of the object with the **scope** attribute.

The iterate Tag

The **iterate** tag wraps content that is repeated for each element of a specified collection. The collection can be any of the following:

- An array of Java objects or primitives (i.e., int, long, and so on).
- An implementation of **java.util.Collection**.
- An implementation of **java.util.Enumeration**.
- An implementation of **java.util.Iterator**.
- An implementation of **java.util.Map**.

Additionally, this tag sets two JSP variables on each iteration through the specified collection's elements. The first variable, whose name is specified by the **id** attribute, stores a reference to the current element of the collection. The second variable, whose name is specified by the **indexId** attribute, stores the numeric index for the current element. Note that each element will be stored as type **Object** unless specified otherwise with use of the **type** attribute. Also note that **java.util.Map**-based collections house **java.util.Map.Entry** elements, which contain the key and value for the given element.

There are three ways you can specify which collection to iterate over, as listed here and shown later in the "Example Usage" section:

- You can use the **collection** attribute to specify a scriptlet that evaluates to a collection object.
- You can use the **name** attribute to specify the name of a collection object that can be in any scope or limited to a specific scope with the **scope** attribute.
- You can use the **name** and **property** attributes in tandem to specify the name of an object and its field whose getter method will be called to return a collection object. Again, the object specified by the **name** attribute can be in any scope or limited to a specific scope with the **scope** attribute.

Note that if none of the aforementioned ways is used to specify the collection that should be iterated over, a **JspException** will be thrown by this tag at run time.

Also note that if the collection you are iterating over can contain **null** values, the loop will still be performed but no page scope attribute will be stored for elements that are **null**.

Attributes

Attribute	Description	Accepts Scriptlet	Required
collection	Specifies a scriptlet that evaluates to an array, **java.util.Collection, java.util.Enumeration, java.util.Iterator,** or **java.util.Map**.	Yes	No
id	Specifies the name for the page scoped JSP variable that will hold a reference to the current element of the collection on each iteration.	No	Yes

Attribute	Description	Accepts Scriptlet	Required
indexId	Specifies the name for the page scoped JSP variable that will hold the current index of the collection on each iteration.	No	No
length	Specifies the maximum number of entries from the collection that will be iterated over. If not specified, all entries in the collection will be iterated over. This attribute can specify an integer value or the name of an **Integer** object (in any scope).	Yes	No
name	Specifies the name of the object that contains the collection that will be iterated over. If the **property** attribute is also specified, one of the fields of the object defined by this attribute will have its getter method called to return the collection that will be iterated over.	Yes	No
offset	Specifies the zero-relative index to start the collection iteration at. If not specified, iteration will start at 0 (the beginning). This attribute can specify an integer value or the name of an **Integer** object (in any scope).	Yes	No
property	Specifies the field of the object specified by the **name** attribute whose getter method will be called to return the collection that will be iterated over.	Yes	No
scope	Specifies the scope (application, page, request, or session) to look in for the object specified by the **name** attribute. If not specified, each scope will be searched, in this order: page, request, session, and then application.	Yes	No
type	Specifies the fully qualified class type (e.g., **java.lang.Integer**) to expose each collection element as, with the **id** attribute. A **ClassCastException** will be thrown at run time if any of the collection's elements are not assignment compatible with this type. If not specified, no type conversions will be performed and each element will be exposed as type **Object**.	Yes	No

Example Usage

As mentioned, there are three basic ways you can use the **iterate** tag. The first way, shown here, uses the **collection** attribute to specify the collection to iterate over:

```
<logic:iterate id="result" collection="<%=results%>">
Result: <%=result%><br>
</logic:iterate>
```

This example assumes you have defined a collection named "results" and then iterates over each result, printing it. Notice that the **collection** attribute was specified with a scriptlet. This attribute only accepts scriptlets. Anything else will result in a **JspException** being thrown at run time.

The second way to use the **iterate** tag is shown here:

```
<logic:iterate id="result" name="results">
Result: <bean:write name="result"/><br>
</logic:iterate>
```

This example is similar to the first example; however, it differs in that the collection to be iterated over is specified with the **name** attribute. Remember that you can explicitly specify the scope of the object, defined by the **name** attribute, with the **scope** attribute.

The following is the third and final way to use the **iterate** tag:

```
<logic:iterate id="result" name="searchObj" property="results">
Result: <bean:write name="result"/><br>
</logic:iterate>
```

In this example, the **name** and **property** attributes are used in tandem to specify the name of an object and its field whose getter method will be called to return a collection to be iterated over. Again, you can explicitly specify the scope of the object with the **scope** attribute.

The lessEqual Tag

The **lessEqual** tag wraps content that is conditionally processed based on whether or not a specified object's value is less than or equal to a specified constant value. This tag works for both numeric and string comparisons.

There are five ways you can use the **lessEqual** tag, as listed here and shown later in the "Example Usage" section:

- You can use the **cookie** attribute to specify the name of an HTTP cookie from the incoming request whose value will be used for the comparison.

- You can use the **header** attribute to specify the name of an HTTP header from the incoming request whose value will be used for the comparison.

- You can use the **parameter** attribute to specify the name of a parameter from the incoming request whose value will be used for the comparison.

- You can use the **name** attribute to specify the name of an object whose value will be used for the comparison. This object can be in any scope or limited to a specific scope with the **scope** attribute.

- You can use the **name** and **property** attributes in tandem to specify the name of an object and its field whose getter method will be called to return an object whose value will be used for the comparison. Again, the object specified by the **name** attribute can be in any scope or limited to a specific scope with the **scope** attribute.

Attributes

Attribute	Description	Accepts Scriptlet	Required
cookie	Specifies the name of the HTTP cookie from the incoming request whose value is used for comparison.	Yes	No
header	Specifies the name of the HTTP header from the incoming request whose value is used for comparison.	Yes	No
name	Specifies the name of an object whose value is used for comparison. If the **property** attribute is also specified, one of the fields of the object defined by this attribute will have its getter method called to return an object whose value is used for comparison.	Yes	No
parameter	Specifies the name of the parameter from the incoming request whose value is used for comparison.	Yes	No
property	Specifies the field of the object specified by the **name** attribute whose getter method will be called to return an object whose value is used for comparison.	Yes	No
scope	Specifies the scope (application, page, request, or session) to look in for the object specified by the **name** attribute. If not specified, each scope will be searched, in this order: page, request, session, and then application.	Yes	No
value	Specifies the constant value to which the value, specified by other attributes of this tag, will be compared.	Yes	Yes

Example Usage

As mentioned, there are five ways you can use the **lessEqual** tag. The first way, shown here, uses the **cookie** attribute to specify the name of an HTTP cookie from the incoming request whose value is compared against the value specified with the **value** attribute:

```
<logic:lessEqual cookie="size" value="0">
Size is invalid.
</logic:lessEqual>
```

If the cookie's value is less than or equal to the **value** attribute's value, the content between the starting and ending **lessEqual** tags will be processed. Otherwise it will be ignored.

The following is the second way to use the **lessEqual** tag:

```
<logic:lessEqual header="Content-Length" value="500">
Page has small amount of content.
</logic:lessEqual>
```

This example compares the incoming request's User-Agent header against the **value** attribute to determine whether or not it is less than or equal to it. If so, the content between the starting and ending **lessEqual** tags will be processed.

The third way to use the **lessEqual** tag is shown here:

```
<logic:lessEqual parameter="catId" value="10">
Category Id is less than or equal to 10.
</logic:lessEqual>
```

This example compares a request parameter from the incoming request against the value of the **value** attribute. If the parameter is less than or equal to the value, the content between the starting and ending **lessEqual** tags will be processed.

The fourth way to use the **lessEqual** tag is shown here:

```
<logic:lessEqual name="resultCount" value="20">
Search returned less than 20 results.
</logic:lessEqual>
```

This example compares the value of the **resultCount** object against the value of the **value** attribute. If the **resultCount** object's value is less than or equal to the value of the **value** attribute, the content between the starting and ending **lessEqual** tags will be processed. Remember that you can explicitly specify the scope of the **resultCount** object with the **scope** attribute.

The following is the fifth and final way to use the **lessEqual** tag:

```
<logic:lessEqual name="employee" property="age" value="20">
Employee is not old enough to drink.
</logic:lessEqual>
```

In this example, the **name** and **property** attributes are used in tandem to specify the name of an object and its field whose getter method will be called to return an object whose value will be compared against that of the **value** attribute. Again, you can explicitly specify the scope of the object with the **scope** attribute.

The lessThan Tag

The **lessThan** tag wraps content that is conditionally processed based on whether or not a specified object's value is less than a specified constant value. This tag works for both numeric and string comparisons.

There are five ways you can use the **lessThan** tag, as listed here and shown later in the "Example Usage" section:

- You can use the **cookie** attribute to specify the name of an HTTP cookie from the incoming request whose value will be used for the comparison.

- You can use the **header** attribute to specify the name of an HTTP header from the incoming request whose value will be used for the comparison.

- You can use the **parameter** attribute to specify the name of a parameter from the incoming request whose value will be used for the comparison.

- You can use the **name** attribute to specify the name of an object whose value will be used for the comparison. This object can be in any scope or limited to a specific scope with the **scope** attribute.

- You can use the **name** and **property** attributes in tandem to specify the name of an object and its field whose getter method will be called to return an object whose value will be used for the comparison. Again, the object specified by the **name** attribute can be in any scope or limited to a specific scope with the **scope** attribute.

Attributes

Attribute	Description	Accepts Scriptlet	Required
cookie	Specifies the name of the HTTP cookie from the incoming request whose value is used for comparison.	Yes	No
header	Specifies the name of the HTTP header from the incoming request whose value is used for comparison.	Yes	No
name	Specifies the name of an object whose value is used for comparison. If the **property** attribute is also specified, one of the fields of the object defined by this attribute will have its getter method called to return an object whose value is used for comparison.	Yes	No
parameter	Specifies the name of the parameter from the incoming request whose value is used for comparison.	Yes	No
property	Specifies the field of the object specified by the **name** attribute whose getter method will be called to return an object whose value is used for comparison.	Yes	No
scope	Specifies the scope (application, page, request, or session) to look in for the object specified by the **name** attribute. If not specified, each scope will be searched, in this order: page, request, session, and then application.	Yes	No
value	Specifies the constant value to which the value, specified by other attributes of this tag, will be compared.	Yes	Yes

Example Usage

As mentioned, there are five ways you can use the **lessThan** tag. The first way, shown here, uses the **cookie** attribute to specify the name of an HTTP cookie from the incoming request whose value is compared against the value specified with the **value** attribute:

```
<logic:lessThan cookie="size" value="1">
Size is invalid.
</logic:lessThan>
```

If the cookie's value is less than the **value** attribute's value, the content between the starting and ending **lessThan** tags will be processed. Otherwise it will be ignored.

The second way to use the **lessThan** tag is shown here:

```
<logic:lessThan header="Content-Length" value="500">
Page has small amount of content.
</logic:lessThan>
```

This example compares the incoming request's User-Agent header against the **value** attribute to determine whether or not it is less than it. If so, the content between the starting and ending **lessThan** tags will be processed.

The following is the third way to use the **lessThan** tag:

```
<logic:lessThan parameter="catId" value="10">
Category Id is less than 10.
</logic:lessThan>
```

This example compares a request parameter from the incoming request against the value of the **value** attribute. If the parameter is less than the value, the content between the starting and ending **lessThan** tags will be processed.

The following is the fourth way to use the **lessThan** tag:

```
<logic:lessThan name="resultCount" value="1">
Search returned no results.
</logic:lessThan>
```

This example compares the value of the **resultCount** object against the value of the **value** attribute. If the **resultCount** object's value is less than the value of the **value** attribute, the content between the starting and ending **lessThan** tags will be processed. Remember that you can explicitly specify the scope of the **resultCount** object with the **scope** attribute.

The fifth and final way to use the **lessThan** tag is shown here:

```
<logic:lessThan name="employee" property="age" value="21">
Employee is not old enough to drink.
</logic:lessThan>
```

PART II

In this example, the **name** and **property** attributes are used in tandem to specify the name of an object and its field whose getter method will be called to return an object whose value will be compared against that of the **value** attribute. Again, you can explicitly specify the scope of the object with the **scope** attribute.

The match Tag

The **match** tag wraps content that is conditionally processed based on whether or not a specified object's value contains, starts with, or ends with a specified constant value. This tag essentially provides a convenient interface to the **String** object's **indexOf( )**, **startsWith( )**, and **endsWith( )** methods. If the **location** attribute of this tag is not specified, an **indexOf( )** match will be performed to see if the specified object's value contains the value specified by the **value** attribute. If the **location** attribute is specified as "start", a **startsWith( )** match will be performed to see if the specified object's value starts with the value specified by the **value** attribute. Finally, if the **location** attribute is specified as "end", an **endsWith( )** match will be performed to see if the specified object's value ends with the value specified by the **value** attribute. Note that all of the matches are case sensitive.

There are five ways you can use the **match** tag, as listed here and shown later in the "Example Usage" section:

- You can use the **cookie** attribute to specify the name of an HTTP cookie from the incoming request whose value will be used to match against.

- You can use the **header** attribute to specify the name of an HTTP header from the incoming request whose value will be used to match against.

- You can use the **parameter** attribute to specify the name of a parameter from the incoming request whose value will be used to match against.

- You can use the **name** attribute to specify the name of an object whose value will be used to match against. This object can be in any scope or limited to a specific scope with the **scope** attribute.

- You can use the **name** and **property** attributes in tandem to specify the name of an object and its field whose getter method will be called to return an object whose value will be used to match against. Again, the object specified by the **name** attribute can be in any scope or limited to a specific scope with the **scope** attribute.

Attributes

Attribute	Description	Accepts Scriptlet	Required
cookie	Specifies the name of the HTTP cookie from the incoming request whose value is matched against.	Yes	No
header	Specifies the name of the HTTP header from the incoming request whose value is matched against.	Yes	No

Attribute	Description	Accepts Scriptlet	Required
location	Accepts "start" or "end" to specify where the match should occur. If not specified, the match can occur at any location.	Yes	No
name	Specifies the name of an object whose value is matched against. If the **property** attribute is also specified, one of the fields of the object defined by this attribute will have its getter method called to return an object whose value is matched against.	Yes	No
parameter	Specifies the name of the parameter from the incoming request whose value is matched against.	Yes	No
property	Specifies the field of the object specified by the **name** attribute whose getter method will be called to return an object whose value is matched against.	Yes	No
scope	Specifies the scope (application, page, request, or session) to look in for the object specified by the **name** attribute. If not specified, each scope will be searched, in this order: page, request, session, and then application.	Yes	No
value	Specifies the constant value to which the value, specified by other attributes of this tag, should contain, start with, or end with.	Yes	Yes

Example Usage

As mentioned, there are five ways you can use the **match** tag. The first way, shown here, uses the **cookie** attribute to specify the name of an HTTP cookie from the incoming request whose value is used to match the value specified with the **value** attribute:

```
<logic:match cookie="roles" value="Manager">
User is a Manager.
</logic:match>
```

If the cookie's value contains the value specified by the **value** attribute, the content between the starting and ending **match** tags will be processed. Otherwise it will be ignored.

The second way to use the **match** tag is shown here:

```
<logic:match header="User-Agent" location="end" value="MSIE">
Browser is Internet Explorer.
</logic:match>
```

This example checks to see if the incoming request's User-Agent header ends with the value specified by the **value** attribute. If so, the content between the starting and ending **match** tags will be processed.

The third way to use the **match** tag is shown here:

```
<logic:match parameter="category" location="start" value="Cloth">
Category is Clothes.
</logic:match>
```

This example checks to see if the parameter from the incoming request starts with the value of the **value** attribute. If so, the content between the starting and ending **match** tags will be processed.

The following is the fourth way to use the **match** tag:

```
<logic:match name="lastName" location="start" value="H">
Last name starts with "H".
</logic:match>
```

This example checks to see if the value of the **lastName** object starts with the value of the **value** attribute. If so, the content between the starting and ending **match** tags will be processed. Remember that you can explicitly specify the scope of the **lastName** object with the **scope** attribute.

The fifth and final way to use the **match** tag is shown here:

```
<logic:match name="employee"
              property="lastName"
              location="start"
              value="H">
Last name starts with "H".
</logic:match>
```

In this example, the **name** and **property** attributes are used in tandem to specify the name of an object and its field whose getter method will be called to return an object whose value will be used to match that of the **value** attribute. Again, you can explicitly specify the scope of the object with the **scope** attribute.

The messagesNotPresent Tag

The **messagesNotPresent** tag wraps content that is conditionally processed based on whether or not Struts' **org.apache.struts.action.ActionErrors** or **org.apache.struts .action.ActionMessages** objects do not have any errors or messages in them, respectively. Additionally, you can optionally specify a particular property to check for the presence of errors or messages with the **property** attribute.

Attributes

Attribute	Description	Accepts Scriptlet	Required
message	Accepts a value of "true" to denote that the presence of messages is checked for. If not specified, the presence of errors will be checked for. If this attribute is set to "true", the **name** attribute will be ignored.	Yes	No
name	Specifies the key to use to look up an **org.apache.struts.action.ActionErrors** or **org.apache.struts.action.ActionMessages** object that will be checked for the presence of errors or messages, respectively.	Yes	No
property	Specifies the name of a particular property to check for the presence of errors or messages. If not specified, the presence of any messages or errors will be checked for.	Yes	No

Example Usage

The following example illustrates the basic usage of the **messagesNotPresent** tag:

```
<logic:messagesNotPresent>
No errors are present.
</logic:messagesNotPresent>
```

This example simply checks if no errors are present. The following example checks if no errors are present for a specific property named "username":

```
<logic:messagesNotPresent property="username">
No errors are present for username property.
</logic:messagesNotPresent>
```

The messagesPresent Tag

The **messagesPresent** tag wraps content that is conditionally processed based on whether or not Struts' **org.apache.struts.action.ActionErrors** or **org.apache.struts.action .ActionMessages** objects have any errors or messages in them, respectively. Additionally, you can optionally specify a particular property to check for the presence of errors or messages with the **property** attribute.

Attributes

Attribute	Description	Accepts Scriptlet	Required
message	Accepts a value of "true" to denote that the presence of messages is checked for. If not specified, the presence of errors will be checked for. If this attribute it set to "true", the **name** attribute will be ignored.	Yes	No
name	Specifies the key to use to look up an **org.apache.struts.action.ActionErrors** or **org.apache.struts.action.ActionMessages** object that will be checked for the presence of errors or messages, respectively.	Yes	No
property	Specifies the name of a particular property to check for the presence of errors or messages. If not specified, the presence of any messages or errors will be checked for.	Yes	No

Example Usage

The following example illustrates the basic usage of the **messagesPresent** tag:

```
<logic:messagesPresent>
Errors are present.
</logic:messagesPresent>
```

This example simply checks if any errors are present. The following example checks if there are any errors present for a specific property named "username":

```
<logic:messagesPresent property="username">
Errors are present for username property.
</logic:messagesPresent>
```

The notEmpty Tag

The **notEmpty** tag wraps content that is conditionally processed based on whether or not the specified object is non-**null** and does not contain an empty (zero length) **String**. Additionally, if the object specified implements **java.util.Collection** or **java.util.Map**, this tag will call the object's **isEmpty( )** method to determine if the object is not empty. If the object is not empty, then the wrapped content will be processed.

Attributes

Attribute	Description	Accepts Scriptlet	Required
name	Specifies the name of an object to check as being not empty. If the **property** attribute is also specified, one of the fields of the object defined by this attribute will have its getter method called to return an object to check as being not empty.	Yes	No
property	Specifies the field of the object specified by the **name** attribute whose getter method will be called to return an object to check as being not empty.	Yes	No
scope	Specifies the scope (application, page, request, or session) to look in for the object specified by the **name** attribute. If not specified, each scope will be searched, in this order: page, request, session, and then application.	Yes	No

Example Usage

There are two ways you can use the **notEmpty** tag. The first way, shown here, uses the **name** attribute to specify the name of an object to check as being not empty:

```
<logic:notEmpty name="results">
Your search returned results!
</logic:notEmpty>
```

If the **results** object is non-**null**, does not contain a zero-length string, and does not contain a **Collection** or **Map** with zero elements, then the content between the starting and ending **empty** tags will be processed. Remember that you can explicitly specify the scope of the object with the **scope** attribute.

The second way to use the **notEmpty** tag is shown here:

```
<logic:notEmpty name="bizObj" property="results">
Your search returned results!
</logic:empty>
```

In this example, the **name** and **property** attributes are used in tandem to specify the name of an object and its field whose getter method will be called to return an object to check as being not empty. Again, you can explicitly specify the scope of the object with the **scope** attribute.

The notEqual Tag

The **notEqual** tag wraps content that is conditionally processed based on whether or not a specified object's value is not equal to a specified constant value. This tag works for both numeric and string comparisons.

There are five ways you can use the **notEqual** tag, as listed here and shown later in the "Example Usage" section:

- You can use the **cookie** attribute to specify the name of an HTTP cookie from the incoming request whose value will be used for the comparison.

- You can use the **header** attribute to specify the name of an HTTP header from the incoming request whose value will be used for the comparison.

- You can use the **parameter** attribute to specify the name of a parameter from the incoming request whose value will be used for the comparison.

- You can use the **name** attribute to specify the name of an object whose value will be used for the comparison. This object can be in any scope or limited to a specific scope with the **scope** attribute.

- You can use the **name** and **property** attributes in tandem to specify the name of an object and its field whose getter method will be called to return an object whose value will be used for the comparison. Again, the object specified by the **name** attribute can be in any scope or limited to a specific scope with the **scope** attribute.

Attributes

Attribute	Description	Accepts Scriptlet	Required
cookie	Specifies the name of the HTTP cookie from the incoming request whose value is used for comparison.	Yes	No
header	Specifies the name of the HTTP header from the incoming request whose value is used for comparison.	Yes	No
name	Specifies the name of an object whose value is used for comparison. If the **property** attribute is also specified, one of the fields of the object defined by this attribute will have its getter method called to return an object whose value is used for comparison.	Yes	No
parameter	Specifies the name of the parameter from the incoming request whose value is used for comparison.	Yes	No
property	Specifies the field of the object specified by the **name** attribute whose getter method will be called to return an object whose value is used for comparison.	Yes	No

Attribute	Description	Accepts Scriptlet	Required
scope	Specifies the scope (application, page, request, or session) to look in for the object specified by the **name** attribute. If not specified, each scope will be searched, in this order: page, request, session, and then application.	Yes	No
value	Specifies the constant value to which the value, specified by other attributes of this tag, will be compared.	Yes	Yes

Example Usage

As mentioned, there are five ways you can use the **notEqual** tag. The first way, shown here, uses the **cookie** attribute to specify the name of an HTTP cookie from the incoming request whose value is compared against the value specified with the **value** attribute:

```
<logic:notEqual cookie="role" value="Manager">
User is NOT a Manager.
</logic:notEqual>
```

If the cookie's value and the **value** attribute's value are not equal, the content between the starting and ending **notEqual** tags will be processed. Otherwise it will be ignored.

The following is the second way to use the **notEqual** tag:

```
<logic:notEqual header="User-Agent" value="MSIE">
Browser is NOT Internet Explorer.
</logic:notEqual>
```

This example compares the incoming request's User-Agent header against the **value** attribute to determine whether or not they are equal. If they are not equal, the content between the starting and ending **notEqual** tags will be processed.

The third way to use the **notEqual** tag is shown here:

```
<logic:notEqual parameter="catId" value="10">
Category Id is NOT 10.
</logic:notEqual>
```

This example compares a request parameter from the incoming request against the value of the **value** attribute. If the two values are not equal, the content between the starting and ending **notEqual** tags will be processed.

The following is the fourth way to use the **notEqual** tag:

```
<logic:notEqual name="resultCount" value="0">
Search returned results.
</logic:notEqual>
```

This example compares the value of the **resultCount** object against the value of the **value** attribute. If the two values are not equal, the content between the starting and ending **notEqual** tags will be processed. Remember that you can explicitly specify the scope of the **resultCount** object with the **scope** attribute.

The fifth and final way to use the **notEqual** tag is shown here:

```
<logic:notEqual name="employee" property="gender" value="male">
Employee is a female.
</logic:notEqual>
```

In this example, the **name** and **property** attributes are used in tandem to specify the name of an object and its field whose getter method will be called to return an object whose value will be compared against that of the **value** attribute. Again, you can explicitly specify the scope of the object with the **scope** attribute.

The notMatch Tag

The **notMatch** tag wraps content that is conditionally processed based on whether or not a specified object's value does not contain, start with, or end with a specified constant value. This tag essentially provides a convenient interface to the **String** object's **indexOf( )**, **startsWith( )**, and **endsWith( )** methods. If the **location** attribute of this tag is not specified, an **indexOf( )** match will be performed to see if the specified object's value does not contain the value specified by the **value** attribute. If the **location** attribute is specified as "start", a **startsWith( )** match will be performed to see if the specified object's value does not start with the value specified by the **value** attribute. Finally, if the **location** attribute is specified as "end", an **endsWith( )** match will be performed to see if the specified object's value does not end with the value specified by the **value** attribute. Note that all of the matches are case sensitive.

There are five ways you can use the **notMatch** tag, as listed here and shown later in the "Example Usage" section:

- You can use the **cookie** attribute to specify the name of an HTTP cookie from the incoming request whose value will be used to match against.

- You can use the **header** attribute to specify the name of an HTTP header from the incoming request whose value will be used to match against.

- You can use the **parameter** attribute to specify the name of a parameter from the incoming request whose value will be used to match against.

- You can use the **name** attribute to specify the name of an object whose value will be used to match against. This object can be in any scope or limited to a specific scope with the **scope** attribute.

- You can use the **name** and **property** attributes in tandem to specify the name of an object and its field whose getter method will be called to return an object whose value will be used to match against. Again, the object specified by the **name** attribute can be in any scope or limited to a specific scope with the **scope** attribute.

Attributes

Attribute	Description	Accepts Scriptlet	Required
cookie	Specifies the name of the HTTP cookie from the incoming request whose value is matched against.	Yes	No
header	Specifies the name of the HTTP header from the incoming request whose value is matched against.	Yes	No
location	Accepts "start" or "end" to specify where the match should occur. If not specified, the match can occur at any location.	Yes	No
name	Specifies the name of an object whose value is matched against. If the **property** attribute is also specified, one of the fields of the object defined by this attribute will have its getter method called to return an object whose value is matched against.	Yes	No
parameter	Specifies the name of the parameter from the incoming request whose value is matched against.	Yes	No
property	Specifies the field of the object specified by the **name** attribute whose getter method will be called to return an object whose value is matched against.	Yes	No
scope	Specifies the scope (application, page, request, or session) to look in for the object specified by the **name** attribute. If not specified, each scope will be searched, in this order: page, request, session, and then application.	Yes	No
value	Specifies the constant value to which the value, specified by other attributes of this tag, should contain, start with, or end with.	Yes	Yes

Example Usage

As mentioned, there are five ways you can use the **notMatch** tag. The first way, shown here, uses the **cookie** attribute to specify the name of an HTTP cookie from the incoming request whose value is used to match the value specified with the **value** attribute:

```
<logic:notMatch cookie="roles" value="Manager">
User is not a Manager.
</logic:notMatch>
```

If the cookie's value does not contain the value specified by the **value** attribute, the content between the starting and ending **notMatch** tags will be processed. Otherwise it will be ignored.

The second way to use the **notMatch** tag is shown here:

```
<logic:notMatch header="User-Agent" location="end" value="MSIE">
Browser is not Internet Explorer.
</logic:notMatch>
```

This example checks to see if the incoming request's User-Agent header does not end with the value specified by the **value** attribute. If so, the content between the starting and ending **notMatch** tags will be processed.

The following is the third way to use the **notMatch** tag:

```
<logic:notMatch parameter="category" location="start" value="Cloth">
Category is not Clothes.
</logic:notMatch>
```

This example checks to see if the parameter from the incoming request does not start with the value of the **value** attribute. If so, the content between the starting and ending **notMatch** tags will be processed.

The following is the fourth way to use the **notMatch** tag:

```
<logic:notMatch name="lastName" location="start" value="H">
Last name does not start with "H".
</logic:notMatch>
```

This example checks to see if the value of the **lastName** object does not start with the value of the **value** attribute. If so, the content between the starting and ending **notMatch** tags will be processed. Remember that you can explicitly specify the scope of the **lastName** object with the **scope** attribute.

The fifth and final way to use the **notMatch** tag is shown here:

```
<logic:notMatch name="employee"
                property="lastName"
                location="start"
                value="H">
Last name starts with "H".
</logic:notMatch>
```

In this example, the **name** and **property** attributes are used in tandem to specify the name of an object and its field whose getter method will be called to return an object whose value will be used to match that of the **value** attribute. Again, you can explicitly specify the scope of the object with the **scope** attribute.

The notPresent Tag

The **notPresent** tag wraps content that is conditionally processed based on whether or not a specified object does not exist. That is, this tag looks up the specified object, and if it is not found, the wrapped content will be processed. If the specified object is found, the content will be skipped.

In addition to the standard existence checks this tag offers, it provides a mechanism for interacting with the J2EE security system to determine if there is an authenticated user with a given name or role. For more information on security in Struts applications, refer to Chapter 19.

There are seven ways you can use the **notPresent** tag, as listed here and shown later in the "Example Usage" section:

- You can use the **cookie** attribute to specify the name of an HTTP cookie from the incoming request whose existence will be checked for.

- You can use the **header** attribute to specify the name of an HTTP header from the incoming request whose existence will be checked for.

- You can use the **parameter** attribute to specify the name of a parameter from the incoming request whose existence will be checked for.

- You can use the **name** attribute to specify the name of an object whose existence will be checked for. This object can be in any scope or limited to a specific scope with the **scope** attribute.

- You can use the **name** and **property** attributes in tandem to specify the name of an object and one of its fields whose existence will be checked for. Again, the object specified by the **name** attribute can be in any scope or limited to a specific scope with the **scope** attribute.

- You can use the **role** attribute to specify a list of roles to check the currently authenticated user against. If the current user is in one of the roles, the existence check passes.

- You can use the **user** attribute to specify a name to compare against the currently authenticated user. If the name matches the user, the existence check passes.

Attributes

Attribute	Description	Accepts Scriptlet	Required
cookie	Specifies the name of the HTTP cookie from the incoming request whose existence is checked for.	Yes	No
header	Specifies the name of the HTTP header from the incoming request whose existence is checked for.	Yes	No

Attribute	Description	Accepts Scriptlet	Required
name	Specifies the name of an object whose existence is checked for. If the **property** attribute is also specified, one of the fields of the object defined by this attribute will have its existence checked for.	Yes	No
parameter	Specifies the name of the parameter from the incoming request whose existence is checked for.	Yes	No
property	Specifies the field of the object specified by the **name** attribute whose existence is checked for.	Yes	No
role	Specifies the list of roles to check the currently authenticated user against. Multiple roles are delimited by commas (i.e., "role1,role2,role3").	Yes	No
scope	Specifies the scope (application, page, request, or session) to look in for the object specified by the **name** attribute. If not specified, each scope will be searched, in this order: page, request, session, and then application.	Yes	No
user	Specifies a name to compare against the currently authenticated user.	Yes	No

Example Usage

As mentioned, there are seven ways you can use the **notPresent** tag. The first way, shown here, uses the **cookie** attribute to specify the name of an HTTP cookie from the incoming request whose existence is checked for:

```
<logic:notPresent cookie="role">
No role cookie exists.
</logic:notPresent>
```

If the incoming request does not have a cookie named "role" in it, the content between the starting and ending **notPresent** tags will be processed. Otherwise it will be ignored.

The second way to use the **notPresent** tag is shown here:

```
<logic:notPresent header="Host">
Host header was not specified.
</logic:notPresent>
```

This example checks the incoming request for a header named "Host". If the header does not exist, the content between the starting and ending **notPresent** tags will be processed.

The following is the third way to use the **notPresent** tag:

```
<logic:notPresent parameter="catId">
Category Id was not specified.
</logic:notPresent>
```

This example checks the incoming request for a parameter name "catId". If the parameter does not exist, the content between the starting and ending **notPresent** tags will be processed.

The fourth way to use the **notPresent** tag is shown here:

```
<logic:notPresent name="results">
Results object exists.
</logic:notPresent>
```

This example looks up an object named "results" to see if it exists. If it does not, the content between the starting and ending **notPresent** tags will be processed. Remember that you can explicitly specify the scope of the **results** object with the **scope** attribute.

The following is the fifth way to use the **notPresent** tag:

```
<logic:notPresent name="employee" property="name">
Employee object does not have a name field.
</logic:notPresent>
```

In this example, the **name** and **property** attributes are used in tandem to specify the name of an object and one of its fields that is checked for existence. Again, you can explicitly specify the scope of the object with the **scope** attribute.

The following is the sixth way to use the **notPresent** tag:

```
<logic:notPresent role="manager">
James is not part of the manager group.
</logic:notPresent>
```

This example checks if the currently authenticated user is associated with the "manager" role. If not, the content between the starting and ending **notPresent** tags will be processed.

The seventh and final way to use the **notPresent** tag is shown here:

```
<logic:notPresent user="jholmes">
James Holmes is not currently logged in.
</logic:notPresent>
```

This example checks if there is currently an authenticated user and if that user's name is "jholmes." If not, the content between the starting and ending **notPresent** tags will be processed. Otherwise the content will be skipped.

The present Tag

The **present** tag wraps content that is conditionally processed based on whether or not a specified object exists. That is, this tag looks up the specified object, and if it is found (regardless of its value), the wrapped content will be processed. If the specified object is not found, the content will be skipped.

In addition to the standard existence checks this tag offers, it provides a mechanism for interacting with the J2EE security system to determine if there is an authenticated user with a given name or role. For more information on security in Struts applications, refer to Chapter 19.

There are seven ways you can use the **present** tag, as listed here and shown later in the "Example Usage" section:

- You can use the **cookie** attribute to specify the name of an HTTP cookie from the incoming request whose existence will be checked for.
- You can use the **header** attribute to specify the name of an HTTP header from the incoming request whose existence will be checked for.
- You can use the **parameter** attribute to specify the name of a parameter from the incoming request whose existence will be checked for.
- You can use the **name** attribute to specify the name of an object whose existence will be checked for. This object can be in any scope or limited to a specific scope with the **scope** attribute.
- You can use the **name** and **property** attributes in tandem to specify the name of an object and one of its fields whose existence will be checked for. Again, the object specified by the **name** attribute can be in any scope or limited to a specific scope with the **scope** attribute.
- You can use the **role** attribute to specify a list of roles to check the currently authenticated user against. If the current user is in one of the roles, the existence check passes.
- You can use the **user** attribute to specify a name to compare against the currently authenticated user. If the name matches the user, the existence check passes.

Attributes

Attribute	Description	Accepts Scriptlet	Required
cookie	Specifies the name of the HTTP cookie from the incoming request whose existence is checked for.	Yes	No
header	Specifies the name of the HTTP header from the incoming request whose existence is checked for.	Yes	No
name	Specifies the name of an object whose existence is checked for. If the **property** attribute is also specified, one of the fields of the object defined by this attribute will have its existence checked for.	Yes	No
parameter	Specifies the name of the parameter from the incoming request whose existence is checked for.	Yes	No
property	Specifies the field of the object specified by the **name** attribute whose existence is checked for.	Yes	No

Attribute	Description	Accepts Scriptlet	Required
role	Specifies the list of roles to check the currently authenticated user against. Multiple roles are delimited by commas (i.e., "role1,role2,role3").	Yes	No
scope	Specifies the scope (application, page, request, or session) to look in for the object specified by the **name** attribute. If not specified, each scope will be searched, in this order: page, request, session, and then application.	Yes	No
user	Specifies a name to compare against the currently authenticated user.	Yes	No

Example Usage

As mentioned, there are seven ways you can use the **present** tag. The first way, shown here, uses the **cookie** attribute to specify the name of an HTTP cookie from the incoming request whose existence is checked for:

```
<logic:present cookie="role">
Role cookie exists.
</logic:present>
```

If the incoming request has a cookie named "role" in it, the content between the starting and ending **present** tags will be processed. Otherwise it will be ignored.

The following is the second way to use the **present** tag:

```
<logic:present header="Host">
Host header was specified.
</logic:present>
```

This example checks the incoming request for a header named "Host". If the header exists, the content between the starting and ending **present** tags will be processed.

The third way to use the **present** tag is shown here:

```
<logic:present parameter="catId">
Category Id was specified.
</logic:present>
```

This example checks the incoming request for a parameter name "catId". If the parameter exists, the content between the starting and ending **present** tags will be processed.

The following is the fourth way to use the **present** tag:

```
<logic:present name="results">
Results object exists.
</logic:present>
```

This example looks up an object named "results" to see if it exists. If it does, the content between the starting and ending **present** tags will be processed. Remember that you can explicitly specify the scope of the **results** object with the **scope** attribute.

The fifth way to use the **present** tag is shown here:

```
<logic:present name="employee" property="name">
Employee object has a name field.
</logic:present>
```

In this example, the **name** and **property** attributes are used in tandem to specify the name of an object and one of its fields that is checked for existence. Again, you can explicitly specify the scope of the object with the **scope** attribute.

The sixth way to use the **present** tag is shown here:

```
<logic:present role="manager">
James is part of the manager group.
</logic:present>
```

This example checks if the currently authenticated user is associated with the "manager" role. If so, the content between the starting and ending **present** tags will be processed.

The seventh and final way to use the **present** tag is shown here:

```
<logic:present user="jholmes">
James Holmes is currently logged in.
</logic:present>
```

This example checks if there is currently an authenticated user and if that user's name is "jholmes." If so, the content between the starting and ending **present** tags will be processed. Otherwise the content will be skipped.

The redirect Tag

The **redirect** tag composes a URL to another page and then redirects to it. The URL is composed by specifying a base URL and optionally specifying an anchor and/or query string parameters to add to the URL.

There are four ways to specify the base URL:

- You can use the **action** attribute to specify the name of an action from the Struts configuration file whose URL will be used.

- You can use the **forward** attribute to specify the name of a forward from the Struts configuration file whose URL will be used.

- You can use the **href** attribute to specify an absolute URL, including protocol (e.g., http://www.yahoo.com/).

- You can use the **page** attribute to specify an application-relative URL.

In addition to specifying the base URL, you have two options for specifying query string parameters to add to the base URL:

- You can use the **paramId** attribute in conjunction with the **paramName** attribute, and optionally the **paramProperty** attribute, to specify a single parameter.

- You can use the **name** attribute, either alone or in tandem with the **property** attribute, to specify a **java.util.Map** object that will be used to add several parameters.

Attributes

Attribute	Description	Accepts Scriptlet	Required
action	Specifies the name of an action from the Action Mappings Configuration section of the Struts configuration file, which contains the URL that will be used as the base of the URL generated by this tag.	Yes	No
anchor	Specifies the anchor (e.g., "#bottom") to be added to the URL generated by this tag. This value should be specified without the leading hash (#) character.	Yes	No
forward	Specifies the name of a forward, from the Global Forwards Configuration section of the Struts configuration file, which contains the URL that will be used as the base of the URL generated by this tag.	Yes	No
href	Specifies the absolute URL (including protocol, such as http://) that will be used as the base of the URL generated by this tag.	Yes	No
name	Specifies the name of the **java.util.Map** object whose elements are added as query string parameters to the URL generated by this tag. If the **property** attribute is also specified, one of the fields of the object defined by this attribute will have its getter method called to return the **java.util.Map** object whose elements are added as query string parameters to the URL generated by this tag.	Yes	No
page	Specifies the application-relative URL (starts with a leading slash, /) that will be used as the base of the URL generated by this tag.	Yes	No
paramId	Specifies the name of a single parameter to add to the URL generated by this tag.	Yes	No

Attribute	Description	Accepts Scriptlet	Required
paramName	Specifies the name of an object whose value will be used as the value for the parameter specified with the **paramId** attribute. If the **property** attribute is also specified, one of the fields of the object defined by this attribute will have its getter method called to return an object whose value will be used as the value for the parameter specified with the **paramId** attribute.	Yes	No
paramProperty	Specifies the field of the object specified by the **name** attribute whose getter method will be called to return an object whose value will be used as the value for the parameter specified with the **paramId** attribute.	Yes	No
paramScope	Specifies the scope (application, page, request, or session) to look in for the object specified by the **paramName** attribute. If not specified, each scope will be searched, in this order: page, request, session, and then application.	Yes	No
property	Specifies the field of the object specified by the **name** attribute whose getter method will be called to return the **java.util.Map** object whose elements are added as query string parameters to the URL generated by this tag.	Yes	No
scope	Specifies the scope (application, page, request, or session) to look in for the object specified by the **name** attribute. If not specified, each scope will be searched, in this order: page, request, session, and then application.	Yes	No
transaction	Accepts "true" or "false" to denote whether or not you want the current transaction token included in the URL generated by this tag.	Yes	No

Example Usage

There are a few different ways to use the **redirect** tag. The first way, shown here, uses the **href** attribute to specify an absolute URL to redirect to:

```
<logic:redirect href="http://www.yahoo.com/"/>
```

Upon this tag's execution, an HTTP redirect response will be sent to the requesting browser. The browser will then request the specified URL.

The following example adds to the first example by specifying a single query string parameter to add to the base URL specified by the **href** attribute:

```
<logic:redirect href="http://www.yahoo.com/"
            paramId="query"
            paramName="queryObj"/>
```

This example takes the base URL specified by the **href** attribute and appends the query string parameter specified by the **paramId** and **paramName** attributes and composes a URL that the tag then redirects to.

Another way to use the **redirect** tag is shown here:

```
<logic:redirect page="/search.jsp" name="params"/>
```

This example uses the **page** attribute to specify an application-relative base URL and the **name** attribute to specify a **java.util.Map** object whose entries are added to the URL as query string parameters.

The Nested Tag Library

I n addition to Struts' core JSP tag libraries—Bean, HTML, and Logic—Struts provides an advanced tag library called Nested that can be used to enhance and simplify JSP development. The Nested Tag Library extends several tags from the Bean, HTML, and Logic tag libraries, giving them the ability to work in a nested context. The Nested Tag Library was initially created by Arron Bates as an add-on to Struts to fill what he saw as a void in the way many of the tags worked in the existing libraries. As his library became popular, it was later integrated into the core Struts framework during the 1.1 release cycle.

Understanding Object Nesting in Struts

The best way to understand the importance of the Nested Tag Library is to begin by reviewing the way nested objects work without it. By default, each of the tags (hereafter referred to as the *base tags*) extended by the Nested Tag Library support the notion of objects nested within other objects. That is, the base tags can access properties of one object nested inside another to any arbitrary level. For example, an **Employee** object might have a nested **Address** object, and the **Address** object may have several fields, such as **Line 1**, **Line 2**, **City**, **State**, and **Zip**. To access an **Employee** object named "employee" with a nested **Address** object named "address" whose **State** field is named "state" with the base Struts tags, you would specify the field as "employee.address.state", as shown in the following example:

```
<html:text property="employee.address.state"/>
```

Struts uses reflection to access the state field. Each level of the nested hierarchy is traversed by calling a getter method for that level's field; thus, in the preceding example, Struts uses reflection to call **getAddress( )** on the employee object and **getState( )** on the address object.

Although the default method of specifying nested references for fields is very useful and greatly simplifies JSP development, it can be problematic for two reasons:

- If an object in a nested hierarchy has its name changed, each nested reference has to be updated. For example, if an **Employee** object had a nested **Address** object named "address" that later becomes "homeAddress", every nested reference that refers to fields in the **Address** object have to be updated to access the fields as "employee.homeAddress.state" instead of "employee.address.state". This is not a huge problem, but it is both time-consuming and error-prone.

- When you are working with a nested object that has several fields, you have to type out the entire nested hierarchy for each field over and over. For example, you have to type "employee.address.line1", "employee.address.line2", "employee.address.city", and so on. Again, this is not a major problem, but it is tedious and is a potential source of errors.

Fortunately, the Nested Tag Library eliminates both problems associated with the default approach to nested tags. The Nested Tag Library allows you to define logical nesting levels and then associate objects with them so that all tags nested inside a level are relative to that level. Therefore, instead of fully qualifying a nested reference within each level of the object hierarchy, you can use the Nested Tag Library's **nest** tag to define each level of the hierarchy. Within each level, you specify the property that you're interested in along with any other tags you need. Here is an example:

```
<nested:nest property="employee">
  <nested:nest property="address">
    Line 1: <nested:text property="line1"/>
    Line 2: <nested:text property="line2"/>
    City: <nested:text property="city"/>
    State: <nested:text property="state"/>
    Zip: <nested:text property="zip"/>
  </nested:nest>
</nested:nest>
```

Notice that the Nested Tag Library's **text** tag was used instead of the HTML Tag Library's **text** tag. The reason is that the base tags are not designed to work with the Nested Tag Library's nesting features. Instead, you must use the Nested Tag Library's extensions to the base tags.

To best understand the benefits of the Nested Tag Library, here is the same example coded without use of the Nested Tag Library:

```
Line 1: <html:text property="employee.address.line1"/>
Line 2: <html:text property="employee.address.line2"/>
City: <html:text property="employee.address.city"/>
```

```
State: <html:text property="employee.address.state"/>
Zip: <html:text property="employee.address.zip"/>
```

As you can see, specifying nested properties without the Nested Tag Library results in more verbose JSP code, which increases the chance for error and the potential for a great deal of maintenance work should the nesting hierarchy change.

Using the Nested Tag Library

To use the Nested Tag Library in a Struts application, you need to include the following snippet in your Web Archive (**.war**) deployment descriptor, **web.xml**:

```
<taglib>
  <taglib-uri>/WEB-INF/tlds/struts-nested.tld</taglib-uri>
  <taglib-location>/WEB-INF/tlds/struts-nested.tld</taglib-location>
</taglib>
```

Recall from the overview of the **web.xml** file in Chapter 2 that **<taglib-uri>** is used to declare the URI (or alias) that will be referenced in each of your JSPs with a **taglib** directive. The **<taglib-location>** tag declares the actual location of the Tag Library Descriptor (**.tld**) file in your Web Archive.

The following snippet illustrates how your JSPs will declare their use of the Nested Tag Library with a JSP **taglib** directive:

```
<%@ taglib uri="/WEB-INF/tlds/struts-nested.tld" prefix="nested" %>
```

Notice that the **uri** attribute specified here is the same as that declared with the **<taglib-uri>** tag in the **web.xml** file. Also, notice that the **prefix** attribute is set to "nested". This attribute can be set to whatever you want; however, "nested" is the accepted default for the Nested Tag Library. The **prefix** attribute declares the prefix that each tag must have when it is used in the JSP, as shown here:

```
<nested:nest property="results">
```

Because "nested" was defined as the prefix, the **nest** tag was used as shown. However, if you choose to use a prefix of "strutsnest", the tag would be used as follows:

```
<strutsnest:nest property="results">
```

The Nested Tag Library Tags

The following table lists each of the tags in the Nested Tag Library and provides a short description of each tag's purpose.

Tag	Description
checkbox	Nesting-enabled version of the HTML Tag Library's **checkbox** tag.
define	Nesting-enabled version of the Bean Tag Library's **define** tag.
empty	Nesting-enabled version of the Logic Tag Library's **empty** tag.
equal	Nesting-enabled version of the Logic Tag Library's **equal** tag.
errors	Nesting-enabled version of the HTML Tag Library's **errors** tag.
file	Nesting-enabled version of the HTML Tag Library's **file** tag.
form	Nesting-enabled version of the HTML Tag Library's **form** tag.
greaterEqual	Nesting-enabled version of the Logic Tag Library's **greaterEqual** tag.
greaterThan	Nesting-enabled version of the Logic Tag Library's **greaterThan** tag.
hidden	Nesting-enabled version of the HTML Tag Library's **hidden** tag.
image	Nesting-enabled version of the HTML Tag Library's **image** tag.
img	Nesting-enabled version of the HTML Tag Library's **img** tag.
iterate	Nesting-enabled version of the Logic Tag Library's **iterate** tag.
lessEqual	Nesting-enabled version of the Logic Tag Library's **lessEqual** tag.
lessThan	Nesting-enabled version of the Logic Tag Library's **lessThan** tag.
link	Nesting-enabled version of the HTML Tag Library's **link** tag.
match	Nesting-enabled version of the Logic Tag Library's **match** tag.
message	Nesting-enabled version of the Bean Tag Library's **message** tag.
messages	Nesting-enabled version of the HTML Tag Library's **messages** tag.
messagesNotPresent	Nesting-enabled version of the Logic Tag Library's **messagesNotPresent** tag.
messagesPresent	Nesting-enabled version of the Logic Tag Library's **messagesPresent** tag.
multibox	Nesting-enabled version of the HTML Tag Library's **multibox** tag.
nest	Defines a logical level in a nesting hierarchy and associates an object with it that all of its nested tags will be relative to.
notEmpty	Nesting-enabled version of the Logic Tag Library's **notEmpty** tag.
notEqual	Nesting-enabled version of the Logic Tag Library's **notEqual** tag.
notMatch	Nesting-enabled version of the Logic Tag Library's **notMatch** tag.
notPresent	Nesting-enabled version of the Logic Tag Library's **notPresent** tag.
options	Nesting-enabled version of the HTML Tag Library's **options** tag.
optionsCollection	Nesting-enabled version of the HTML Tag Library's **optionsCollection** tag.
password	Nesting-enabled version of the HTML Tag Library's **password** tag.
present	Nesting-enabled version of the Logic Tag Library's **present** tag.
radio	Nesting-enabled version of the HTML Tag Library's **radio** tag.

Tag	Description
root	Defines the root object of a nested hierarchy of objects.
select	Nesting-enabled version of the HTML Tag Library's **select** tag.
size	Nesting-enabled version of the Bean Tag Library's **size** tag.
submit	Nesting-enabled version of the HTML Tag Library's **submit** tag.
text	Nesting-enabled version of the HTML Tag Library's **text** tag.
textarea	Nesting-enabled version of the HTML Tag Library's **textarea** tag.
write	Nesting-enabled version of the Bean Tag Library's **write** tag.
writeNesting	Renders or creates a JSP scripting variable for a string representation of the object related to the current nesting level.

As mentioned, the majority of the tags in the Nested Tag Library are simply tags from the Bean, HTML, and Logic tag libraries to which support for nesting has been added. Thus, they are not individually covered in detail here. Instead, the basic concepts of nesting are discussed because they apply to all the extended tags in the same way. For nonnesting-related information on each of the extended tags, see the descriptions of their base tags in their respective chapters.

The remainder of this section discusses in detail each of the tags that are specific to the Nesting Tag Library, including a complete description of the tag, a table listing each of the tag's attributes, and a usage example for the tag. In the tables that describe each tag's attributes, pay special attention to the Required and Accepts Scriptlet columns.

The Required column simply denotes whether or not the given attribute is required when using the tag. If an attribute is required and you do not specify it when using the tag, the tag will throw a **javax.servlet.jsp.JspException** at run time. Note that you can declare an error page in your JSP with a **page** directive to capture any **JspExceptions** that might be thrown, as shown here:

```
<%@ page errorPage="error.jsp" %>
```

If an exception occurs, the page specified by the **errorPage** attribute will be internally redirected to display an error page.

The Accepts Scriptlet column denotes whether or not the given attribute's value can be specified with a JSP scriptlet. If a JSP scriptlet is used to specify an attribute value, the scriptlet must comprise the complete value, quote (") to quote ("), as shown here.

Correct:

```
<nested:nest property="<%=result%>">
```

Incorrect:

```
<nested:nest property="<%=result%>-result">
```

Notice in the incorrect example that "-result" is used as part of the value for the **property** attribute following the scriptlet. This is invalid because there are extra characters between the end of the scriptlet and the ending quote.

A corrected version of the incorrect example follows:

```
<nested:nest property="<%=result + "-result"%>"/>
```

The concatenation of "-result" is now part of the scriptlet and the scriptlet comprises the complete value for the attribute.

The nest Tag

The **nest** tag is used to define a logical level in a nesting hierarchy and associate an object with it that all of its nested tags are relative to.

Attribute

Attribute	Description	Accepts Scriptlet	Required
property	Specifies the name of the object (in any scope) to associate with this logical nesting level.	Yes	No

Example Usage

The following example illustrates how to use the **nest** tag:

```
<nested:nest property="address">
   Line 1: <nested:text property="line1"/>
   Line 2: <nested:text property="line2"/>
   City: <nested:text property="city"/>
   State: <nested:text property="state"/>
   Zip: <nested:text property="zip"/>
</nested:nest>
```

Because the **nest** tag specifies the object that all of its nested tags are relative to, the nested tags only have to specify properties of the nested object.

The equivalent without the Nested Tag Library is shown here:

```
Line 1: <html:text property="address.line1"/>
Line 2: <html:text property="address.line2"/>
City: <html:text property="address.city"/>
State: <html:text property="address.state"/>
Zip: <html:text property="address.zip"/>
```

As you can see, nesting simplifies JSP development for even this short example; however, the real benefit comes when you have several layers of nesting to handle.

The root Tag

The **root** tag is used to define the root object of a nested hierarchy of objects. Typically, tags from this tag library and the HTML Tag Library are nested inside the HTML Tag Library's **form** tag and use the form's Form Bean object as the root of the nested hierarchy. However, the **root** tag can be used to explicitly set the hierarchy's root object, effectively overriding the Form Bean object.

Attribute

Attribute	Description	Accepts Scriptlet	Required
name	Specifies the name of an object (in any scope) to set as the root of a nested hierarchy.	Yes	No

Example Usage

The following example illustrates how to use the **root** tag:

```
<nested:root name="employee">
  <nested:nest property="address">
    Line 1: <nested:text property="line1"/>
    Line 2: <nested:text property="line2"/>
    City: <nested:text property="city"/>
    State: <nested:text property="state"/>
    Zip: <nested:text property="zip"/>
  </nested:nest>
</nested:root>
```

All tags nested inside the **root** tag will use its associated object as the root object for a nested hierarchy. Thus, in the example, the nested **text** tags will actually be accessing "employee.address.line1" even though they only specify "line1".

The writeNesting Tag

The **writeNesting** tag is used to render or create a JSP scripting variable for a string representation of the object related to the current nesting level.

Attributes

Attribute	Description	Accepts Scriptlet	Required
property	Specifies the name of a property of the current nesting level's object.	Yes	No
id	Specifies the name of the JSP variable that will hold a reference to the object related to the current nesting level.	Yes	No
filter	Accepts "true" or "false" to denote whether or not HTML-sensitive characters should be converted to their entity equivalents. For example, if this attribute is enabled, the less than sign (<) would get converted to < before it is rendered. Defaults to "true."	Yes	No

Example Usage

The following snippet shows the basic usage of the **writeNesting** tag:

```
<nested:nest property="address">
  Line 1: <nested:writeNesting property="line1"/>
</nested:nest>
```

This example will generate the following output:

```
Line 1: address.line1
```

Essentially, this tag generates the fully qualified nested reference for the given property.

Using JSTL with Struts

A key advantage of working with Struts is its support for the View layer of MVC applications. At the foundation of this support is its JSP tag libraries. As you've seen in the previous four chapters, the tag libraries greatly simplify JSP development and reduce the need to use JSP scriptlets. At the time of their creation, the Struts tag libraries filled a void in JSP functionality. They provided a simple and convenient interface for getting and setting data on Java beans, implementing simple conditional logic, and accessing Web application attributes. Although an important part of Struts, today large portions of the Struts tag libraries have been superceded by the JSP Standard Tag Library (JSTL). Here's why.

Like Struts, many other frameworks and development teams implemented a set of tag libraries to accomplish basic Java bean manipulation and conditional logic functionality inside JSPs. Although several of those implementations are quite similar, each is a little different in the scope of what it can do and each uses different names for its tags and attributes. Because of the duplication of effort across multiple projects, the need arose for a common, standardized set of tag libraries that could be used universally. Having a standardized set of tags would eliminate the need to learn the details of several different tag libraries as well as curtail the duplication of effort across projects. To meet this need, the JSP Standard Tag Library was created. JSTL is an extension to JSP technology that provides a set of standardized tag libraries and a simple expression language (EL) for accessing objects in JSPs.

Because JSTL offers a standardized set of tags, it is now the preferred approach for JSP development with Struts. Thus, applications should use the JSTL tag libraries and expression language instead of the Struts tags wherever possible. This chapter provides a brief introduction to JSTL, a list of the Struts tags that can be replaced by JSTL, and information on the Struts EL tag libraries that support the JSTL expression language.

JSTL Overview

JSTL can be broken into two functional areas: a set of tag libraries and an expression language. The tag libraries provide a set of tags that implement general-purpose functionality for iteration and conditional processing, data formatting and localization,

XML manipulation, and database access. The expression language simplifies access to Java language constructs within JSPs. Together, the two make up a powerful set of functionality for developing applications with JSPs.

JSTL arose out of the Java Community Process (JCP) and thus had the input and forethought of many high-profile organizations and influential individuals in the industry. In June of 2000, the first JSTL specification was finalized and targeted to work with the JSP 1.2 and Servlet 2.3 specifications. Since then, a maintenance release (1.1) became available in January of 2004. Currently, JSTL expressions can only be used as an attribute value with Tag Library tags that support them. However, when JSP 2.0 is finalized, expressions will be supported throughout JSPs. This means that the expressions will be usable anywhere inside the JSP and will not be limited to just JSTL-enabled tags as they are now.

You can download JSTL from Sun's Web site at **http://java.sun.com/products/ jsp/jstl/**.

The JSTL Expression Language

JSTL's greatest strength lies in its expression language. The expression language simplifies access to Java language constructs from within JSPs and provides the foundation for the JSTL tag libraries' usefulness. With the expression language, you create simple expressions that return a value. For example, one expression might retrieve the value of a request parameter. Another might evaluate a conditional expression that returns a **boolean** result. This latter use is extremely helpful when conditionally processing portions of a JSP.

JSTL expressions are surrounded by an opening ${ and a closing }, as shown in the following snippet:

```
<c:out value="${userObj}"/>
```

Everything between the opening ${ and closing } constitutes the expression. Expressions can contain references to JSP page-scoped objects and implicit objects and can use operators to traverse the objects and manipulate them. The following sections describe the details of the expression language.

Accessing Objects

The JSTL expression language provides a simple mechanism for accessing objects and their properties. The dot (.) operator is used to traverse object hierarchies and access properties. The following snippet illustrates a basic example of the dot operator's usage:

```
<c:out value="${customer.address.city}"/>
```

In this example, the dot operator is used to access the **customer** object's **address** property and then the **address** object's **city** property. Each instance of the dot operator in the expression evaluates to a getter method call for the property on the left of the operator. Thus, the first dot will call a **getAddress( )** method on the **customer** object.

The second dot will then call a **getCity( )** method on the object returned from the **getAddress( )** call. In order for the dot operator to work, the object on the right of the operator must have a getter method for the property on the left of the operator. Otherwise, the operator will fail.

As you can see, this method of traversing object hierarchies is quick and simple. Without JSTL, you'd have to use a JSP expression similar to the following to access properties down a hierarchy:

```
<%= customer.getAddress().getCity() %>
```

The dot operator is great for accessing simple properties; however, it doesn't allow you to access elements of arrays or collections. For that, JSTL has the brackets ([ ]) operator. The brackets operator allows you to specify the index of an element you want to access, as shown next:

```
<c:set var="highBid" value="${bids[0]}"/>
```

This approach works for arrays and list-based collections. For map-based collections, you specify the key for the element you want to access, as shown next:

```
<c:set var="color" value="${param['color']}"/>
```

Implicit Objects

JSTL makes several objects available to the expression language as *implicit objects*. The implicit objects are built in and can be used by any expression without having to be initialized or otherwise set up. They are available by default. Utilizing an implicit object is as simple as referencing its name in an expression, as shown here:

```
<c:out value="${header['User-Agent']}"/>
```

In this example, the Core Tag Library's **out** tag is used to output the value of the "User-Agent" HTTP header. The **header** implicit object is a **java.util.Map** instance containing the incoming request's HTTP headers.

The following table lists and describes each of the JSTL implicit objects.

Category	Implicit Object	Description
Cookies	cookie	A **java.util.Map** instance containing the current request's cookies
Initialization parameters	initParam	A **java.util.Map** instance containing the Web application's context initialization parameters specified in **web.xml**
JSP	pageContext	A **javax.servlet.jsp.PageContext** instance for the current page

Category	Implicit Object	Description
Request headers	header	A **java.util.Map** instance containing the primary values for the current request's HTTP headers
	headerValues	A **java.util.Map** instance containing all the values for the current request's HTTP headers
Request parameters	param	A **java.util.Map** instance containing the primary values for the current request's parameters
	paramValues	A **java.util.Map** instance containing all the values for the current request's parameters
Scopes	applicationScope	A **java.util.Map** instance containing application-scoped attributes
	pageScope	A **java.util.Map** instance containing page-scoped attributes
	requestScope	A **java.util.Map** instance containing request-scoped attributes
	sessionScope	A **java.util.Map** instance containing session-scoped attributes

Using Operators

The JSTL expression language supports several operators for comparing and manipulating data in expressions. When expressions contain operators, the operators are applied to the operands and the resulting value is used as the expression's value. Take for example the following snippet:

```
<c:set var="sqrFt" value="${width * length}"/>
```

This example uses the asterisk (*) multiplication operator to multiply a **width** variable times a **length** variable and stores the result in a JSP scripting variable.

Operators can also be combined to create complex expressions, as shown next:

```
<c:set var="halfSqrFt" value="${(width * length) / 2}"/>
```

Here, **width** and **length** are multiplied and then divided and the resulting value is stored.

Logical and relational operators work the same; however, their results are often used with conditional tags, as shown here:

```
<c:if test="${count == 5}">
Count equals 5.
</c:if>
```

This example compares the value of the **count** object to 5 to see if they match. If they do, the text enclosed between the opening and closing **if** tags is processed. Otherwise it is skipped.

The following table lists each of the JSTL expression language operators.

Category	Operators
Arithmetic	**+, −, *, /** (or **div**), **%** (or **mod**)
Logical	**&&** (or **and**), **||** (or **or**), **!** (or **not**)
Relational	**==** (or **eq**), **!=** (or **ne**), **<** (or **lt**), **>** (or **gt**), **<=** (or **le**), **>=** (or **ge**)
Validation	empty

As mentioned, multiple operators can be used together in a single expression. The following lists the order of precedence of operators:

- [], .
- ( )
- unary −, not, !, empty
- *, /, div, %, mod
- +, binary −
- <, >, <=, >=, lt, gt, le, ge
- ==, !=, eq, ne
- &&, and
- \|\|, or

The JSTL Tag Libraries

JSTL's tag libraries provide a common thread for JSP applications to be sewn from, offering the base functionality needed by most applications. The JSTL tag libraries work like any other JSP tag libraries with the added functionality of supporting JSTL expressions for tag attribute values. The following table lists each of the JSTL tag libraries. The following sections describe the tags in each library.

Library	Taglib Prefix	Description
Core	c	Provides tags for conditional logic, loops, output, variable creation, text imports, and URL manipulation
Format	fmt	Provides tags for formatting dates and numbers and for localizing text messages
SQL	sql	Provides tags for making SQL queries to databases
XML	x	Provides tags for parsing of XML documents, selection of XML fragments, flow control based on XML, and XSLT transformations

The Core Tag Library Tags

The following table lists each of the tags in the Core Tag Library and provides a short description of each tag's purpose.

Tag	Description
catch	Catches and optionally exposes any exception (i.e. anything derived from **java.lang.Throwable**) that may be thrown from nested instances of other tags in this library.
choose	Establishes a context for mutually exclusive conditional operations, marked by nested **when** and **otherwise** tags.
forEach	Iterates over each element in a collection.
forTokens	Iterates over tokens, separated by the supplied delimiters.
if	Evaluates its body if the supplied condition is true and optionally exposes a **java.lang.Boolean** scripting variable representing the evaluation of this condition.
import	Retrieves an absolute or relative URL and exposes its contents to the page, a **String** specified by its **var** attribute, or a **Reader** specified by its **varReader** attribute.
out	Outputs JSTL expressions. Equivalent to JSP's **<%= ... >** for JSTL expressions.
otherwise	Subtag of **choose** that follows **when** tags and runs only if all of the prior conditions evaluate to false.
param	Adds a parameter to a containing **import** tag's URL.
redirect	Redirects to a new URL.
remove	Removes a scoped variable (from a particular scope, if specified).
set	Sets the result of an expression evaluation in a scope.
url	Creates a URL with optional query parameters.
when	Subtag of **choose** that includes its body if its condition evaluates to true.

The Format Tag Library Tags

The following table lists each of the tags in the Format Tag Library and provides a short description of each tag's purpose.

Tag	Description
bundle	Loads a resource bundle to be used by nested instances of other tags in this library.
formatDate	Formats a date and/or time using the supplied styles and pattern.
formatNumber	Formats a numeric value as a number, currency, or percentage.
message	Specifies a localized message from the current bundle and performs parametric replacement on it and then outputs it.
param	Supplies an argument for parametric replacement to a containing **message** tag.

Tag	Description
parseDate	Parses the string representation of a date and/or time.
parseNumber	Parses the string representation of a number, currency, or percentage.
requestEncoding	Sets the request character encoding.
setBundle	Loads a resource bundle and stores it in the named scoped variable or the bundle configuration variable.
setLocale	Stores the given locale in the locale configuration variable.
setTimeZone	Stores the given time zone in the time zone configuration variable.
timeZone	Specifies the time zone for any time formatting or parsing tags nested in its body.

The SQL Tag Library Tags

The following table lists each of the tags in the SQL Tag Library and provides a short description of each tag's purpose.

Tag	Description
dateParam	Sets a parameter in an SQL statement to the specified **java.util.Date** value.
param	Sets a parameter in an SQL statement to the specified value.
query	Executes the SQL query defined in its body or through its **sql** attribute.
setDataSource	Specifies a JDBC data source for which nested instances of other tags in this library will use when to execute SQL statements.
transaction	Provides nested instances of other tags in this library with a shared connection, set up to execute all statements as one transaction.
update	Executes the SQL update defined in its body or through its **sql** attribute.

The XML Tag Library Tags

The following table lists each of the tags in the XML Tag Library and provides a short description of each tag's purpose.

Tag	Description
choose	Establishes a context for mutually exclusive conditional operations, marked by **when** and **otherwise**.
forEach	Iterates over a collection of XML tags.
if	Evaluates its body if the supplied XPath expression evaluates to true.
otherwise	Subtag of **choose** that follows **when** tags and runs only if all of the prior conditions evaluated to false.
out	Outputs XPath (XML Path) expressions. Equivalent to JSP's **<%= ... >** for XPath expressions. XPath is a set of syntax rules for defining parts of an XML document.
param	Adds a parameter to a containing **transform** tag.

Tag	Description
parse	Parses XML content from a specified **source** attribute or from body content.
set	Saves the result of an XPath expression evaluation in a scope.
transform	Conducts a transformation given a source XML document and an XSLT stylesheet.
when	Subtag of **choose** that includes its body if its expression evaluates to true.

Using JSTL with Struts

Using JSTL with Struts is as simple as adding the JSTL **.jar** files (**jstl.jar** and **standard.jar**) to your Web application's library directory (**/WEB-INF/lib**) and then referencing the Tag Library Descriptors (**.tld**s) from your JSPs. There are two ways that you can reference JSTL **.tld**s in your JSPs. First, you can use an absolute URI to Sun's site, as shown next:

```
<%@ taglib prefix="c" uri="http://java.sun.com/jstl/core" %>
```

Second, you can employ the approach used by the Struts tag libraries: an entry is made in the **web.xml** file and then the URI assigned in the file is used by JSPs. If you choose to take this route, you need to copy the JSTL **.tld** files into your Web application's **WEB-INF** directory so that you can reference them.

The following table lists the absolute URI for each of the libraries, should you choose to reference the **.tld**s in that way.

Library	Prefix	URI
Core	c	http://java.sun.com/jstl/core
Format	fmt	http://java.sun.com/jstl/fmt
SQL	sql	http://java.sun.com/jstl/sql
XML	x	http://java.sun.com/jstl/xml

Struts-EL

As previously mentioned, with the advent of JSTL, the Struts tag library tags should now be used only when there is not a JSTL equivalent tag to replace them. This ensures that JSPs are as portable as possible and shields your application from being too heavily tied to Struts-specific facilities. The following table lists each of the Struts tag library tags that can be replaced by JSTL tags and their corresponding replacements.

Struts Tag Library	Tag	JSTL Replacement
Bean	cookie	c:set
Bean	define	c:set
Bean	header	c:set

Struts Tag Library	Tag	JSTL Replacement
Bean	include	c:import
Bean	parameter	c:set
Bean	write	c:out
Logic	empty	c:if, c:when
Logic	equal	c:if, c:when
Logic	greaterEqual	c:if, c:when
Logic	greaterThan	c:if, c:when
Logic	iterate	c:forEach
Logic	lessEqual	c:if, c:when
Logic	lessThan	c:if, c:when
Logic	notEmpty	c:if, c:when
Logic	notEqual	c:if, c:when

As you can see, JSTL can be used in lieu of many of the Struts tag library tags. However, you may have noticed that none of the tags from the Struts HTML Tag Library has an equivalent JSTL tag. JSTL does not have a tag library for rendering HTML form elements, thus the absence of Struts tag replacements. For the HTML tags and all the tags in the Bean and Logic tag libraries that do not have JSTL replacements, a project called Struts-EL was created. Struts-EL was created by David Karr and is currently distributed with Struts in the distribution's **contrib** folder. It is likely that Struts-EL will eventually become part of the Struts core.

The Struts-EL project is an extension to Struts that provides a JSTL expression language–enabled version of each Struts tag for which no JSTL replacement exists. Most of the base Struts tag library tags' attributes accept values represented as scriptlet expressions. This allows the tags to have dynamic attribute values. For example, the Bean Tag Library's **message** tag accepts scriptlet expressions for its **key** attribute, as shown here:

```
<bean:message key="<%=messageKey%>"/>
```

This example uses the value of the **messageKey** JSP scripting variable as the value for the **message** tag's **key** attribute. Notice that the JSP scripting variable had to be specified within the scriptlet expression identifiers <%= and %>.

The following example shows the Struts-EL equivalent of the previous example using a JSTL expression to specify a dynamic value for the **key** attribute:

```
<bean-el:message key="${messageKey}"/>
```

As you can see, the JSTL expression syntax is a little shorter and is cleaner looking.

As mentioned, the basic concepts of using JSTL expressions apply to all the Struts-EL tags in the same way. Any tag attribute that accepts a scriptlet expression with the base tags will accept a JSTL expression with the Struts-EL tags.

JSTL Replacement Examples

The following sections provide examples for replacing Struts tag library tags with their JSTL equivalents. Remember that not all the Bean, HTML, and Logic tags can be replaced by JSTL tags.

bean:cookie Replacement Example

The following snippet shows the basic usage of the **cookie** tag from the Bean Tag Library:

```
<bean:cookie id="category" name="cat"/>
```

The JSTL equivalent is as follows:

```
<c:set var="category" value="${cookie['cat'].value}"/>
```

This example accesses the **cat** cookie with a JSTL expression that makes use of the JSTL implicit **cookie** object.

bean:define Replacement Example

The following snippet shows the basic usage of the **define** tag from the Bean Tag Library:

```
<bean:define id="name" name="nameObj"/>
```

The JSTL equivalent is as follows:

```
<c:set var="name" value="${nameObj}"/>
```

bean:header Replacement Example

The following snippet shows the basic usage of the **header** tag from the Bean Tag Library:

```
<bean:header id="browser" name="User-Agent"/>
```

The JSTL equivalent is as follows:

```
<c:set var="browser" value="${header['User-Agent']}"/>
```

This example accesses the "User-Agent" header with a JSTL expression that makes use of the JSTL implicit **header** object.

bean:include Replacement Example

The following snippet shows the basic usage of the **include** tag from the Bean Tag Library:

```
<bean:include id="yahooContents" href="http://www.yahoo.com/"/>
```

The JSTL equivalent is as follows:

```
<c:import var="yahooContents" url=" http://www.yahoo.com/"/>
```

bean:parameter Replacement Example

The following snippet shows the basic usage of the **parameter** tag from the Bean Tag Library:

```
<bean:parameter id="color" name="clr"/>.
```

The JSTL equivalent is as follows:

```
<c:set var="color" value="${param['clr']}"/>
```

This example accesses the **clr** parameter with a JSTL expression that makes use of the JSTL implicit **param** object.

bean:write Replacement Example

The following snippet shows the basic usage of the **write** tag from the Bean Tag Library:

```
<bean:write name="bizObj"/>
```

The JSTL equivalent is as follows:

```
<c:out value="${bizObj}" />
```

logic:empty Replacement Example

The following snippet shows the basic usage of the **empty** tag from the Logic Tag Library:

```
<<logic:empty name="results">
Your search yielded no results.
</logic:empty>
```

The JSTL equivalent is as follows:

```
<c:if test="${empty results}">
Your search yielded no results.
</c:if>
```

logic:equal Replacement Example
The following snippet shows the basic usage of the **equal** tag from the Logic Tag Library:

```
<logic:equal name="count" value="0">
Count is zero.
</logic:equal>
```

The JSTL equivalent is as follows:

```
<c:if test="${count == 0}">
Count is zero.
</c:if>
```

bean:greaterEqual Replacement Example
The following snippet shows the basic usage of the **greaterEqual** tag from the Logic Tag Library:

```
<logic:greaterEqual name="count" value="5">
Count is greater than or equal to five.
</logic:greaterEqual>
```

The JSTL equivalent is as follows:

```
<c:if test="${count >= 5}">
Count is greater than or equal to five.
</c:if>
```

logic:greaterThan Replacement Example
The following snippet shows the basic usage of the **greaterThan** tag from the Logic Tag Library:

```
<logic:greaterThan name="count" value="5">
Count is greater than five.
</logic:greaterThan>
```

The JSTL equivalent is as follows:

```
<c:if test="${count > 5}">
Count is greater than five.
</c:if>
```

logic:iterate Replacement Example
The following snippet shows the basic usage of the **iterate** tag from the Logic Tag Library:

```
<logic:iterate id="result" collection="<%=results%>">
Result: <%=result%><br>
</logic:iterate>
```

The JSTL equivalent is as follows:

```
<c:forEach var="result" items="${results}">
Result: <c:out value="${result}"/>
</c:forEach>
```

logic:lessEqual Replacement Example

The following snippet shows the basic usage of the **lessEqual** tag from the Logic
Tag Library:

```
<logic:lessEqual name="count" value="5">
Count is less than or equal to five.
</logic:lessEqual>
```

The JSTL equivalent is as follows:

```
<c:if test="${count <= 5}">
Count is less than or equal to five.
</c:if>
```

logic:lessThan Replacement Example

The following snippet shows the basic usage of the **lessThan** tag from the Logic
Tag Library:

```
<logic:lessThan name="count" value="5">
Count is less than five.
</logic:lessThan>
```

The JSTL equivalent is as follows:

```
<c:if test="${count < 5}">
Count is less than five.
</c:if>
```

logic:notEmpty Replacement Example

The following snippet shows the basic usage of the **notEmpty** tag from the Logic
Tag Library:

```
<logic:notEmpty name="results">
Your search returned results!
</logic:notEmpty>
```

The JSTL equivalent is as follows:

```
<c:if test="${!empty results}">
Your search returned results!
</c:if>
```

logic:notEqual Replacement Example

The following snippet shows the basic usage of the **notEqual** tag from the Logic Tag Library:

```
<logic:notEqual name="count" value="0">
Count is not equal to zero.
</logic:notEqual>
```

The JSTL equivalent is as follows:

```
<c:if test="${count != 0}">
Count is not equal to zero.
</c:if>
```

Using the Struts-EL Tag Libraries

To use the Struts-EL tag libraries in a Struts application, you need to include the following snippet in your Web Archive (**.war**) deployment descriptor, **web.xml**:

```
<taglib>
  <taglib-uri>/WEB-INF/struts-bean-el.tld</taglib-uri>
  <taglib-location>/WEB-INF/struts-bean-el.tld</taglib-location>
</taglib>
<taglib>
  <taglib-uri>/WEB-INF/struts-html-el.tld</taglib-uri>
  <taglib-location>/WEB-INF/struts-html-el.tld</taglib-location>
</taglib>
<taglib>
  <taglib-uri>/WEB-INF/struts-logic-el.tld</taglib-uri>
  <taglib-location>/WEB-INF/struts-logic-el.tld</taglib-location>
</taglib>
```

Of course, if you only want to use one or two of the libraries, you could place just their **taglib** definitions in **web.xml**.

Recall from the overview of the **web.xml** file in Chapter 2 that **<taglib-uri>** is used to declare the URI (or alias) that will be referenced in each of your JSPs with a **taglib** directive. The **<taglib-location>** tag declares the actual location of the Tag Library Descriptor (**.tld**) file in your Web Archive.

The following snippet illustrates how your JSPs will declare their use of the Struts-EL tag libraries with JSP **taglib** directives:

```
<%@ taglib uri="/WEB-INF/struts-bean-el.tld" prefix="bean-el" %>
<%@ taglib uri="/WEB-INF/struts-html-el.tld" prefix="html-el" %>
<%@ taglib uri="/WEB-INF/struts-logic-el.tld" prefix="logic-el" %>
```

Notice that the **uri** attributes specified here are the same as those declared with the **<taglib-uri>** tags in the **web.xml** file. Also, notice that the **prefix** attributes are set to "bean-el", "html-el", and "logic-el", respectively. These attributes can be set to whatever you want; however, "bean-el", "html-el", and "logic-el" are the accepted defaults for the Struts-EL tag libraries. The **prefix** attribute declares the prefix that each tag must have when it is used in the JSP, as shown here:

```
<bean-el:message key="label.search.name">
```

Because "bean-el" was defined as the prefix, the **message** tag was used as shown. However, if you chose to use a prefix of "strutsbean-el", the tag would be used in the following way:

```
<strutsbean-el:message key="label.search.name">
```

The Struts-EL Tag Library Tags

As mentioned, each of the tags in the Struts-EL tag libraries is simply a tag from the Bean, HTML, Logic, or Tiles tag libraries to which support for JSTL expressions has been added. Thus, they are not individually covered in detail here. Instead, the basic concepts of using JSTL expressions with the tags were discussed because they apply to all the extended tags in the same way. For non-Struts-EL-related information on each of the extended tags, see the descriptions of their base tags in their respective chapters.

The remainder of this section lists each Struts-EL library-specific tag and the base tag from which it has been extended. Remember that not all of the Bean, HTML, Logic, and Tiles tags have been extended to support JSTL expressions. Only those tags whose functionality cannot be wholly replaced by a JSTL tag have been extended.

The Struts-EL Bean Tag Library Tags

The following table lists each of the tags in the Struts-EL Bean Tag Library and provides a short description of each tag's purpose.

Tag	Description
include	Expression language–enabled version of the Bean Tag Library's **include** tag.
message	Expression language–enabled version of the Bean Tag Library's **message** tag.
page	Expression language–enabled version of the Bean Tag Library's **page** tag.
resource	Expression language–enabled version of the Bean Tag Library's **resource** tag.
size	Expression language–enabled version of the Bean Tag Library's **size** tag.
struts	Expression language–enabled version of the Bean Tag Library's **struts** tag.

The Struts-EL HTML Tag Library Tags

The following table lists each of the tags in the Struts-EL HTML Tag Library and provides a short description of each tag's purpose.

Tag	Description
base	Expression language–enabled version of the HTML Tag Library's **base** tag.
button	Expression language–enabled version of the HTML Tag Library's **button** tag.
cancel	Expression language–enabled version of the HTML Tag Library's **cancel** tag.
checkbox	Expression language–enabled version of the HTML Tag Library's **checkbox** tag.
errors	Expression language–enabled version of the HTML Tag Library's **errors** tag.
file	Expression language–enabled version of the HTML Tag Library's **file** tag.
form	Expression language–enabled version of the HTML Tag Library's **form** tag.
frame	Expression language–enabled version of the HTML Tag Library's **frame** tag.
hidden	Expression language–enabled version of the HTML Tag Library's **hidden** tag.
html	Expression language–enabled version of the HTML Tag Library's **html** tag.
image	Expression language–enabled version of the HTML Tag Library's **image** tag.
img	Expression language–enabled version of the HTML Tag Library's **img** tag.
javascript	Expression language–enabled version of the HTML Tag Library's **javascript** tag.
link	Expression language–enabled version of the HTML Tag Library's **link** tag.
messages	Expression language–enabled version of the HTML Tag Library's **messages** tag.
multibox	Expression language–enabled version of the HTML Tag Library's **multibox** tag.
option	Expression language–enabled version of the HTML Tag Library's **option** tag.
options	Expression language–enabled version of the HTML Tag Library's **options** tag.
optionsCollection	Expression language–enabled version of the HTML Tag Library's **optionsCollection** tag.
password	Expression language–enabled version of the HTML Tag Library's **password** tag.
radio	Expression language–enabled version of the HTML Tag Library's **radio** tag.
reset	Expression language–enabled version of the HTML Tag Library's **reset** tag.
rewrite	Expression language–enabled version of the HTML Tag Library's **rewrite** tag.
select	Expression language–enabled version of the HTML Tag Library's **select** tag.
submit	Expression language–enabled version of the HTML Tag Library's **submit** tag.
text	Expression language–enabled version of the HTML Tag Library's **text** tag.
textarea	Expression language–enabled version of the HTML Tag Library's **textarea** tag.
xhtml	Expression language–enabled version of the HTML Tag Library's **xhtml** tag.

The Struts-EL Logic Tag Library Tags

The following table lists each of the tags in the Struts-EL Logic Tag Library and provides a short description of each tag's purpose.

Tag	Description
forward	Expression language–enabled version of the Logic Tag Library's **forward** tag.
iterate	Expression language–enabled version of the Logic Tag Library's **iterate** tag.
match	Expression language–enabled version of the Logic Tag Library's **match** tag.
messagesNotPresent	Expression language–enabled version of the Logic Tag Library's **messagesNotPresent** tag.
messagesPresent	Expression language–enabled version of the Logic Tag Library's **messagesPresent** tag.
notMatch	Expression language–enabled version of the Logic Tag Library's **notMatch** tag.
notPresent	Expression language–enabled version of the Logic Tag Library's **notPresent** tag.
present	Expression language–enabled version of the Logic Tag Library's **present** tag.
redirect	Expression language–enabled version of the Logic Tag Library's **redirect** tag.

The Struts-EL Tiles Tag Library Tags

The following table lists each of the tags in the Struts-EL Tiles Tag Library and provides a short description of each tag's purpose.

Tag	Description
add	Expression language–enabled version of the Tiles Tag Library's **add** tag.
definition	Expression language–enabled version of the Tiles Tag Library's **definition** tag.
get	Expression language–enabled version of the Tiles Tag Library's **get** tag.
getAsString	Expression language–enabled version of the Tiles Tag Library's **getAsString** tag.

Tag	Description
importAttribute	Expression language–enabled version of the Tiles Tag Library's **importAttribute** tag.
initComponentDefinitions	Expression language–enabled version of the Tiles Tag Library's **initComponentDefinitions** tag.
insert	Expression language–enabled version of the Tiles Tag Library's **insert** tag.
put	Expression language–enabled version of the Tiles Tag Library's **put** tag.
putList	Expression language–enabled version of the Tiles Tag Library's **putList** tag.
useAttribute	Expression language–enabled version of the Tiles Tag Library's **useAttribute** tag.

PART

Struts Configuration Files

The Struts
Configuration File

One of the core benefits to using the Struts framework is that a great deal of your application's configuration can be specified declaratively in an external configuration file instead of being hard-coded into the application. This greatly simplifies development because many changes can be made to the application without having to recompile any code. Upon application startup, Struts loads its configuration file(s) and creates a series of configuration objects that correspond to the settings in the file. Struts then uses those configuration objects to guide its behavior.

The Struts configuration file is XML-based and its format is governed by a Document Type Definition (DTD) file that specifies how the configuration tags must be ordered in the file, what settings are required, and so on. Each Struts configuration file declares its conformance to the DTD by having the following DOCTYPE definition at the top of the file:

```
<!DOCTYPE struts-config PUBLIC
  "-//Apache Software Foundation//DTD Struts Configuration 1.1//EN"
  "http://jakarta.apache.org/struts/dtds/struts-config_1_1.dtd">
```

When Struts reads the configuration file, its XML parser uses the DOCTYPE definition to determine the DTD that the XML file must conform to. If configured to do so, the XML parser will validate the XML file's conformance to the DTD.

Understanding XML DTDs

Because DTD conformance is important for Struts tags, a brief overview of how XML DTDs work is given here. DTDs specify a set of tags and attributes that make up a specific XML document type. DTDs also specify the order in which tags must be placed in the file, and the relationship between tags. For example, a tag definition defines what other tags can be nested inside of it, how many occurrences can be nested, and in what order the nesting can occur. Additionally, DTDs define which tag attributes are required and which are optional.

Each tag described in this chapter has a DTD Definition section that lists the tag's definition in the Struts configuration file DTD. The definitions will be similar to the one shown in the following snippet:

```
<!ELEMENT form-bean (icon?, display-name?, description?, set-property*, form-property*)>
```

This example defines a **form-bean** tag and the tags that can be nested inside of it. According to the definition, the tag can have nested **icon**, **display-name**, **description**, **set-property**, and **form-property** tags. The question mark (?) and asterisk (*) characters following the nested tags' names indicate the number of times the nested tag can be nested. The question mark character indicates that the tag can be nested zero or one time. The asterisk character indicates that the tag can be nested zero or more (unlimited) times. A plus (+) character indicates that the tag must be nested at least once and as many times as you'd like. The lack of a trailing character means that the tag must be nested exactly once and no more. If no tags can be nested inside the defined tag, EMPTY will be used to denote that:

```
<!ELEMENT set-property EMPTY>
```

Configuring the web.xml Deployment Descriptor

As explained in Chapter 2, Struts configuration files are specified inside in the **web.xml** deployment descriptor file when defining the use of Struts' **ActionServlet**, as shown here:

```
<!DOCTYPE web-app
    PUBLIC "-//Sun Microsystems, Inc.//DTD Web Application 2.2//EN"
    "http://java.sun.com/j2ee/dtds/web-app_2_2.dtd">

<web-app>
  <servlet>
    <servlet-name>action</servlet-name>
    <servlet-class>org.apache.struts.action.ActionServlet</servlet-class>
    <init-param>
      <param-name>config</param-name>
      <param-value>/WEB-INF/struts-config.xml</param-value>
    </init-param>
    <load-on-startup>1</load-on-startup>
  </servlet>

  ...

</web-app>
```

The Struts configuration file is specified by declaring a servlet initialization parameter named **config**. The **config** parameter must be set to the Web application-relative path of your configuration file, which will be underneath the protected **/WEB-INF/** directory so that it can be accessed only from server-side applications.

As of version 1.1, Struts supports the use of multiple configuration files. This way, configuration settings can be broken down into separate files, which allows teams of developers to work on an application in parallel without having the configuration file be a point of contention. To specify multiple configuration files, simply list each configuration file delimited by commas, as shown here:

```
<init-param>
  <param-name>config</param-name>
  <param-value>
    /WEB-INF/struts-config.xml,
    /WEB-INF/struts-config2.xml,
    /WEB-INF/struts-config3.xml,
  </param-value>
</init-param>
```

When Struts loads the configuration files, if there is any overlap among the files' settings, Struts will use the last settings specified. For example, if configuration file A specifies a setting and then configuration file B specifies the same setting with a different value, the setting in configuration file B will override the one in configuration file A, provided that file B is loaded after file A.

In addition to support for multiple configuration files, Struts version 1.1 added support for application modules. The module feature allows applications to be broken down into discreet chunks and can be thought of as being almost a mini-application inside of a large application. Using modules requires you to create a separate configuration file for each module, as shown here:

```
<servlet>
  <servlet-name>action</servlet-name>
  <servlet-class>org.apache.struts.action.ActionServlet</servlet-class>
  <init-param>
    <param-name>config</param-name>
    <param-value>/WEB-INF/struts-config.xml</param-value>
  </init-param>
  <init-param>
    <param-name>config/ModuleA</param-name>
    <param-value>/WEB-INF/struts-config-moduleB.xml</param-value>
  </init-param>
  <init-param>
    <param-name>config/ModuleB</param-name>
```

```
<param-value>/WEB-INF/struts-config-moduleA.xml</param-value>
</init-param>
<load-on-startup>1</load-on-startup>
</servlet>
```

Notice that the second and third **init-param** definitions specify parameters named **config/moduleA** and **config/ModuleB**, respectively. Struts uses the part of the name following the slash (/) as the logical name for the module and loads and associates the specified configuration file with that module. Thus, for a parameter named **config/ModuleA**, the module's name is **ModuleA**. For module configuration files, parameter names must begin with **config/** in order for Struts to recognize them. When using modules, you still need to define a default configuration file for your application with the **config** parameter, as you would with a nonmodular application.

NOTE *For more information on using Struts modules, refer to Chapter 9.*

The Struts Configuration File Tags

Table 16-1 lists and describes each of the tags used to configure the Struts configuration file.

Tag	Description
action	Maps an application URL either to an **Action** object that will be executed when the specified URL is requested or to another URL that will be forwarded to.
action-mappings	Encapsulates the set of actions the application will have.
controller	Defines several global configuration settings for a Struts application.
data-source	Defines a Java data source that an application can use to access a database or similar resource.
data-sources	Encapsulates the set of data sources the application will have.
exception	Defines an exception handler to process a specific exception thrown by an **Action**.
form-bean	Defines a Form Bean and assigns a logical name to it.
form-beans	Encapsulates the set of Form Beans the application will have.
form-property	Defines a form property for dynamic Form Beans.
forward	Defines a logical name for a URL, thus allowing code to reference the logical name and not the URL itself.
global-exceptions	Encapsulates a set of exception handlers, defined by **exception** tags, which are global to the application.
global-forwards	Encapsulates a set of forwards, defined by **forward** tags, which are global to the application.

TABLE 16-1   Struts Configuration File Tags

Tag	Description
message-resources	Defines a resource bundle that Struts will use when looking up externalized strings, messages, and labels.
plug-in	Defines a plugin that Struts loads at application startup and unloads at application shutdown.
set-property	Defines a property and its value.
struts-config	Is the root tag for the Struts configuration file and thus encapsulates all other tags in the file.

TABLE 16-1   Struts Configuration File Tags *(continued)*

The remainder of this chapter discusses each tag in detail, including a complete description of the tag, the tag's DTD definition, a table that lists each of the tag's attributes (if the tag has attributes), and a usage example for the tag. In the tables that describe each tag's attributes, pay special attention to the Required column, which denotes whether or not the given attribute is required when using the tag. If an attribute is required and you do not specify it when using the tag, the Struts framework will not be properly configured and, consequently, will not function properly.

The action Tag

The **action** tag is used to map an application URL to an **Action** object that will be executed when the specified URL is requested or to map the URL to another URL to forward the request to.

There are three ways you can use the **action** tag, as listed here and shown later in the "Example Usage" section.

- You can use the **type** attribute to map an **org.apache.struts.action.Action** subclass to the application URL specified by the **path** attribute.

- You can use the **forward** attribute to specify a URL to forward to with a call to **RequestDispatcher.forward( )** when the URL specified by the **path** attribute is matched.

- You can use the **include** attribute to specify a URL to forward to with a call to **RequestDispatcher.include( )** when the URL specified by the **path** attribute is matched.

DTD Definition

Following is the definition for the **action** tag from the Struts configuration file DTD:

```
<!ELEMENT action (icon?, display-name?, description?, set-property*, exception*,
forward*)>
```

Attributes

Attribute	Description	Required
attribute	Specifies the name of the request- or session-scope attribute under which the Form Bean associated with this action is stored. Normally the name specified with the **name** attribute is used to look up the Form Bean; however, if this attribute is used, it will be used instead. This attribute is only valid if the **name** attribute is specified.	No
className	Specifies the fully qualified class name of the configuration object to instantiate for this **Action** definition. Defaults to **org.apache.struts.config.ActionConfig**.	No
forward	Specifies a module-relative URL to forward to when this **Action** mappings path is matched. Uses **RequestDispatcher.forward( )** to perform forward. Only this attribute or one of the **include** or **type** attributes can be specified at a time.	No
include	Specifies a module-relative URL to forward to when this **Action** mappings path is matched. Uses **RequestDispatcher.include( )** to perform forward. Only this attribute or one of the **forward** or **type** attributes can be specified at a time.	No
input	Specifies a module-relative URL to which control will be forwarded if the Form Bean associated with this **Action** is set to be validated and the validation process fails. This attribute is only valid if the **name** attribute is specified.	No
name	Specifies the logical name of a Form Bean, defined with a **form-bean** tag, which will be associated with this action.	No
path	Specifies the module-relative URL to map to.	Yes
parameter	Specifies a value that will be passed as a general-purpose configuration parameter to the **Action** object defined by the **type** attribute upon each execution of the action.	No
prefix	Specifies the prefix to add to request parameter names when populating this **Action**'s associated Form Bean. Thus, a request parameter named "username" coupled with this attribute set to "search" would try to call a method called **setSearchUsername( )** on the Form Bean. This attribute is only valid if the **name** attribute is specified.	No
roles	Specifies a comma-delimited list of security roles that are allowed to access this **Action**.	No
scope	Specifies the scope ("request" or "session") that will be used to access the Form Bean associated with this action with the **name** attribute. This attribute is only valid if the **name** attribute is specified.	No

Attribute	Description	Required
suffix	Specifies the suffix to add to request parameter names when populating this **Action**'s associated Form Bean. Thus, a request parameter named "username" coupled with this attribute set to "search" would try to call a method called **setUsernameSearch( )** on the Form Bean. This attribute is only valid if the **name** attribute is specified.	No
type	Specifies the fully qualified class name for the **org.apache.struts.action.Action** subclass to associate with this **Action** mapping. Only this attribute or one of the **forward** or **include** attributes can be specified at a time.	No
unknown	Accepts "true" or "false" to denote whether or not this action will be set as the default action for the application. If set to "true", any application URLs that don't match another mapping will be handled by this action definition. Only one **action** definition per module configuration should have this set to true. Defaults to "false".	No
validate	Accepts "true" or "false" to denote whether or not the Form Bean specified by the **name** attribute will have its **validate( )** method invoked before this **Action** is executed. This attribute is only valid if the **name** attribute is specified. Defaults to "true".	No

Example Usage

As mentioned, there are three ways you can use the **action** tag. The first way, shown here, defines a global exception handler:

```
<action-mappings>
  <action path="/search"
          type="com.xyzcorp.app.SearchAction"/>
</action-mappings>
```

This example uses the **type** attribute to specify an **Action** object that will be executed when the specified path is matched.

The second way to use the **action** tag is shown here:

```
<action-mappings>
  <action path="/search"
       forward="/search.jsp"/>
</action-mappings>
```

This example uses the **forward** attribute to specify that the "/search.jsp" URL will be forwarded by using **RequestDispatcher.forward( )** when the specified path is matched.

The following snippet shows the third general way to use the **action** tag:

```
<action-mappings>
  <action path="/search"
      include="/search.jsp"/>
</action-mappings>
```

This example uses the **include** attribute to specify that the "/search.jsp" URL will be forwarded by using **RequestDispatcher.include( )** when the specified path is matched.

The action-mappings Tag

The **action-mappings** tag is used to encapsulate the set of actions the application will have. This tag is simply a container for **action** tags.

DTD Definition

Following is the definition for the **action-mappings** tag from the Struts configuration file DTD:

```
<!ELEMENT action-mappings (action*)>
```

Attribute

Attribute	Description	Required
type	Deprecated Use the **action** tag's **className** attribute instead.	No

Example Usage

The following example illustrates how to use the **action-mappings** tag:

```
<action-mappings>
  <action path="/search"
        type="com.xyzcorp.app.SearchAction"/>
</action-mappings>
```

The controller Tag

The **controller** tag is used to define several global configuration settings for your Struts application. In earlier versions of Struts, many of these settings were configured via the Web deployment descriptor **web.xml** by specifying initialization parameters for Struts' **ActionServlet**. However, when Struts added support for application modules in version 1.1, these settings were moved to the Struts configuration file so that they could be configured on a per-module basis.

DTD Definition

Following is the definition for the **controller** tag from the Struts configuration file DTD:

```
<!ELEMENT controller (set-property*)>
```

Attributes

Attribute	Description	Required
bufferSize	Specifies the input buffer size that will be used for file uploads. Defaults to 4096 bytes.	No
className	Specifies the fully qualified class name of the configuration object to instantiate for this controller definition. Defaults to **org.apache.struts.config.ControllerConfig**.	No
contentType	Specifies the content type (and optional character encoding) that will be set on each HTTP response. Note that this setting can be overridden by an **Action**, JSP, or similar resource that a request is forwarded to. Defaults to "text/html".	No
debug	Deprecated Configure your underlying logging library instead.	No
forwardPattern	Specifies the pattern for how the **path** attribute of **forward** tags is mapped to URLs. $M Replaced by this module's prefix. $P Replaced by the **path** attribute of the selected forward. $$ Causes a literal dollar sign ($) to be used. All other $x variables, where x is variable, are reserved for future use and will be silently ignored. Defaults to "MP".	No
inputForward	Accepts "true" or "false" to denote whether or not the **action** tag's **input** attribute will be treated as the name of a forward whose path will be used. If set to "false" (the default), the **action** tag's **input** attribute will be taken as the literal path. Defaults to "false".	No
locale	Accepts "true" or "false" to denote whether or not a **java.util.Locale** object will be stored in users' sessions. Defaults to "true".	No
maxFileSize	Specifies the maximum size, in bytes, for file uploads. Alternatively, if you add "K", "M", or "G" to the end of the value, it will be interpreted as kilobytes, megabytes, or gigabytes, respectively. Defaults to "250M".	No

PART III

Attribute	Description	Required
memFileSize	Specifies the maximum size in bytes for file uploads that will be kept in memory. Alternatively, if you add "K", "M", or "G" to the end of the value, it will be interpreted as kilobytes, megabytes, or gigabytes, respectively. Files larger than this threshold will be written to disk. Defaults to "256K".	No
multipartClass	Specifies the fully qualified class name of the object to use for handling file uploads. Defaults to **org.apache.struts.upload.CommonsMultipartRequestHandler**.	No
nocache	Accepts "true" or "false" to denote whether or not HTTP headers will be added to each response to disable browser caching. Defaults to "false".	No
pagePattern	Specifies the pattern for how the **page** attribute of Struts' tag library tags is mapped to URLs. $M Replaced by this module's prefix. $P Replaced by the **page** attribute of the selected tag. $$ Causes a literal dollar sign ($) to be used. All other $x variables, where x is variable, are reserved for future use and will be silently ignored. Defaults to "MP".	No
processorClass	Specifies the fully qualified class name for the **RequestProcessor** subclass that will be used for this module. Defaults to **org.apache.struts.action.RequestProcessor**.	No
tempDir	Specifies a temporary directory to use to store data during file uploads.	No

Example Usage
There are many different ways that the **controller** tag can be used because it has several attributes, all of which are optional. Following is an example usage that specifies the maximum file size for file uploads:

```
<controller maxFileSize="3M"/>
```

This example sets the maximum size for file uploads to three megabytes.

The data-source Tag
The **data-source** tag is used to define a Java data source that your application can use to access a database or similar resource. The use of nested **set-property** tags configures the data source.

DTD Definition
Following is the definition for the **data-source** tag from the Struts configuration file DTD:

```
<!ELEMENT data-source (set-property*)>
```

Attributes

Attribute	Description	Required
className	Specifies the fully qualified class name for the configuration object to instantiate for this data source definition. Defaults to **org.apache.struts.config.DataSourceConfig**.	No
key	Specifies the servlet context attribute key under which this data source will be stored. If using application modules, the module prefix will be appended to the key (e.g., "${key}${prefix}"). Defaults to the value specified by the constant **org.apache.struts.Globals.DATA_SOURCE_KEY**.	No
type	Specifies the fully qualified class name for the object that will be instantiated for this data source. Must implement **javax.sql.DataSource**.	No

Example Usage
The following example illustrates the basic usage of the **data-source** tag:

```
<data-sources>
  <data-source>
    <set-property property="driverClass"
                  value="org.postgresql.Driver"/>
    ...
  </data-source>
</data-sources>
```

Typically, you will not have to set any attributes on the **data-source** tag itself unless you are defining multiple data sources. All you have to do is configure your data source with nested **set-property** tags. The **set-property** tags will be used to invoke setter methods on the data source when it is initialized.

The data-sources Tag
The **data-sources** tag is used to encapsulate the set of Data Sources the application will have. This tag is simply a container for **data-source** tags.

DTD Definition

Following is the definition for the **data-sources** tag from the Struts configuration file DTD:

```
<!ELEMENT data-sources (data-source*)>
```

Example Usage

The following example illustrates how to use the **data-sources** tag:

```
<data-sources>
  <data-source>
    <set-property property="driverClass"
                     value="org.postgresql.Driver"/>
    ...
  </data-source>
</data-sources>
```

The exception Tag

The **exception** tag is used to define an exception handler to process a specific exception thrown by an **Action**. This feature allows you to assign a different handler to each type of exception that is thrown by actions.

There are two ways you can use the **exception** tag, as listed here and shown later in the "Example Usage" section:

- You can define global exception handlers by placing the **exception** tags inside the **global-exceptions** tag. Global exception handlers apply to all actions.

- You can define action-specific exception handlers by nesting **exception** tags underneath an **action** tag. Action-specific exception handlers can only be "seen" by the enclosing action and will override any global exception handlers with the same target exception.

DTD Definition

Following is the definition for the **exception** tag from the Struts configuration file DTD:

```
<!ELEMENT exception (icon?, display-name?, description?, set-property*)>
```

Attributes

Attribute	Description	Required
bundle	Specifies the servlet context attribute key for a resource bundle, defined with the **message-resources** tag, which will be used to retrieve the message for the key specified by the **key** attribute.	No

Attribute	Description	Required
className	Specifies the fully qualified class name for the configuration object to instantiate for this exception definition. Defaults to **org.apache.struts.config.ExceptionConfig**.	No
handler	Specifies the fully qualified class name for this exception handler.	No
key	Specifies the resource bundle message key to use with this handler.	Yes
path	Specifies the module-relative URL to redirect to if this exception handler is triggered.	No
scope	Specifies the scope ("request" or "session") that will be used to access the **org.apache.struts.action.ActionError** object for this exception.	No
type	Specifies the fully qualified class name of the exception class that this handler is for.	Yes

Example Usage

As mentioned, there are two ways you can use the **exception** tag. The first way, shown here, defines a global exception handler:

```
<global-exceptions>
   <exception type="com.xyzcorp.app.DateFormatException"
             key="errors.date.format"
             path="/error.jsp"/>
</global-exceptions>
```

The following is the second way to use the **exception** tag:

```
<action-mappings>
   <action path="/search"
          type="com.xyzcorp.app.SearchAction">
    <exception type="com.xyzcorp.app.DateFormatException"
              key="errors.date.format"
              path="/searchError.jsp"/>
   </action>
</action-mappings>
```

This example defines an action-specific exception handler. Only the enclosing action can "see" this exception handler and it will override a global exception handler targeted at the same exception.

The form-bean Tag

The **form-bean** tag is used to define a Form Bean and assign a logical name to it. Struts uses Form Beans to capture form data when a form is submitted and to populate forms before being displayed.

There are two ways you can use the **form-bean** tag, as listed here and shown later in the "Example Usage" section:

- You can define a concrete Form Bean by specifying its concrete class with the **type** attribute. This requires creating a class that subclasses **org.apache.struts.action.ActionForm** and creating all the getter and setter methods.

- You can define a dynamic Form Bean by using the **type** attribute to specify that its type is **org.apache.struts.action.DynaActionForm** or a subclass thereof. With this approach, you specify each of the Form Bean's fields in the configuration file with **form-property** tags.

DTD Definition

Following is the definition for the **form-bean** tag from the Struts configuration file DTD:

```
<!ELEMENT form-bean (icon?, display-name?, description?, set-property*, form-
property*)>
```

Attributes

Attribute	Description	Required
className	Specifies the fully qualified class name of the configuration object to instantiate for this Form Bean definition. Defaults to **org.apache.struts.config.FormBeanConfig**.	No
dynamic	Deprecated This is now determined based on whether or not the class specified with the **type** attribute is a subclass of **org.apache.struts.action.DynaActionForm**.	No
name	Specifies the logical name for the Form Bean.	Yes
type	Specifies the fully qualified class name for the Form Bean class.	Yes

Example Usage

As mentioned, there are two ways you can use the **form-bean** tag. The first way, shown here, defines a concrete Form Bean:

```
<form-beans>
  <form-bean name="logonForm"
             type="com.xyzcorp.app.LogonForm"/>
</form-beans>
```

The following is the second way to use the **form-bean** tag:

```
<form-beans>
  <form-bean name="logonForm"
            type="org.apache.struts.action.DynaActionForm">
    <form-property name="username"
                   type="java.lang.String"/>
    <form-property name="password"
                   type="java.lang.String"/>
  </form-bean>
</form-beans>
```

This example defines a dynamic Form Bean whose properties are specified with the nested **form-property** tags. Notice that the **type** attribute is set to **org.apache.struts.action.DynaActionForm**. This informs Struts that the Form Bean's properties are defined in the configuration file.

The form-beans Tag

The **form-beans** tag is used to encapsulate the set of Form Beans the application will have. This tag is simply a container for **form-bean** tags.

DTD Definition

Following is the definition for the **form-beans** tag from the Struts configuration file DTD:

```
<!ELEMENT form-beans (form-bean*)>
```

Attribute

Attribute	Description	Required
type	Deprecated Use the **form-bean** tag's **className** attribute instead.	No

Example Usage

The following example illustrates how to use the **form-beans** tag:

```
<form-beans>
  <form-bean name="searchForm"
            type="com.xyzcorp.app.SearchForm"/>
</form-beans>
```

The form-property Tag

The **form-property** tag is used to define form properties for dynamic Form Beans. Dynamic Form Beans allow you to define a form's properties in the Struts configuration file instead of in a concrete class. Use of this tag will be ignored if the enclosing **form-bean** tag's **type** attribute is not **org.apache.struts.action.DynaActionForm** or a subclass of it.

DTD Definition

Following is the definition for the **form-property** tag from the Struts configuration file DTD:

```
<!ELEMENT form-beans (form-bean*)>
```

Attributes

Attribute	Description	Required
className	Specifies the fully qualified class name of the **FormPropertyConfig** subclass to use for this property. Defaults to **org.apache.struts.config.FormPropertyConfig**.	No
initial	Specifies the initial value of the property. If not specified, primitives will be initialized to 0 and objects will be initialized with their default constructor (thus, **String**s will be initialized to "").	No
name	Specifies the name of the property.	Yes
size	Specifies the size of the array to create if the **type** attribute specifies an array and the **initial** attribute is omitted.	No
type	Specifies the fully qualified class name for the property's underlying field. Optionally, [] can be appended to the type declaration to denote that the field is indexed (e.g., **java.lang.String[ ]**).	Yes

Example Usage

The following example illustrates the basic usage of the **form-property** tag:

```
<form-beans>
  <form-bean name="logonForm"
             type="org.apache.struts.action.DynaActionForm">
    <form-property name="username"
                   type="java.lang.String"/>
    <form-property name="password"
                   type="java.lang.String"/>
  </form-bean>
</form-beans>
```

Instead of specifying a concrete class for your Form Bean definition, you set its type to **org.apache.struts.action.DynaActionForm** or a subclass and then list each of its properties with the **form-property** tag.

The forward Tag

The **forward** tag is used to define a logical name for a URL, thus allowing code and so on to reference the logical name and not the URL itself.

There are two ways you can use the **forward** tag, as listed here and shown later in the "Example Usage" section:

- You can define global forwards by placing the **forward** tags inside the **global-forwards** tag. Global forwards are accessible by any action.

- You can define action-specific forwards by nesting **forward** tags underneath an **action** tag. Action-specific forwards can only be "seen" by the enclosing action and will override any global forwards with the same logical name.

DTD Definition

Following is the definition for the **forward** tag from the Struts configuration file DTD:

```
<!ELEMENT forward (icon?, display-name?, description?, set-property*)>
```

Attributes

Attribute	Description	Required
className	Specifies the fully qualified class name for the configuration object to instantiate for this forward definition. Defaults to **org.apache.struts.config.ForwardConfig**.	No
contextRelative	Accepts "true" or "false" to denote whether or not the URL specified with the **path** attribute will be application-relative when using application modules. Defaults to "false".	No
name	Specifies the logical name for the forward.	Yes
path	Specifies the URL for this forward.	Yes
redirect	Accepts "true" or "false" to denote whether or not an HTTP redirect will be executed for this forward's URL. Defaults to "false".	No

Example Usage

As stated, there are two ways you can use the **forward** tag. The first way, shown here, defines a global forward:

```
<global-forwards>
  <forward name="success"
           path="/success.jsp"/>
</global-forwards>
```

PART III

The second way to use the **forward** tag is shown here:

```
<action-mappings>
  <action path="/search"
          type="com.xyzcorp.app.SearchAction">
    <forward name="success"
             path="/results.jsp"/>
  </action>
</action-mappings>
```

This example defines an action-specific forward. Only the enclosing action can "see" this forward and it will override a global forward with the same logical name if present.

The global-exceptions Tag

The **global-exceptions** tag is used to encapsulate a set of exception handlers, defined by **exception** tags, which are global to the application. This set of global exception handlers will be used to handle any exceptions being thrown from actions unless an action's corresponding **action** tag overrides one or more of the global exception handlers by nesting **exception** tags underneath it.

DTD Definition

Following is the definition for the **global-exceptions** tag from the Struts configuration file DTD:

```
<!ELEMENT global-exceptions (exception*)>
```

Example Usage

The following example illustrates how to use the **global-exceptions** tag:

```
<global-exceptions>
  <exception type="com.xyzcorp.app.DateFormatException"
             key="errors.date.format"
             path="/error.jsp"/>
</global-exceptions>
```

This tag simply encapsulates the set of exception handlers that are global to the application.

The global-forwards Tag

The **global-forwards** tag is used to encapsulate a set of forwards, defined by **forward** tags, which are global to the application. Unless an action defines a forward with a nested **forward** tag that overrides one or more of these global forwards, the global forward will be used to determine where to forward when an action finishes executing.

DTD Definition

Following is the definition for the **global-forwards** tag from the Struts configuration file DTD:

```
<!ELEMENT global-forwards (forward*)>
```

Attribute

Attribute	Description	Required
Type	Deprecated Use the **forward** tag's **className** attribute instead.	No

Example Usage

The following example illustrates the basic usage of the **global-forwards** tag:

```
<global-forwards>
  <forward name="success" path="/success.jsp"/>
  <forward name="failure" path="/failure.jsp"/>
</global-forwards>
```

This tag simply encapsulates the set of forwards that will be global to the application.

The message-resources Tag

The **message-resources** tag is used to define a resource bundle that Struts will use when looking up externalized strings, messages, and labels.

DTD Definition

Following is the definition for the **message-resources** tag from the Struts configuration file DTD:

```
<!ELEMENT message-resources (set-property*)>
```

Attributes

Attribute	Description	Required
className	Specifies the fully qualified class name of the configuration object to instantiate for this message resource's definition. Defaults to **org.apache.struts.config.MessageResourcesConfig**.	No

Attribute	Description	Required
factory	Specifies the fully qualified class name of the **MessagesResourcesFactory** subclass that will be used to create this message resource instance. Defaults to **org.apache.struts.util.PropertyMessageResourcesFactory**.	No
key	Specifies the servlet context attribute key under which this message resource instance will be stored. If using application modules, the module prefix will be appended to the key (e.g., "${key}${prefix}"). Defaults to the value specified by the constant **org.apache.struts.Globals.MESSAGES_KEY**.	No
null	Accepts "true" or "false" to denote whether or not missing messages should return null.	No
parameter	Specifies a configuration parameter value that will be passed to the **createResources( )** method of the factory object specified by the **factory** attribute.	Yes

Example Usage

The following example illustrates the basic usage of the **message-resources** tag:

```
<message-resources
    parameter="com.xyzcorp.app.ApplicationResources"/>
```

This example specifies that Struts should use a file called **ApplicationResources .properties** from the **com.xyzcorp.app** package as its resource bundle. Notice that the ".properties" portion of the filename is not specified with the tag; Struts automatically appends that to the name of the file that you specify with the **parameter** attribute.

    Sometimes it's useful or necessary to have more than one resource bundle. You can accomplish that by using multiple **message-resources** tags in your configuration file, as shown here:

```
<message-resources
    parameter="com.xyzcorp.app.ApplicationResources"/>

<message-resources
    parameter="com.xyzcorp.app.AlternateApplicationResources"
        key="alternate"/>
```

Each instance of the **message-resources** tag must specify a unique key with the **key** attribute to identify it, unless it's for the default resource bundle, which does not require an explicit key.

The plug-in Tag

The **plug-in** tag is used to define a plugin that Struts loads at application startup and unloads at application shutdown. Among other things, plugins are useful for loading persistent resources at application startup. Each plugin class must implement Struts' **org.apache.struts.action.PlugIn** interface. Upon application startup, the plugin's **init( )** method will be called. Upon application shutdown, the plugin's **destroy( )** method will be called.

DTD Definition

Following is the definition for the **plug-in** tag from the Struts configuration file DTD:

```
<!ELEMENT plug-in (set-property*)>
```

Attribute

Attribute	Description	Required
className	Specifies the fully qualified class name for the plugin. This class must implement the **org.apache.struts.action.PlugIn** interface.	Yes

Example Usage

The following example illustrates the usage of the **plug-in** tag:

```
<plug-in className="org.apache.struts.validator.ValidatorPlugIn">
  <set-property property="pathnames"
                value="/WEB-INF/validator-rules.xml,
                       /WEB-INF/validation.xml"/>
</plug-in>
```

The **plug-in** tag is quite simple because it has only one attribute. In most cases, there will be nested **set-property** tags to dynamically configure the plugin. Each plugin defines its own set of properties that can be configured via **set-property** tags.

The set-property Tag

The **set-property** tag is used to define a property and its value. Several of the other Struts configuration file tags allow instances of this tag to be nested inside them to specify properties that will be set when the tags' corresponding configuration objects are instantiated. Struts uses reflection to look up and invoke a setter method (e.g., **setMyProp( )** for a property called **myProp**) on the configuration object based on the name specified with this tag's **property** attribute.

DTD Definition

Following is the definition for the **set-property** tag from the Struts configuration file DTD:

```
<!ELEMENT set-property EMPTY>
```

Attributes

Attribute	Description	Required
property	Specifies the name of the property.	Yes
value	Specifies the value of the property.	Yes

Example Usage

The following example illustrates the basic usage of the **set-property** tag:

```
<plug-in className="org.apache.struts.tiles.TilesPlugin">
  <set-property property="definitions-config"
                value="/WEB-INF/tiles-defs.xml"/>
  <set-property property="moduleAware" value="true"/>
</plug-in>
```

At run time, when Struts parses a configuration file with a definition similar to this, it will use reflection to look up and invoke the **setDefinitionsConfig( )** and **setModuleAware( )** methods of the class specified by the **plug-in** tag's **className** attribute, passing them the defined values.

The struts-config Tag

The **struts-config** tag is the root tag for the Struts configuration file and thus encapsulates all other tags in the file. This tag has no other use than to denote the beginning and end of configuration data.

DTD Definition

Following is the definition for the **struts-config** tag from the Struts configuration file DTD:

```
<!ELEMENT struts-config (data-sources?, form-beans?, global-exceptions?, global-
forwards?, action-mappings?, controller?, message-resources*, plug-in*)>
```

Example Usage

The following snippet illustrates how to use the **struts-config** tag:

```
<struts-config>
  <form-beans>
    ...
```

```
    </form-beans>
    <action-mappings>
      ...
    </action-mappings>
</struts-config>
```

Metadata Tags

Several of the tags for the Struts configuration file give you the option to nest metadata tags. The metadata tags exist solely for adding extra information to the configuration file that will show up in GUI tools and the like; Struts itself ignores the metadata tags. None of the metadata tags has any attributes; thus, you just add text between opening and closing tags to specify their value, as shown here:

```
<action path="/search"
        type="com.xyzcorp.app.SearchAction">
  <icon>
    <small-icon>small.gif</small-icon>
    <large-icon>large.gif</large-icon>
  </icon>
  <display-name>Search Action</display-name>
  <description>Search Action searches for employees.</description>
</action>
```

The following table lists and describes each of the metadata tags.

Tag	Description
description	Defines descriptive text for the enclosing tag.
display-name	Defines a short description (or name) for the enclosing tag.
icon	Encapsulates an instance of the **large-icon** and the **small-icon** tags.
large-icon	Defines the location for a large (32×32 pixel) icon to associate to the enclosing tag.
small-icon	Defines the location for a small (16×16 pixel) icon to associate to the enclosing tag.

Editing Struts Configuration Files with Struts Console

As you can imagine, trying to remember every tag's list of attributes as well as its proper order inside the configuration file can be cumbersome. If you make a mistake in typing any of the tag's or attribute's names, your Struts application will not be configured properly. To simplify the creation and modification of Struts configuration files, you can use a GUI tool called Struts Console. Struts Console is a stand-alone Java Swing application that provides a graphical editor for Struts configuration files.

Additionally, Struts Console can be used as a plugin with several major Java IDEs, providing a seamless Struts development experience.

Struts Console is free software and can be downloaded from

http://www.jamesholmes.com/struts/

which has all the information you need to configure Struts Console to work with your favorite Java IDE. In addition, this book's appendix provides a Struts Console quick reference.

Figure 16-1 shows Struts Console running as a stand-alone application.

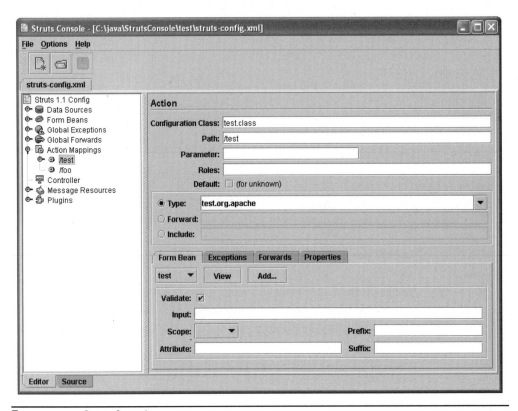

FIGURE 16-1   Struts Console

17
CHAPTER

The Tiles Configuration File

The Tiles framework, which supports the creation of regions within a page, provides a rich JSP templating system that extends beyond JSP's built-in include mechanism. Like the include mechanism, Tiles templates can be defined and accessed via JSP Tag Library tags. However, Tiles takes it one step further by allowing your application's configuration to be specified declaratively in an external configuration file instead of being hard-coded into JSPs. This greatly simplifies development because many changes can be made to the application without having to recompile any code.

The Tiles configuration file is XML-based and its format is governed by a Document Type Definition (DTD) file that specifies how the configuration tags must be ordered in the file, what settings are required, and so on. Each Tiles configuration file declares its conformance to the DTD by having the following DOCTYPE definition at the top of the file:

```
<!DOCTYPE tiles-definitions PUBLIC
  "-//Apache Software Foundation//DTD Tiles Configuration 1.1//EN"
  "http://jakarta.apache.org/struts/dtds/tiles-config_1_1.dtd">
```

When Tiles reads the configuration file, its XML parser uses the DOCTYPE definition to determine to which DTD the XML file must conform. If configured to do so, the XML parser will validate the XML file's conformance to the DTD.

NOTE *An in-depth discussion of the Tiles framework is found in Chapter 7.*

Understanding XML DTDs

Because DTD conformance is important for Tiles tags, a brief overview of how XML DTDs work is given here. DTDs specify a set of tags and attributes that make up a specific XML document type. DTDs also specify the order in which tags must be placed in the file, and the relationship between tags. For example, a tag definition defines what other tags can be

377

nested inside of it, how many occurrences can be nested, and in what order the nesting can occur. Additionally, DTDs define which tag attributes are required and which are optional.

Each tag described in this chapter has a DTD Definition section that lists the tag's definition in the Tiles configuration file DTD. The definitions will be similar to the one shown in the following snippet:

```
<!ELEMENT definition (icon?,display-name?,description?,put*,putList*)>
```

This example defines a "definition" tag and the tags that can be nested inside of it. According to the definition, the tag can have nested **icon**, **display-name**, **description**, **put**, and **putList** tags. The question mark (?) and asterisk (*) characters following the nested tags' names indicate the number of times the nested tag can be nested. The ? character indicates that the tag can be nested zero or one time. The * character indicates that the tag can be nested zero or more (unlimited) times. A plus (+) character indicates that the tag must be nested at least once and as many times as you'd like. No trailing character means that the tag must be nested exactly once and no more. If no tags can be nested inside the defined tag, EMPTY is used to denote that, as shown next:

```
<!ELEMENT set-property EMPTY>
```

Enabling the Tiles Plugin

Although the Tiles framework comes packaged with Struts, by default Tiles is not enabled. In order to enable and use Tiles, you have to add the following **<plug-in>** definition to your application's Struts configuration file:

```
<!-- Tiles Configuration -->
<plug-in className="org.apache.struts.tiles.TilesPlugin">
  <set-property property="definitions-config"
                value="/WEB-INF/tiles-defs.xml"/>
</plug-in>
```

This definition causes Struts to load and initialize the Tiles plugin for your application. Upon initialization, the plugin loads the comma-delimited list of Tiles configuration files specified by the "definitions-config" property. Each configuration file's path must be specified using a Web application–relative path, as shown in the preceding example.

Note that your application's Struts configuration file must conform to the Struts configuration file DTD, which specifies the order in which elements are to appear in the file. Because of this, you must place the Tiles **<plug-in>** definition in the proper place in the file. The easiest way to ensure that you are properly ordering elements in the file is to use a tool, such as Struts Console, that automatically formats your configuration file so that it conforms to the DTD.

TABLE 17-1
Tiles Configuration
File Tags

Tag	Description
add	Defines an entry for a list created with the **putList** tag.
bean	Defines an entry (of the specified type) for a list created with the **putList** tag.
definition	Defines a "tile" and assigns a logical name to it.
item	Defines a **MenuItem** entry for a list created with the **putList** tag.
put	Defines an attribute (or parameter) for a definition.
putList	Defines a list attribute (of **java.util.List** type) containing an ordered collection of individual attributes.
set-property	Defines a property and its value for a bean defined with the **bean** tag.
tiles-definitions	Is the root tag for the Tiles configuration file and thus encapsulates all other tags in the file.

The Tile Configuration File Tags

Table 17-1 (above) lists each of the tags used to configure the Tiles configuration file and provides a short description of each tag's purpose.

The remainder of this chapter discusses each tag in detail, including a complete description of the tag, the tag's DTD definition, a table that lists each of the tag's attributes (if the tag has attributes), and a usage example for the tag. In the tables that describe each tag's attributes, pay special attention to the Required column, which denotes whether or not the given attribute is required when using the tag. If an attribute is required and you do not specify it when using the tag, the Tiles framework will not be properly configured and, consequently, will not function properly.

The add Tag

The **add** tag is used to define an entry for a list created with the **putList** tag. There are two ways that the value for the entry can be specified. The value can be specified with the **value** attribute, or the value can be placed between opening and closing **add** tags, as shown next:

```
<add>value goes here</add>
```

DTD Definition

Following is the definition for the **add** tag from the Tiles configuration file DTD:

```
<!ELEMENT add (#PCDATA)>
```

Attributes

Attribute	Description	Required
content	Deprecated Originally for compatibility with the now defunct Template Tag Library. Use the **value** attribute instead.	No
direct	Deprecated Originally for compatibility with the now defunct Template Tag Library. Use the **type** attribute set to "string" instead.	No
type	Specifies the type (string, page, or definition) of the value. If present, it indicates how the value specified with the **value** attribute is treated.	No
value	Specifies the value for this entry.	No

Example Usage

The following example illustrates the basic usage of the **add** tag:

```
<definition name="mainLayout"
             path="/layouts/main.jsp">
  <putList name="urls">
    <add value="http://www.google.com/"/>

    <add value="http://www.yahoo.com/"/>
  </putList>
</definition>
```

Each **add** definition is added to the enclosing list in the order specified.

The bean Tag

The **bean** tag is used to define an entry (of the specified type) for a list created with the **putList** tag.

DTD Definition

Following is the definition for the **bean** tag from the Tiles configuration file DTD:

```
<!ELEMENT bean (set-property*)>
```

Attribute

Attribute	Description	Required
classtype	Specifies the fully qualified class name for the bean.	Yes

Example Usage

The following snippet illustrates how to use the **bean** tag:

```
<definition name="mainLayout"
            path="/layouts/main.jsp">
  <putList name="items">
    <bean classtype="org.apache.struts.tiles.beans.SimpleMenuItem">
      <set-property property="link" value="aLink1"/>
      <set-property property="value" value="aValue1"/>
    </bean>
  </putList>
</definition>
```

Beans defined with the **bean** tag can have their properties initialized at creation by nesting **set-property** tags with the name of the property and the value to be initialized.

The definition Tag

The **definition** tag is used to define a tile (which is a region within a page) and assign a logical name to it.

DTD Definition

Following is the definition for the **definition** tag from the Tiles configuration file DTD:

```
<!ELEMENT definition (icon?, display-name?, description?, put*, putList*)>
```

Attributes

Attribute	Description	Required
controllerClass	Specifies the fully qualified class name of a controller object that is executed before this definition is inserted.	No
controllerUrl	Specifies the URL for a controller that is executed before this definition is inserted.	No
extends	Specifies the name of another definition that this definition is to extend.	No

Attribute	Description	Required
name	Specifies the logical name for the definition.	Yes
page	Deprecated Use the **path** attribute instead.	No
path	Specifies the URL for the tile.	No
role	Specifies a role to check against the currently authenticated user. If the user is not in the specified role, this definition will not be inserted.	No
template	Deprecated Originally for compatibility with the now defunct Template Tag Library. Use the **path** attribute instead.	No

Example Usage

The following example illustrates the basic usage of the **definition** tag:

```
<definition name="mainLayout"
            path="/layouts/main.jsp">
  <put name="header" value="/layouts/header.jsp"/>
  <put name="footer" value="/layouts/footer.jsp"/>
</definition>
```

Each of the attributes nested underneath the **definition** tag can be accessed by the JSP specified with the **path** attribute.

The item Tag

The **item** tag is used to define a **MenuItem** entry for a list created with the **putList** tag.

DTD Definition

Following is the definition for the **item** tag from the Tiles configuration file DTD:

```
<!ELEMENT item (#PCDATA)>
```

Attributes

Attribute	Description	Required
classtype	Specifies the fully qualified class name of the item. If specified, it must be a subclass of **org.apache.struts.tiles.beans.MenuItem**.	No
icon	Specifies the value to set the bean's **icon** property to.	No
link	Specifies the value to set the bean's **link** property to.	Yes

Attribute	Description	Required
tooltip	Specifies the value to set the bean's **tooltip** property to.	No
value	Specifies the value to set the bean's **value** property to.	Yes

Example Usage

The following example illustrates the basic usage of the **item** tag:

```
<definition name="mainLayout"
            path="/layouts/main.jsp">
  <putList name="items">
    <item value="Home" link="/index.jsp"/>
    <item value="Search" link="/search.jsp"/>
  </putList>
</definition>
```

The values specified with the **value** and **link** attributes are used to initialize the corresponding properties on the **MenuItem** object.

The put Tag

The **put** tag is used to define an attribute (or parameter) for a definition. There are two ways that the value for the attribute can be specified. The value can be specified with the **value** attribute, or the value can be placed between opening and closing **put** tags, as shown next:

```
<put name="header">value goes here</put>
```

DTD Definition

Following is the definition for the **put** tag from the Tiles configuration file DTD:

```
<!ELEMENT put (#PCDATA)>
```

Attributes

Attribute	Description	Required
content	Deprecated Originally for compatibility with the now defunct Template Tag Library. Use the **value** attribute instead.	No
direct	Deprecated Originally for compatibility with the now defunct Template Tag Library. Use the **type** attribute set to "string" instead.	No

PART III

Attribute	Description	Required
name	Specifies the name for the attribute.	Yes
type	Specifies the type (string, page, or definition) of the value. If present, it indicates how the value specified with the **value** attribute is treated.	No
value	Specifies the value for the attribute.	No

Example Usage
The following example illustrates the basic usage of the **put** tag:

```
<definition name="mainLayout"
            path="/layouts/main.jsp">
  <put name="header" value="/layouts/header.jsp"/>
  <put name="footer" value="/layouts/footer.jsp"/>
</definition>
```

Defining attributes with the **put** tag is as simple as specifying their names and values.

The putList Tag

The **putList** tag is used to define a list attribute (of **java.util.List** type) containing an ordered collection of individual attributes. The list can be populated with **add**, **item**, or **bean** definitions or any combination thereof.

DTD Definition
Following is the definition for the **putList** tag from the Tiles configuration file DTD:

```
<!ELEMENT putList ((add*|item*|bean*|putList*)+)>
```

Attribute

Attribute	Description	Required
name	Specifies the name of the list.	Yes

Example Usage
The following example illustrates the basic usage of the **putList** tag:

```
<definition name="mainLayout"
            path="/layouts/main.jsp">
  <putList name="urls">
    <add value="http://www.google.com/"/>
    <add value="http://www.yahoo.com/"/>
  </putList>
</definition>
```

Each tag nested between opening and closing **putList** tags will be added to the backing **java.util.List** instance in the order specified.

The set-property Tag

The **set-property** tag is used to define a property and its value for a bean defined with the **bean** tag. The Tiles framework uses reflection to look up and invoke a setter method (e.g., **setMyProp( )** for a property called **myProp**) on the enclosing bean based on the name specified with this tag's **property** attribute.

DTD Definition

Following is the definition for the **set-property** tag from the Tiles configuration file DTD:

```
<!ELEMENT set-property EMPTY>
```

Attributes

Attribute	Description	Required
property	Specifies the name of the property.	Yes
value	Specifies the value of the property.	Yes

Example Usage

The following example illustrates the basic usage of the **set-property** tag:

```
<definition name="mainLayout"
            path="/layouts/main.jsp">
  <putList name="items">
    <bean classtype="org.apache.struts.tiles.beans.SimpleMenuItem">
      <set-property property="link" value="aLink1"/>
      <set-property property="value" value="aValue1"/>
    </bean>
  </putList>
</definition>
```

At run time, when the Tiles framework parses a configuration file with a definition similar to this, it will use reflection to look up and invoke the **setLink( )** and **setValue( )** methods of the class specified by the **bean** tag's **classtype** attribute, passing them the defined values.

The tiles-definitions Tag

The **tiles-definitions** tag is the root tag for the Tiles configuration file and thus encapsulates all other tags in the file. This tag has no other use than to denote the beginning and end of configuration data.

DTD Definition

Following is the definition for the **tiles-definitions** tag from the Tiles configuration file DTD:

```
<!ELEMENT tiles-definitions (definition+)>
```

Example Usage

The following snippet illustrates how to use the **tiles-definitions** tag:

```
<tiles-definitions>
  <definition …/>
  <definition …/>

  …
</tiles-definitions>
```

Metadata Tags

Several of the tags for the Tiles configuration file give you the option to nest metadata tags. The metadata tags exist solely for adding extra information to the configuration file that will show up in GUI tools and the like; the Tiles framework, itself, ignores the metadata tags. None of the metadata tags has any attributes, thus you just add text between opening and closing tags to specify their value, as shown here:

```
<action path="/search"
        type="com.xyzcorp.app.SearchAction">
  <icon>
    <small-icon>small.gif</small-icon>
    <large-icon>large.gif</large-icon>
  </icon>
  <display-name>Search Action</display-name>
  <description>Search Action searches for employees.</description>
</action>
```

The following table lists each of the metadata tags and its description.

Tag	Description
description	Defines descriptive text for the enclosing tag.
display-name	Defines a short description (or name) for the enclosing tag.
icon	Encapsulates an instance of the **large-icon** and **small-icon** tags.
large-icon	Defines the location for a large (32×32 pixel) icon to associate to the enclosing tag.
small-icon	Defines the location for a small (16×16 pixel) icon to associate to the enclosing tag.

Editing Tiles Configuration Files with Struts Console

As you can imagine, trying to remember every tag's list of attributes as well as its
proper order inside the configuration file can be cumbersome. If you make a mistake
in typing any of the tag's or attribute's names, your Struts application will not be
configured properly. To simplify the creation and modification of Tiles configuration
files, you can use a GUI tool called Struts Console. Struts Console is a stand-alone
Java Swing application that provides a graphical editor for Tiles configuration files.
Additionally, Struts Console can be used as a plugin with several major Java IDEs,
providing a seamless Struts development experience.

Struts Console is free software and can be downloaded from

http://www.jamesholmes.com/struts/

This Web site has all the information for configuring Struts Console to work with your
favorite Java IDE. In addition, this book's appendix provides a Struts Console quick
reference. Figure 17-1 shows Struts Console running as a stand-alone application.

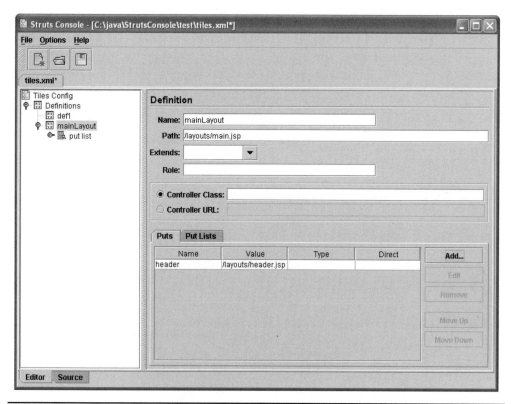

FIGURE 17-1   Struts Console running as a stand-alone application

The Validator
Configuration Files

The Validator framework is designed to enable you to specify validations declaratively in external configuration files instead of having to hard-code validation logic into the application. This simplifies development because validations can be changed, added, or removed as necessary without having to recompile any code. Using configuration files also enables a significant amount of code reuse for the validation routines.

The Validator configuration files are XML-based and their formats are governed by a Document Type Definition (DTD) file that specifies how the configuration tags must be ordered in each file, what settings are required, and so on. Each Validator configuration file declares its conformance to the DTD by having the following DOCTYPE definition at the top of the file:

```
<!DOCTYPE form-validation PUBLIC
  "-//Apache Software Foundation//DTD Commons
  Validator Rules Configuration 1.0//EN"
  "http://jakarta.apache.org/commons/dtds/validator_1_0.dtd">
```

When Validator reads the configuration file, its XML parser uses the DOCTYPE definition to determine the DTD that the XML file must conform to. If configured to do so, the XML parser will validate the XML file's conformance to the DTD.

NOTE *An in-depth discussion of using the Validator framework is found in Chapter 6.*

Two Configuration Files

In general, Validator uses two XML configuration files to tell it which validation routines should be "installed" and how they should be applied for a given application, respectively. The first configuration file, **validator-rules.xml**, declares the validation routines that are plugged into the framework and assigns logical names to each of the validations. Additionally, the **validator-rules.xml** file is used to define client-side JavaScript code for each validation routine. If configured to do so, Validator will emit this JavaScript code to the browser so that validations are performed on the client side as well as the server side. The second configuration file, **validation.xml**, defines which validation routines are applied to which Form Beans. The definitions in this file use the logical names of Form Beans from the Struts configuration file along with the logical names of validation routines from the **validator-rules.xml** file to tie the two together.

Although it is standard to use two configuration files for Validator, it is not technically required. Both configuration files must conform to the same DTD and thus could be combined into one large file that specifies both the validation routines and their use with forms. However, it's advantageous to have the individual files because you can reuse the **validation-rules.xml** file in multiple applications. Similarly, if your application uses the Struts module feature, then you will likely have a **validation.xml** file for each module. Embedding the contents of **validator-rules.xml** in **validation.xml** would result in a great deal of redundancy in this scenario.

Understanding XML DTDs

Because DTD conformance is important for Validator tags, a brief overview of how XML DTDs work is given here. DTDs specify a set of tags and attributes that make up a specific XML document type. DTDs also specify the order in which tags must be placed in the file, and the relationship between tags. For example, a tag definition defines what other tags can be nested inside of it, how many occurrences can be nested, and in what order the nesting can occur. Additionally, DTDs define which tag attributes are required and which are optional.

Each tag described in this chapter has a DTD Definition section that lists the tag's definition in the Struts configuration file DTD. The definitions will be similar to the one shown in the following snippet:

```
<!ELEMENT form-bean
  (icon?, display-name?, description?, set-property*, form-property*)>
```

This example defines a **form-bean** tag and the tags that can be nested inside of it. According to the definition, the tag can have nested **icon**, **display-name**, **description**, **set-property**, and **form-property** tags. The question mark (?) and asterisk (*) characters following the nested tags' names indicate the number of times the nested tag can be nested. The ? character indicates that the tag can be nested zero or one time. The * character indicates that the tag can be nested zero or more (unlimited) times. A plus (+) character indicates that the tag must be nested at least once and as many times as you'd like. No trailing character means that the tag must be nested exactly once and no more. If no tags can be nested inside the defined tag, EMPTY is used to denote that, as shown next:

```
<!ELEMENT arg1 EMPTY>
```

Enabling the Validator Plugin

Although the Validator framework comes packaged with Struts, by default Validator is not enabled. In order to enable and use Validator, you have to add the following **<plug-in>** definition to your application's Struts configuration file:

```
<!-- Validator Configuration -->
<plug-in className="org.apache.struts.validator.ValidatorPlugIn">
  <set-property property="pathnames"
                value="/WEB-INF/validator-rules.xml,
                       /WEB-INF/validation.xml"/>
</plug-in>
```

This definition causes Struts to load and initialize the Validator plugin for your application. Upon initialization, the plugin loads the comma-delimited list of Validator configuration files specified by the "pathnames" property. Each configuration file's path must be specified using a Web application–relative path, as shown in the preceding example.

Note that your application's Struts configuration file must conform to the Struts configuration file DTD, which specifies the order in which elements are to appear in the file. Because of this, you must place the Validator **<plug-in>** definition in the proper place in the file. The easiest way to ensure that you are properly ordering elements in the file is to use a tool, such as Struts Console, that automatically formats your configuration file so that it conforms to the DTD.

The Validator Configuration File Tags

Table 18-1 lists each of the tags used to configure the Validator configuration file and provides a short description of each tag's purpose.

The remainder of this chapter discusses each tag in detail, including a complete description of the tag, the tag's DTD definition, a table that lists each of the tag's attributes (if the tag has attributes), and a usage example for the tag. In the tables that describe a tag's attributes, pay special attention to the Required column, which denotes whether or not the given attribute is required when using the tag. If an attribute is required and you do not specify it when using the tag, the Validator framework will not be properly configured and, consequently, will not function properly.

PART III

Tag	Description
arg0	Defines the first replacement value, **{0}**, for a validation's error message.
arg1	Defines the second replacement value, **{1}**, for a validation's error message.
arg2	Defines the third replacement value, **{2}**, for a validation's error message.
arg3	Defines the fourth replacement value, **{3}**, for a validation's error message.
constant	Defines a named value that can be used as a replacement parameter within the **field** tag's nested tags.
constant-name	Defines the **constant** tag's constant name.
constant-value	Defines the **constant** tag's constant value.
field	Defines the set of validations that will be applied to a form's field.
form	Defines a Form Bean whose set of fields will be validated based on rules defined by nested **field** tags.
form-validation	Is the root tag for the Validator configuration file and thus encapsulates all other tags in the file.
formset	Defines validations for a set of forms.
global	Encapsulates the set of validations and the set of constants that Validator will use.
javascript	Defines client-side JavaScript code for a validation.
msg	Defines an error message that will override a validation's default message.
validator	Defines a validation routine and assigns it a logical name.
var	Defines a variable that will be passed to each of a field's validators at run time.
var-name	Defines the **var** tag's variable name.
var-value	Defines the **var** tag's variable value.

TABLE 18-1   Validator Configuration File Tags

The arg0, arg1, arg2, and arg3 Tags

The **arg** tags are used to define values for a validation's error message. There are four **arg** tags and they are shown here:

- **arg0**   The first replacement value, specified by {0}
- **arg1**   The second replacement value, specified by {1}
- **arg2**   The third replacement value, specified by {2}
- **arg3**   The fourth replacement value, specified by {3}

Before the specified validation's error message is generated, it is parsed and any {N} reference is replaced with the message specified by the corresponding tag. Following is an example resource bundle message that contains a {0} reference:

```
errors.required={0} is a required field
```

At run time, when Validator uses this error message, it will attempt to replace any parametric references with the values specified by their respective **arg0 – arg3** tags. Thus, if "Username" was specified with the **arg0** tag, the preceding message would be turned into the following message:

```
Username is a required field
```

DTD Definition
Following is the definition for the **arg** tags from the Validator configuration file DTD:

```
<!ELEMENT argN EMPTY>
```

Attributes

Attribute	Description	Required
key	Specifies a key for a resource bundle message that will be used as the replacement value.	No
name	Specifies the logical name of the validation that this tag will be applied to.	No
resource	Accepts "true" or "false" to denote whether or not the **key** attribute's value will be taken as a literal value rather than a message key. Defaults to "true".	No

Example Usage
The following example illustrates the basic usage of the **arg2** tag:

```
<field property="zipCode"
        depends="required,mask">
  <arg2 key="prompt.zipCode"/>
  <var>
    <var-name>mask</var-name>
    <var-value>>^\d{5}\d*$</var-value>
  </var>
</field>
```

This example specifies the {2} replacement value to use for each of the validations specified by the **field** tag's **depends** attribute. Alternatively, the **arg** tag can be configured to apply to only a specific validation's error message by using the **name** attribute, as shown next:

```
<arg2 name="required" key="prompt.zipCode"/>
```

In this example, the replacement value will be applied only to the **required** validation's error message.

The constant Tag

The **constant** tag is used to define a named value that can be used as a replacement parameter within the **field** tag's nested tags. For example, constants can be used to define an often used regular expression for the configurable **mask** validation, as shown here:

```
<constant>
  <constant-name>zip</constant-name>
  <constant-phone>^\d{5}\d*$</constant-phone>
</constant>
```

Each time a ZIP code needs to be validated with the **mask** validation, the constant can be used to specify the regular expression to use, instead of having to specify the regular expression itself, as shown next:

```
<field property="zipCode"
       depends="required,mask">
  <var>
    <var-name>mask</var-name>
    <var-value>${zip}</var-value>
  </var>
</field>
```

To use constants, you simply enclose the constant name with an opening ${ and a closing }.

DTD Definition

Following is the definition for the **constant** tag from the Validator configuration file DTD:

```
<!ELEMENT constant (constant-name, constant-value)>
```

Example Usage

The following snippet illustrates how to use the **constant** tag:

```
<global>
  <constant>
    <constant-name>zip</constant-name>
    <constant-value>^\d{5}\d*$</constant-value>
  </constant>
</global>
```

The **constant** tag can be used an unlimited number of times. Each use of the **constant** tag must have nested **constant-name** and **constant-value** tags.

The constant-name Tag

The **constant-name** tag is used to define the **constant** tag's constant name. This tag must be nested exactly once underneath the **constant** tag.

DTD Definition

Following is the definition for the **constant-name** tag from the Validator configuration file DTD:

```
<!ELEMENT constant-name (#PCDATA)>
```

Example Usage

The following snippet illustrates how to use the **constant-name** tag:

```
<global>
  <constant>
    <constant-name>zip</constant-name>
    <constant-value>^\d{5}\d*$</constant-value>
  </constant>
</global>
```

The constant-value Tag

The **constant-value** tag is used to define the **constant** tag's constant value. This tag must be nested exactly once underneath the **constant** tag.

DTD Definition

Following is the definition for the **constant-value** tag from the Validator configuration file DTD:

```
<!ELEMENT constant-value (#PCDATA)>
```

Example Usage

The following snippet illustrates how to use the **constant-value** tag:

```
<global>
  <constant>
    <constant-name>zip</constant-name>
    <constant-value>^\d{5}\d*$</constant-value>
  </constant>
</global>
```

PART III

The field Tag

The **field** tag is used to define the set of validations that will be applied to a form's field.

DTD Definition

Following is the definition for the **field** tag from the Validator configuration file DTD:

```
<!ELEMENT field (msg|arg0|arg1|arg2|arg3|var)*>
```

Attributes

Attribute	Description	Required
depends	Specifies the comma-delimited list of validations that will be applied to this field.	No
indexedListProperty	Specifies the name of a collection field whose elements will be validated. If this attribute is specified, the value specified with the **property** attribute will be used as the name of the property that will be validated on each object in the collection.	No
page	Specifies a value that will be compared against the enclosing Form Bean's "page" property if it has one. If the value matches, then this field definition's validations will be applied. If not, they will be bypassed. This feature is useful for wizard-style forms where fields need to be conditionally validated based on which page the wizard is currently on.	No
property	Specifies the name of the form field.	Yes

Example Usage

The following example illustrates the basic usage of the **field** tag:

```
<field property="zipCode"
       depends="required,mask">
  <arg0 key="prompt.zipCode"/>
  <var>
    <var-name>mask</var-name>
    <var-value>>^\d{5}\d*$</var-value>
  </var>
</field>
```

Each validation specified with the **depends** attribute will be executed in order. Consequently, if a validation fails, the remaining validations will be skipped. Additionally, each validation can be globally or individually customized with nested **arg0 – arg3**, **msg**, and **var** tags.

The form Tag

The **form** tag is used to define a Form Bean whose set of fields will be validated based on rules defined by nested **field** tags.

DTD Definition

Following is the definition for the **form** tag from the Validator configuration file DTD:

```
<!ELEMENT form (field+)>
```

Attribute

Attribute	Description	Required
name	Specifies the name of the form.	Yes

Example Usage

The following snippet illustrates how to use the **form** tag:

```
<form name="logonForm">
  <field property="username" depends="required">
    <arg0 key="prompt.username"/>
  </field>
  <field property="password" depends="required">
    <arg0 key="prompt.password"/>
  </field>
</form>
```

The name specified with the **name** attribute must match the logical name of a Form Bean from the Struts configuration file. Similarly, each of the form's nested **field** tags must match a property of the Form Bean.

The form-validation Tag

The **form-validation** tag is the root tag for the Validator configuration file and thus encapsulates all other tags in the file. This tag has no other use than to denote the beginning and end of configuration data.

DTD Definition

Following is the definition for the **form-validation** tag from the Validator configuration file DTD:

```
<!ELEMENT form-validation (global*,formset*)>
```

Example Usage

The following snippet illustrates how to use the **form-validation** tag:

```
<form-validation>
  <global>
    ...
  </global>
  <formset>
    ...
  </formset>
</form-validation>
```

The formset Tag

The **formset** tag is used to define validations for a set of forms. By default, the validations are applied to the enclosing forms for users within any locale. However, you can optionally use the **country** and **language** attributes to tailor a set of validations to a specific locale. The **formset** definition without the **country** or **language** attribute specified is considered the default set of validations. Any other **formset** definitions with one or both of the locale-narrowing attributes will override any overlapping forms. That is, if the default (or master) form set defines three forms and a locale-specific form set overrides one of the forms for French users, only the one form will be overridden for French users—not every form defined by the default form set.

DTD Definition

Following is the definition for the **formset** tag from the Validator configuration file DTD:

```
<!ELEMENT formset (constant*, form+)>
```

Attributes

Attribute	Description	Required
country	Specifies the country code that this form set's definitions will be applied to.	No
language	Specifies the language code that this form set's definitions will be applied to.	No

Example Usage

The following example illustrates the basic usage of the **formset** tag:

```
<formset>
  <form name="logonForm">
    ...
  </form>
  <form name="searchForm">
    ...
  </form>
</formset>
```

Because this example omits the **country** and **language** attributes, the enclosed validations will be applied to users within any locale unless specifically overridden with other **formset** definitions.

   If desired, one or more forms' validations can be overridden by specifying additional form sets for specific locales, as shown next:

```
<formset language="fr">
  <form name="logonForm">
    ...
  </form>
</formset>
```

This example provides validation settings for all users whose locale has French as its language. The **country** and **language** attributes can be used in tandem or individually based on how specific or broad the validation settings will be.

The global Tag

The **global** tag is used to encapsulate the set of validations and the set of constants that Validator will use. This tag is simply a container for **validator** and **constant** tags.

DTD Definition

Following is the definition for the **global** tag from the Validator configuration file DTD:

```
<!ELEMENT global (validator*, constant*)>
```

Example Usage

The following example illustrates the basic usage of the **global** tag:

```
<global>
  <constant>
    <constant-name>zip</constant-name>
    <constant-value>^\d{5}\d*$</constant-value>
  </constant>
</global>
```

The javascript Tag

The **javascript** tag is used to define client-side JavaScript code for a validation. The code placed between opening and closing **javascript** tags will be used to perform a preliminary client-side (browser) validation if Validator is configured to do so.

DTD Definition

Following is the definition for the **javascript** tag from the Validator configuration file DTD:

```
<!ELEMENT javascript (#PCDATA)>
```

Example Usage

The following example illustrates how to use the **javascript** tag:

```
<validator name="minlength"
      classname="org.apache.struts.validator.FieldChecks"
        method="validateMinLength"
  methodParams="java.lang.Object,
               org.apache.commons.validator.ValidatorAction,
               org.apache.commons.validator.Field,
               org.apache.struts.action.ActionErrors,
               javax.servlet.http.HttpServletRequest"
           msg="errors.minlength">
  <javascript>
    <![CDATA[
      function validateMinLength(form) {
        var isValid = true;
        var focusField = null;
        var i = 0;
        var fields = new Array();
        oMinLength = new minlength();
        for (x in oMinLength) {
          var field = form[oMinLength[x][0]];
          if (field.type == 'text' ||
              field.type == 'textarea') {
            var iMin = parseInt(oMinLength[x][2]("minlength"));
            if ((trim(field.value).length > 0) &&
                (field.value.length < iMin)) {
              if (i == 0) {
                focusField = field;
              }
              fields[i++] = oMinLength[x][1];
              isValid = false;
            }
          }
        }
```

```
      }
      if (fields.length > 0) {
        focusField.focus();
        alert(fields.join('\n'));
      }
      return isValid;
    }
  ]]>
  </javascript>
</validator>
```

Notice that the JavaScript code is enclosed in a **<![CDATA[ ]]>** tag. This is an XML
facility that is used to notify XML parsers that the enclosed text should be taken as is
and should not be parsed. Normally, parsers would parse the text for other tags or
XML entities; however, sometimes it's necessary to specify text that has XML-like
references in it, but that should not be parsed. The **<![CDATA[ ]]>** tag makes that
possible.

The msg Tag

The **msg** tag is used to define an error message that will override a validation's default
message. When validations are defined with the **validator** tag, they define a resource
bundle message key for an error message that will be used when the validation fails.
Sometimes, however, it's necessary to use an error message other than the default for a
validation. The **msg** tag makes this possible by allowing for an alternative message to
be set for a specific use of the validation.

DTD Definition

Following is the definition for the **msg** tag from the Validator configuration file DTD:

```
<!ELEMENT msg EMPTY>
```

Attributes

Attribute	Description	Required
key	Specifies a resource bundle message key that the specified validation will use for its error message instead of its default message.	No
name	Specifies the logical name of the validation whose error message will be overridden.	No
resource	Accepts "true" or "false" to denote whether or not the **key** attribute's value will be taken as a literal value rather than a message key. Defaults to "true".	No

Example Usage
The following example illustrates the basic usage of the **msg** tag:

```
<field property="ssNum"
       depends="required,mask">
  <msg name="mask" key="errors.ssNum"/>
  <arg0 key="ssNum.prompt"/>
  <var>
    <var-name>mask</var-name>
    <var-value></var-value>
  </var>
</field>
```

In this example, the **mask** validation is overridden to use the **errors.ssNum** message key instead of the one defined by the validation. As you can see, the **msg** tag is useful for specifying custom error messages for validations.

The validator Tag

The **validator** tag is used to define a validation routine and assign it a logical name. Each definition specifies the Java class, method, and method arguments for the validation routine. Once defined, the validation routine can be applied to form fields using its logical name.

DTD Definition
Following is the definition for the **validator** tag from the Validator configuration file DTD:

```
<!ELEMENT validator (javascript?)>
```

Attributes

Attribute	Description	Required
classname	Specifies the name of the class that houses the validation routine.	Yes
depends	Specifies a comma-delimited list of other validations defined by the **validator** tag that must pass before this validation is executed.	No
jsFunctionName	Specifies an alternate method name to use for the JavaScript code generated by this tag if client-side validation is enabled.	No
method	Specifies the name of the validation routine's method in the class specified by the **classname** attribute.	Yes

Attribute	Description	Required
methodParams	Specifies the comma-delimited list (in order) of the validation routine's arguments.	Yes
msg	Specifies a resource bundle message key for the error message that will be generated if this validation fails.	Yes
name	Specifies the logical name for the validation.	Yes

Example Usage

The following example illustrates the basic usage of the **validator** tag:

```
<validator name="minlength"
      classname="org.apache.struts.validator.FieldChecks"
        method="validateMinLength"
  methodParams="java.lang.Object,
              org.apache.commons.validator.ValidatorAction,
              org.apache.commons.validator.Field,
              org.apache.struts.action.ActionErrors,
              javax.servlet.http.HttpServletRequest"
           msg="errors.minlength"/>
```

Each validation definition specifies the Java class, method, and method arguments for the validation. Validator uses reflection to instantiate and invoke the validation at run time.

The var Tag

The **var** tag is used to define a variable that will be passed to each of a field's validations at run time. This allows validations to be configurable. For example, the maximum length validation has a variable that specifies its maximum length that must be set using this tag. Additionally, variables defined with the **var** tag can be used by the **arg0 – arg3** and **msg** tags, as shown here:

```
<arg1 name="maxlength" key="${var:maxlength}" resource="false"/>
```

To reference variables defined by the **var** tag from other tags, you must use this form: **${var:varName}** (where **varName** is the name of the defined variable).

The variable's name and value are defined with nested **var-name** and **var-value** tags, respectively.

DTD Definition

Following is the definition for the **var** tag from the Validator configuration file DTD:

```
<!ELEMENT var (var-name,var-value)>
```

Example Usage

The following snippet illustrates how to use the **var** tag:

```
<field property="username"
        depends="required,maxlength">
  <arg0 key="prompt.username"/>
  <var>
    <var-name>maxlength</var-name>
    <var-value>16</var-value>
  </var>
</field>
```

The **var** tag can be nested underneath the **field** tag an unlimited number of times. Each use of the **var** tag must have nested **var-name** and **var-value** tags.

The var-name Tag

The **var-name** tag is used to define the **var** tag's variable name. This tag must be nested exactly once underneath the **var** tag.

DTD Definition

Following is the definition for the **var-name** tag from the Validator configuration file DTD:

```
<!ELEMENT var-name (#PCDATA)>
```

Example Usage

The following snippet illustrates how to use the **var-name** tag:

```
<field property="username"
        depends="required,maxlength">
  <arg0 key="prompt.username"/>
  <var>
    <var-name>maxlength</var-name>
    <var-value>16</var-value>
  </var>
</field>
```

The var-value Tag

The **var-value** tag is used to define the **var** tag's variable value. This tag must be nested exactly once underneath the **var** tag.

DTD Definition

Following is the definition for the **var-value** tag from the Validator configuration file DTD:

```
<!ELEMENT var-value (#PCDATA)>
```

Example Usage

The following snippet illustrates how to use the **var-value** tag:

```
<field property="username"
       depends="required,maxlength">
  <arg0 key="prompt.username"/>
  <var>
    <var-name>maxlength</var-name>
    <var-value>16</var-value>
  </var>
</field>
```

Editing Validator Configuration Files with Struts Console

As you can imagine, trying to remember every tag's list of attributes as well as its proper order inside the configuration file can be cumbersome. If you make a mistake in typing any of the tag's or attribute's names, your Struts application will not be configured properly. To simplify the creation and modification of Validator configuration files, you can use a GUI tool called Struts Console. Struts Console is a stand-alone Java Swing application that provides a graphical editor for Validator configuration files. Additionally, Struts Console can be used as a plugin with several major Java IDEs, providing a seamless Struts development experience.

Struts Console is free software and can be downloaded from

http://www.jamesholmes.com/struts/

This Web site has all the information for configuring Struts Console to work with your favorite Java IDE. In addition, this book's appendix provides a Struts Console quick reference. Figure 18-1 (next page) shows Struts Console running as a stand-alone application.

FIGURE 18-1 Struts Console running as a stand-alone application

Applying Struts

Securing Struts Applications

M ost Web applications require certain aspects of the system to be secured in some manner. Security requirements are often specified at both the system and functional levels. System requirements may dictate, for example, that entry of sensitive information should be performed over a secure HTTP connection (HTTPS). On a higher level, functional requirements may dictate that only users with administrative privileges can access certain pages and menu items. From a developer's perspective, the critical task is to identify which of the requirements can be satisfied using standard security mechanisms, and which requirements require a customized security solution. Quite often, security requirements dictate some sort of customization. In some cases, you can use a combination of standard security mechanisms and customization to achieve the desired security policy.

Levels of Security

Security is a fairly broad topic and may encompass everything from encryption to personalization, depending on how "security" is defined. This chapter focuses on the levels of security that you can implement to secure your Struts applications, beginning in this section with an overview of the various security levels. That is followed by sections that look in depth at using container-managed security and application-managed security, the two primary ways to secure your Struts applications.

- Transport-level security using HTTPS
- Authentication and authorization
- Role-based access control
- Container-managed security
- Application-managed security

Some aspects of personalization will also be covered, specifically some techniques for hiding or displaying content based on a user's authorization.

Providing Secure Communications

Data can be securely transmitted by using HTTP over Secure Socket Layer (referred to as HTTPS). HTTPS secures data by encrypting the protocol at the transport level. In other words, the entire HTTP conversation between the client browser and the Web server is encrypted. Struts applications, like most Web applications, can send data over HTTPS without modification.

HTTPS does impact performance, however. There is an order of magnitude of performance penalty when using HTTPS. To reduce the impact on performance, it is common for applications to switch the protocol between HTTP and HTTPS. The typical scenario uses the HTTPS protocol for application login and submission of sensitive data. Once the data is entered, the protocol is switched back to HTTP. While on the surface this seems like a good approach, it leaves open a serious security hole whereby the user's session can be hijacked. Sensitive user information, such as a credit card number, may be stored in that session. A network snoop could use the session ID to spoof a valid user session. Due to this risk, container-managed security does not support protocol switching. However, if you need protocol switching and can accept the security risks, there are mechanisms for doing so that integrate with Struts, as you will see in "Integrating Struts with SSL," later in this chapter.

Authentication and Authorization

Authentication is the process of proving to an application that you are who you say you are. For Web applications, this process is most commonly associated with entering a username and password. If you are registered as a user of the application and you provide a valid password, the application allows access to privileged features of the application. In contrast, if you cannot provide valid credentials, you are allowed access only to the public areas of the site. In fact, many Web applications may only allow authenticated access—with the only public page being the login screen. Authentication can be provided through custom coding for the application, or by using container-managed security services.

Authorization is how the application determines which aspects of the Web application you are allowed to access. Generally speaking, determining a user's authorization requires the user to first be authenticated. Once authenticated, application-provided or container-managed security can be used to determine a user's authorization.

Role-based Access Control

Role-based access control (RBAC) is a common scheme for implementing authorization. Users are assigned roles through a container-specific means. When a user is authenticated, the user's roles are associated with the HTTP request. Given this information, access to certain pages or user interface components can be allowed or disallowed based on the user's roles. In most cases, a user is allowed to have multiple roles. However, roles are typically flat; that is, there is no hierarchical relationship between roles.

Container- vs. Application-Managed Security

Servlet containers provide security as specified by the servlet specification. Container-managed security allows the developer to declaratively specify how authentication is to be performed and how authorization is to be granted. Container-managed security provides an easy, unobtrusive way of adding security to an application. This mechanism of implementing security provides the following benefits:

- It is declarative. Authentication and authorization are specified in the **web.xml** file. Container-specific details, such as the security realm, typically are configured in server-specific XML configuration files.

- It supports multiple authentication schemes, such as password authentication, FORM-based authentication, authentication using encrypted passwords, and authentication using client-side digital certificates.

- Using container-specific security realms, user data can be provided by a variety of stores, including flat files, relational databases, and Lightweight Directory Access Protocol (LDAP) servers.

- Redirects are handled automatically. In other words, the container determines when a user is accessing a protected URL, prompts for user credentials, and, if authenticated, redirects to the requested page. This is a powerful mechanism, particularly for applications that publish links to protected pages in e-mail communications.

Containers are, however, somewhat limiting because of the following:

- The implementation of container-managed security varies by container. An application using container-managed security generally requires modification at some level when ported from one application server to another.

- The login flow does not allow easy custom processing of login requests. In other words, additional processing cannot be performed in the authentication process.

- Authorization can only use a flat, role-based approach. Access to Web pages cannot be granted based on multiple factors, for example, a managerial level and a department number.

- FORM-based login forces a workflow that uses a separate page for login. This limits the flexibility of the application.

- Container-managed authentication requires changes to the application server's configuration that may not be allowed in a hosted environment.

These limitations can be overcome by using application-managed security. However, using application-managed security means that custom code must be designed and written. The decision of which approach to take should be driven by the requirements.

While container-managed security is simpler to implement, it does restrict the flexibility of your security policy. One container's security implementation may be different from another's, making your application less portable. Also, container-managed security limits you to a specific login workflow that may not be what you want for your application.

Application-managed security, on the other hand, allows you to implement your security policy as needed at the price of requiring more custom code. Struts mitigates this problem by allowing for customized role processing via a custom request processor. Also, servlet filters can be used to apply across-the-board security policies. Cookies can be used to persist user login information between sessions. In addition, there are Struts extensions that permit finer-grained control of the use of HTTPS.

One last point: there is a somewhat hybrid approach that allows programmatic access to the methods that are usually only available when using container-managed security. This interesting mechanism will be covered later in the chapter, in the "Using Servlet Filters for Security" section.

Using Container-Managed Security

To explain how to use container-managed security, this section describes how you would apply container-managed security to the Mini HR application, introduced in Chapter 2, to fulfill a particular security requirement. Assume that Mini HR resides on ABC, Inc.'s corporate intranet. The application allows anyone to access the employee search. However, only *administrators* can add or remove employees from the database. If someone attempts to perform an administrator function, that user is prompted to input a username and password. If the password is valid, and the user is an administrator, the application will display the requested page.

Although this security requirement can be completely fulfilled without making any modifications to Java code or JSP pages, as you will see, it is often better to group URLs under role-specific path prefixes. Therefore, you must change the location of **add.jsp** and **add.do** to **/admin/add.jsp** and **/admin/add.do**, respectively. This also means that you need to change the **index.jsp** page and **struts-config.xml**. Making these changes may seem burdensome, but it will make implementing security easier. Following are the additions needed to **web.xml** to implement container-managed security:

```
<web-app>
    [... snipped ...]
    <security-constraint>
        <web-resource-collection>
            <web-resource-name>AdminPages</web-resource-name>
            <description>Administrator-only pages</description>
            <url-pattern>/admin/*</url-pattern>
        </web-resource-collection>
        <auth-constraint>
            <role-name>administrator</role-name>
        </auth-constraint>
```

```
    </security-constraint>
    <login-config>
        <auth-method>BASIC</auth-method>
        <realm-name>MiniHRRealm</realm-name>
    </login-config>
    <security-role>
        <description>HR Administrator</description>
        <role-name>administrator</role-name>
    </security-role>
</web-app>
```

The three XML elements (**security-constraint**, **login-config**, and **security-role**) that were added define the security requirements. The **security-constraint** element associates a collection of pages with a role. The pages are identified using URL patterns. If a user attempts to access a page that matches one of the patterns and the user has the associated role, then the user is allowed access. If the user has not yet been authenticated, the user is prompted to log in according to the settings of the **login-config** element. If the user authenticates and has the *administrator* role, then the user is redirected to the requested page.

Before discussing the login configurations, a quick detour is necessary to describe URL patterns. These patterns, also known as *URL mappings*, are dictated by the Java servlet specification. Four types of patterns are searched, in the following order:

- **Explicit mapping**   No wildcards are used (e.g., **/add.jsp** or **/admin/remove.do**).

- **Path prefix mapping**   Contains a **/**, then a path prefix, then a **/***. This mapping can be used to specify an entire subbranch of your Web application (e.g., **/admin/*** or **/search/company/***).

- **Extension mapping**   Contains ***.** followed by a prefix. This mapping can be used to specify all files of a certain type (e.g., ***.jsp**). It is also often used to map Struts actions (e.g., ***.do**).

- **Default mapping /**   Matches all URLs for the Web application. This mapping matches any URL of the Web application. Any URL beginning with the context path of the Web application will match this pattern.

As you can see, these patterns are not very flexible. You cannot, for example, specify a pattern of **/add.***. If you did not place the administrative URLs under a specific path prefix, you would have to explicitly list each constrained URL. From a security perspective, partitioning your application using role-based paths makes securing the application much easier. Even if you are not using container-managed security, this approach has benefits, as you will discover later, in the section "Using Servlet Filters for Security."

PART IV

If you decide to use Struts modules, then you have already established some partitioning for your application. Each module will be in its own path off the context root. Organizing modules by role is a reasonable approach—therefore, the use of Struts modules generally will make implementing your security policy easier.

Login Configurations

The **login-config** element indicates the type of authentication to be performed and where the user information can be found. A Web application can have only one login configuration. The **auth-method** nested element indicates the type of authentication and accepts the values listed and described in the following table.

Authentication	Description
BASIC	The browser pops up a dialog box that allows the user to enter a username and password. The username and password are encoded using the Base-64 algorithm and sent to the server. The Base-64 algorithm is a common Web encoding scheme that is often used to encode e-mail attachments and so on.
FORM	Allows for a custom form to be specified. The form must contain a **j_username** field for the username and a **j_password** field for the password. The form must submit to **j_security_check**. The username and password are Base-64 encoded.
DIGEST	Similar to BASIC authentication except that the username and password are encrypted into a message digest value. This configuration may not be supported by all browsers.
CLIENT-CERT	The client is required to provide a digital certificate for authentication. This is the most secure configuration. However, it also is the most costly. Certificates for production use must be purchased from a certificate authority.

In addition to specifying the type of login, the login configuration may also specify a security realm. A *security realm* is essentially the store from which a Web application retrieves and verifies user credentials. In addition, a realm provides a mechanism for specifying the roles that users may have. For the login configuration, no details of the realm can be provided other than the realm name. That name refers, either directly or indirectly, to a container-specific security realm implementation.

DIGEST authentication provides the same basic user experience as BASIC. However, because DIGEST authentication may not be supported by all browsers, it is not discussed further here. There are ways of encrypting the user credentials without requiring DIGEST. CLIENT-CERT requires the user to have a digital certificate. This chapter discusses only BASIC and FORM-based login because these are the authentication methods that are encountered in most situations.

BASIC Login

The simplest way to get started with container-managed security is to use BASIC authentication, which involves the use of the security realm. The security realm serves as a reference to container-specific security storage. The mechanism for associating this logical realm to the concrete realm varies by container. Typically, realms can be based on flat files (for example, property files or XML files), a relational database, or an LDAP server. Some containers, such as JBoss, provide a mapping between a realm and a Java Authentication and Authorization Service (JAAS) implementation.

For simplicity, the security realm for ABC, Inc. will be implemented using the Tomcat **UserDatabase** realm. By its default configuration, Tomcat supports this realm for all applications. The realm retrieves usernames, passwords, roles, and role assignments from the **tomcat-users.xml** file.

You will add three users to the system to test the functionality—two of the users will be assigned the administrator role. The third user will be defined using a non-administrator role. This third user is defined for testing and illustrative purposes. Add the following four elements (in bold) to the **<TOMCAT_HOME>/conf/tomcat_users.xml** file:

```
<tomcat-users>
  <role name="administrator"/>
  <user name="bsiggelkow" password="thatsme" roles="administrator" />
  <user name="jholmes"  password="maindude" roles="administrator"  />
  <user name="gburdell"   password="gotech" roles="employee" />
</tomcat-users>
```

Now, deploy this new version of the Mini HR application. You need to restart Tomcat to enable the new functionality. Then, browse to the welcome page, **index.jsp**. You should see no differences here. Next, click the Add an Employee link. Your browser will display a dialog box similar to that shown in Figure 19-1.

Entering a valid username and password of a user with the administrator role displays the requested page. If the user does not have the administrator role but is otherwise valid, an HTTP status of 403 (Access Denied) is the response. Likewise, if you click Cancel, an HTTP status of 401 (Authentication Required) is returned. If a matching username and password are not found, then the dialog box simply redisplays.

Once a user has been authenticated, the Web application can glean useful user data from the HTTP request. The two methods of interest are **getUserPrincipal( )**, which can be used to acquire the username, and **isUserInRole( )**, which can be used to determine if a user has a specified role. These methods can be used in the **Action** classes to perform such things as the following:

- Load the user's profile and store it in the session
- Render a specific response or redirect to a certain URL based on the user's role

FIGURE 19-1
Browser-provided
authentication
dialog box

In addition to the programmatic uses of this data, Struts applications can also use this information to do the following:

- Allow role-based access to **Action** classes configured in the **struts-config.xml** file.
- Dynamically hide or display presentation components (links, buttons, menus, etc.) based on the user's role using the **<logic:present>** and **<logic:notPresent>** tags.

The first two programmatic uses are available to any JSP/servlet-based application. The Struts-specific uses, however, warrant more discussion.

Action mappings in the **struts-config.xml** file have an optional **roles** attribute, which accepts a comma-separated list of roles. If a user has any one of those roles, the user can access the action. Otherwise, access is denied. This attribute provides a much more natural way of granting/denying access than using the URL patterns. Note, however, that using the action mappings only restricts access to URLs served through the Struts controller (e.g., ***.do**). It does not restrict access to JSP pages or static HTML pages. The following snippet from the **struts-config.xml** file shows the use of the **roles** attribute:

```
<action path="/add"
        type="com.jamesholmes.minihr.AddAction"
        name="addForm"
        scope="request"
        validate="true"
        input="/add.jsp"
        roles="administrator">
</action>
```

If your Web application places the JSP pages under the **WEB-INF** folder and *all* requests are handled by the Struts controller, the **roles** attribute can be used to completely control access to Web resources.

As mentioned, the rendering of portions of a JSP page can be based on role using the **<logic>** tags. Considering the main page, it might be worthwhile to display only the Add an Employee link if the user is an administrator. Such a page might look something like the following:

```
<logic:present role="administrator"/>
<a href="admin_login.jsp">Administrator Login</a>
</logic:present>
<ul>
  <li><html:link forward="add">Add an Employee</html:link></li>
  <li><html:link forward="search">Search for Employees</html:link></li>
</ul>
```

However, this approach leads to a common problem with container-managed security. You want to show the link only if the user is an administrator, but you don't know if the user is an administrator unless the user selects the link and is authenticated. There are several alternatives that you can use to solve this problem. One alternative is to force all users to log in—obviously leading to disgruntled users if the login does not add value. Another alternative is to provide a means for a user to proactively log in.

The proactive login behavior can still be accomplished by using container-managed security—albeit through some trickery. What you will do is create a link on the main page (**index.jsp**) to a security-constrained JSP page (**/admin/admin_login.jsp**). This page will simply redirect back to the main page. Since it will be a protected page, the user will be forced to log in.

The **admin_login** JSP page is as simple as the following:

```
<%@ taglib uri="/WEB-INF/tlds/struts-logic.tld" prefix="logic" %>
<logic:redirect page="/index.jsp"/>
```

The **redirect** tag results in an HTTP redirect response. The **page** attribute of the tag indicates where to redirect the response. In this example, this will result in a redirect to the main page of the application. Since this page is put under the **/admin** path, no changes are necessary to the security constraint in the **web.xml** file.

The user experience now is as follows:

1. When the index page is first displayed, the user does not see the Add an Employee link, but can log in.

2. Upon login, the index is redisplayed, this time displaying the administrative link.

3. Upon selecting this link, the user does not have to reauthenticate.

FORM-Based Login

FORM-based login is another variant of a container-managed login configuration. With FORM-based login, you supply a Web page (either a JSP or static HTML page) that contains the login form and a page to display if an error occurs. This provides a much more consistent look and feel for your application. The behavior of FORM-based login when a user is trying to access protected resources is similar to the behavior of BASIC login. To implement FORM-based login, you supply a Web page that has a form for login that must follow specific guidelines. The form must submit two parameters with the names **j_username** and **j_password**, holding the username and password respectively, to the **j_security_check** URL. Optionally, you can also specify a Web page that will be displayed if a login error occurs. Here's the **login_form.html** page:

```
<html>
<head>
<title>ABC, Inc. Human Resources Portal</title>
</head>
<body>
  <font size="+1">ABC, Inc. Human Resources Portal Login</font><br>
  <hr width="100%" noshade="true">
  <form action="j_security_check">
    Username: <input type="text" name="j_username"/><br/>
    Password: <input type="password" name="j_password"/><br/>
    <input type="submit" value="Login"/>
  </form>
</body>
</html>
```

Next, change the **login-config** element of **web.xml** to use FORM-based authentication:

```
<login-config>
  <auth-method>FORM</auth-method>
  <realm-name>MiniHRRealm</realm-name>
  <form-login-config>
    <form-login-page>/login_form.html</form-login-page>
    <form-error-page>/login_error.html</form-error-page>
  </form-login-config>
</login-config>
```

Now, instead of displaying the standard dialog box, the browser displays the new page (albeit a little bland in this case). Once authenticated, the user is taken back to the index page, where the hidden link is now displayed.

A natural progression of these modifications is to place the login form on the main index page, thereby reducing an extra mouse click and page display. This approach is quite common in Web applications. Often, the main pages of applications have a login form on the welcome page. The main page provides lots of information to anyone. When you log in, however, the user experience becomes personalized for you. However, if you move the login form to the Mini HR index page, you will find that it will not work. When you submit your username and password, an error will occur. Tomcat generates the following error:

HTTP Status 400 – Invalid direct reference to form login page

Tomcat raises this error because the login page can only be managed by the container. Access by a user to a protected page is the only mechanism that should trigger display of the login page. In the container-managed authentication workflow, once a user is authenticated, the client is then redirected to the requested protected page. If the user browses directly to the login page, the protected resource to redirect to is undefined. In other words, if the user were to submit the form, the container would not know where to redirect the request.

There is no good work-around for this problem. This is one of the frustrations with FORM-based authentication and container-managed security—a simple change in requirements (e.g., put the login on the main page) causes you to rethink your security implementation. However, if you and your users can live with the constraints of container-managed security, it is a great way to provide robust security with minimal coding.

Container-Managed Secure Transport

The last container-managed security service to be discussed concerns transport-level security. This service operates by declaratively specifying whether pages should be accessed using HTTPS. This is specified using the **user-data-constraint** subelement of the **security-constraint** element. Following is a sample from **web.xml**:

```
<security-constraint>
  <web-resource-collection>
    <web-resource-name>AdminPages</web-resource-name>
    <description>Administrator-only pages</description>
    <url-pattern>/admin/*</url-pattern>
  </web-resource-collection>
  <auth-constraint>
    <role-name>administrator</role-name>
  </auth-constraint>
  <user-data-constraint>
    <transport-guarantee>
      CONFIDENTIAL
    </transport-guarantee>
  </user-data-constraint>
</security-constraint>
```

PART IV

The key here is the **transport-guarantee** element. The values accepted are the following:

- **NONE** No restrictions, normal HTTP
- **INTEGRAL** Use HTTPS
- **CONFIDENTIAL** Use HTTPS

It is important to note that the use of the **user-data-constraint** subelement does *not* require specification of an authentication constraint. This means that you can define Web resources that are secure but do not require authentication. This is useful, for example, when you are using application-managed authentication but still want to use a container-managed protocol. At one time, the servlet specification did not indicate how this constraint was to be handled. Some servers would not automatically redirect to HTTPS but instead would simply report an error and leave the user dumbfounded.

Tomcat 4 does redirect to HTTPS; however, it does not always redirect back to HTTP after leaving the constrained page. Also, the behavior seems to vary by browser. Fortunately, there is a more flexible solution for Struts applications, which is described in "Integrating Struts with SSL" later in this chapter. For the time being, you may want to experiment using Tomcat with HTTPS and setting the transport guarantee. Like other container-managed services, if you can get it to work for you without having to compromise your requirements, then it is worth pursuing.

Application-Managed Security

If container-managed security is not sufficient for your application, then you need consider creating your own security structure. Generally, you need to address the same issues in application-managed security that are addressed in container-managed security:

- How and when do you authenticate the users?
- What determines the authorization levels?
- Is there a guest user and, if so, what privileges does that user have?
- Does the application need to support HTTPS for transmission of sensitive data?

The following sections look at several ways of handling these issues. As you read through them, you will apply your knowledge to the Mini HR application. Most of this discussion applies to Java-based Web applications in general—not just Struts-based applications.

Creating a Security Service

Using application-managed security requires different skills and knowledge than are required to use a container-managed approach. For application-managed security, you need to rely on traditional "best practices" development. For use with Mini HR, you will create a **SecurityService** interface API that will act as a façade for whatever underlying implementations exist. The definition of the interface to meet the needs of the Mini HR application is shown here:

```
package com.jamesholmes.minihr.security;

public interface SecurityService {
  public User authenticate(String username, String password)
    throws AuthenticationException;
}
```

Next is a sample implementation that uses a **HashMap** to store the user data in memory. Of course, a real implementation would retrieve this data from a persistent store such as a file system, relational database, or LDAP server.

```
package com.jamesholmes.minihr.security;

import java.util.HashMap;
import java.util.Map;

public class SecurityServiceImpl implements SecurityService {
  private Map users;
  private static final String ADMIN_ROLE = "administrator";

  public SecurityServiceImpl() {
    users = new HashMap();
    users.put("bsiggelkow",
      new User( "bsiggelkow","Bill", "Siggelkow",  "thatsme",
        new String[] {ADMIN_ROLE}));
    users.put("jholmes",
      new User( "jholmes","James", "Holmes",  "maindude",
        new String[] {ADMIN_ROLE}));
    users.put("gburdell",
      new User( "gburdell","George", "Burdell",  "gotech",
        new String[] {ADMIN_ROLE}));
  }

  public User authenticate(String username, String password)
    throws AuthenticationException
  {
    User user = (User) users.get(username);
    if (user == null)
      throw new AuthenticationException("Unknown user");
    boolean passwordIsValid = user.passwordMatch(password);
    if (!passwordIsValid)
```

PART IV

```
      throw new AuthenticationException("Invalid password");
    return user;
  }
}
```

This interface provides the basic security services. The **authenticate( )** method
verifies the user's password and returns an object that represents the user. For the
authorization needs of the application, there are different alternatives. While it may be
tempting to engineer a complete role-based infrastructure, a more pragmatic approach
is to provide a mechanism to determine if a user is an administrator. Following is the
object that will hold the user data:

```
package com.jamesholmes.minihr.security;

import java.io.Serializable;

public class User implements Serializable {
  private String firstName;
  private String lastName;
  private String username;
  private String password;
  private String[] roles;

  public User(String name, String fName, String lName,
    String pwd, String[] assignedRoles) {
    username = name;
    firstName = fName;
    lastName  = lName;
    password  = pwd
    roles = assignedRoles;
  }

  public String getUsername() {
    return username;
  }

  public String getFirstName() {
    return firstName;
  }

  public String getLastName() {
    return lastName;
  }

  public boolean passwordMatch(String pwd) {
    return password.equals(pwd);
```

```
    }

  public boolean hasRole(String role) {
    if (roles.length > 0) {
      for (int i=0; i<roles.length; i++) {
        if (role.equals(roles[i])) return true;
      }
    }
    return false;
  }

  public boolean isAdministrator() {
    return hasRole("administrator");
  }
}
```

Notice that some basic information that can be used for personalization, such as the user's first and last name, has been included. In addition, the **isAdministrator( )** method indicates whether or not the user is an administrator. Also a **hasRole( )** method has been implemented that will indicate whether or not a user has been assigned a given role. This method will be useful with customized Struts role processing. To tie this custom security service into the application, you also need to create a **LoginAction** that will process the user login, as shown in the following code. A **LogoutAction** that allows a user to log out of the application is also created by the following code. A logout action typically needs to just invalidate the user's session. While you cannot force a user to log out, it is important to provide this feature, particularly if your application is accessible from a public terminal.

```
package com.jamesholmes.minihr;

import javax.servlet.http.*;
import org.apache.commons.beanutils.PropertyUtils;
import org.apache.struts.action.*;
import com.jamesholmes.minihr.security.*;

public final class LoginAction extends Action {
  public ActionForward execute(ActionMapping mapping,
    ActionForm form,
    HttpServletRequest request,
    HttpServletResponse response)
    throws Exception
  {
    HttpSession session = request.getSession();
    String username =
      (String) PropertyUtils.getSimpleProperty(form, "username");
    String password =
      (String) PropertyUtils.getSimpleProperty(form,"password");
```

```
        SecurityService service = new SecurityServiceImpl();
        User user = service.authenticate(username, password);
        session.setAttribute("User", user);
        // Forward control to this Action's success forward
        return mapping.findForward("success");
    }
}
```

First, the action gets the username and password from the login form. Then, it calls the **authenticate** method of the security service. The returned user is then stored in the session. The exception handling is performed using Struts' declarative exception handling. Back at the index page, you need to change it from the container-managed implementation as shown in the following example. In this case, you want to check the **administrator** bean property of the user and display the link only if the value is *true*. Note also that you must explicitly check whether the User object is in the session. This handles the case where the user has not yet been authenticated.

```
<%@ taglib uri="/WEB-INF/tlds/struts-html.tld" prefix="html" %>
<%@ taglib uri="/WEB-INF/tlds/struts-logic.tld" prefix="logic" %>

<html>
<head>
  <title>ABC, Inc. Human Resources Portal</title>
</head>
<body>
<font size="+1">ABC, Inc. Human Resources Portal</font><br>

<logic:notPresent name="user" scope="session">
<hr width="100%" noshade="true">
<html:form action="/login">
Username: <html:text property="username"/><br/>
Password: <html:password property="password"/><br/>
<html:submit value="Login"/>
</html:form>
<html:errors/>
</logic:notPresent>

<hr width="100%" noshade="true">
<ul>
<logic:present name="user" scope="session">
<logic:equal name="user" property="administrator" value="true">
<li><html:link forward="add">Add an Employee</html:link></li>
</logic:equal>
</logic:present>
<li><html:link forward="search">Search for Employees</html:link></li>
```

```
</ul>
</body>
</html>
```

The important modification to this index page is the use of the **<logic:present>** tag to hide or show the login form. In addition, the **<logic:equal>** tag is used to hide or show the Add an Employee link. You are not finished, however. First, remove (or comment out) the container-managed security sections from the **web.xml** file. Then, remove the **roles** attribute from the **add.do** action mapping.

You are not done yet, however. Notice that there is now nothing to prevent someone who is not an administrator from adding a new employee. Anyone can browse directly to the Add an Employee page and submit the form. In addition, although securing the **add.jsp** page is not critical, it is imperative that you secure the **AddAction (add.do)**. What you need to do is implement the checks that were in place with container-managed security. There are several alternatives to consider.

Page/Action-Level Security Checks

You want to disallow access to the JSP page and, more importantly, the **AddAction** (**add.do**). The JSP page can be checked by adding in JSP logic, similar to the index page, that looks for the User object in the session and checks whether the user is an administrator. If the user is not an administrator, a **redirect** tag can be used to send the user back to the index page. To protect the action, the most obvious solution is to add these same checks into the **AddAction** class. If the checks fail, the user can be redirected to a page where an error could be displayed, or an exception can be thrown, or an appropriate HTTP status (e.g., 400) can be set in the response. While this solution works for one JSP and one action, it will not scale when many pages and actions are involved.

One mechanism for making this solution scale for the action is to place the authorization check in a base **Action** class. If, however, you still want to use role-based access for authorization, a better solution is to extend the Struts request processor.

Extending Struts' Request Processing

Struts' request processing can be customized by extending **RequestProcessor**. Specifically, security customizations can be brought into play in particular methods of **RequestProcessor**. The **processRoles( )** method determines how roles, specified for an action mapping via the **roles** attribute, are handled. Its purpose is to ensure that a user who is accessing an action with assigned roles has at least one of those roles. The method returns true to continue processing normally or false to stop processing and return an appropriate response. The default implementation uses the **HttpServletRequest.isUserInRole( )** method to determine if a user has a particular role. This can be used with container-managed security. For application-managed security, you need to override this method in a custom **RequestProcessor**. For your implementation, you will get the **User** object from the session and then call the

User.hasRole( ) method. The custom request processor with the overridden method is shown here:

```
package com.jamesholmes.minihr;

import java.io.IOException;
import javax.servlet.ServletException;
import javax.servlet.http.*;
import org.apache.struts.action.*;
import com.jamesholmes.minihr.security.User;

public class CustomRequestProcessor extends RequestProcessor {
  protected boolean processRoles(HttpServletRequest request,
    HttpServletResponse response, ActionMapping mapping)
    throws IOException, ServletException
  {
    // Is this action protected by role requirements?
    String roles[] = mapping.getRoleNames();
    if ((roles == null) || (roles.length < 1)) {
      return (true);
    }
    // Check the current user against the list of required roles
    HttpSession session = request.getSession();
    User user = (User) session.getAttribute("user");
    if (user == null) {
      return false;
    }
    for (int i = 0; i < roles.length; i++) {
      if (user.hasRole(roles[i])) {
        return (true);
      }
    }
    response.sendError(HttpServletResponse.SC_BAD_REQUEST,
                       getInternal().getMessage("notAuthorized",
                       mapping.getPath()));
    return (false);
  }
}
```

Now, you can add the **roles** attribute back to your action mapping and the action will be protected. Of course, you also need to plug the customized request processor into the Struts configuration file. That still leaves the somewhat nagging problem of unauthorized users gaining access to the JSP pages. One solution is to place all the JSP pages under **WEB-INF** and route all JSP page requests through the **ActionServlet** by using **ForwardAction**s. This is an appealing solution, because you can then use the **roles** attribute on these actions. This does mean a fairly drastic change to the organization of a Web application and may require substantial modification of your JSP pages.

However, as you will see in the following section, servlet filters can be used to implement security policies that can be applied to related Web resources.

In addition to the **processRoles( )** method, there is a more generic **processPreprocess( )** method. That method should return true to continue standard processing or false to indicate that the response is complete. That method is a good place to put security checks that cannot be implemented using roles alone.

Using Servlet Filters for Security

Servlet filters were introduced as part of the Servlet 2.3 specification. They provide a powerful mechanism for creating customized request and response processing that can be applied across many Web resources. You can create a filter and then map it to a collection of URLs by using the URL mapping discussed earlier in the chapter. Filters can alter a request before it arrives at its destination and, likewise, can modify the response after it leaves a destination. Filters can be applied to static HTML pages, JSP pages, Struts actions—essentially, any resource that you can specify with a URL.

You can use a filter to implement role-based access controls. The filter in effect performs the same checks that were implemented in the custom **RequestProcessor**. The filter determines if a user is allowed access to a given Web resource. It checks if the user has been authenticated and if the user has one of the required roles. If either of these checks fails, the filter stores an appropriate error message in the request and forwards the request to a URL. Initialization parameters are used to specify the authorization as well as the page to forward to if an error occurs. As you can see, the initialization parameters enable the creation of filter classes that can easily be reused. Here is the complete implementation for the authorization filter that Mini HR will be using:

```
package com.jamesholmes.minihr.security;

import java.io.IOException;
import javax.servlet.*;
import javax.servlet.http.*;
import org.apache.struts.Globals;
import org.apache.struts.action.*;

public class AuthorizationFilter implements Filter {
  private String[] roleNames;
  private String onErrorUrl;

  public void init(FilterConfig filterConfig)
      throws ServletException {
    String roles = filterConfig.getInitParameter("roles");
    if (roles == null || "".equals(roles)) {
      roleNames = new String[0];
    }
    else {
      roles.trim();
      roleNames = roles.split("\\s*,\\s*");
```

```
    }
    onErrorUrl = filterConfig.getInitParameter("onError");
    if (onErrorUrl == null || "".equals(onErrorUrl)) {
      onErrorUrl = "/index.jsp";
    }
  }

  public void doFilter(ServletRequest request,
                       ServletResponse response,
                       FilterChain chain)
                 throws IOException, ServletException {
    HttpServletRequest req = (HttpServletRequest) request;
    HttpServletResponse res = (HttpServletResponse) response;

    HttpSession session = req.getSession();
    User user = (User) session.getAttribute("user");
    ActionErrors errors = new ActionErrors();
    if (user == null) {
      errors.add(ActionErrors.GLOBAL_ERROR,
        new ActionError("error.authentication.required"));
    }
    else {
      boolean hasRole = false;
      for (int i=0; i<roleNames.length; i++) {
        if (user.hasRole(roleNames[i])) {
          hasRole = true;
          break;
        }
      }
      if (!hasRole) {
        errors.add(ActionErrors.GLOBAL_ERROR,
          new ActionError("error.authorization.required"));
      }
    }
    if (errors.isEmpty()) {
      chain.doFilter(request, response);
    }
    else {
      req.setAttribute(Globals.ERROR_KEY, errors);
      req.getRequestDispatcher(onErrorUrl).forward(req, res);
    }
  }

  public void destroy() {
  }
}
```

First, notice that the **AuthorizationFilter** class implements **Filter**. Thus, it must implement the **init( )**, **doFilter( )**, and **destroy( )** methods. The comma-separated list of roles and the URL of the error page to forward to are retrieved from the initialization parameters in the **init( )** method. The **doFilter( )** method first checks if there is a **User** in the session. If not, an appropriate **ActionError** is created and no further checks are performed. Otherwise, it iterates through the list of roles to determine if the user has any of them. If not, an **ActionError** is created. If any errors were created, then a **RequestDispatcher** is created to forward to the given URL; otherwise, the **doFilter( )** method calls **chain.doFilter( )** to continue normal processing. This implementation also demonstrates the ability to integrate filters with Struts. You could have provided a more generic implementation, by calling the **sendError( )** method of the **HttpServletResponse** class with an appropriate HTTP status code (e.g., 401).

Filters are configured and deployed like servlets. In the **web.xml** file, you can specify the filter name and class, and initialization parameters. Then, associate the filter with a URL pattern in a filter mapping. The following is the snippet from the **web.xml** file that shows the necessary changes for this filter:

```
<filter>
  <filter-name>adminAccessFilter</filter-name>
  <filter-class>
    com.jamesholmes.minihr.security.AuthorizationFilter
  </filter-class>
  <init-param>
    <param-name>roles</param-name>
    <param-value>administrator</param-value>
  </init-param>
  <init-param>
    <param-name>onError</param-name>
    <param-value>/index.jsp</param-value>
  </init-param>
</filter>

<filter-mapping>
  <filter-name>adminAccessFilter</filter-name>
  <url-pattern>/admin/*</url-pattern>
</filter-mapping>
```

As you can see, the **AuthorizationFilter** is fairly generic. There is, in fact, an open-source security filter known as **SecurityFilter** that is worth considering. This filter permits implementation of a custom security policy, yet still allows programmatic access to role and user information (i.e., the **request.isUserInRole( )** and **request.getUserPrincipal( )** methods) that is generally only available when using container-managed authentication. It performs this magic by using wrapper classes around the **HttpServletRequest**. **SecurityFilter** is configured using a separate configuration file that is very similar to the standard **security-constraint** element of the **web.xml** file. It provides the benefits of application-managed security while still enabling standard role processing without modification. There is no need to extend the Struts **RequestProcessor** for role handling, and the **<logic:equal>** tag with the **role** attribute will also work correctly. **SecurityFilter** is implemented similarly to **AuthorizationFilter**. You will want to understand how the filter works and its limitations before migrating your application.

Like servlets and Struts actions, filters are extremely powerful. You have complete access to the Java API that can be applied as needed using URL patterns. However, to truly integrate filters with Struts, you may need to delve into Struts implementation details as was shown in the **AuthorizationFilter**.

Using Cookies

A cookie consists of name-value data that can be sent to a client's browser and then read back again at a later time. Persistent cookies are stored by the client's browser. Cookies can be read only by the same server or domain that originated them. Also, a cookie can have an expiration period. Cookies are supported by most major browsers. However, cookies are often considered a privacy risk and can be disabled by the client. A good approach is to design your Web application to use cookies to improve the user experience, but not to require or force users to allow cookies.

For application-managed security, you can use cookies to allow users automatic logins. Specifically, you can create a persistent cookie that contains the user's username and password. Then, when a user accesses the application, you can check for those cookie values. If present, the values can be used to log the user in without requiring them to fill out a login form. Using a servlet filter, or some JavaScript, you could log in a user automatically. Alternatively, you may want to just prepopulate the login form with the values from the cookie.

To illustrate the use of cookies, Mini HR will be changed to use them as follows:

1. Once a user logs in, Mini HR creates persistent cookies containing the username and password.

2. Mini HR uses the cookie support of the Struts tags to set the initial values for the login form.

For the login action, this means adding the following lines *after* the authentication check has been performed:

```
Cookie usernameCookie = new Cookie("MiniHRUsername", username);
usernameCookie.setMaxAge(60 * 60 * 24 * 30); // 30 day expiration
response.addCookie(usernameCookie);
Cookie passwordCookie = new Cookie("MiniHRPassword", password);
passwordCookie.setMaxAge(60 * 60 * 24 * 30); // 30 day expiration
response.addCookie(passwordCookie);
```

This code creates cookies for holding the username and password. Each cookie has an expiration of 30 days. Each cookie is then added to the response.

Next, use the Struts bean tags to retrieve the cookie values and write the values to the login form:

```
<logic:notPresent name="user" scope="session">
  <bean:cookie id="uname" name="MiniHRUsername" value=""/>
  <bean:cookie id="pword" name="MiniHRPassword" value=""/>
  <hr width="100%" noshade="true">
  <html:form action="/login">
    Username: <html:text property="username"
               value="<%=uname.getValue()%>"/><br/>
    Password: <html:password property="password"
               value="<%=pword.getValue()%>"/><br/>
    <html:submit value="Login"/>
  </html:form>
  <html:errors/>
</logic:notPresent>
```

The **cookie** tags retrieve the cookie values from the request and store them in page scope variables. These variables are then used as the initial values for the login form fields. However, this example is too simplistic for production use. Generally, using cookies without input from the user is considered overly presumptuous. A good Web application lets the user specify whether they want their user data stored as a cookie. It is also reasonable to let the user specify the length of time before the cookie expires. This type of information is easily gathered and stored by an application. Typically, this information is collected at registration time and stored as part of the user's profile.

In addition, the data sent in the cookies should be secured or encrypted. A simple encryption scheme, such as MD5 or a variant of the Secure Hash Algorithm (SHA), can be used to encrypt the cookie value when it is created. Since the server creates the cookie and is the only party to legitimately use the data, it can encrypt and decrypt the data using the algorithm of its own choosing. Alternatively, cookies can be configured to only be transmitted over HTTPS—thereby providing encryption/decryption at the transport level.

Integrating Struts with SSL

Web applications often need to allow certain operations to be performed under secure processing—that is, using HTTPS. Users have come to expect sensitive data such as their usernames, passwords, and credit card numbers to be transmitted over a secure channel. As was noted earlier, the use of HTTPS for specific URLs can be specified using a user data constraint within a security constraint in the **web.xml** file. This declarative mechanism can be used to restrict URLs to SSL (by specifying a transport guarantee of INTEGRAL or CONFIDENTIAL). However, this approach does not address all the issues when using SSL. As a container-managed service, the implementation and behavior with SSL can vary by container. If the service is not used carefully and with a full understanding of its nuances, it is easy to code an application that will only run in a specific container—even when using services that are defined via an industry-accepted specification.

Therefore, HTTPS typically is used only when passing sensitive data, and otherwise HTTP is used. This requires redirecting from nonsecure pages to secure pages and then back again. Performing this redirection requires changing the protocol scheme on a URL from **http** to **https** on each redirection. The biggest problem with needing to do this protocol switching is that absolute URLs must be hard-coded into JSP pages and **Action** classes. This quickly leads to deployment and maintenance problems that arise when server names are different between development, integration test, and production servers. Some techniques for overcoming this problem are described shortly.

More pragmatically, programming an application to use HTTPS has other, more mundane but nevertheless equally frustrating issues. A common one is that the **https** protocol of the URL must often be hard-coded into a page. In fact, generally if you create HTML links that reference HTTPS, you must specify a fully qualified absolute URL. This makes it difficult to develop an application that is easy to migrate between deployment servers. Also, because switching the protocol requires an HTTP redirect, request attributes for the current request cannot be propagated to the secure URL. Thankfully, there is an open-source solution for handling these types of problems.

SSLEXT to the Rescue

The SSL Extension to Struts (SSLEXT) is an open-source plug-in for Struts. This software was created and is maintained by Steve Ditlinger (and others). It is hosted at SourceForge, **http://sslext.sourceforge.net**. It is the recommended approach for integrating Struts with SSL processing. Its features include:

- The ability to declaratively specify in the Struts configuration file whether or not an action mapping should be secure. This feature allows your application to switch protocols between actions and JSP pages.

- Extensions of the Struts JSP tags that can generate URLs that use the **https** protocol.

SSLEXT consists of a plug-in class for initialization, a custom extension to the Struts **RequestProcessor**, and a custom extension of the Struts **ActionMapping**. In addition, custom JSP tags, which extend the Struts tags, are provided for protocol-specific URL generation. SSLEXT also includes an additional JSP tag that lets you specify whether an entire JSP page is secure. SSLEXT depends on the Java Secure Socket Extension (JSSE), which is included with JDK 1.4 and later. Finally, you need to enable SSL for your application server. For Tomcat, this can be found in the *Tomcat SSL How-To* documentation.

SSLEXT works by intercepting the request in its **SecureRequestProcessor**. If the request is directed toward an action that is marked as **secure**, the **SecureRequestProcessor** generates a redirect. The redirect changes the protocol to **https** and the port to a secure port (e.g., 443 or 8443). This sounds simple enough; however, a request in a Struts application usually contains request attributes. These attributes are lost on a redirect. SSLEXT solves this problem by temporarily storing the request attributes in the session.

SSLEXT does not include a lot of documentation but it comes with a sample application that demonstrates its use and features. To try SSLEXT, you can modify Mini HR to use it by changing the login behavior so that the **LoginAction** occurs over HTTPS. Once logged in, the protocol should be switched back to HTTP. Take the following steps to set up SSLEXT for the Mini HR application:

1. Copy the **sslext.jar** file into the **MiniHR19\WEB-INF\lib** folder.

2. Copy the **sslext.tld** file into the **MiniHR19\WEB-INF\tlds** folder.

3. Add a **taglib** declaration in the **web.xml** for the **sslext** tag library as follows:

```
<taglib>
  <taglib-uri>/WEB-INF/tlds/sslext.tld</taglib-uri>
  <taglib-location>/WEB-INF/tlds/sslext.tld</taglib-location>
</taglib>
```

Now, make the following changes to the **struts-config.xml** file:

1. Add the **type** attribute to the **action-mappings** element to specify the custom secure action mapping class as follows:

```
<action-mappings type="org.apache.struts.config.SecureActionConfig">
```

2. Add the **controller** element configured to use the **SecureRequestProcessor**. If you are already using a custom request processor, change it to extend the **SecureRequestProcessor**.

```
<controller
  processorClass="org.apache.struts.action.SecureRequestProcessor"/>
```

3. Add the **plug-in** declaration to load the SSLEXT code:

```
<plug-in className="org.apache.struts.action.SecurePlugIn">
  <set-property property="httpPort" value="8080"/>
  <set-property property="httpsPort" value="8443"/>
  <set-property property="enable" value="true"/>
  <set-property property="addSession" value="true"/>
</plug-in>
```

4. Set the **secure** property to true for the **login** action mapping by adding the following element:

```
<set-property property="secure" value="true"/>
```

5. Finally, you need to configure the **index.jsp** page to always run on **http**, not **https**. Otherwise, after you log in, the protocol will remain on **https**. Add the

following **taglib** directive and custom tag to the **index.jsp** page (after the existing **taglib** directives):

```
<%@ taglib uri="/WEB-INF/tlds/sslext.tld" prefix="sslext"%>
<sslext:pageScheme secure="false"/>
```

This tag is only needed for those JSP pages that are not accessed through your actions.

Now all you need to do is rebuild and redeploy the application. When you click the login link, the protocol will switch to **https** and the port will switch to 8443. After you log in, you should be redirected back to the **index.jsp** page and the protocol and port should switch back to **http** and 8080. You should experiment with using the **<sslext:link>** tag to create links to secure actions. You will find that using SSLEXT is much easier than using the **user-data-constraint** subelement of the **web.xml** file. It gives you fine-grained control where you need it through the tags. At the same time, it leverages the **struts-config.xml** file to enable simple declarative configuration for secure request processing.

Testing Struts Applications

Testing, and unit testing in particular, has become a hot topic in software development in recent years. Spurred on by the advent of agile methodologies such as Extreme Programming and Scrum, developers are placing a greater emphasis on software testing. Successful iterative development hinges on having repeatable tests that can be run with every build. Because of this need, this chapter covers testing Struts applications. Before you read about how to test a Struts application, however, take a look at the types of testing that are applicable.

Types of Testing

There are different levels, or types, of testing. Each type serves different purposes. Traditionally, testing is viewed as a quality control function. However, unit testing is considered to be in the development domain. This chapter covers testing from both of these perspectives. However, the primary focus will be on the types of tests run by developers.

Unit Testing

Unit testing refers to independent testing of individual software units. In Java development, a unit is typically associated with a Java class. Unit testing is normally performed by the developer, not the quality assurance or quality control department. The goal of unit testing is to ensure that the unit under test does what it is supposed to do. More specifically, the developer specifies in a unit test what the expected output or behavior of individual methods is for a given set of inputs. Unit testing is typically associated with the xUnit family of software testing frameworks led by the JUnit framework.

The folks at the Cactus project (**http://jakarta.apache.org/cactus**), a testing framework covered in the "Using Cactus for Integration Unit Testing" section, refer to the following three specific types of unit testing:

- **Code logic testing** The traditional view of unit testing, where the unit is completely isolated.

435

- **Integration unit testing**   Testing of a unit that is not in isolation; that is, the unit communicates with other units.

- **Functional unit testing**   An integrated unit test that verifies the output of a unit for a known input. The unit in this case is typically not a software unit per say, but an application unit (for example, a Web page). Functional unit testing can be considered black-box integration testing.

This chapter covers several tools and techniques that assist with unit testing.

Functional Testing

Functional testing is driven by requirements and use cases and is usually performed by a quality control group. Functional tests ensure that the application performs the functions specified by the requirements. Functional tests are typically focused on verifying that the application or components of the application respond with the expected output when given known input. For Web applications, functional tests can be automated using testing tools.

System Testing

Performance is an important aspect of most applications. System testing is concerned with measuring and verifying the response of the system when the application is run under varying loads. System responses include such things as performance/latency, throughput, and memory consumption. At the end of this chapter, two open-source tools are presented that can measure and analyze this type of data.

Unit Testing Struts Applications

If a developer follows the best practices of Web application design—specifically, use of the Model-View-Controller (MVC) design pattern supported by Struts—most of the critical unit tests will be written for testing the model, and the Struts-specific tests will be only a small portion of the application's unit test suite. A well-designed Struts application promotes the definition of actions that delegate processing to business components and services that reside in the model. The **Action** classes are responsible only for transferring data from the View layer to the Model layer and vice versa.

The bulk of the unit tests required for a Struts application should be for the business components and services. JUnit (**http://www.junit.org**), developed by Erich Gamma and Kent Beck, is an excellent framework for unit testing these types of Java objects. This framework provides the software infrastructure for developing tests. It has become the *de facto* standard for Java unit testing. JUnit provides a base test class that is extended by the developer to create a specific unit test. The developer then writes test methods in this new test class. The test methods exercise the class to be tested and verify that the class being tested behaves as expected.

JUnit provides several features that make writing and running these tests simple. First, JUnit treats any method in the test class that begins with the word "test" as a method to run. Therefore, the developer uses that convention to name the test methods (e.g., *test*SearchByName, *test*Success). Within the test, JUnit provides methods for performing the verifications. These methods are referred to as *assertions.* An assertion simply expresses a Boolean (true/false) relationship. For example, you may assert that a value returned from a method is not null, or that the returned value has a specific value. If an assertion fails, that particular test method fails. Finally, JUnit provides several test runners that run the tests and report the test results. The following section describes how JUnit can be applied to the sample Mini HR application.

Testing the Model

The **EmployeeSearchService** class, first introduced in Chapter 2, is the primary business component of the Mini HR application. It provides methods to search for employees by name or social security number. Following is a JUnit unit test for this service. Note that the unit test can be run independently of the Web application and servlet container. Its only dependency is to the class being tested.

```
package com.jamesholmes.minihr;

import java.util.ArrayList;
import junit.framework.TestCase;

public class EmployeeSearchServiceTest extends TestCase {
  private EmployeeSearchService service;

  public EmployeeSearchServiceTest(String arg0) {
    super(arg0);
  }

  public void setUp() {
    service = new EmployeeSearchService();
  }
  public void tearDown() {
    super.tearDown();
  }

  public void testSearchByName() {
    String name ="Jim";
    ArrayList l = service.searchByName(name);
    assertEquals("Number of results", 2, l.size());
  }

  public void testSearchBySSN() {
```

```
      String ssn ="333-33-3333";
      ArrayList l = service.searchBySsNum(ssn);
      assertEquals("Number of results", 1, l.size());
      Employee e = (Employee) l.get(0);
      assertEquals("SSN", ssn, e.getSsNum());
    }

  public void testSearchByUnknownSSN() {
      String ssn ="999099-49493939";
      ArrayList l = service.searchBySsNum(ssn);
      assertEquals("Number of results", 0, l.size());
    }
}
```

First, notice that the test class is in the same package as the **EmployeeSearchService** class and uses the *Class under test*Test naming convention. If the test class were in a different package, only public methods could be tested. The next thing to notice is the **setUp( )** method, which is used to prepare each test. Here, this method creates the **EmployeeSearchService** object and stores a reference to it in an instance variable. As a corollary, a **tearDown( )** method can be implemented to perform any test cleanup. That would be the place, for example, to close a database connection or file resource used by the test.

A JUnit test runner actually runs the test. JUnit includes three test runner user interfaces—one based on Java AWT, one based on Java Swing, and a text-based runner that can be run from the command line. In addition, many Java IDEs provide some level of integration with JUnit. The test runner first creates a new instance of the test class. Then, for *each* test method (i.e., each method that begins with "test"), the runner calls **setUp( )**, then the test method itself, and then **tearDown( )**. This approach allows for the creation of independent, repeatable tests. Each test method should be capable of running separately, with the **setUp( )** and **tearDown( )** methods performing the initialization and cleanup.

The actual verification part of the test is encapsulated in the individual test methods. Generally speaking, there should be at least one test method for each method of the external interface of a class under test. The test method should create the input values, call the appropriate method, and then verify the results. This verification may include examining any returned values as well as checking any expected state changes. Each verification is implemented using one or more of the JUnit **assert( )** methods. For example, if a search by social security number is performed using a value for which there is no match, then an assertion can be made that the returned collection should be empty. This type of negative test is illustrated in the **EmployeeSearchServiceTest** class in the **testSearchByUnknownSSN( )** method.

To run this test, ensure that the **junit.jar** file and the application classes are on your classpath. Then, simply execute the following command:

```
java junit.swingui.TestRunner
```

This displays the JUnit graphical user interface (GUI), shown in Figure 20-1, which allows you to select the test to run. You can then run the test and view the results. If you get a green bar, then all tests succeeded. If the test fails, you can change the code to make it work—then rerun the test. Usually, you do not need to restart the JUnit Swing user interface because it incorporates a mechanism for reloading classes.

Now that you've seen how to write a unit test, you need to integrate unit testing into the build process. Apache Ant (**http://ant.apache.org**) is a Java-based build tool that provides support for integrating testing into an application's build cycle. An Ant build is driven by an XML-based build file. The build file includes specific targets that correspond to steps in the build process, such as compiling classes, creating the distribution (such as a **.jar** file), and deploying the application. Testing can be added to the build cycle by including testing targets in the application's Ant build script. This

FIGURE 20-1   A successful test run using the JUnit Swing test runner

chapter will not go into complete details of integrating JUnit with Ant; however, it is fairly straightforward and the Ant support for unit testing is well documented in Ant's documentation set. Following is the Ant build script, **build.xml**, that will be used and expanded throughout this chapter. The test target is the last target in this file.

```xml
<project name="MiniHR20" default="dist" basedir=".">
  <property environment="env"/>
  <property name="build.compiler" value="javac1.4"/>
  <!-- set global properties for this build -->
  <property name="src" location="src"/>
  <property name="webinf.dir" location="web/WEB-INF"/>
  <property name="build.dir" location="build"/>
  <property name="dist.dir"  location="dist"/>
  <property name="server.dir" location="${env.CATALINA_HOME}"/>
  <property name="servlet.jar"
  <property name="test.dir" location="test"/>
  <property name="deploy.dir" location="${server.dir}/webapps"/>

  <target name="clean">
    <delete dir="${build.dir}"/>
    <delete dir="${dist.dir}"/>
  </target>

  <target name="init">
    <mkdir dir="${build.dir}"/>
    <mkdir dir="${dist.dir}"/>
  </target>

  <target name="compile" depends="init"
        description="compile the source ">
    <javac srcdir="${src}:${test.dir}/src"
          destdir="${build.dir}" debug="on">
      <classpath>
        <pathelement path="${classpath}"/>
        <pathelement location="${servlet.jar}"/>
        <fileset dir="${webinf.dir}/lib">
          <include name="**/*.jar"/>
         </fileset>
      </classpath>
    </javac>

    <copy todir="${build.dir}">
      <fileset dir="${src}">
        <include name="**/*.properties"/>
      </fileset>
    </copy>
  </target>
```

```
    <target name="dist" depends="compile">
      <war destfile="${dist.dir}/${ant.project.name}.war"
           webxml="${webinf.dir}/web.xml">
        <webinf dir="${webinf.dir}">
          <include name="struts-config.xml"/>
          <include name="validation.xml"/>
          <include name="validator-rules.xml"/>
        </webinf>
        <classes dir="${build.dir}"/>
        <fileset dir="web" excludes="WEB-INF/**.*"/>
      </war>
    </target>

    <target name="deploy" depends="dist">
      <unjar src="${dist.dir}/${ant.project.name}.war"
             dest="${deploy.dir}/${ant.project.name}"/>
    </target>

    <target name="test" depends="compile">
      <mkdir dir="${test.dir}/results"/>
      <junit printsummary="yes" fork="no" haltonfailure="no"
             errorProperty="test.failed" failureProperty="test.failed">
        <formatter type="xml" />
        <classpath>
          <pathelement path="${build.dir}"/>
        </classpath>
        <batchtest todir="${test.dir}/results">
          <fileset dir="${build.dir}">
            <include name="**/*Test.class" />
          </fileset>
        </batchtest>
      </junit>
      <junitreport todir="${test.dir}/reports">
        <fileset dir="${test.dir}/results">
          <include name="TEST-*.xml"/>
        </fileset>
        <report format="frames" todir="${test.dir}/reports"/>
      </junitreport>
      <fail message="JUnit tests failed. Check reports." if="test.failed"/>
    </target>
</project>
```

The test target in the preceding build script integrates testing into the build. The **junit** task is used to run tests and generate the results. The **junitreport** task is used to accumulate and generate an HTML report from those results. These tests are run by simply typing **ant test** at a command prompt. The reports are generated into the

test/reports directory. The generated report includes information about which tests passed, which ones failed, and the specific assertions that failed. If an exception was thrown, the stack trace is included with the report. In addition, some basic timing information is also recorded. As mentioned previously, testing the model should be the top priority when determining what aspects of the system to test first.

Testing Controller Behavior

Assuming that unit tests have been completed for the Model portion of the application, the next step is to test Controller behavior. Here the focus is on verifying the behavior of Struts actions. You want to check that an action performs as expected. This includes ensuring that the action does such things as the following:

- Receives the data it needs from the request or session
- Handles cases properly where required input is missing or invalid
- Calls the model passing the correct data
- Marshals and transforms as needed the data from the model
- Stores the data in the appropriate context or scope
- Returns the correct action response

These types of tests can be performed in a running container (i.e., a servlet engine such as Tomcat) or outside of the container in a normal client JVM. This is an important distinction. Test execution outside the container allows you to isolate the class under test from outside dependencies. When the test fails, you know that the failure is in the class under test, not a problem with the container.

In-container tests are a form of integrated unit tests. Integrated unit tests can be valuable for verifying that the class being tested will work in an actual deployed environment. Practically speaking, in-container tests are more complex to set up and run and generally take more CPU time than tests run independently of a container. On the other hand, outside-the-container tests often require creation of mock objects to stand in for container-provided software entities such as the servlet request and response objects, the servlet context, and the HTTP session.

Using StrutsTestCase

StrutsTestCase (**http://strutstestcase.sourceforge.net**) is an open-source JUnit extension that provides a framework of Java classes specifically for testing Struts actions. It provides support for unit testing Struts actions outside of a servlet container using mock objects. These objects are provided as stand-ins for the servlet request and response, and context components such as the servlet context and the HTTP session. Test cases using the mock objects use information from your application's configuration files—specifically the **web.xml** file and the **struts-config.xml** file. In addition, StrutsTestCase also supports in-container testing through integration with the Cactus framework. In-container testing will be covered in "Using Cactus for Integration Unit Testing" later in this chapter.

Since StrutsTestCase extends JUnit, the tests can be run using the JUnit test-running tools. Consider a unit test for the **SearchAction** class of the sample application. This action performs the following steps:

1. Gets the entered name from the form.
2. Determines whether the search is by name (i.e., a name was entered) or by social security number.
3. Performs the search using **EmployeeSearchService**.
4. Stores the results back in the form.
5. Forwards the request back to the input page.

Here's a unit test that verifies this behavior:

```
package com.jamesholmes.minihr;

import servletunit.struts.MockStrutsTestCase;

public class SearchActionTest extends MockStrutsTestCase {
  public SearchActionTest(String testName) {
    super(testName);
  }

  public void setUp() throws Exception {
    super.setUp();
    setRequestPathInfo("/search");
  }

  public void testSearchByName() throws Exception {
    addRequestParameter("name","Jim");
    actionPerform();
    assertNotNull("Results are null",
      ((SearchForm) getActionForm()).getResults());
    verifyInputForward();
  }
}
```

First, notice that the class inherits from **servletunit.struts.MockStrutsTestCase**, which in turn inherits from the JUnit **TestCase** (**junit.framework.TestCase**). This relationship allows access to all the assertion methods provided by JUnit. Next, in the **setUp( )** method, the parent's **setUp()** method is called and the request path is set. Both of these steps are critical. If you override **setUp( )**, you must call **super.setUp( )**. Setting the request path ensures that the desired action is called. Notice that the **.do** extension mapping is not included in the request path. StrutsTestCase uses the **web.xml** file to determine this. Note also that there is no reference in the test to the **SearchAction** class itself. StrutsTestCase actually relies on the action mappings in the **struts-config.xml** file to determine which action to call. So, in reality, you are testing not just the **SearchAction** class, but the entire action configuration.

The test method itself is relatively simple. First, a request parameter is added that represents the data that would be submitted from the HTML form on the **search.jsp** page. Next, **actionPerform( )** actually executes the action. After that, the resultant behavior is verified. Specifically, the **results** property of the **SearchForm** object is checked for null. In addition, the forward back to the input page (**search.jsp**) is verified using the **verifyInputForward( )** method.

To run this test, some changes need to be made to the **test** target of the Ant script. Since StrutsTestCase relies on the XML configuration files of the application, the parent directory of the application's **WEB-INF** directory must be on the classpath. The following three entries should be added to the **classpath** element of the **junit** task:

```
<fileset dir="${webinf.dir}/lib"/>
<pathelement location="${servlet.jar}"/>
<pathelement path="web"/>
```

The first entry adds all **.jar** files in the **WEB-INF/lib** folder. The second element adds the **servlet.jar** file. Finally, the third element specifies the directory that contains the **WEB-INF** directory.

The use of StrutsTestCase for mock testing is extremely powerful. The underlying mock implementation allows your test to focus on the specific unit being tested. In addition, the tests can be run without requiring a running container with the application deployed. If you are in an environment where the container is running on a different server, likely even a different operating system, you can still unit test your actions on your local development computer. That being said, these unit tests do not take into account deployment issues, container dependencies, and other run-time behaviors that can only be tested with a running application. Fortunately, there is a tool that can help with this testing also.

Using Cactus for Integration Unit Testing

Some would consider *integration unit testing* a bit of an oxymoron. Typically, unit tests should be written such that they are isolated from outside dependencies. Isolating the unit test makes it much easier to identify the cause of errors when a test fails. However, there certainly is a place for integrated testing. A counter-argument can be made that an integrated unit test gives you a more realistic test. For some types of objects, say for example, Enterprise Java Beans, certain aspects of the objects can only be tested in the container. Container-provided services such as transactions and persistence are not easily mocked up. Another case where integration tests are invaluable is with regression testing. Deployments to different application servers and different operating systems can be verified using integrated unit tests.

Cactus was developed to provide these types of unit tests. It was originally developed to test Enterprise JavaBeans but is equally up to the task of testing servlets, servlet filters, and JSPs. In fact, Cactus can be used to test any type of behavior that relies on a J2EE/servlet container. As will be shown later in this section, Struts actions can be tested through interaction with Struts' **ActionServlet**. However, these tests do come at a cost of increased complexity and slower performance. Cactus tests are fairly easy to write, but configuration and deployment can be complex. If you are running your unit tests frequently as part of your build process, you may find that your build takes far too long. The reason Cactus tests take longer is that Cactus starts your application server every time it runs its suite of tests. A good option is to only run Cactus periodically, such as on nightly automated builds. Here are some guidelines to help you decide what type of testing to use and when:

- *Concentrate on unit tests for the model, first.* That is where most of the business logic is and that should be the focus.

- *Use the StrutsTestCase with mock objects to test your **Action** classes.* Tests using mock objects can be run much faster, and do not require a servlet container.

- *Use Cactus testing for those classes that rely on container-provided services.* For example, if you are using JNDI, or testing behavior based on container-managed security, you should use Cactus.

In addition, the Cactus site itself includes an even-handed comparison of mock object testing to Cactus in-container tests.

To get started with Cactus, you need to download the distribution. As of this writing, Cactus 1.5 was the latest release build. Cactus can run tests via integration with your IDE; however, the preferred approach is via Ant. First, you need to define the task definitions for the Ant tasks that Cactus provides:

```
<path id="cactus.classpath">
  <fileset dir="cactus/lib">
    <include name="*.jar"/>
  </fileset>
</path>
<taskdef resource="cactus.tasks"
  classpathref="cactus.classpath"/>
```

This defines a path containing the Cactus **.jar** files and creates the Cactus task definitions.

Next, add the Cactus classpath to the classpath of the **compile** target. Use **cactus .classpath** as the reference ID for the **path** element. As stated, Cactus tests will make the build slower; therefore, create a separate **test.cactus** target. In addition, provide a **test** wrapper target for running both test sets. The **test.cactus** target performs the following:

1. Instruments the application's **.war** file for testing by creating a new **.war** file. This process is referred to as *cactifying* the **.war** file.

2. Runs the unit tests. This is done using the *cactus* task. The **containerset** element indicates the container to run the tests against. This task extends the **junit** task.

It uses the same subelements for specifying the results format and the set of tests to run.

3. Creates an HTML report of the results. This is done using the **junitreport** task that was shown previously.

Now the test case needs to be written. Cactus is an extension of JUnit. Cactus provides base classes that extend **junit.framework.TestCase**. If you have written a JUnit test, Cactus tests will be familiar. However, since Cactus runs on both the client and server, there are some additional APIs that are of use. Before delving into test code, a review of how Cactus works is in order.

One of the most important aspects of Cactus to understand is that a Cactus test runs in two JVMs. Specifically, there is a copy of the test on the client JVM, and a copy on the server JVM (that is, the JVM running the J2EE/servlet container). From Figure 20-2 you can see that Cactus provides hooks on both the server and client side. The server-side hooks are the standard JUnit fixture methods—**setUp( )** and **tearDown( )**. These methods are run, on the server, before and after execution of each **test***YourMethod***( )** method. The **begin( )** and **end( )** methods are unique to Cactus. These methods are executed on the client side—before the request is sent, and after the response is received. Since there are two copies of the test, instance variables set in the **begin( )** method are not set on the server side. Likewise, variables set in **setUp( )** and **tearDown( )** are not available in the client-side **begin( )** and **end( )** methods.

These optional methods can be used to simulate the request and interrogate the response. Think of these methods as the browser side of the test. To make things concrete, the **SearchActionTest** class, implemented before as a **MockStrutsTestCase**, is reimplemented in the following code as a Cactus **ServletTestCase**. As mentioned, Cactus does not provide a direct way of testing a Struts action, as StrutsTestCase

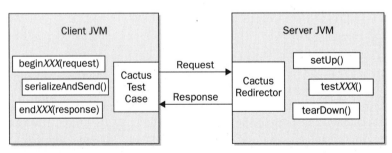

1. The **begin***XXX***( )** method is called to set up the Web request.

2. Cactus serializes the request and sends it (using HttpClient).

8. The **end***XXX***( )** method is called and passed the Web response.

3. Redirector receives the request.

4. Redirector calls the **setUp( )** method.

5. Redirector calls the **test***XXX***( )** method.

6. Redirector calls the **tearDown( )** method.

7. Redirector returns the response.

FIGURE 20-2   Cactus architecture

does. Struts actions are tested indirectly by interacting with the **ActionServlet**. Here is the Cactus unit test for testing the **SearchAction** class:

```
package com.jamesholmes.minihr;

import org.apache.cactus.ServletTestCase;
import org.apache.cactus.WebRequest;
import org.apache.struts.action.ActionServlet;

public class SearchActionCactusTest extends ServletTestCase {
  private ActionServlet servlet;

  public SearchActionCactusTest(String theName) {
    super(theName);
  }

  public void setUp() throws Exception {
    servlet = new ActionServlet();
    servlet.init(config);
  }

  public void beginSuccess(WebRequest request) {
    request.setURL(null, // server name (e.g. 'localhost:8080')
    null, // context (e.g. '/MiniHR20')
    "/search.do", // servlet path
    null,         // extra path info
    "name=Jim");   // query string
  }

  public void testSuccess() throws Exception {
    servlet.doGet(request, response);
    SearchForm form = (SearchForm) request.getAttribute("searchForm");
    assertNotNull(form.getResults());
  }

  public void tearDown() throws Exception {
    servlet.destroy();
  }
}
```

There are key differences between this test and the previous mock test. First, notice that the **setUp()** method creates an instance of the Struts **ActionServlet** itself. Then, in the **beginSuccess( )** method, the URL of the request object is set to the page to access and the query string. The **SearchAction** class is executed indirectly by calling the **doGet( )** method of the **ActionServlet**. Essentially, the test is emulating the behavior of the container. Also notice that the request path must include the **.do** extension—Cactus knows nothing about Struts or the **ActionServlet**'s mapping. Finally, in the **testSuccess( )**

method, the request is queried for the form. Note that the attribute name "searchForm" had to be hard-coded into the test. Using StrutsTestCase, this information was pulled from the **struts-config.xml** file. Simply changing the name of the form in the **struts-config.xml** file will break this Cactus test.

As you might suspect, these tests can become rather brittle. The tests are dependent on configuration settings that are outside the scope of the test. It would be preferable if there were a base class that could get configuration information from Struts. Fortunately, StrutsTestCase provides just that.

Using StrutsTestCase with Cactus

StrutsTestCase actually provides two base classes that can be used to create **Action** tests. **MockStrutsTestCase**, which extends the JUnit **TestCase**, has already been demonstrated. Tests that extend this class can be run outside the container. For in-container tests, StrutsTestCase includes the **CactusStrutsTestCase** base class. This class extends the Cactus **ServletTestCase**. The UML diagram in Figure 20-3 shows how these objects relate.

A **MockStrutsTestCase** can easily be turned into a container-driven Cactus test case by simply changing the class it extends to the **CactusStrutsTestCase**. You may find that you will want to have both forms of these tests. In fact, you could probably refactor the

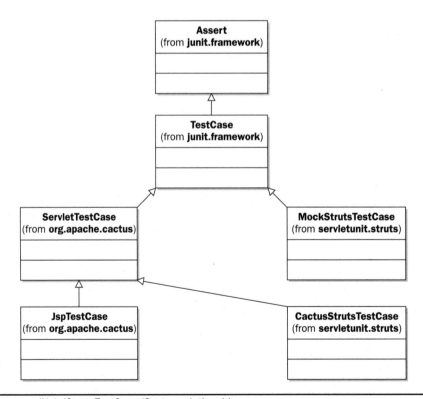

FIGURE 20-3   JUnit/StrutsTestCase/Cactus relationships

common test behavior (that is, the setup, assertions, and verifications) into a common class that is used by both the mock test and the in-container test. The previous StrutsTestCase can be changed to run under Cactus by simply changing it to extend from **CactusStrutsTestCase**—the rest is the same.

```
package com.jamesholmes.minihr;

import servletunit.struts.CactusStrutsTestCase;

public class SearchActionStrutsTest extends CactusStrutsTestCase {
  public SearchActionStrutsTest(String testName) {
    super(testName);
  }

  public void setUp() throws Exception {
    super.setUp();
    setRequestPathInfo("/search");
  }

  public void testSearchByName() throws Exception {
    addRequestParameter("name","Jim");
    actionPerform();
    assertNotNull("Results are null",
      ((SearchForm) getActionForm()).getResults());
    verifyInputForward();
  }
}
```

As you can see, the code is much simpler and easier to maintain than the same test written using the Cactus framework alone. Moreover, because it extends the Cactus classes, the test can easily be run as an in-container test that more closely tests actual deployment.

Now that you know how to test actions both in and out of the container, you should consider the additional verifications that StrutsTestCase provides. Both **MockStrutsTestCase** and **CactusStrutsTestCase** extend **TestCase** and therefore offer all the standard assertion methods that are available with the JUnit API. In addition, several Struts-specific assertions are available in both of the StrutsTestCase base classes. All of these methods begin with *verify*:

- **verifyActionErrors( )** Verifies that a specific set of error messages, identified by key, were sent

- **verifyNoActionErrors( )** Verifies that no errors were sent

- **verifyActionMessages( )** Verifies that a specific set of action messages, identified by key, were sent

- **verifyNoActionMessages( )** Verifies that no action messages were sent

- **verifyForward( )**   Verifies that the controller forwarded to a specified logical forward name, global or local, as specified in the Struts configuration file

- **verifyForwardPath( )**   Verifies that the controller forwarded to a specified absolute path

- **verifyInputForward( )**   Verifies that the controller forwarded to the path identified by the action mappings **input** attribute

- **verifyTilesForward( )**   Verifies that the controller forwarded to a specified logical forward name from the Struts configuration and a Tiles definition name from the Tiles configuration

- **verifyInputTilesForward( )**   Verifies that the controller forwarded to the defined input of a specified Tiles definition

Before leaving the subject of in-container tests, it is worth mentioning that Cactus also provides a base class for testing servlet filters. This could be used, for example, to test the authorization filter used in Chapter 19.

Testing the View

Verifying that an application's presentation is correct is a critical step in software development. You are never quite sure if the view is appropriate until you put it before the customer. All too frequently, countless hours are spent building a complex system without regard to the presentation. Testing these views typically falls under the heading of functional testing and acceptance testing. However, there is important behavior that a view provides that can be unit tested. Most Struts applications leverage the rich Struts tag library in JSP pages to provide dynamic HTML rendering. The Logic Tag Library tags, for example, can be used to selectively render HTML markup in a JSP page. Such pages can be unit tested by supplying the appropriate inputs to the page, accessing the page, and then verifying the response. The difficulty comes in two areas. First, the inputs may come from the container-managed objects such as the HTTP request, **HttpSession** or **ServletContext**. Second, the response is generally in HTML— verifying that the correct HTML was rendered involves complex parsing.

Cactus helps address the first problem, as was shown earlier in the **SearchAction CactusTest**. These tests can be run in the container and the tests have access to the container-managed context objects. For parsing HTML, HttpUnit can be used. HttpUnit (**http://httpunit.sourceforge.net**) is a Java-based open-source framework for functional testing of Web sites. It provides Java APIs for accessing all aspects of the HTTP interaction. HttpUnit refers to this as the *Web conversation*.

One aspect of Cactus that has not been demonstrated is use of the **WebResponse** object provided by the **endTest( )** method. Cactus supports two versions of this method. The first method provides access to a simple object, **org.apache.cactus .WebResponse**, which represents the HTTP response. With this object you can check the HTTP response status code and headers, check cookies, and assert actions based on the content. The content of the response is returned as a simple string. For a complex

Web site, the returned content could be quite large. The other accepted version of the **endTest( )** method receives an HttpUnit **WebResponse** object, **com.meterware .httpunit.WebResponse**. Contrary to the Cactus **WebResponse**, this object provides a rich API for accessing the HTML content of the returned response. Through this integration with HttpUnit, Cactus tests can navigate through the response in an object-oriented fashion, verifying that the response contains specific HTML details such as HTML tables, links, and forms.

Consider a unit test for the **index.jsp** page of the Mini HR application. The dynamic aspects of this page are conditioned on the presence of a **User** object in the session. An additional link is rendered if the user is an administrator, enabling the administrator to add an employee. A unit test for this JSP allows for these assertions. Here is a Cactus unit test that includes a test method that performs these assertions. This test allows the JSP to be tested in isolation.

```java
package com.jamesholmes.minihr;

import org.apache.cactus.JspTestCase;
import com.jamesholmes.minihr.security.User;
import com.meterware.httpunit.WebLink;
import com.meterware.httpunit.WebResponse;

public class IndexJspTest extends JspTestCase {
  public IndexJspTest(String theName) {
    super(theName);
  }

  public void testAdministratorAccess() throws Exception {
    User user = new User("bsiggelkow","Bill", "Siggelkow", "thatsme",
                          new String[] {"administrator"});
    session.setAttribute("user", user);
    pageContext.forward("/index.jsp");
  }

  public void endAdministratorAccess(WebResponse response)
            throws Exception {
    // verify that the login form is not displayed
    assertNull("Login form should not have rendered",
    response.getFormWithName("loginForm"));
    //verify that the proper links are present
    WebLink[] links = response.getLinks();
    assertTrue("First link is admin/add.jsp",
      links[0].getURLString().startsWith("/test/admin/add.jsp"));
    assertTrue("Second link is search.jsp",
      links[1].getURLString().startsWith("/test/search.jsp"));
  }
}
```

The first thing you should notice is that the test imports the HttpUnit classes. HttpUnit is bundled with Cactus. (You may also want to get the latest HttpUnit distribution and documentation at **http://httpunit.sourceforge.net**.) Note also that the class extends **JspTestCase** instead of **ServletTestCase**. **JspTestCase**, which inherits from **ServletTestCase**, allows a JSP to be tested in isolation. The JSP page context can be accessed by the test class as needed. The test method was named to indicate that it is testing the display of the index page for a logged-in user with administrative privileges. Other conditions should also be modeled as test methods as appropriate. The first thing that the **testAdministratorAccess( )** method does is instantiate a **User** object that is assigned the **administrator** role. This object is placed in the **HttpSession** under the name by which it will be accessed on the page. The page is then rendered by forwarding to the **index.jsp** page. The implicit **PageContext** object performs the job of forwarding the request.

The actual test assertions and verifications are now performed in the **endAdministratorAccess( )** method. Remember that this method is executed in the client-side JVM after the request is processed. If a **User** object is in the session, the login form should not be displayed. The first assertion verifies this by asserting that the response does not contain a form named **loginForm**. Next, the set of links contained in the response is retrieved. Assertions are made that the first link is to the **Add an Employee** page (**/admin/add.jsp**), and that the second link is to the Search page (**search.jsp**). Initially, these assertions were written using the **assertEquals( )** method as follows:

```
assertEquals("Check first link", "/test/admin/add.jsp",
  links[0].getURLString());
```

At first glance, this appears correct; however, if you run the test using this assertion, it most likely will fail, because the servlet container may append a session identifier string to the link. In this case, the actual value of the URL was the following:

```
/test/admin/add.jsp;jsessionid=0E5EFB6F64C01749EE94E3A57BDEBD21
```

Therefore, the assertion was changed to verify that the URL *starts with* the expected result.

While the tests just demonstrated certainly are useful, they are getting more into the realm of functional testing than unit testing. HttpUnit can be used for broader functional testing—not just unit testing JSPs. HttpUnit provides full support for the entire Web conversation. The API provides methods for constructing requests, following links, and populating and submitting forms. Tests can be written using this API that mimic expected usage scenarios of the Web application. However, the amount of code to support such a test can be extensive. Also, this code can be extremely sensitive to simple changes in presentation. In the following section, a better approach for this type of functional testing is presented.

Use-Case-Driven Testing

The classical view of testing, from a quality control perspective, is use-case driven. That is, test cases are derived from use cases. For example, the following is a use case for the Mini HR "Search by Name" feature.

Precondition:

- The user has browsed to the Mini HR main page.

Primary Flow:

1. Click the Search link on the main page.
2. On the Search page, choose to Search by Name.
3. Enter all or part of an employee's name.
4. Submit the form.
   If a username was not entered, a validation error is displayed.
5. All employees that match the input name are displayed on the page. For each user, the employee name and social security number are listed.
   If no employees match, a message is displayed indicating that no matches exist.

This use case is straightforward and easy to understand. It is complete in that it specifies what must happen prior to the scenario (preconditions), all steps that the user must take, and the results of those steps.

Creating Test Cases

Specific test cases can be easily derived from this use case. A test case is generally more explicit than the use case in that it may describe specific test data to be used. In addition, alternate use-case flows are often modeled as separate test cases. The test explicitly states the steps that must be taken to test the functionality described by the use case. In addition, it explicitly states what the results should be. Think of a test case as a set of steps that you would hand to someone who is testing a certain function or feature of the application. The following are the two test cases for Search by Name—the key differences from the use case are in bold.

Test Case: Search by Name with Matches
Preconditions:

- The employee database is preloaded with test data.
- The browser location is the Mini HR main page.

Primary Flow:

1. Click the Search link on the main page.

2. **Verify that the Search page is displayed.**

3. On the Search page, choose to Search by Name.

4. **Enter "Jim" in the username field.**

5. Submit the form.

6. **Verify that the results are displayed with a table like the following:**

Jim Smith	123-45-6789
Will Jimmerson	987-65-4321

Test Case: Search by Name with No Matches
Preconditions:

- The employee database is preloaded with test data.
- **The browser location is the Mini HR main page.**

Primary Flow:

1. Click the Search link on the main page.

2. **Verify that the Search page is displayed.**

3. On the Search page, choose to Search by Name.

4. **Enter "Fred" in the username field.**

5. Submit the form.

6. **Verify that the "No Employees Found" message is displayed.**

These test cases now provide the test engineer with a *script* to follow for testing. While manual testing is important, it would also be beneficial if test cases like these could be automated. Automated testing would permit regression tests of an application anytime such testing is needed. For example, these tests would be run whenever a new version of the application was deployed to the QA server. The next section demonstrates a tool for automating these types of tests.

Using Canoo WebTest

Canoo WebTest, developed by Canoo Engineering, was designed to test Web applications. It is distributed as free open-source software. WebTest uses the Ant build utility as a test driver and HttpUnit to interact with an HTTP server. It works off an XML-based test specification. Test cases can be easily modeled using this test description. These tests are functional tests, not unit tests. The expected behavior is specified as a set of steps. These steps closely match the steps in a test case. Ant is used to execute the tests. You can create these tests in your normal Ant build script. However, it is better if they are separated out into separate files. They can always be integrated into a build, say for use by Quality Control, using Ant's **ant** task (which can execute a target of another build file). To demonstrate WebTest, a functional test for the "Search by Name" test case from the preceding section will be created.

First, download Canoo WebTest (**http://webtest.canoo.com**). Extract the distribution into a directory and create the environment variable *WEBTESTHOME* that refers to that directory. You can test the installation by running the *WEBTESTHOME***doc****samples****installTest.xml** file with Ant as follows:

```
cd WEBTESTHOME\doc\samples
ant -f installTest.xml
```

However, this test may fail on certain systems. As suggested in the WebTest installation instructions, HttpUnit (which is used internally by WebTest) may not handle the **file** protocol. To verify the installation, make a copy of **installTest.xml**. In the copied file, change the host, port, and protocol to valid values for your application server. For example, if you are running Tomcat locally on port 8080, you would change the **checkWebTest** element to the following:

```
<target name="checkWebTest">
  <testSpec name="check calling and parsing a local file">
    <config host="" port="8080" basepath="/" summary="false"
            verbose="true" saveresponse="false" haltonfailure="true"
            protocol="http" />
    <steps>
      <invoke stepid="get local file" url="/index.jsp" />
      <verifytitle stepid="check the title is parsed correctly"
                   text="Apache Tomcat" regex="true" />
    </steps>
  </testSpec>
</target>
```

An important item to note here is that the **checkWebTest** target is a regular Ant target. The first nested element of the **testSpec** element is **config**. This element is required. It defines the location of the application under test. **Host** defaults to **localhost** if not specified. Following the **config** element are the steps of the test specification. The steps consist of a sequential set of nested elements that define the actions that the test is to take. These steps can generally be categorized as either *action* steps or *verification* steps. Action steps include such things as accessing a URL, clicking a link or button, and typing text on a form. Verification steps are used like assertions in a JUnit unit test. They define steps that evaluate to true or false.

Once WebTest is up and running, you will want to create the test specifications for the test cases. The following test specification is used to test the two Search by Name test cases. A target is created for each test case. These test targets can be run by simply calling Ant, passing the build filename using the **–buildfile testfile.xml** (or **–f testfile.xml**) option. Likewise, if your IDE provides Ant integration (as most IDEs do), you can run the tests from your IDE in the same manner that you run an Ant build script.

PART IV

```xml
<?xml version="1.0"?>
<!DOCTYPE project SYSTEM "WebTest.dtd"[
   <!ENTITY definition SYSTEM "includes/definition.xml">
   <!ENTITY config      SYSTEM "includes/config.xml">
   <!ENTITY getSearchPage    SYSTEM "includes/getSearchPage.xml">]>
<project name="MiniHR20-SearchTest" basedir="." default="all">
  <property name="webtest.home" value="../../canoo"/>
  &definition;
  <target name="all" depends="nameSearchWithResults, nameSearchNoResults"/>
  <target name="nameSearchWithResults">
    <testSpec name="Perform a Search by Name">
      &config;
      <steps>
        &getSearchPage;
        <setinputfield stepid="Enter 'Jim' into Name field"
                       name="name" value="Jim"/>
        <clickbutton stepid="Submit the 'search by' form"
                     label="Submit"/>
        <verifyxpath stepid="Verify xpath 'Jim Smith'"
                     xpath="/html/body/table/tr/td[1]"
                     text="[Jj][Ii][Mm]"
                     regex="true"/>
      </steps>
    </testSpec>
  </target>
  <target name="nameSearchNoResults">
    <testSpec name="Perform a Search by Name with No Results">
      &config;
      <steps>
        &getSearchPage;
        <setinputfield stepid="Enter 'Morty' into Name field"
                       name="name" value="Morty"/>
        <clickbutton stepid="Submit the 'search by' form"
                     label="Submit"/>
        <verifytext stepid="Verify 'No Employees Found'"
                    text="No Employees Found"/>
      </steps>
    </testSpec>
  </target>
</project>
```

As you can see in the DOCTYPE declaration, this test makes extensive use of XML entities to bring in shared XML fragments. The first entity, **definition**, defines an entity that contains the task definitions for Canoo.

includes/definition.xml:

```xml
<taskdef file="${webtest.home}/webtestTaskdefs.properties">
  <classpath>
```

```
    <pathelement path="${webtest.home}/lib"/>
    <fileset dir="${webtest.home}" includes="**/lib/*.jar"/>
  </classpath>
</taskdef>
```

This fragment is generic to most any use of Canoo WebTest.

The second entity, **config**, is specific to the application being tested. In this case, the XML fragment defines the **config** element specifically for accessing the Mini HR application running on Tomcat.

includes/config.xml:

```
<config host="" port="8080" basepath="/MiniHR20" summary="false"
    verbose="true" saveresponse="false" haltonfailure="true"
    protocol="http"/>
```

You can reuse this element for any test specification of your application.

The final entity, **getSearchPage**, is specific to this test set. It defines the steps that are necessary to get the Search page. These steps include accessing the application's main page, clicking the Search link, and then verifying that the Search page is displayed. While the steps could have been duplicated for each target, creating the entity allows reuse of this functionality for additional tests that need to get the Search page. Those tests may be added to this set of specifications or to new sets of specifications.

includes/getSearchPage.xml:

```
<invoke stepid="Get main page" url="/index.jsp" />
<verifytitle stepid="Check that title is correct"
    text="ABC, Inc. Human Resources Portal"/>
<clicklink stepid="Click Search for Employees link"
    label="Search for Employees"/>
<verifytext stepid="Find 'Employee Search' text"
    text="Employee Search"/>
```

The first step of this fragment, **Get main page**, uses the **invoke** task to access the page of the application. The URL is relative to the settings in the **config** element. Next, the title of the displayed page is verified. Following that, the Search link is clicked. Finally, the text "Employee Search" is searched for and verified. This XML fragment is used in both of the test targets.

The test case to Search by Name uses these entities. First, the **config** entity is referenced to indicate the basic configuration. Next, the **getSearchPage** entity is used. At this point in the test, the Search page should be displayed. Next, the **setinputfield** element is used to emulate a user typing "Jim" into the **name** field. The **clickbutton** task is then used to submit the form. The last step is the most interesting. Canoo allows you to use XPath expressions to identify and verify portions of the expected response. In this case, the XPath attribute of the **verifyxpath** task refers to the first table data cell of the first row in the table. The **text** attribute indicates what the expected value should be. The **text** attribute can be either normal text to search for or a regular expression. Here, a regular expression is used to indicate that the table data cell referenced by the XPath expression should contain the text "JIM" regardless of case.

The second test target, **nameSearchNoResults**, verifies proper behavior when the search results in no matches for the entered name. This target reuses the **getSearchPage** steps. Also, it uses the simpler **verifytext** task to check if the resulting response contains the expected message—No Employees Found.

As you can see, Canoo WebTest is very powerful. Test cases map to automated test specifications in a natural and easy-to-understand fashion. The test specification tasks are well documented and can be written by nondevelopers. WebTest also provides the capability to generate test reports for a test specification. These reports, generated in XML, can then be rendered in HTML using an XSLT stylesheet. Check the Canoo WebTest samples for examples of how to utilize this functionality. Finally, the use of Ant as the underlying framework means easier integration with cross-platform build processes.

The one aspect that WebTest does not easily provide verifications for is presentation and layout. These verifications can be made using XPath; however, wholesale use of XPath to verify the presentation of a page can get extensive and difficult to maintain. Depending on the size of your application, you may want to consider a testing tool that provides record and playback capability. Such tools are usually not open source or free; however, they are usually quite powerful and may be necessary for large sites— particularly if those sites use a lot of JavaScript and other Dynamic HTML techniques.

Testing Application Performance

A final and sometimes overlooked area of testing is performance. Too often, an application is rolled out to production only to find that the performance of the application is unacceptable. For Struts applications, the first step to good performance is proper design and planning. Developers should plan for the expected number of concurrent users. Testing should be performed on a platform that is as similar as possible to the production environment. Developers are not often called on to test their applications for performance. However, tools are available that allow a developer to measure and test the performance of their application. One such tool, JUnitPerf, allows for performance tests to be run against existing JUnit tests. JUnitPerf accomplishes this by *decorating* a unit test. In other words, it wraps an existing test with a test that measures the performance of the wrapped test methods.

JUnitPerf (**http://www.clarkware.com/software/JUnitPerf.html**) was written and is maintained by Mike Clark of Clarkware Consulting. It can be downloaded and used free of charge. There are two main types of performance tests that JUnitPerf supports:

- **Timed tests**   Measure the amount of time that a test takes. Assertions can be made about the maximum amount of time that the test should take. If the test takes longer than that, then the assertion fails.

- **Load tests**   Allow the test writer to indicate the number of concurrent users (threads) that are running the test and optionally the number of times to execute the test.

To start, the following code defines a timed test for the simple JUnit **EmployeeSearchServiceTest** class that was created earlier in the "Testing the Model" section. Of course, the test execution should be integrated into the Ant build.

```
package com.jamesholmes.minihr;

import com.clarkware.junitperf.TimedTest;
import junit.framework.Test;
import junit.framework.TestSuite;

public class EmployeeSearchServicePerfTest {
  public static final long toleranceInMillis = 10;

  public static Test suite() {
    long maxElapsedTimeInMillis = 10 + toleranceInMillis;
    Test timedTest = new TimedTest(
        new TestSuite( EmployeeSearchServiceTest.class ),
                       maxElapsedTimeInMillis);
    TestSuite suite = new TestSuite();
    suite.addTest(timedTest);
    return suite;
  }
}
```

As you can see, this class is somewhat atypical of previous unit tests in that it does not extend **TestCase**. It does, however, provide a **suite** method that returns a **Test**. This method creates a test suite of a JUnitPerf **TimedTest** by wrapping a test suite created from the original **EmployeeSearchServiceTest**. The maximum time that the test should take to run is passed in as the second parameter to the **TimedTest**. This test can be run just as any other JUnit test—that is, using the JUnit test runners, IDE/JUnit integration, or via an Ant task.

Another tool, in the open-source domain, for testing and measuring the performance of Web applications is Apache JMeter (**http://jakarta.apache.org/jmeter**). JMeter allows a developer to create and run test plans against running applications. It was originally designed for testing Web sites so it is well suited for most Struts applications. JMeter provides a Java Swing user interface for creating and running test plans. Performance metrics are gathered and can be visualized graphically as well as in other formats. To get started, you need to first download JMeter and install it. Follow the provided documentation to create a test plan. You can create thread groups that simulate a number of concurrent users. Then, you can specify the details of an HTTP request to test. Figure 20-4 shows an HTTP request configured to access the Search by Name feature of the Mini HR application.

FIGURE 20-4 JMeter HTTP request

The request is configured to access the **URL http://localhost:8080/MiniHR20/search.do**. In addition, request parameters can be specified. In this case, the query string **name=Jim** will be added to the request.

The test can then be run against the running server and the results are accumulated for each result listener. Figure 20-5 shows the display using the Graph Results listener. The thread group, in this case, was configured to run with 20 concurrent users, each making 25 requests to the Search page—a total of 500 data points.

From the results, you can see that on average the search could be performed in a bit over 50 milliseconds, with some requests taking as long as 120 milliseconds. JMeter is a powerful tool and has a great deal more capabilities than described here. It is well documented and has many additional features that you may want to use.

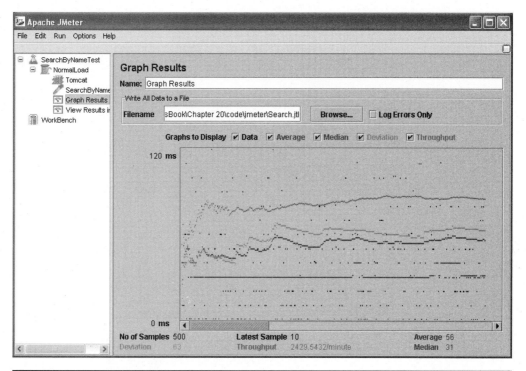

FIGURE 20-5   JMeter Graph Results

Performance is an area of your application that should not be overlooked—particularly if the application is targeted for high-volume, high-performance Web sites. As was shown above, JUnitPerf and Apache JMeter can be used to test the performance of your Web application under simulated loads. These tools can be used to help identify those areas of your application that are bottlenecks. Once identified, profiling tools should be used to focus the performance analysis.

Appendix

Struts Console
Quick Reference

A fundamental advantage of using the Struts framework for Java Web application development is its declarative nature. Instead of binding components of an application together in code, Struts applications use a centralized XML configuration file to declaratively connect components together. Unfortunately, modifying Struts configuration files by hand can be tedious and error prone. If you mistakenly leave off a closing bracket for a tag or misspell a tag or attribute name, Struts is unable to parse the configuration file and thus does not function properly. Trying to correct errors like these for a typical application, whose configuration file is usually quite long, can be time consuming because of the many details involved. For this reason, I created the Struts Console GUI tool to simplify the creation and maintenance of the Struts configuration file. Struts Console provides a simple and intuitive graphical interface with which to edit Struts configuration files.

Struts Console has evolved significantly since its initial release and continues to evolve today. Originally, Struts Console supported editing of only Struts configuration files. Since then Struts Console has been updated to support editing of Tiles and Validator configuration files as well as JSP Tag Library Descriptor (.tld) files. Struts Console is written in Java and thus can be run on any platform that supports Java GUI applications (e.g., Microsoft Windows, Macintosh, Linux, and so on). In its original release, Struts Console could be run only as a stand-alone application. Subsequently, Struts Console has been updated to support being run as a plugin in most of the major Java IDEs. Following is the list of IDEs that Struts Console can be used with:

- Borland JBuilder (versions 4.0 and later)

- Eclipse (versions 1.0 and later)

- IBM WebSphere Studio Application Developer (WSAD) (versions 4.0.3 and later)

- IntelliJ IDEA (versions 3.0 build 668 and later)

- NetBeans (versions 3.2 and later)
- Sun Java Studio (previously known as Forte or Sun ONE Studio) (versions 3.0 and later)
- Oracle JDeveloper (versions 9*i* and later)

The following sections explain how to acquire, install, and use Struts Console, both as a stand-alone application and as a plugin inside all the supported IDEs. Because IDEs are continually evolving, some of the instructions for using Struts Console inside the IDEs may change over time. If any of the instructions found in this appendix do not work for you, visit my Web site at **http://www.jamesholmes.com/struts/** for the most up to date instructions.

Supported Configuration Files

As explained, the current version of Struts Console supports editing not only Struts configuration files, but also Tiles and Validator configuration files, plus the JSP Tag Library Descriptor (**.tld**) files. All of these files are XML-based. In order for Struts Console to distinguish these files from any random XML file, they must have a proper XML **<!DOCTYPE>** declaration. The **<!DOCTYPE>** declaration specifies the Document Type Definition (DTD) to which the file must conform. Following is a list of the configuration files supported by Struts Console and their **<!DOCTYPE>** definitions.

Struts 1.2 Configuration File

```
<!DOCTYPE struts-config PUBLIC
   "-//Apache Software Foundation//DTD Struts Configuration 1.2//EN"
   "http://jakarta.apache.org/struts/dtds/struts-config_1_2.dtd">
```

Struts 1.1 Configuration File

```
<!DOCTYPE struts-config PUBLIC
   "-//Apache Software Foundation//DTD Struts Configuration 1.1//EN"
   "http://jakarta.apache.org/struts/dtds/struts-config_1_1.dtd">
```

Struts 1.0 Configuration File

```
<!DOCTYPE struts-config PUBLIC
   "-//Apache Software Foundation//DTD Struts Configuration 1.0//EN"
   "http://jakarta.apache.org/struts/dtds/struts-config_1_.dtd">
```

Tiles 1.1 Configuration File

```
<!DOCTYPE tiles-definitions PUBLIC
  "-//Apache Software Foundation//DTD Tiles Configuration 1.1//EN"
  "http://jakarta.apache.org/struts/dtds/tiles-config_1_1.dtd">
```

Validator 1.1 Configuration File

```
<!DOCTYPE form-validation PUBLIC
   "-//Apache Software Foundation//DTD Commons
   Validator Rules Configuration 1.1//EN"
   "http://jakarta.apache.org/commons/dtds/validator_1_1.dtd">
```

Validator 1.0 Configuration File

```
<!DOCTYPE form-validation PUBLIC
   "-//Apache Software Foundation//DTD Commons
   Validator Rules Configuration 1.0//EN"
   "http://jakarta.apache.org/commons/dtds/validator_1_0.dtd">
```

JSP Tab Library 1.2 File

```
<!DOCTYPE taglib PUBLIC
  "-//Sun Microsystems, Inc.//DTD JSP Tag Library 1.2//EN"
  "http://java.sun.com/dtd/web-jsptaglibrary_1_2.dtd">
```

JSP Tab Library 1.1 File

```
<!DOCTYPE taglib PUBLIC
  "-//Sun Microsystems, Inc.//DTD JSP Tag Library 1.1//EN"
  "http://java.sun.com/j2ee/dtds/web-jsptaglibrary_1_1.dtd">
```

NOTE *Your configuration file must contain one of the preceding* **<!DOCTYPE>** *declarations or Struts Console will be unable to load your configuration file.*

Acquiring and Installing Struts Console

Struts Console is free software and can be used both noncommercially and commercially free of charge. However, Struts Console is not open source software like Struts itself. Struts Console can be acquired from my Web site at

http://www.jamesholmes.com/struts/

Struts Console comes packaged as both a Zip file (**.zip**) and a Gzipped Tar file (**.tar.gz**). Select your desired packaging and download the file. Once you have downloaded Struts Console, installing it is straightforward. Because Struts Console is simply packaged in an archive file and not as an executable installation program, all you have to do is unpack the archive file into your desired installation directory. All the files inside the archive file are beneath a version-specific directory (e.g., **struts-console-4.4**), thus when you unpack them into your desired directory, they will all be beneath the version-specific directory. For example, if you were to download version 4.4 of Struts Console and unpack its archive to **c:\java**, the Struts Console files would all be located at **c:\java\struts-console-4.4**. That's all you have to do to install Struts Console.

NOTE   *Because Struts Console does not use an installer to place any special files into system directories, multiple versions of Struts Console can be installed on the same machine if necessary or desired.*

Using Struts Console as a Stand-alone Application

Most often, Struts Console is used as an IDE plugin because of the convenience of working seamlessly inside one tool. However, Struts Console can just as easily be run as a stand-alone application. Before running Struts Console as a stand-alone application, you must set the **JAVA_HOME** environmental variable. Many JDKs set this for you when you install them; however, if it is not set on your machine, you have to set it before you run Struts Console. The **JAVA_HOME** variable must be set to the directory where you have your JDK installed. For example, if you have JDK 1.4.1_03 installed at **c:\java\j2sdk1.4.1_03**, your **JAVA_HOME** variable should be set to **c:\java\ j2sdk1.4.1_03**.

Once you have set the **JAVA_HOME** environmental variable, you are ready to run Struts Console. Simply navigate to the directory where you installed Struts Console (e.g., **c:\java\struts-console-4.4**) and then navigate into the **bin** directory. The **bin** directory contains two files: **console.bat** and **console.sh**. If you are on a Microsoft

Windows machine, run **console.bat**. However, if you are on Linux, Unix, or Macintosh, run **console.sh**.

Once Struts Console is up and running, you can open an existing configuration file or create a new configuration file for editing. Figure A-1 shows Struts Console in action as a stand-alone application. Notice that open files have an Editor and a Source tab at the bottom. The Source tab shows you the source XML for the configuration file. Unlike many of the Struts Console IDE plugins, you cannot edit the XML source directly. This, however, may be a new feature in the future.

FIGURE A-1   Struts Console in action as a stand-alone application

---

NOTE   *On Linux, Unix, and Macintosh you have to set the executable flag on the **console.sh** file before it can be executed.*

Using Struts Console Inside Borland JBuilder

Struts Console can be run as a plugin inside Borland JBuilder versions 4.0 and later. To do so, you first must install the Struts Console JBuilder plugin. Following is the list of steps for installing the Struts Console JBuilder plugin:

1. Shut down JBuilder if it is currently running.

2. Navigate to the directory in which you have JBuilder installed (e.g., **c:\Program Files\JBuilder**) and then navigate into the **lib** directory.

3. In another window, navigate to the directory in which you installed Struts Console (e.g., **c:\java\struts-console-4.4**) and then navigate into the **com.jamesholmes.console.struts** directory and then into the **lib** directory.

4. Copy the **xerces.jar** file from the Struts Console **lib** directory (e.g., **c:\java\ struts-console-4.4\lib**) into the JBuilder **lib** directory (e.g., **c:\Program Files\JBuilder\lib**), *if and only if **xerces.jar** does not already exist in the JBuilder lib directory.*

NOTE   *This step should only be necessary for JBuilder version 4.*

---

5. Navigate into the **ext** directory (e.g., **c:\Program Files\JBuilder\lib\ext**) from the JBuilder **lib** directory.

6. Copy the **struts-console.jar** file from the Struts Console **lib** directory into the JBuilder **ext** directory.

After you have installed the Struts Console JBuilder plugin, you must restart JBuilder.

Once JBuilder is running, to use Struts Console, simply open a valid configuration file supported by Struts Console. Struts Console will be a tab option for the file, as shown in Figure A-2. You can edit the configuration file using Struts Console or you can edit the file by hand from the Source tab. Changes made in either tab are automatically reflected in the other tab.

Struts Console also allows you to modify some of its configuration settings from inside JBuilder. To access the Struts Console configuration settings, select

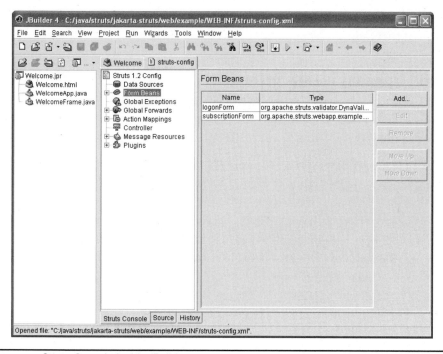

FIGURE A-2   Struts Console inside JBuilder

Tools | IDE Options. The following illustration shows the Struts Console IDE Options dialog box.

For more information on these configuration settings, see the "Configuring the Struts Console Output Options" section later in this appendix.

Using Struts Console Inside Eclipse

Struts Console can be run as a plugin inside Eclipse versions 1.0 and later. To do so, you first have to install the Struts Console Eclipse plugin. Following is the list of steps for installing the Struts Console Eclipse plugin:

1. Shut down Eclipse if it is currently running.

2. Navigate to the directory in which you have Eclipse installed (e.g., **c:\Program Files\eclipse**) and then navigate into the **plugins** directory.

3. In another window, navigate to the directory in which you installed Struts Console (e.g., **c:\java\struts-console-4.4**).

4. Copy the **com.jamesholmes.console.struts** directory from the Struts Console installation directory into the Eclipse **plugins** directory.

5. *If and only if you are running Eclipse versions 3.0m7 or later*, rename the **plugin.xml** file beneath the Eclipse **plugins** directory to **plugin.xml.bak**. Next, rename **plugin-3.0.xml** to **plugin.xml**. This step is necessary because there are two Struts Console Eclipse plugins, one for Eclipse versions 3.0m7 and later and one for earlier versions of Eclipse.

After you have installed the Struts Console Eclipse plugin, you must restart Eclipse. Once Eclipse is running, to use Struts Console, simply right-click on a valid configuration file and select Open With | Struts Console, as shown here:

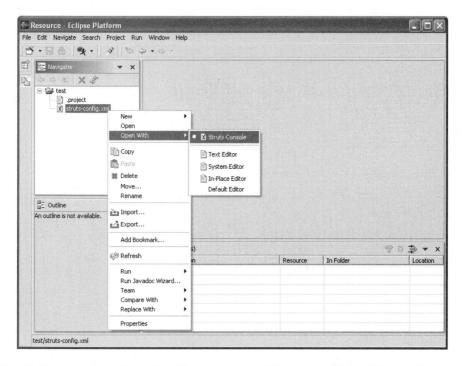

For Eclipse versions 3.0m7 and later, after you have opened the file, it will load into the Struts Console editor inside of Eclipse, as shown in Figure A-3. You can edit the configuration file using Struts Console or you can edit the file by hand from the Source tab. Changes made in either tab are automatically reflected in the other tab. For versions of Eclipse prior to 3.0m7, the file will load into a separate Struts Console window, as shown in Figure A-4.

NOTE *The Struts Console Eclipse plugin requires that your configuration files have specific filenames in order for the plugin to recognize them. Struts configuration files must be named **struts-config.xml**; Tiles configuration files must be named **tiles.xml**; and Validator configuration files must be named **validation.xml**. JSP TLD files only need to have a file extension of **.tld**.*

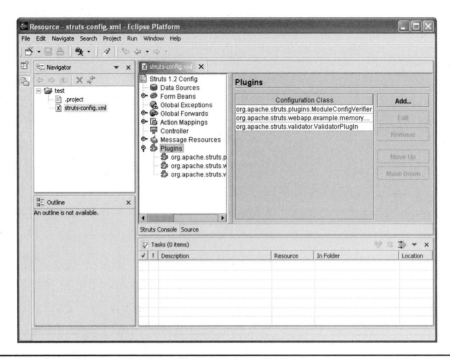

FIGURE A-3 Struts Console editor inside Eclipse

FIGURE A-4 Struts Console editor in a separate window

Struts Console also allows you to modify some of its configuration settings from inside Eclipse. To access the Struts Console configuration settings, select Window | Preferences. The following illustration shows the Struts Console Preferences dialog box.

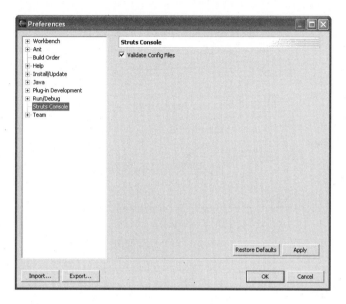

For more information on these configuration settings, see the "Configuring the Struts Console Output Options" section later in this appendix.

Using Struts Console Inside IBM WebSphere Studio Application Developer

Struts Console can be run as a plugin inside IBM WebSphere Studio Application Developer (WSAD) versions 4.0.3 and later. To do so, you first have to install the Struts Console Eclipse plugin. Following is the list of steps for installing the Struts Console WSAD plugin:

1. Shut down WSAD if it is currently running.

2. Navigate to the directory in which you have WSAD installed (e.g., **c:\Program Files\IBM\WebSphere Studio**) and then navigate into the **eclipse** directory and then into the **plugins** directory.

3. In another window, navigate to the directory in which you installed Struts Console (e.g., **c:\java\struts-console-4.4**).

FIGURE A-5   Struts Console editor in a separate window

For more information on these configuration settings, see the "Configuring the Struts Console Output Options" section later in this appendix.

Using Struts Console Inside IntelliJ IDEA

Struts Console can be run as a plugin inside JetBrains' IntelliJ IDEA versions 3.0 build 668 and later. To do so, you first have to install the Struts Console IDEA plugin. Following is the list of steps for installing the Struts Console IntelliJ IDEA plugin:

1. Shut down IntelliJ IDEA if it is currently running.

2. Navigate to the directory in which you have IntelliJ IDEA installed (e.g., **c:\Program Files\IntelliJ-IDEA-4.0**) and then navigate into the **plugins** directory.

3. In another window, navigate to the directory in which you installed Struts Console (e.g., **c:\java\struts-console-4.4**) and then navigate into the **com.jamesholmes.console.struts** directory and then into the **lib** directory.

4. Copy the **struts-console.jar** file from the Struts Console **lib** directory into the IDEA **plugins** directory.

After you have installed the Struts Console IDEA plugin, you must restart IDEA.

Once IDEA is running, to use Struts Console, simply right-click on a valid configuration file and select Edit With Struts Console, as shown here:

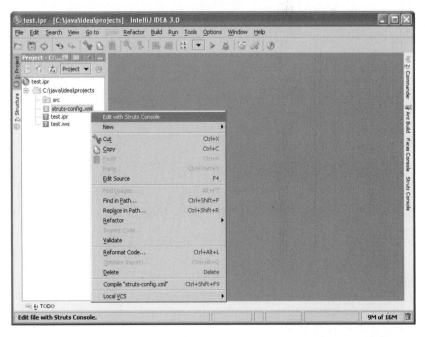

After you have opened the file, it will load into the Struts Console editor, as shown in Figure A-6.

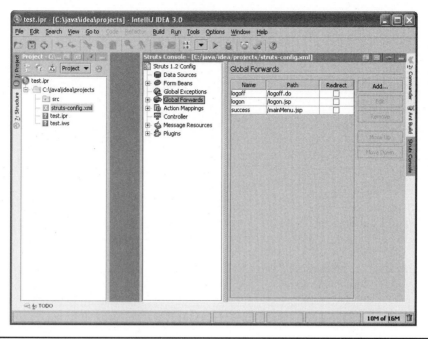

FIGURE A-6   Struts Console editor inside IDEA

Struts Console also allows you to modify some of its configuration settings from inside IDEA. To access the Struts Console configuration settings, select Options | IDE Settings. Here is the Struts Console IDE Settings dialog box:

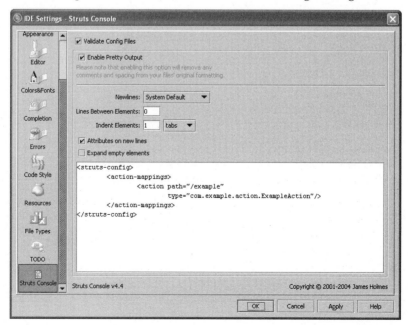

For more information on these configuration settings, see the "Configuring the Struts Console Output Options" section later in this appendix.

Using Struts Console Inside NetBeans and Sun Java Studio

Struts Console can be run as a plugin inside NetBeans versions 3.2 and later and inside Sun Java Studio versions 3.0 and later. To do so, you first have to install the Struts Console NetBeans plugin. Following is the list of steps for installing the Struts Console NetBeans plugin:

1. Start up NetBeans if it is not currently running.

2. Select Tools | Options. In the Options dialog box, navigate to the Options | IDE Configuration | System | Modules node in the tree on the left and then right-click it and select Add | Module, as shown here:

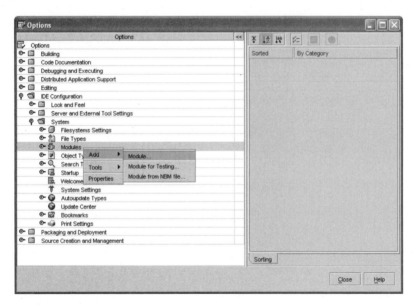

3. Using the file chooser, navigate to the directory in which you installed Struts Console (e.g., **c:\java\struts-console-4.4**) and then navigate into the **com.jamesholmes.console.struts** directory and then into the **lib** directory.

4. Select the **struts-console.jar** file and then click the Install button, as shown here.

After you have installed the Struts Console NetBeans plugin, you must restart NetBeans.

Once NetBeans is running, to use Struts Console, simply open a valid configuration file supported by Struts Console. The file will load into the Struts Console editor inside of NetBeans, as shown in Figure A-7.

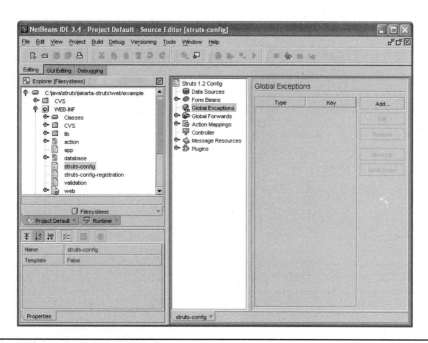

FIGURE A-7   Struts Console inside NetBeans

Using Struts Console Inside Oracle JDeveloper

Struts Console can be run as a plugin inside Oracle JDeveloper versions 9*i* and later. To do so, you first have to install the Struts Console JDeveloper plugin. Following is the list of steps for installing the Struts Console JDeveloper plugin:

1. Shut down JDeveloper if it is currently running.

2. Navigate to the directory in which you have JDeveloper installed (e.g., **c:\Program Files\JDeveloper**) and then navigate into the **jdev** directory and then into the **lib** directory and then into the **ext** directory.

3. In another window, navigate to the directory in which you installed Struts Console (e.g., **c:\java\struts-console-4.4**) and then navigate into the **com.jamesholmes.console.struts** directory and then into the **lib** directory.

4. Copy the **struts-console.jar** file from the Struts Console **lib** directory into the JDeveloper **ext** directory.

After you have installed the Struts Console JDeveloper plugin, you must restart JDeveloper.

Once JDeveloper is running, to use Struts Console, simply right-click on a valid configuration file and select Struts Console Editor, as shown here:

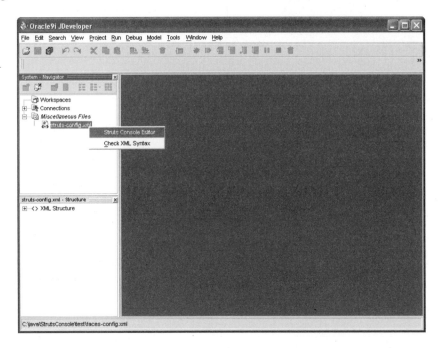

After you have opened the file, it will load into the Struts Console editor inside of JDeveloper, as shown in Figure A-8.

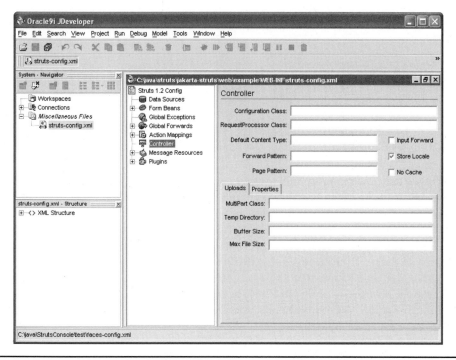

FIGURE A-8   Struts Console editor inside JDeveloper

Struts Console also allows you to modify some of its configuration settings from inside JDeveloper. To access the Struts Console configuration settings, select Tools | Preferences. Here is the Struts Console Preferences dialog box:

For more information on these configuration settings, see the next section, "Configuring the Struts Console Output Options."

Configuring the Struts Console Output Options

Struts Console uses an XML parser to read in XML configuration files and then it manipulates the files in memory. Because XML parsers do not retain all of a file's original formatting when the file is parsed, the files are often poorly formatted when they are saved. By default, Struts Console simply persists the in-memory representation of configuration files, which results in poorly formatted XML files. To get around the limitation of XML parsers not retaining complete formatting information, Struts Console has a feature called Pretty Output that allows the format configuration of an XML file to be saved.

The Pretty Output options can be configured in the stand-alone version of Struts Console as well as from inside IDEs that Struts Console plugs into. (For information on how to access the configuration settings for the Pretty Output options in a supported IDE, see that IDE's section in this appendix.) To configure the Pretty Output options in the stand-alone version of Struts Console, select Options | Output. This opens the dialog box shown here with options for specifying the details of how XML files should be formatted when they are saved.

Following is an explanation of each of the output options:

- **Enable Pretty Output**   Enables and disables the use of Pretty Output options.

- **Newlines**   Specifies the type of newline character to use. System Default is the default and recommended setting. System Default defaults to the newline character for the given system on which the application is running. For example, if run on Windows, System Default uses Windows-style newline characters.

- **Lines Between Elements**   Specifies the number of new lines to place in between tags.

- **Indent Elements**   Specifies the number and type of indenting to use. Indenting is used for tags and is hierarchical. Each level in the tag hierarchy is a level of indenting.

- **Attributes on New Lines**   Specifies whether a tag's attributes should each be placed on a new line or if each should be placed on the same line as the tag.

- **Expand Empty Elements**   Specifies whether or not empty tags (that is, tags without nested tags) should be expanded (e.g., **<tag/>** versus **<tag></tag>**).

- **Bottom pane**   Shows an example of how the output will look with the current output options applied. This changes as you change the output options.

NOTE   *Enabling Pretty Output removes any XML comments (e.g., **<!-- -->**) and formatting from your original configuration files.*

Index

INTERNATIONAL CONTACT INFORMATION

AUSTRALIA
McGraw-Hill Book Company
Australia Pty. Ltd.
TEL +61-2-9900-1800
FAX +61-2-9878-8881
http://www.mcgraw-hill.com.au
books-it_sydney@mcgraw-hill.com

CANADA
McGraw-Hill Ryerson Ltd.
TEL +905-430-5000
FAX +905-430-5020
http://www.mcgraw-hill.ca

**GREECE, MIDDLE EAST, & AFRICA
(Excluding South Africa)**
McGraw-Hill Hellas
TEL +30-210-6560-990
TEL +30-210-6560-993
TEL +30-210-6560-994
FAX +30-210-6545-525

MEXICO (Also serving Latin America)
McGraw-Hill Interamericana Editores
S.A. de C.V.
TEL +525-1500-5108
FAX +525-117-1589
http://www.mcgraw-hill.com.mx
carlos_ruiz@mcgraw-hill.com

SINGAPORE (Serving Asia)
McGraw-Hill Book Company
TEL +65-6863-1580
FAX +65-6862-3354
http://www.mcgraw-hill.com.sg
mghasia@mcgraw-hill.com

SOUTH AFRICA
McGraw-Hill South Africa
TEL +27-11-622-7512
FAX +27-11-622-9045
robyn_swanepoel@mcgraw-hill.com

SPAIN
McGraw-Hill/
Interamericana de España, S.A.U.
TEL +34-91-180-3000
FAX +34-91-372-8513
http://www.mcgraw-hill.es
professional@mcgraw-hill.es

**UNITED KINGDOM, NORTHERN,
EASTERN, & CENTRAL EUROPE**
McGraw-Hill Education Europe
TEL +44-1-628-502500
FAX +44-1-628-770224
http://www.mcgraw-hill.co.uk
emea_queries@mcgraw-hill.com

ALL OTHER INQUIRIES Contact:
McGraw-Hill/Osborne
TEL +1-510-420-7700
FAX +1-510-420-7703
http://www.osborne.com
omg_international@mcgraw-hill.com

Sound Off!

Visit us at **www.osborne.com/bookregistration** and let us know what you thought of this book. While you're online you'll have the opportunity to register for newsletters and special offers from McGraw-Hill/Osborne.

We want to hear from you!

Sneak Peek

Visit us today at **www.betabooks.com** and see what's coming from McGraw-Hill/Osborne tomorrow!

Based on the successful software paradigm, Bet@Books™ allows computing professionals to view partial and sometimes complete text versions of selected titles online. Bet@Books™ viewing is free, invites comments and feedback, and allows you to "test drive" books in progress on the subjects that interest you the most.